Joy and Laughter in Nietzsche's Philosophy

Also available from Bloomsbury

Conflict and Contest in Nietzsche's Philosophy, edited by
Herman Siemens and James Pearson
Nietzsche and Epicurus, edited by Vinod Acharya and Ryan J. Johnson
Nietzsche and Friendship, by Willow Verkerk
'The Gift' in Nietzsche's Zarathustra, by Emilio Corriero
The Parallel Philosophies of Sartre and Nietzsche, by Nik Farrell Fox

Joy and Laughter in Nietzsche's Philosophy

Alternative Liberatory Politics

Edited by
Paul E. Kirkland and Michael J. McNeal

BLOOMSBURY ACADEMIC
LONDON • NEW YORK • OXFORD • NEW DELHI • SYDNEY

BLOOMSBURY ACADEMIC
Bloomsbury Publishing Plc
50 Bedford Square, London, WC1B 3DP, UK
1385 Broadway, New York, NY 10018, USA
29 Earlsfort Terrace, Dublin 2, Ireland

BLOOMSBURY, BLOOMSBURY ACADEMIC and the Diana logo are
trademarks of Bloomsbury Publishing Plc

First published in Great Britain 2022
This paperback edition published 2023

Copyright © Paul E. Kirkland, Michael J. McNeal and Contributors, 2022

Paul E. Kirkland and Michael J. McNeal have asserted their right under the Copyright,
Designs and Patents Act, 1988, to be identified as Editors of this work.

For legal purposes the Acknowledgments on p. vii constitute an
extension of this copyright page.

Cover image: Comedians' Handbill (1938), Paul Klee
(© agefotostock / Alamy Stock Photo)

All rights reserved. No part of this publication may be reproduced or transmitted in
any form or by any means, electronic or mechanical, including photocopying,
recording, or any information storage or retrieval system, without prior
permission in writing from the publishers.

Bloomsbury Publishing Plc does not have any control over, or responsibility for, any
third-party websites referred to or in this book. All internet addresses given in this
book were correct at the time of going to press. The author and publisher regret any
inconvenience caused if addresses have changed or sites have ceased to exist, but
can accept no responsibility for any such changes.

A catalogue record for this book is available from the British Library.

A catalog record for this book is available from the Library of Congress.

ISBN: HB: 978-1-3502-2523-7
PB: 978-1-3502-2527-5
ePDF: 978-1-3502-2524-4
eBook: 978-1-3502-2525-1

Typeset by Newgen KnowledgeWorks Pvt. Ltd., Chennai, India

To find out more about our authors and books visit www.bloomsbury.com
and sign up for our newsletters.

Contents

Acknowledgments — vii
Abbreviations and References for Nietzsche's Texts — viii

Introduction — 1
    Paul E. Kirkland and Michael J. McNeal

Part 1   Joy and Knowledge

1   A Gay Science *Avant La Lettre*? Knowledge and Joy in *Human, All too Human* — 11
    Ruth Abbey

2   Aesthetics of Joy and Levity for Nietzsche's Free Spirit — 27
    Paul E. Kirkland

Part 2   Nietzsche's Joyful Teachings

3   Nietzsche's *Übermensch*: From Shared Suffering to Shared Joy — 47
    Melanie Shepherd

4   "Is the Sea Not Full of Verdant Islands?": Zarathustra on Passing by the Great City — 65
    Peter S. Groff

5   Why "All Joy Wills Eternity" for Nietzsche — 85
    Richard J. Elliott

Part 3   Predecessors and Heirs

6   "What Do I Matter!": Nietzsche on Pascal, Self-Obsession, and Good Cheer — 105
    Jamie Parr

7   Schopenhauer's Jokes and Nietzsche's Riddles: Toward a Morphology of Laughter — 123
    Glen Baier

8   Subversive Playfulness in Nietzsche and Dada — 143
    Philip Mills

Part 4 Perspectives on Laughter

9   On Nietzsche's "Teachings" about Learning to Laugh at Oneself:
    A Critical Approach   161
    Katia Hay
10 Nietzsche on Masculinity: The Joys of Danger and Play   179
    Jeffrey Church
11 The Free Spirit's Dionysian Mirth: A Laughing Storm to Herald
    Philosophers of the Future   191
    Michael J. McNeal

Notes on Contributors   215
Name Index   217
Subject Index   221

Acknowledgments

In assembling and editing this book, we have accrued debts of gratitude for the institutional and individual support we have received along the way. We are thankful for one another and those who participated, including Professor Daniel Conway and Assistant Professor George Shea, in our panel, "The Political Significance of Joyfulness in Nietzsche's Thought," at the 2019 *Southern Political Science Association* conference, at which some contributions to this volume were initially presented. In addition, we thank those who attended our respective presentations at the 2019 *Friedrich Nietzsche Society* conference for their feedback, the discussions that ensued, and for considerable laughter and joy. Dr. Kirkland thanks his partner H. Abbie Erler for her ongoing support throughout this process. Dr. McNeal thanks his partner Kurt Holzberlein for his support and expresses gratitude to the editors of the *Southwest Philosophy Review*. We are also indebted to our blind reviewers and all those at Bloomsbury Academic who assisted in the realization of this volume, particularly Jade Grogan and Suzie Nash. Finally, we are grateful to each of the contributors to this volume for their work.

Abbreviations and References for Nietzsche's Texts

German Editions Utilized

KGB   Nietzsche, Friedrich (1975–), *Briefwechsel. Kritische Studienausgabe*, ed. Giorgio Colli and Mazzino Montinari, *Berlin: de Gruyter*
KGW   Nietzsche, Friedrich (1967–), *Werke Kritische Gesamtausgabe*, ed. Giorgio Colli and Mazzino Montinari, Berlin: de Gruyter.
KSA   Nietzsche, Friedrich (1980), *Kritische Studienausgabe in 15 Banden*, ed. Giorgio Colli and Mazzino Montinari, Berlin: de Gruyter.

Abbreviations

Standardized abbreviations of Nietzsche's works in English translation are utilized throughout this volume. Where necessary, numerically distinct books, parts or sections, and abbreviated section titles are employed.

A	*The Antichrist*
AOM	*Assorted Opinions and Maxims*
BGE	*Beyond Good and Evil*
BT	*The Birth of Tragedy*
CW	*The Case of Wagner*
D	*Dawn*
EH	*Ecce Homo*
GM	*On the Genealogy of Morality*
GS	*The Gay Science*
HH	*Human, All Too Human*
HL	*On the Use and Disadvantage of History for Life*
M	*Morgenroete*
NL	*Nachlass Notes*
PPP	*The Pre-Platonic Philosophers*
RWB	*Richard Wagner in Bayreuth*
TI	*Twilight of the Idols*
TL	"On Truth and Lies in an Extra-Moral Sense"
UM	*Untimely Meditations*
WS	*The Wanderer and His Shadow*
Z	*Thus Spoke Zarathustra*

English Translations of Nietzsche's Texts

Along with their own translations, authors have drawn from a wide range of translations of Nietzsche's writings, modifying them and combining them as they considered appropriate. The following translations are used:

Nietzsche, Friedrich (1968), *The Antichrist*, trans. Walter Kaufmann, in *The Portable Nietzsche*, ed. Walter Kaufmann, New York: Viking Press.

Nietzsche, Friedrich (2005), *The Anti-Christ: A Curse on Christianity*, in *The Anti-Christ, Ecce Homo, Twilight of the Idols and Other Writings*, ed. Aaron Ridley and Judith Norman, trans. Judith Norman, Cambridge: Cambridge University Press.

Nietzsche, Friedrich (1966), *Beyond Good and Evil, Prelude to a Philosophy of the Future*, trans. Walter Kaufmann, New York: Random House, 1966.

Nietzsche, Friedrich (2002), *Beyond Good and Evil, Prelude to a Philosophy of the Future*, ed. Rolf-Peter Horstmann and Judith Norman, trans. Judith Norman, Cambridge: Cambridge University Press.

Nietzsche, Friedrich (2014), *Beyond Good and Evil, Prelude to a Philosophy of the Future*, in *Beyond Good and Evil, / On the Genealogy of Morality*, trans. Adrian Del Caro, Stanford, CA: Stanford University Press.

Nietzsche, Friedrich (1967), *The Birth of Tragedy*, in *The Birth of Tragedy and The Case of Wagner*, trans. Walter Kaufmann, New York: Random House.

Nietzsche, Friedrich (1999), *The Birth of Tragedy and Other Writings*, ed. Raymond Geuss and Ronald Speirs, trans. Ronald Speirs, Cambridge: Cambridge University Press.

Nietzsche, Friedrich (1967), *The Case of Wagner: A Musicians' Problem*, trans. Walter Kaufmann, New York: Random House.

Nietzsche, Friedrich (2011), *Dawn: Thoughts on the Presumptions of Morality*, trans. Brittain Smith, Stanford, CA: Stanford University Press.

Nietzsche, Friedrich (1982), *Daybreak: Thoughts on the Prejudices of Morality*, trans. R. J. Hollingdale, Cambridge: Cambridge University Press.

Nietzsche, Friedrich (1967), *Ecce Homo: How One Becomes What One Is*, trans. Walter Kaufmann, New York: Random House.

Nietzsche, Friedrich (2005), *Ecce Homo: How to Become What you Are*, in *The Anti-Christ, Ecce Homo, Twilight of the Idols and Other Writings*, ed. Aaron Ridley and Judith Norman, trans. Judith Norman, Cambridge: Cambridge University Press.

Nietzsche, Friedrich (1974), *The Gay Science, with a Prelude of Rhymes and an Appendix of Songs*, trans. Walter Kaufmann, New York: Random House.

Nietzsche, Friedrich (2001), *The Gay Science, with a Prelude of Rhymes and an Appendix of Songs*, ed. Bernard Williams, trans. Josefine Nauckhoff, with poems translated by Adrian Del Caro, Cambridge: Cambridge University Press.

Nietzsche, Friedrich (1986), *Human, All Too Human: A Book for Free Spirits*, trans. R. J. Hollingdale, Cambridge: Cambridge University Press.

Nietzsche, Friedrich (1995), *Human, All Too Human: A Book for Free Spirits*, vol. 1, trans. Gary Handwerk, Stanford, CA: Stanford University Press.

Nietzsche, Friedrich (2013), *Human, All Too Human: A Book for Free Spirits*, vol. II, and *Unpublished Fragments from the Period of Human, All Too Human II*, trans. Gary Handwerk, Stanford, CA: Stanford University Press.

Nietzsche, Friedrich (2005), *Nietzsche contra Wagner: From the Files of a Psychologist*, in *The Anti-Christ, Ecce Homo, Twilight of the Idols and Other Writings*, ed. Aaron Ridley and Judith Norman, trans. Judith Norman, Cambridge: Cambridge University Press.

Nietzsche, Friedrich (1967), *On the Genealogy of Morality, A Polemic*, trans. Walter Kaufmann and R. J. Hollingdale, New York: Random House.

Nietzsche, Friedrich (1994), *On the Genealogy of Morality, A Polemic*, ed. Keith Ansell-Pearson, trans. Carol Diethe, Cambridge: Cambridge University Press.

Nietzsche, Friedrich (2014), *On the Genealogy of Morality, A Polemic*, in *Beyond Good and Evil/On the Genealogy of Morality*, trans. Adrian Del Caro, Stanford, CA: Stanford University Press.

Nietzsche, Friedrich (1999), *Philosophy and Truth, Selections from Nietzsche's Notebooks of the Early 1870's*, ed. and trans. Daniel Breazeale, Amherst, NY: Humanity Books.

Nietzsche, Friedrich (2001), *The Pre-Platonic Philosophers*, trans. and ed. Greg Whitlock, Urbana: University of Illinois Press.

Nietzsche, Friedrich (2005), *Prefaces to Unwritten Works*, trans. and ed. Michael W. Grenke, with additional prefaces by Matthew K. Davis and Lise van Boxel, South Bend, IN: St. Augustine's Press.

Nietzsche, Friedrich (1968), *Thus Spoke Zarathustra: A Book for All and None*, trans. Walter Kaufmann, in *The Portable Nietzsche*, New York: Viking Press.

Nietzsche, Friedrich (2005), *Thus Spoke Zarathustra: A Book for All and None*, trans. Graham Parkes, Oxford: Oxford University Press.

Nietzsche, Friedrich (2006), *Thus Spoke Zarathustra: A Book for All and None*, ed. Adrian Del Caro and Robert Pippen, trans. Adrian Del Caro, Cambridge: Cambridge University Press.

Nietzsche, Friedrich (1998), *Twilight of the Idols, or How One Philosophizes with a Hammer*, trans. Duncan Large, Oxford: Oxford University Press.

Nietzsche, Friedrich (2005), *Twilight of the Idols, or How to Philosophize with a Hammer*, in *The Anti-Christ, Ecce Homo, Twilight of the Idols and Other Writings*, ed. Aaron Ridley and Judith Norman, trans. Judith Norman, Cambridge: Cambridge University Press.

Introduction

Paul E. Kirkland and Michael J. McNeal

In his song of eternal recurrence, Zarathustra proclaims, "Joy wants eternity" (*Lust will Ewigkeit*)" (Z III Other Dance-Song), giving pride of place to joy (*Lust*) as the affect suited to the most life-affirming teaching of eternal recurrence. In launching the project of a new approach to philosophical wisdom and scientific understanding in *The Gay Science* (GS), Nietzsche writes, "Even laughter may yet have a future" (GS 1), signaling an important place for laugher in both the life of communities and the life of the mind. As the affirmation of life emerges in Nietzsche's work as a measure of vitality and orientation toward life, the affirmative dispositions—joy, cheerfulness, laughter, and gaiety—become central to an adequate understanding of Nietzsche's aims. Especially attentive to the political ramifications of these issues, the essays comprising this volume examine, in disparate ways, those dispositions as a path into Nietzsche's thought, providing fresh approaches to understanding key ideas in his philosophy that indicate their relevance to political thought. These themes include how joy and laughter came to serve a central role in Nietzsche's thought, the ways in which the disposition they commend informs future possibilities for philosophy, and how they may enable the emergence of new forms of life. What is this place for laughter? How is joy the source for affirmative ways of living and living together? This volume takes up these questions, among others, through a variety of scholarly approaches to Nietzsche's thought.

When Nietzsche writes of the "eternal joy (*Lust*) of becoming" as the key to the Dionysian and to the psychology of the tragic poet, he describes this capacity as one that can move us "beyond all terror and pity" (TI Ancients 5). He treats joy as the comprehensive state most conducive to affirming life. Insofar as he regards joy as related to tragedy, it is insufficient to understand it conventionally, as an affect or attitude equivalent to others, for the capacity for the sort of joy he advocates includes the embrace of suffering. Therefore, such joy should properly be understood as integral to the affirmation of life that Nietzsche claims is his central teaching. By extension, this conception of joy informs his encouragement of cheerfulness, laughter, and gaiety, and each of these related affects ramify it in turn. He anticipates that this joyfulness will foster philosophical life, shape social relations, and give rise to unanticipated liberatory political possibilities.

Replete with consideration of the interrelated subjects of joy, cheerfulness, gaiety, and laughter (*Freude, Heiterkeit, Frolichkeit, Lachen*), Nietzsche's work calls attention to the role of related affects, dispositions, and attitudes in his work. A few prominent examples show the vital place of these affects and related considerations in Nietzsche's thought. In the first aphorism of GS, Nietzsche suggests that laughter can overcome "the age of tragedy, the age of moralities and religions," giving it a crucial place in his aim of overcoming morality. He offers an evaluation of science in accordance with its capacity to foster joy (*Freude*) (GS 12) and teaches *Mitfreude* (shared joy) as a means of overcoming of Mitleid (pity). The supplement to GS (Part Five) opens with a consideration of the "meaning of our cheerfulness" (*Heiterkeit*) and its possibility for opening new seas. Zarathustra claims to teach the higher men to "learn to laugh" in Part Four of *Thus Spoke Zarathustra* (Z), in a passage that Nietzsche quotes in his 1886 preface to *The Birth of Tragedy* (BT Preface 7) to reframe the arguments of that early work with laughter. As Nietzsche connects laughter to tragedy, gaiety to science (knowledge), cheerfulness to daring experiments, and joy to human relations, he offers an affirmative framework that encourages lightness in the pursuit of serious goals. Furthermore, his presentation of heretofore unseen paths to new forms of life underscores what an innovative thinker he was with regard to the sociopolitical realm of human existence and how thoroughly this aspect of this thought ought to be taken. Giving due attention to these themes illuminates the affirmative possibilities of Nietzsche's project in a way that notably advances scholarship on Nietzsche's thought.

Nietzsche remarked on the way that "serious" philosophy has excluded laughter, noting that "'where laughter and gaiety are found, thinking does not amount to anything', that is the prejudice of this beast against all 'gay science' (*fröliche Wissenschaft*)—Well then, let us prove that this is a prejudice" (GS 327). With this he playfully suggested that the serious pursuit of knowledge, which has historically harbored a prejudice against what is light, has been inconsistent with itself. He worked to demonstrate the value of levity to knowledge, in order to overcome this prejudice, aiming thereby to legitimate previously excluded methods of scholarship. Among other things, this volume explicates the important role that gaiety played in Nietzsche's thought, along with the transformative potentials he attached to it.

Given the centrality of joy and laughter in Nietzsche's thought, it is surprising that the subject has not received more attention in the secondary literature. Scholars have examined the comic elements of Nietzsche's thought, principally by scrutinizing individual texts (e.g., Higgins 2000, More 2014), and other noteworthy efforts have prepared the way for a fuller examination of the significance of laughter in Nietzsche's thought to political themes (e.g., Hatab 1988, Lippitt 1992, Lampert 1999). For example, Alex McIntyre has argued that "communion in joy" (2012: 150) constitutes Nietzsche's principle of sovereignty and the aim of his great politics, which could serve as a basis for reorienting political philosophy. Launching from such contributions, the essays herein feature a variety of fresh approaches to the ways in which joy and laughter might shape human communities.

As the primary theme of this volume is the political significance of high spirits and comprehensive joy in Nietzsche's thought, the contributors address a range of subjects, from the efficacy of mirth to new experiments in living and Nietzsche's project of revaluating all values. Thinkers from Aristotle to Foucault taught that the political was the crucial dimension of all human relationships. Whether pertaining to the self, the structure of power relations, or the character of a regime, political questions inform myriad aspects of human life, be they mundane or profound. This volume takes the political in the broadest sense, from conceptions of the individual, modes of communal life, relations of power, liberatory possibilities, self-creation, and sources of authority and value.

While there have been no scholarly examinations of the political implications of the themes of joy and laughter in Nietzsche's thought, rather than reexamining familiar matters such as Nietzsche's opposition to Bismarck's nationalist cultural politics (e.g., Drochon 2016) or the significance of his admiration of Napoleon (e.g., Dombowsky 2014), the essays here deal with issues pertaining to the affective disposition that compels their disruptive laughter and creation of affirming forms of life toward the aim of comprehensive revaluation. In so doing, they treat the themes of joy and laughter in connection to his larger aims with a multiplicity of approaches to its political implications. When Nietzsche connects great politics with "a war of the spirits" (EH Destiny 1), much of his project of revaluation and the affirmative possibilities to which it may give rise takes on a political cast. Without rejecting the role of immediate political conditions to Nietzsche's thinking about politics and culture, it is possible to focus on the aims of revaluation and affirmation, beyond conflicts among great powers, rancorous partisan discourse, or the shape of practical rule.[1] Nietzsche's campaign against morality, his aims of liberation, and his project of revaluation all show the way in which political concerns include aims beyond those of specific states, parties, and institutions.[2] The scholars in this volume do not speak univocally about the character of the political ramifications of these goals. Instead, they show the way in which Nietzsche's experiments with high spirits might offer preludes and launch new directions in the study of Nietzsche and political theory.

The goal of liberation from decadent values and the rule of their promoters is clearly one of Nietzsche's aims, yet he is emphatically opposed to liberalism as a basis for political organization, political theory, or emancipation. He goes so far as to argue that liberalism runs counter to its own aims of freedom (TI Skirmishes 38) and dismisses it, along with modern political ideologies and parties, in favor of liberation from the inheritance of Christian European values and their political legacies (GS 377).[3] Such elevating liberation indicates a distinct approach to political matters and new possibilities for political thought. Rather than a single avenue of liberation or transformation, Nietzsche's work directs his readers beyond liberal notions of freedom and into explorations of potentially new forms of life.[4]

The essays in this volume consider a variety of ways in which a new politics might emerge from careful consideration of Nietzsche's account of high spirits and comprehensive joy. Specifically, they examine how the interventions of laughter may reshape communities and provide shared joy as a new basis for human relations. Whereas some authors argue the Nietzschean mirth can play a strategic political role while also providing a source of affirmation, others argue that joy requires a great distance from political life. Nietzsche's key affirmative teachings provide the basis for some of the reflections on the place of joy and laughter in this thought. Other essays explore the way in which laughter and joy can supply means of liberation from otherworldly hopes, inherited morality, pity, and secular dogmas. Some examine the free spirit ideal as one that aims to liberate the pursuit of knowledge from positivism, scientism, and a morality of probity. Together, the essays variously consider alternative liberatory paths revealed by considerations of joy and laughter in Nietzsche's thought. With attention to joyful affirmation, they connect these political possibilities with Nietzsche's core philosophical themes and his aim of revaluation.

Each chapter in this volume explores, in its own way, the prospects Nietzsche's joyful orientation may provide for new modes of judgment about political life and, as aforementioned, new kinds of human community. Moreover, the contributors treat joy's relation to aesthetic judgment and relationality, the affirmation of joyful solitude, and cheerfulness and laughter as inherently political strategies for the basis of a future (distant) political order. They show the way in which joy, laughter, and cheerfulness connect to his major teachings, including self-overcoming, *amor fati*, the Übermensch, and eternal recurrence. Rather than offering uniform conclusions, the contributors limn the difficulties involved in Nietzsche's affirmative vision for new social orders. They raise questions about his notion of joy and the corresponding role of laughter in forming future social orders, highlighting his contribution to an affirmative human future.

Beginning with an examination of joyful ways of living and the pursuit of knowledge, the chapters of the book move toward the implications of joy for human communities and then the specifically political implications of the affects, dispositions, and modes of life Nietzsche's joy commends. The first section addresses science and aesthetics in Nietzsche's liberatory project as they pertain to his free spirit ideal. In the first chapter, Ruth Abbey argues that *Human, All Too Human* (HH) should not be viewed, as some have, as a work committed to positivism. She demonstrates that it already includes the possibility of a science that will be joyful. The chapter demonstrates that the seeker after truth experiences purified affects and that Nietzsche's account of such commitment to truth includes an image of the good life. Abbey argues that Nietzsche promotes a historically aware pursuit of knowledge, attentive to a view of happiness rather than a mechanistic account of nature. Instead of finding positivism in HH, Abbey finds a clear connection between the pursuit of knowledge and questions of ethics and affects. Her essay elucidates Nietzsche's considerations of joyful ways of living with truth and anticipating the possibility of a gay science in HH. Continuing the examination of Nietzsche's views of a gay science in the second chapter, Paul Kirkland takes up the role of aesthetics in the project of the free spirit trilogy, primarily treating GS. Kirkland addresses Nietzsche's call for an alliance between laughter and wisdom. Arguing that the distance provided by art offers a perspective serving knowledge rather than one simply concealing deadly truths, the chapter shows that Nietzsche moves from an aesthetics oriented toward freedom to one that finds beauty in necessity. The levity of laughter and artist's perspectives act as counterforces to the weight of probity and knowing, and Nietzsche's imagery of beautiful monsters provides a model for combining levity and gravity that makes it possible to pursue wisdom with joy.

The next section takes up the place of joy in Nietzsche key teachings—Übermensch, eternal recurrence, and solitude. The chapters therein treat the role of Nietzsche's affirmative teachings in shaping new forms of community and consider relational joy as a form of political engagement in life affirmation. Melanie Shepherd considers the issue of joy as the basis for a new relational structure. It examines the matter of pity (*Mitleid*) and shared joy (*Mitfreude*), arguing that shared joy is the basis for *übermenschlichkeit* relations. By tracing Zarathustra's efforts to replace pity with shared joy, the essay demonstrates specific limitations of relations based in suffering alongside the expansive possibilities in shared joy. It thereby finds a non-egoistic reading of Nietzsche's understanding of *Übermensch* and the significance of the teaching of eternal recurrence. By treating relationships and their structure as fundamental rather than merely instrumental in Nietzsche's thought, it brings to light the burden of resistance involved in cultivating friendships and an orientation of shared joy. Beyond the bounds of pity or individualized overcoming of it, Shepherd argues, a culture of shared joy provides the possibility for a new and affirmative mode of relationality. Where Shepherd finds a new basis for relationality in *Mitfreude*, Peter Groff reflects on the primacy of joy in solitude in Zarathustra's "passing by" in which he finds a key instance of Nietzsche's presentation of the enduring conflict between the city and philosophy. Groff's close examination of the teaching of "passing by" distinguishes Zarathustra's view from constant combat and disgust with the city, on the one hand, and hopes for grand transformation through a project of philosophical legislation, on the other. With an approach that negates only in "looking away," Zarathustra's relation to the city can include affirmation without defining itself in terms of the petty politics of the feverish city or the great politics of transforming humanity. Instead, its affirmation, Groff shows, consists in joy found primarily in solitude, a joy that sees the beautiful in the necessary, and prepares the way for supra-political teachings of *amor fati* and eternal recurrence. In the fifth chapter, Richard Elliott explores Nietzsche's uses of the motifs of eternity and infinity to track the three developmental stages of nihilism. These motifs serve to demonstrate, first, disorientation, second, an active confrontation by means of a new experimental freedom, then, third, a form of life-affirmation as instantiated in willing eternal recurrence. These steps of engagement with (and through) nihilism, Elliott argues, correspond to the three metamorphoses of spirit set out in Z and show a specific affect of a form of joy as integral to the third stage's ability to "will eternity."

Through an examination of Nietzsche's predecessors and heirs, the third section elucidates the role of joy and laughter in orienting alternative models for liberation from inherited values and new ways of shaping political communities. Jamie Parr's chapter examines the refrain "What do I matter!," which appears multiple times in Nietzsche's texts. Nietzsche claims that the investigation of the problem of the world must now be pursued on the basis of a new and "*more magnanimous*" feeling. The chapter examines Pascal's laughter of self-importance and Nietzsche's relation to Pascal. Parr argues that the self-relationship expressed by "What do I matter!" exposes one of the complex positive results of the collapse of the Christian god: it captures a vision of the human as a creature actively eschewing the fear and self-obsession bred into it by Christianity and striving instead to lead a humble, patient, cheerful existence in which laughter again finds a central place. It shows how the new orientation might shape contemporary social and political relations. Investigating means of overcoming pessimism, Glen Baier's chapter investigates Schopenhauer's definitions of jokes, irony, and humor, as formulated in *The World as Will and Representation*, as a means for understanding Nietzsche's utilization of riddles in Z. He finds Nietzsche's treatment of laughter to be compatible with Schopenhauer's stipulation of the causes of laughter and shows that both subscribe to a version of what is typically called an "incongruity theory." While Schopenhauer finds the use of jokes and humor to be specifically human, Baier points out that Nietzsche's use of humor takes on greater existential significance. A key difference between Nietzsche and Schopenhauer emerges in Nietzsche's defense of a laughter that sustains cheerfulness as a counter to Schopenhauer's pessimism. Baier argues that this allows an overcoming of Schopenhauer that uses Schopenhauer's view of humor, jokes, and riddles against his pessimism. Turning to heirs of Nietzsche's thought, Philip Mills examines its influence on Dadaism, analyzing how Nietzsche's lampooning of ascetic priests, jokes about conventional (scholarly) philosophers, and self-parody (as in *Ecce Homo*) inspired the movement's founders. Examining the manifestos of Hugo Ball and Tristan Tzara, he considers how Nietzsche's ethos of playfulness informed their conception of the movement. Mills demonstrates that the Dadaists offered a politically subversive response to Nietzsche's call for a revaluation of values, undermining plebeian expectations of artworks as they reconceived the aesthetic. He argues that their Nietzschean challenge provocatively exposed the meaninglessness and nihilism of late modernity's dissipative values.

The final set of chapters address the significance of Nietzsche's thought on laughter, playfulness, and joy, both for life and the socio-cultural and political transformation of societies. The section sketches paths toward an alternative liberatory politics that connect aspirations for new values and forms of emancipation from decadent values with corresponding modes of life. Katia Hay's chapter examines the extent to which Nietzsche's "philosophy of laughter" can help us think about the tension between laughter and politics today. She argues that addressing humor in the context of free speech has proved to be insufficient if not totally counterproductive, precisely because it does not enable us to address the complex nature of comedy nor the violent, disruptive or transgressive potential of humor and laughter in general, demonstrating the overcoming of the opposition between laughter and seriousness in the project of gay science. Laughter enables us to play with and test our preconceptions concerning the things that are closest and most dear to us, without totally undermining or negating their value. She thus shows that laughing at ourselves makes it possible to question ourselves and our values without falling into despair. Destabilizing the perspective of the laughter itself, Hay shows, can open the possibility of reconfiguring communities and identities with new forms of inclusion that are never entirely stabilized. Jeffrey Church finds a complex tension within a particular situation of masculinity, constructive for facing contemporary political life, rather than a simple assertion in the face of nihilism. Presenting something of a dialectical overcoming of the opposition represented by master and slave morality in *On the Genealogy of Morality*, Church looks to the treatment of personal relationships in Z and political exemplars in *Beyond Good and Evil* for models that synthesize the disparity. He finds in relations of love a context for reconciling the conflicting ends of danger and play, and in the political action of Frederick the Great a model for a synthesizing the exertion of will and skeptical distance. Church suggests a more nuanced understanding of masculinity, compatible with contemporary liberal democratic societies, that takes joy in the risks that combining assertion and skepticism entails. In the concluding chapter,

Michael McNeal considers the affective disposition characteristic of and cultivated by Nietzsche's free spirits, which McNeal dubs "Dionysian mirth," and its role in realizing their revaluation of all values. Examining laughter's role in confronting ascetic life-denial and a corresponding Nietzschean praxis of life-affirmation, he demonstrates the significance of this temperament to the free spirit's identification of their task and enactment of the practices it commends. He then assesses how their inimitable laughter challenges the efficacy of decadence values and disrupts them like a storm, arguing that it is the key means by which they overcome those values. In so doing, he demonstrates the importance of the free spirit's Dionysian mirth to Nietzsche's lived philosophy and project of transfiguring humanity.

Notes

1. For a recent account connecting great power contests and Nietzsche's version of great politics, see Drochon (2016), and on Nietzsche's conflation of spiritual and concrete politics, see Gillespie (2017). Kirkland (2020), by contrast, argues that Nietzsche sees an enduring tension between philosophical and political life.
2. On Nietzsche's "campaign against morality," framed in political language and its liberatory aim in free spirit period, see Ansell-Pearson and Bamford (2021). On liberation and Nietzsche's long-term political strategy of revaluation, see Conway (1997: 148–57, 194–206; 2019: 182). On the role of individual self-overcoming and the revaluation of values, and the prospects they raise for a broader transfiguration of political life, see Strong (2000).
3. While Tamsin Shaw (2007) argues that Nietzsche's skepticism about all political forms leaves him unable to provide a normative basis for authority, Jeffrey Church claims that Nietzsche's early cultural views provide an argument against state power that would support a kind of liberalism (2015: 224).
4. On the subversive role of Nietzsche's conception of joyfulness as a practice in eroding the efficacy of life-denying ascetic values, see Michael McNeal (2019). David Owen (2002) challenges liberal pluralism while Lawrence Hatab (2008) argues that an agonistic theory can displace social contract theory and the need for justification of political authority in a manner that serves constitutional democracy.

References

Ansell-Pearson, Keith, and Rebecca Bamford (2021), *Nietzsche's Dawn: Philosophy, Ethics, and the Passion of Knowledge*, Hoboken, NJ: Wiley.

Church, Jeffrey (2015), *Nietzsche's Culture of Humanity: Beyond Aristocracy and Democracy in the Early Period*, New York: Cambridge University Press.

Conway, Daniel W. (2019), "Resurgent Nobility and the Problem of False Consciousness," in *Nietzsche and The Antichrist: Religion, Politics, and Culture in Late Modernity*, ed. Daniel Conway, 181–203, London: Bloomsbury Academic.

Conway, Daniel W. (1997), *Nietzsche's Dangerous Game: Philosophy in the Twilight of the Idols*, New York: Cambridge University Press.

Dombowsky, Don (2014), *Nietzsche and Napoleon: A Dionysian Conspiracy*, Chicago: University of Chicago Press.
Drochon, Hugo (2016), *Nietzsche's Great Politics*, Princeton, NJ: Princeton University Press.
Gillespie, Michael Allen (2017), *Nietzsche's Final Teaching*, Chicago: University of Chicago Press.
Hatab, Lawrence (2008), "Breaking the Social Contract," in *Nietzsche, Power, and Politics*, ed. Herman W. Siemens and Vasti Roodt, 169–88, Berlin: Walter de Gruyter.
Hatab, Lawrence (1988), "Laughter in Nietzsche's Thought: A Philosophical Tragicomedy," *International Studies in Philosophy* 20 (2): 67–79.
Higgins, Kathleen (2000), *Comic Relief: Nietzsche's Gay Science*, New York: Oxford University Press.
Kirkland, Paul E. (2020), "Nietzsche, Agonistic Politics, and Spiritual Enmity," *Political Research Quarterly* 73 (1): 3–14.
Lampert, Laurence (1999), "Nietzsche's Best Jokes," in *Nietzsche's Futures*, ed. John Lippitt, 68–91, London: Palgrave Macmillan.
Lippitt, John (1992), "Nietzsche, Zarathustra, and the Status of Laughter," *British Journal of the History of Aesthetics* 32 (1): 39–49.
McIntyre, Alex (2012), *The Sovereignty of Joy: Nietzsche's View of Grand Politics*, Toronto: University of Toronto Press.
McNeal, Michael J. (2019), "Subversive Joy: Nietzsche's Practice of Life-Enhancing Cheerfulness," *Southwest Philosophy Review* 35 (1): 207–16.
More, Nicholas D. (2014), *Nietzsche's Last Laugh: Ecce Homo as Satire*, New York: Cambridge University Press.
Owen, David (2002), "Equality, Democracy, and Self-Respect: Reflections on Nietzsche's Agonal Perfectionism," *Journal of Nietzsche Studies* 24: 113–31.
Shaw, Tamsin (2007), *Nietzsche's Political Skepticism*, Princeton, NJ: Princeton University Press.
Strong, Tracy B. (2000), *Friedrich Nietzsche and the Politics of Transfiguration*, Urbana: University of Illinois Press.

Part One

Joy and Knowledge

1

A Gay Science *Avant La Lettre*? Knowledge and Joy in *Human, All too Human*

Ruth Abbey

In an overview of Nietzsche's oeuvre, Andrew Huddleston repeats and seems to endorse the view of *Human, All too Human* (HH) as one of Nietzsche's positivist works. Although he provides no clear definition of positivism, Huddleston seems to mean three things by this: (1) "physiological or mechanistic explanations of a variety of phenomena," (2) a sober approach, and (3) "the simplistic assumption that … everything we do is ultimately driven by a desire for our own satisfaction" (2019: 346). Huddleston contrasts HH with *The Gay Science* (GS) where Nietzsche moves away from this putative positivism to seek "a form of 'science' [*Wissenschaft*] that will be joyful, centred in particular around the idea of *life affirmation*—finding life as something valuable to be celebrated" (2019: 348, emphasis in original).

Space does not permit me to outline why the imputation of each of these three features of positivism to HH is misleading at best and distortive at worst. For present purposes, I explore the possibility that, pace Huddleston, Nietzsche's quest for a gay science is already present in HH. While the term *fröhliche* itself does not appear, there are a number of cognate or comparable terms that signal that in HH, Nietzsche is already reaching for a way in which knowledge seekers can experience some joy or happiness, even if the truths they uncover are not particularly salutary or reassuring.

I start by noting that a number of scholars join Huddleston in characterizing HH as positivist. I consider whether there is any justification for this, based on the way Nietzsche introduces this work in its first chapter and reviewing his remarks about science there. Moving mostly chronologically through HH, I bring to light some of Nietzsche's profound concerns with the possible deleterious consequences of seeking and finding the truth. Yet I go on to identify those moments where he allows that finding truth might also spark joy, without losing sight of truth's difficult and perhaps dreadful nature. Moving through Nietzsche's remarks on knowledge and joy chronologically rather than thematically allows us to track some of twists and turns this work takes along its way. I point out what a high note HH ends on, a note more positive than positivist. I conclude by recommending that we henceforth banish the term "positivist" when describing HH while also noting what a difficult, if not impossible, text this is to summarize, given its highly experimental and volatile character.

My discussion is confined to the work originally entitled *Human, All Too Human*, which, in Keith Ansell-Pearson's estimation, shows Nietzsche "clearly … at his most positivistic" (2018: 8). HH was published in early 1878. *Assorted Opinions and Maxims* (AOM) appeared in 1879 and *The Wanderer and His Shadow* (WS) in 1880. These latter two works were, at the suggestion of Nietzsche's publisher, amalgamated to form volume 2 of HH in 1886 (Handwerk 2013: 561). At that time, Nietzsche appended a preface to each volume. In recognition of this publication history, I approach these three works separately and, due to constraints of space, can give only the first work the attention it deserves. The preface to volume 1, having been appended eight years later, is not treated here either.[1]

1. Positivism

Huddleston is not, as just noted, the only scholar to have dubbed HH positivist. As Ansell-Pearson conveys, HH "is typically construed as … being his most positivistic text in which the scientific interpretation of the world is privileged and guides the inquiry into religion, metaphysics, art and culture" (2018: 17).[2] Ansell-Pearson reads Nietzsche as negotiating "the competing claims of the positivist goal of science and eudaemonistic philosophy by aligning himself with the former" (2018: 8, cf. 18, 31). Maudemarie Clark and Brian Leiter describe HH as "the high watermark of Nietzsche's 'positivist' phase in which he accepted, somewhat uncritically, that science was the paradigm of all genuine knowledge" (1997: vii). Jonathan Cohen sees Nietzsche as embracing his own form of positivism in HH, taking Nietzsche's brand of positivism to mean the belief that science can contribute to reliable human knowledge and to human flourishing (1999: 101).[3] Julian Young writes of Nietzsche's "turn to positivism," according to which "*nothing* exists 'behind' nature; nothing exists *but* nature … nothing is beyond the reach of natural science, nothing is knowable save that which is, in principle, knowable by science" (2010: 242, emphasis original). More generally, Young identifies the "defining presupposition" of HH's new research program as "the potential omniscience of science" (2010: 243).

The progenitor of this idea that HH embraces positivism is probably Lou Andreas Salomé. Her *Friedrich Nietzsche in seinen Werken* was published in 1894, and the section on HH in her chapter entitled "Nietzsche's Transitions" contains several references to positivism. She claims, for example, that after his break with Wagner, "Nietzsche's intellectual development took a sudden turn toward the positivistic philosophy of the English and the French" (Salomé 2001: 53, cf. 59–60). She further maintains that Nietzsche was influenced by Paul Rée in this regard and indicates that for both of them, positivism's appeal lay in its promise of answering "the question about the origin of the moral phenomenon" (2001: 63). At this time Nietzsche became a "historian who planted his feet on the firm ground of positivism" (2001: 63, cf. 73, 81, 82, 85).

2. The Status of Science

As a way of trying to understand why scholars might characterize HH as positivist, it is instructive to start with the book's very first chapter, which reflects quite explicitly and consistently on the nature of knowledge and makes a number of comments in praise of science. HH opens by observing how much the philosophical project of Nietzsche's own time resembles that of the Ancient Greeks. "At almost every point, philosophical problems are once again assuming the same form for their questions as they did two thousand years ago" (HH 1). For someone trained as a classical philologist, this could be the ideal opportunity, as his expertise in Greek thought and culture could afford him an immediate relevance to and credibility within the philosophical debates of his time. Not so for Nietzsche, who roundly condemns this sort of "metaphysical philosophy" that treats these traditional questions as if they were of unchanging relevance and importance. He prefers "historical philosophy [*historische Philosophie*]" that is more cognizant of and responsive to the reality of change. He aligns this "historical philosophy" closely with "natural science [*Naturwissenschaft*]" (HH 1).[4]

HH's very next passage, however, initially effaces this promising subcategory of historical philosophy by accusing "all philosophers" of adopting an ahistorical approach to the human being. Devoid of all sense of history, philosophers confuse "the most recent shape of human beings" for their "fixed form" (HH 2). Yet Nietzsche insists, contrariwise, that everything "has become;[5] there are no eternal facts just as there are no absolute truths" (HH 2). Because of this, he once again invokes "historical philosophizing" as the more promising path to knowledge and in doing so tacitly corrects his earlier suggestion that all philosophy is ahistorical. The clear implication is that Nietzsche will not only be championing, but also doing, this sort of historically aware philosophy, which, as we just saw from HH 1, he associates with natural science.

Yet the possibility of this sort of historically aware philosophy is once again effaced when, just a few passages later, Nietzsche contrasts science with philosophy in general to posit an "antagonism between the individual fields of science and philosophy" (HH 6). By this rendering, all philosophy is metaphysical philosophy, and one of its preoccupations is to endow human life with "as much depth and meaning as possible." This is one of the reasons why throughout HH, metaphysical philosophy is associated with aesthetics and religion, for both of those latter endeavors also impute depth and meaning to human life. Science, unlike all these other approaches, "seeks knowledge and nothing further—whatever may come of it" (HH 6). From a remark like this last one, we can see why HH can be associated with positivism.

Science and philosophy are once again posed as antagonists in the very next passage that illustrates one of the ways in which philosophy has striven to provide depth and meaning to life. Nietzsche claims that since the Socratic school in Ancient Greece, philosophy has sought "that knowledge of the world and of life by which human beings will live most happily [*am glücklichsten lebt*]" (HH 7). The implication is that philosophers have subordinated truth to happiness whereas science, by contrast, has been unconcerned with the impact of its findings on human well-being. And once again we are led to infer that Nietzsche's own approach to knowledge will be closer to science than to philosophy.[6] Later in HH he asserts as a "fundamental Insight" that "there is no preestablished harmony between the furthering of truth and the well-being of humanity" (517). But the implication of this fundamental insight is that, conversely, there is no preestablished disharmony between truth and well-being. One cannot assume automatically that truth will lead either to happiness or to misery. As

I read Nietzsche, he is calling for an open, scientific approach to the truth rather than an a priori one. While some truths might prove fatal, others could be salutary.

This idea that science is historically aware and informed in a way that philosophy has not been returns in section 16, which announces that "the steady and laborious process of science … will someday finally celebrate its highest triumph in a genetic history of thought." This passage confidently predicts that this genetic history of thought will vindicate Nietzsche's claims that so far most philosophical knowledge has been a form of wishful thinking and built on a series of unsupportable premises and false dichotomies, such as those outlined in HH 1. Section 18 refers again to this "genetic history of thinking" that will bear out Nietzsche's claims and show that "all metaphysics" has been "the science that deals with the fundamental errors of human beings, but does so as if they were fundamental truths" (HH 18).[7] The fact that metaphysics is here referred to as a science should alert us to the fact that not all of Nietzsche's uses of the term "science" are meant to evoke the modern natural sciences or even forms of knowledge of which he approves.[8] Conversely, many of the errors he associates with metaphysics are not confined to that area of inquiry; they also infect mathematics (HH 19) and even language itself (HH 11).

Much of what is going on in these early sections of HH is an attack on the idea that we know the world in itself, in a way that is devoid of or detached from its meanings for humans. Metaphysics has mistaken the representational world, the world as it is for us, with the way it necessarily is, in itself. But in section 9, Nietzsche suggests that such a mistake might be inevitable: "We see all things through the human head and cannot cut this head off" (HH 9). He goes on to muse that anything we could know about the world in itself, separate from human understanding, would be irrelevant anyway.[9]

There are, however, times when Nietzsche suggests that the developments of the modern natural sciences and a greater historical awareness might free us from these errors and get us closer to an understanding of the world as it is. But he is also conscious that this task will not be easy, and however much it might increase our grasp of the truth, it might not be conducive to human happiness or well-being.[10] We get some inkling of the risks associated with seeking and finding truth in HH 22 where he sketches one of the disadvantages that might ensue from "the cessation of metaphysical views." He fears that this could foreshorten people's horizons, such that they focus only on the short term and fail to build for a longer future. Concerns about the consequences of knowing the truth recur when HH 29 cautions that "anyone who disclosed to us the essence of the world would cause us all the most unpleasant disillusionment." Section 31, entitled "Being Illogical Necessary," voices related worries and opens by declaring that "among the things that can bring a thinker to despair is the knowledge that being illogical is necessary for human beings, and that from being illogical arises much that is good." In all of these passages, Nietzsche is wringing his hands about what might happen if humans really did uncover the truth about themselves and their world. If, per HH 6, science "seeks knowledge and nothing further—whatever may come of it," then Nietzsche is not doing science here—or he is not doing just science because he repeatedly reflects upon the impact that finding the truth will have on human well-being.

At chapter 1's conclusion, a long passage reflects on the dilemma these ideas about knowledge and truth have brought Nietzsche to: how to live with the realization that "all of human life is sunk deeply into untruth." Are despair at the personal level and destruction at the philosophical level the only options for the pellucid thinker (HH 34)? He answers his own question by claiming that there is no definitive response: the way anyone reacts to these truths depends upon personal temperament. The right temperament allows thinkers to see religion and metaphysics for the beautiful illusions that they are, and to live unaided by them without descending into despondency at life's meaninglessness. For those with a good temperament, this knowledge, and indeed the commitment "to live only in order to know better" can even bring advantages. It can result in "a much simpler life," enabling them to live with some detachment and to view their lives as they would a play (*einem Schauspiel*). The knowledge such types are committed to pursuing cleanses them of the push, pull, and intensity of clashing desires. They are able to cast off a slew of negative emotions such as fear, blame, grumbling, sullenness, envy, and irritation. Such a person needs "a stable, mild and basically cheerful soul [*eine gefestete, milde und im Grunde frohsinnige Seele*]." The state of detachment and freedom they can achieve is one of "joy [*Freude*]," and this joy can be shared with others.[11] So already, by the conclusion of HH's first chapter, Nietzsche is adumbrating "a form of science [*Wissenschaft*], that will be joyful" (Huddleston 2019: 348). We don't need to wait for GS to encounter this possibility in his thinking.

Ansell-Pearson acknowledges this passage, even though it troubles his distinction between positivist science on the one hand, and eudemonistic philosophy on the other, and threatens his interpretation that HH pursues the former over the latter. But he finds it to be a "curiously passionless joy, one that divorces scientific practice and knowledge from the ends of eudaemonia or human flourishing" (2018: 8).[12] A close reading of the passage suggests otherwise to me. As I indicate above, the seeker after truth experiences joy and cheer but is largely free of the disruptive passions listed above. The seeker's life is "more purified of affects" but not affect-less; over time he becomes subject to less "intense desire" but he is not devoid of desire.[13] He does, after all, desire "to know better" (HH 34). Such a person is slow to judge and looks upon himself and other humans "without praise, reproaches or excessive zeal." He is likewise free of "emphasis" and accepts himself and all humans as part of nature. All of these attainments enhance the thinker's well-being. As such a person looks upon their own life and that of others, they feast "upon the sight of many things that had previously only made us afraid."[14] This might not be a picture of the good life that appeals to Ansell-Pearson (or many others), but that it is an image of the good life, rather than an expression of positivist science, seems hard to deny.

This possibility that seekers after truth have their own distinctive form of happiness recurs in a charming passage entitled "Vegetation of Happiness [*Glückes*]" (HH 591), which outlines the various ways in which humans seek happiness despite suffering, sorrow, and devastation. They lay out their little, and different, gardens of happiness (*kleinen Gärtens des Glückes*) with two of the three types of gardeners depicted there having the features Nietzsche associates with free spirits. There are, for instance, those who "observe life with the eye of someone who wants knowledge alone from experience" and there are those who rejoice "in difficulties that have been overcome"

(HH 591). In these cases, happiness can sprout alongside misfortune, and it might be that the greater the misfortune, the greater the happiness. But Nietzsche insists that the happiness does not justify the misfortune and suffering. Passages like these suggest to me that, pace Ansell-Pearson, there is a concern with eudaimonia in HH. It might be primarily a concern for the well-being of free spirits, but we can read Nietzsche as trying to articulate, protect, and promote their distinctive form of happiness. As we read in HH 438, free spirits do have their own idea of happiness, one that seems to be entwined with their own idea of seriousness (*Ernst*). Their idea of happiness is quite different from that of most people (*ihr Glück ist ein anderer Begriff*), but it is still an idea of happiness.

By the time we arrive at the end of the first of HH's nine chapters, we can see what a poor fit the positivist label is for this work. Pace Huddleston, there is no evidence that Nietzsche is advocating physiological or mechanistic explanations for all things—instead he insists upon a historically aware approach to knowledge. Nietzsche is not pitting science against philosophy in any implacable sense but rather urging philosophers to become less metaphysical and more scientific and thus more historical in their thinking. As this indicates, not all philosophy need be metaphysical; rather, metaphysical philosophy is one subcategory of philosophy and historical philosophy is another. This latter is, in Nietzsche's view, a better type of philosophy because it is more attuned to and able to accommodate findings from the natural sciences. This gives him hope for the prospect of "a truly liberating philosophical science [*eine wirklich befreiende philosophische Wissenschaft*]" (HH 27).

However, while such a philosophy might free its practitioners from false and ahistorical beliefs about human beings and from metaphysical binaries, Nietzsche is also predicting and evaluating the possible consequences of an increase in true knowledge, both for the individuals who attain it and for the wider culture, should these findings become widely disseminated and accepted. Thus, while Cohen is correct that Nietzsche believes that science can contribute to reliable human knowledge, it is less clear that this knowledge contributes to human flourishing, for he indicates clearly the many ways in which it can jeopardize such flourishing. The evidence from HH so far must also complicate Clark and Leiter's claim that this book takes science to be the paradigm of all genuine knowledge, along with Young's view that Nietzsche has faith in its "potential omniscience" (2010: 243). Read in the round, the sort of knowledge that Nietzsche is promoting in HH points simultaneously to what science does not know and cannot tell us along with what it can teach. For this reason, we must also question Ansell-Pearson's claim that HH privileges science over other forms of knowledge and thus provides the standpoint from which its inquiries into religion, metaphysics, art, and culture proceed. While there is some accuracy to this depiction when it comes to HH's critiques of religion, art, and metaphysics, it is also the case, once again, that Nietzsche draws attention to the things that science cannot do and cannot provide that religion, art, and metaphysics can. The evaluation of these different forms of knowledge and their effects is not one way with religion, metaphysics, and art sitting in the dock to be evaluated by science as judge, jury, and executioner. While there is a lot of that style of critique, we must not be blind to the fact that science is also found wanting by Nietzsche in multiple ways when considered from the vantage point of religion, metaphysics, and art. He is keenly aware that its truths could lead many into despair, and, as noted above, only the right temperament will prevent "our philosophy" from turning into "tragedy" (HH 34).

3. Sparking Joy

Huddleston is closer to the mark when he detects "a sober approach" in HH, but even then, as we have seen witnessed in section 34, sober is not solemn and sobriety need not preclude gaiety. We can see, moreover, that such attention to the place of joy in the truth-seeker's experience is not Nietzsche's first and last word on this issue. For example, not all of the truths that Nietzschean knowers uncover will be dangerous or dispiriting, as the remarkable, overlooked, and seemingly most un-Nietzschean passage on "Benevolence" (HH 49) testifies.[15] Nietzsche recommends benevolence (*Wohlwollen*) as something to which science should pay more attention, and when it does, "it will find much more happiness [*Glück*] in the world than melancholy eyes see" (HH 49). By benevolence, he means "those expressions of friendly sentiment in social interaction, that smile of the eyes, that shaking of hands, that comfortable pleasure with which almost all human actions are ordinarily entwined." Not limited to associations of intimates or familiars, benevolence also manifests itself among teachers and officials, seasoning the conduct of their duties. But Nietzsche goes on to make it an even more pervasive social sentiment than this: benevolence "is the continual activity of human nature, the waves of its light … in which everything grows." These small, everyday expressions of benevolence such as "good naturedness, friendliness, politeness of the heart" that are "the ever-flowing streams of the unegotistical drive" are more effective and more genuine forms of fellow feeling than forces such as "sympathy, compassion and sacrifice." This latter trio are, of course, the things that religion and conventional morality have attended to, while the power, fertility, and quotidian beauty of benevolence has been overlooked. Although Nietzsche goes on to clarify that "there is not actually much that is unegotistical" in benevolence, this does not detract from its value or importance. Instead, expressions of benevolence contribute to the "moments of comfortable pleasure in which every day of every human life, even the most distressed one, is rich." (HH 49) As this wonderfully lyrical passage conveys, recognition of the reality of benevolence in human life is a truth that is bound to bring joy to those who see it.

Lest this passage on benevolence and its fruits be dismissed as either insincere or a moment of Nietzschean self-forgetfulness, this image of benevolence bringing pleasure to other people, no matter how closely connected we are to them, reappears in passing in HH 89. It is also relevant that Nietzsche's long, loving, and lovely account of benevolence belongs to a chapter that opens by praising the perspicacity of the French moralist tradition of psychology (HH 35). Debating with himself, Nietzsche goes on to weigh the pros and cons of such psychological acuity, just as in chapter 1 he weighs and measures the consequences of truth-seeking. On the one hand, psychological observation in the moralist tradition is a gain for truth, but there are also disadvantages attendant upon this. He worries, for example, that this can implant "a sense of diminishment and suspicion in the souls of human beings" (HH 36). Insight into humans' true motivations can corrode belief in their goodness, diminish their happiness, and even reduce the amount of goodness in the world by making people mutually mistrustful. So, there is a trade-off between illusion, happiness, trust in one's fellows, and "philanthropy" (*Menschenfreundlichkeit*), on the one hand, and truth and "the spirit of science" (*Geiste der Wissenschaft*) on the other (HH 36). Despite these dangers, Nietzsche ultimately welcomes a revival of psychological observation in this tradition: "For what rules here is the science that inquires about the origin and history of the so-called moral sensations" (HH 37). He sees his friend and collaborator Paul Rée as spearheading this historical approach to morality (HH 36–7). When the passage on benevolence is restored to this context within HH, we can reliably infer that Nietzsche is offering a sincere and clear-sighted account of this sentiment and its social benefits.

The possibility that knowing the truth is inimical to human happiness returns, however, early in chapter 3 when Nietzsche cites a bracing passage from Lord Byron's dramatic prose poem, *Manfred*. Borrowing Bryon's words to entitle the passage "Sorrow is Knowledge," Nietzsche reflects on the demise of religious belief and the loss of its consolations. The truths that will replace religion will not be edifying or salutary; instead, we will discover, in Manfred's words, "the fatal truth [that] the tree of knowledge is not that of life." Nietzsche also moots "the danger … that humanity may bleed to death from recognizing truth" (HH 109). But Nietzsche's invocation of *Manfred*, which he quotes in English, is quite selective and somewhat misleading when placed in the overall context of Byron's poem. The eponymous Manfred has done something terrible—exactly what is not specified, as Manfred cannot bring himself to speak it. But because of this deed, the poem's protagonist longs for oblivion. Unable to sleep, he can find refuge in no activity or distraction. He therefore summons the immortal spirits of the universe to help him attain forgetfulness. Even if Manfred is making a claim about the nature of truth when he equates sorrow and knowledge, its significance fades by contrast with his own personal torture. It is the memory of this deed that he is desperately seeking relief from, rather than the lethal nature of truth. Indeed, Manfred draws this contrast between the tree of knowledge and that of life but observes that he can subject philosophy and science to his own mind whereas he cannot gain control over the knowledge of his terrible deed. He lists the other things he has done in life—good to some and harm to enemies. Yet the full gamut of his experience is as nothing compared to his current torment and he cannot exercise any mental dominion or even sway over this. Instead, he is utterly consumed by it.

However selective and unrepresentative Nietzsche's invocation of Bryon's poem might be, the passage in HH soon conjures a Horatian ideal of "festive levity [*feierlichen Leichtsinn*]" (HH 109) as an antidote to this rumination on the possibly fatal nature of truth. R. J. Hollingdale translates this as "solemn frivolity," which is quite different from Handwerk's "festive levity," but the passage from Horace cited in the text (*Odes*, 2, 11) is more in accord with levity than solemnity. As an alternative to burdening one's mortal mind with thoughts of eternity, this passage invites its addressee, Quinctius, to come and lie under a tree and drink wine, which strikes a note more festive than solemn (to me at least). In this context we see not so much that knowledge can be a source of joy but that solace in the comforts of ordinary human life can be a counterweight to the heavy burdens of truth.

However we interpret this Horatian turn, it is noteworthy that Nietzsche refers in this passage to the work of two poets—one modern, one ancient—as he reflects upon how to carry on in the face of truths that might prove fatal. This illustrates anew one of my claims above about the status of science in HH. Because Nietzsche sources poetry to convey his thinking about the challenges of living with the truth, science cannot be "the paradigm of all genuine knowledge" (Clark and Leiter 1997: vii) nor the "interpretation of the world [that] is privileged and guides the inquiry into religion, metaphysics, art and culture" (Ansell-Pearson 2018: 17). Science is not sitting in judgment on art here; instead, resources from poetry are drawn upon to inform his discussion of how to live with the truths that science uncovers. Even when scientific discoveries such as the recognition of benevolence as described above can bring pleasure and satisfaction, Nietzsche fears that once science's findings become commonplace, they will supply less and less pleasure to their recipients, while at the same time robbing them of the pleasures and satisfactions that metaphysics, religion, and art once afforded. In this dire scenario, "the greatest source of pleasure, the one to which humanity owes almost all it means to be human, will be impoverished" (HH 251). As this passage soon reveals, that greatest source of pleasure is "illusion, error, and fantasy [*die Illusion, der Irrthum, die Phantastik*]" rather than reason, truth, or science.

Reflecting explicitly on the "future of science," Nietzsche's solution to this threat to that greatest source of pleasure is for people to develop "a dual brain, two compartments of the brain … the one to experience science, the other to experience nonscience: lying next to each other, without confusion, separable, each able to be closed off from the other" (HH 251). The nonscience side of the brain is "the power source [*die Kraftquelle*]": fueled by "illusions, one-sidedness, and passions [*Illusionen, Einseitigkeiten, Leidenschaften*]," it generates heat. The scientific side of the brain is "the regulator" that prevents "the dangerous consequences of overheating." Should this bicameral brain not be developed, society will regress horribly:

> The interest in what is true will cease to the extent that it provides less pleasure; illusion, error, and fantasy will reconquer step by step the terrain they once controlled, because they are associated with pleasure: the ruination of the sciences and a sinking back into barbarism will result. (HH 251)

Among other things, this remarkable passage illustrates that in HH, scientific thinking need not and should not drive out its opposite; on the contrary, it is essential that nonscientific thinking and experiences remain part of the higher culture of the future, whatever form they take. The role of science is to regulate these other forces, to moderate but not extirpate or even dominate them. He evokes a fearful image of barbaric backsliding into a state where the achievements of the present are forfeited or at least buried if the nonscience side of the human brain is not given adequate recognition and avenues for its creativity.[16] It is really hard to see how this picture of the scientific and nonscientific parts of the brain working together is compatible with any model of positivism or any belief in the omniscience of science. But it also shows Nietzsche being more accepting than he sometimes is of the persistence of error, illusion, and fantasy. Sometimes in HH this realization is a cause for gloom, but here it is accepted not only as an essential ingredient of being human but also as "the greatest source of pleasure [*Lust*]" (HH 251). Nietzsche carves out a place for this in the future that gives full rein to its creativity while also mitigating some of its dangers.

The final section of chapter 5, which contains this passage on the bicameral brain, starts on an upbeat note. Addressing seekers of knowledge directly, it exhorts them to move "forward on the track of wisdom [*Weisheit*] with a firm step and steady confidence" (HH 292). Shifting the imagery from marching to climbing, Nietzsche assures them that "you have in yourself a ladder with a hundred rungs on which you can climb to knowledge [*Erkenntniss*]" (HH 292). He comforts his audience about the interregnum they live in where old forms of knowledge such as metaphysics and religion are being discredited while new forms are still being built. Rather than regret this, he urges them to see this as an advantage: "You have it in your own hands to succeed in dissolving everything you live through … into your goal without any remainder" (HH 292). He acknowledges that this path might feel too demanding and too unrewarding for some but assures them that "no honey is sweeter than that of knowledge and that the clouds of affliction hanging over you must serve as the udder from which you will squeeze the milk for your own refreshment" (HH 292). To those having doubts and second or third thoughts about persisting in their quest for knowledge, Nietzsche promises a metaphorical land of milk and honey!

He also urges them to look ahead to their own old age for the rewards that their quest will ultimately afford. Looking back from that projected vantage point, they will be able to appreciate "how you have given ear to the voice of nature, the nature that rules the whole world through appetite [*Lust*]." For present purposes, it is interesting to note that Handwerk translates *Lust* as "pleasure" here; Hollingdale as joy. But I am taking *Lust* to mean a more generic "appetite," so that Nietzsche seems to be saying that seekers after knowledge have followed the voice of nature by pursuing their appetite for truth. It would seem that in doing so I am weakening the value of this passage as evidence for my thesis that HH harbors glimpses of a gay science. But what follows these lines cannot be mistaken, for these imagined matured free spirits will bask in "the gentle sunshine of a continuous spiritual joyfulness [*in jenem milden Sonnenglanz einer beständigen geistigen Freudigkeit*]."[17] Although death might be imminent, their "final movement" is one "toward the light"; their "final sound" is "an exulting shout of knowledge" (HH 292). Nietzsche's term here, *Jauchzen*, can be translated as "to shout with joy" when used as a verb, which perhaps explains why Hollingdale translates this as "a joyful shout of knowledge." Replete with this remarkable imagery, including some with Platonic resonances, chapter 5 thus ends on a note that is not just upbeat but triumphant. Whatever else we make of this fascinating section, it is clear that Nietzsche is assuring his followers that their quest for knowledge, whatever its challenges and difficulties, will ultimately yield them joy and self-affirmation.[18]

For the purposes of this chapter, it is important to note that HH as a whole ends on a very high note, with its final passage offering a vignette of the person pursuing the sort of scientific knowledge that this book advocates. Using the analogy of a journey to describe what the seeker of knowledge experiences, Nietzsche does not shy away from or understate the travails involved. Not only does this wandering seeker after truth not know his final destination, he does not even see himself as having one. He journeys on, absorbing all he sees around him, without becoming rooted in or attached to any locale. This journey will know its share of difficulties, and there will be times when the wanderer feels oppressed by his journey and all it reveals to him, and yearns to cease moving. "Then the terrible night will sink over him like a second desert upon the desert and his heart will be weary of wandering" (HH 638). In some cases, the dawn of day will bring further ugly and painful things to light, so that "the day may be almost worse than the night" (HH 638).

But to leaven this very real and extensive suffering, there will be other mornings in other places that are "delightful [*wonnevollen*],"[19] disclosing swarms of dancing muses to the wanderer's eyes. At yet other times, his soul will experience "equanimity [*Gleichmass*]" and "nothing but good and bright things are thrown out to him … the gifts of all those free spirits who are at home amid the mountains, woods and solitude." Not only do they have "good and bright things [*gute und helle Dinge*]" to dispense, but those fellow and perhaps former free spirits are described as sometimes "joyful" (HH 638). HH's remarkably fecund conclusion reveals that this work is clearly ruminating on the thread that has run through my chapter—how to live with truths that are difficult and disturbing and what the impact on the seeker after truth of these discoveries will be. From this final passage we can see that Nietzsche is already envisaging a form of gay science—one that will be gay in the face of very difficult truths. Fellow free spirits who follow or have followed this difficult route will ultimately have some "good and bright things" to bestow as gifts (*die Geschenke*) and will possess the generosity to do just that.

Conclusion

This chapter has charted a course through HH guided by Nietzsche's remarks about knowledge and joy. We have witnessed some of his expressions of profound concern with the possible deleterious consequences of seeking and finding the truth. But we have also witnessed some moments when, notwithstanding its difficult and perhaps dreadful nature, finding truth can engender joy.

Of the handful of scholars who have grappled with these issues, my interpretation is closest to that of Michael Ure who reads Nietzsche as extracting an emancipatory or therapeutic value from science in HH and who is aware of the damaging consequences that uncovering the truth could have in Nietzsche's estimation (2013: 118–19). However, Ure discerns a stronger presence of positivism in HH than do I, describing Nietzsche as trying to "convert his newly discovered positivist value neutrality into an ethical stance" (2013: 118, cf. 124). Ure helpfully dramatizes the very real tension between these two strands more fully than does Ansell-Pearson and does not, as I read him, suggest that HH prioritizes positivism over eudaimonia (Ure 2013: 112–21). I have addressed above why I find Ure's claim, reiterated by Ansell-Pearson, that HH 34's view of "joyful science is a curiously joyless affair" (2013: 123) to be unconvincing. Ure's chapter draws from fewer of HH's passages than I do here,[20] in part because he casts his net more widely to include WS, *Dawn* (D), and GS. He finds a changed relationship between science and philosophical passions in D such that Nietzsche now recognizes that science "satisfies certain kinds of passions, particularly a certain kind of joy or delight" (2013: 126). However, as evidenced above, I see this connection already in HH rather than being new to D. Moreover, as his title—"Nietzsche's 'View from Above'"—signals, Ure's organizing focus is different from mine, for he attributes considerable significance to HH 34's image of the hovering philosopher looking over reality from above and is constantly tracing Nietzsche's outlook in HH back to ancient antecedents.

In contrast to most of HH's commentators, I propose that henceforth we banish the term "positivism" from our lexicon for describing this book. It is noteworthy that the term does not appear anywhere in the text. Indeed, the term does not appear in any of Nietzsche's published works until GS where section 347 uses the term "positivist [*positivistisch*]" in conjunction with "scientific [*wissenschaftlich*]." The term *positivismus* is used in Nietzsche's notebooks in 1876 and 1877, indicating that it was part of his vocabulary.[21] Had Nietzsche wanted to call HH positivist he could have. Indeed, according to Erich Heller (1996: xii–xii), the 1877 notebook reference comes from an unused introduction to HH, which illustrates that Nietzsche ultimately elected not to use this term to describe his work.

In *Nietzsche's Enlightenment*, Paul Franco distinguishes Nietzsche's "Enlightenment Project," which begins in HH, from positivism. Franco argues that whereas positivism rejects metaphysics, Nietzsche reflects upon what happens once we go beyond metaphysics (2011: 22–3). I echo Franco's view that the term "positivism" is misleading in this context (Franco 2011: x) and share his preference for the term "enlightenment" when describing HH (Abbey 2020: 7). As Domenico Losurdo also contends, "the science of Nietzsche as a philosopher of the 'Enlightenment' had nothing to do with the sort of science valued by positivism a la Comte" (2019: 288).[22] And it is noteworthy that unlike "positivist," "enlightenment" is a term that Nietzsche uses to characterize his work at this time (HH 26). However, even here, Nietzsche's use of the term "enlightenment" is quite idiosyncratic, as Franco observes (2011: ix). I suspect that no single term can capture what is going on in HH. As I have argued elsewhere, this is a highly experimental work that entertains and explores a number of different ideas and possibilities. Rather than advocating or practicing positivism, Nietzsche is "conducting an honest, searching and troubled conversation with himself about the implications of treading the scientific path to knowledge" (Abbey 2020: 13, cf. 31).

My purpose here is not to suggest that HH's agenda is that same as that of GS. HH's agenda is, for one thing, too manifold and mobile to mount such a claim. And Nietzsche changes some of his views between HH and AOM and WS, so it is very likely that he will have changed some views again by the time he gets to GS. My point is the more modest one that understanding what joyful knowing requires for Nietzsche need not start with GS; we can get some premonitions of this from HH. As Ansell-Pearson says when discussing the "Vegetation of Happiness" (HH 591) passage outlined above, "the longing for 'blissful' and 'serene' mobility seems to provide the kind of happiness or joy sought by the wandering free spirit prized in the middle period texts and anticipates something of the character of the joyful wisdom of the gay science" (Ansell-Pearson

2017: 47). But rather than describing HH's many reflections on joyful knowledge as "anticipating" GS, I propose that GS elaborates these earlier possibilities.

Notes

1. Unless noted, I cite Gary Handwerk's 1995 translation of HH.
2. Cf. Magnus and Higgins (1996: 31) and Fortier (2020: 4–5). Jeremy Fortier wrongly characterizes me as applying the positivist label to this work (and the other middle period writings). On the page he cites to support this claim (2020: 166, n11), I simply observe that these works "are sometimes labeled positivist" (Abbey 2000: 87). Although I do not prosecute there the critique of calling HH positivist that I offer here, I do not endorse that label, and the index to that work incudes no entry for positivism.
3. Nadeem Hussain (2004) discusses whether some of Nietzsche's later writings can be considered positivist.
4. Although Matthew Meyer (2019: 89) contends that Nietzsche's intervention in this debate is directly informed by his knowledge of ancient thought, from this perspective he is effectively capitalizing on his expertise as a classical philologist.
5. Handwerk renders "*Alles ... ist geworden*" as "Everything ... has come to be" (1995: 17) whereas I follow R. J. Hollingdale's "everything has become" (1986: 13).
6. Ansell-Pearson (2018: 29) also discusses this passage.
7. Ansell-Pearson (2018: 28) also discusses this idea but cites HH 17–18 whereas I track this phrase to sections 16 and 18.
8. As Robin Small points out, "when Nietzsche refers to science (*Wissenschaft*) ... he is invoking a concept of disciplined inquiry which applies to classical philology as much as to the investigation of natural phenomena" (2005: 9).
9. This point is a bit different from Young's claims that "*nothing* exists 'behind' nature; nothing exists *but* nature" and that "Nietzsche's strategy is not to refute metaphysics but to show that the metaphysical world is a superfluous hypothesis" (2010: 24). Here Nietzsche is allowing that the world in itself might exist, behind and beyond nature. But knowledge of it, were it possible, would be useless for us. So while hypothesizing its existing might not be superfluous, anything we could know about it would be unusable information.
10. Ansell-Pearson (2018: 32) and Michael Ure (2013) also recognize this dilemma. I compare my approach and finding's to Ure's in the concluding section of this chapter.
11. Meyer (2019: 90–8) provides a very helpful tour of chapter 1 and a discussion of its connections with Nietzsche's earlier thought.
12. Reiterating this idea (2018: 31), Ansell-Pearson attributes it to Ure (2013: 123).
13. Ansell-Pearson's (2019: 79–80) reading of this passage acknowledges this.
14. For an explanation as to why I refer to the free spirit figure in HH as masculine, see Abbey (2020: 123–4).
15. I discuss this remarkable passage in Abbey (2000: 65–6) but have seen no other Nietzsche commentator refer to it.
16. Ansell-Pearson (2018: 20) also discusses this passage.
17. Ansell-Pearson is aware of this passage (2018: 9) but does not consider its significance for his thesis about HH's preference for positivism over eudaimonia.
18. In this way it echoes an earlier, shorter passage from chapter 4, "Joy in Old Age [*Freude im Alter*]" (HH 209), where Nietzsche describes the joy that the ageing

thinker or artist can experience, notwithstanding their physical and mental decay. That person's "better self has taken refuge in his works," and so the damage that the thief of time can do to the body and the spirit poses no threat to the works. However, as he describes that joy as "almost malicious [*boshafte*]," I do not include it in the catalog of passages that support my thesis about HH's gay science.
19. Handwerk renders this as "rapturous", Hollingdale as "joyful."
20. He cites HH 7, 30, 33, 34, 517.
21. Nietzschesource shows the term *positivismus* appearing in two places in Nietzsche's writings around this time: *Nachgelassene Fragmente Winter 1876–1877*, 20 (19) and *Nachgelassene Fragmente Frühling–Sommer 1877*, 22 (37).
22. Chapters 7–9 of Losurdo's book trace the enlightenment theme through Nietzsche's middle period works.

References

Abbey, Ruth (2000), *Nietzsche's Middle Period*, Oxford: Oxford University Press.
Abbey, Ruth (2020), *Human All too Human: A Critical Introduction and Guide*, Edinburgh University Press, Edinburgh.
Ansell-Pearson, Keith (2017), "On Nietzsche's Search for Happiness and Joy: Thinking with Epicurus", *The Agonist*, X, II, Spring, pp. 41–58.
Ansell-Pearson, Keith (2018), *Nietzsche's Search for Philosophy: On the Middle Writings*, London: Bloomsbury.
Ansell-Pearson, Keith (2019), "Nietzsche on Transforming the Passions into Joys: On the Middle Writings and *Thus Spoke Zarathustra*," in *Nietzsche, penseur de l'affirmation: Relecture de Ainsi parlait Zarathoustra*, ed. Clément Bertot, Jean Leclercq, N. Monseu, and Patrick Wotling, 73–90, Louvain, Presses Universitaires de Louvain.
Clark, Maudemarie, and Brian Leiter (1997), "Introduction," in *Nietzsche: Daybreak: Thoughts on the Prejudices of Morality*, vii–xxxiv, Cambridge: Cambridge University Press.
Cohen, Jonathan R. (1999), "Nietzsche's Fling with Positivism," in *Nietzsche, Epistemology, and Philosophy of Science: Nietzsche and the Sciences II*, ed. Babette Babich, 101–7, Dordrecht: Kluwer.
Franco, Paul (2011), *Nietzsche's Enlightenment: The Free Spirit Trilogy of the Middle Period*, Chicago: University of Chicago Press.
Fortier, Jeremy (2020), *The Challenge of Nietzsche: How to Approach His Thought*, Chicago: University of Chicago Press.
Handwerk, Gary (2013), "Translator's Afterword," in *Human, All Too Human II and Unpublished Fragments from the Period*, trans. Gary Handwerk, 555–84, Stanford: Stanford University Press.
Heller, Erich (1996), "Introduction," in Nietzsche, Friedrich (1986), *Human, All Too Human*, trans. R. J. Hollingdale, New York: Cambridge University Press, vii–xix.
Huddleston, Andrew (2019), "The Value of Our Values: Nietzsche," in *A Companion to Nineteenth Century Philosophy*, ed. John Shand, 339–64, Oxford: John Wiley and Sons.
Hussain, Nadeem J. Z. (2004), "Nietzsche's Positivism," *European Journal of Philosophy* 12 (3): 326–68.
Losurdo, Domenico (2019), *Nietzsche, the Aristocratic Rebel: Intellectual Biography and Critical Balance Sheet*, trans. Gregor Benton, with an introduction by Harrison Fluss, Leiden: Brill.

Magnus, Bernd, and Higgins, Kathleen (1996), "Nietzsche's Work and Their Themes," in *The Cambridge Companion to Nietzsche*, ed. Bernd Magnus and Kathleen Higgins, 22–70, Cambridge: Cambridge University Press.

Meyer, Matthew (2019), *Nietzsche's Free Spirit Works: A Dialectical Reading*, Cambridge: Cambridge University Press.

Salomé, Lou Andreas (2001), *Nietzsche*, trans. and ed. Siegfried Mandel, Urbana: University of Illinois Press.

Small, Robin (2005), *Nietzsche and Rée: A Star Friendship*, New York: Oxford University Press.

Ure, Michael (2013), "Nietzsche's 'View from Above,'" in *Nietzsche's Therapeutic Teaching*, ed. Horst Hutter and Eli Friedland, 117–41, London: Bloomsbury Press.

Young, Julian (2010), *Friedrich Nietzsche: A Philosophical Biography*, New York: Cambridge University Press.

2

Aesthetics of Joy and Levity for Nietzsche's Free Spirit

Paul E. Kirkland

Nietzsche's *The Gay Science* (GS) completes a series of books that he conceived as trilogy of works dedicated to building an ideal of the free spirit.[1] Some scholars have viewed this "middle period" of Nietzsche's work as a rejection of the aestheticism of the early period.[2] The books he published between 1878 and 1882 (*Human, All Too Human* [HH] and its sequels, *Dawn* [D] and GS) exhibit a development in the role that art plays for the free spirit. Rather than a full rejection of his earlier aesthetic views in favor of an embrace of positivism, we can see the move, especially as manifest in GS, as one from the tragic to the comic. In its opening section, Nietzsche raises the prospect—"Even laughter may yet have a place" (GS 1)—and suggests that laughter and wisdom might form an alliance that produces a gay science. The shift is toward attention to the possibility of the sort of joy that takes delight in the world. Nietzsche scholars who have systematically addressed works of the free spirit period have noted the development across the time of this set of works.[3] After what appears to be a very clear break with the aesthetic enthusiasms of the early period,[4] the role of art develops from HH to GS. I argue that Nietzsche's second aesthetics emerges in GS as a play of levity and gravity, giving art a vital role in serving the possibility of knowledge and liberation characteristic of the free spirit.

The role of art moves from one that is preparatory to science in HH to that of a counterforce to the ethic of scientific inquiry in GS. By the culminating work of the free spirit period, Nietzsche demonstrates the important role art has to play in this dynamic. While Nietzsche's view develops across his free spirit works,[5] this chapter focuses on GS and its aesthetic themes that serve the goal of making joyful knowledge possible. After briefly touching on the role of art from the beginning of free spirit works, I turn to Nietzsche's comic framing of aesthetic considerations in GS. I then take up "the appearance of freedom" as a definition of beauty that Nietzsche adopts from earlier German aesthetics and transforms into a fitting element of freedom of spirit. Across GS, Nietzsche moves from "the beautiful unnaturalness" of artistic appearances to an agonistic naturalism that presents art as a needed counterforce to rigorous science that challenges its moral commitments. Next, I examine the ways that Nietzsche's aesthetics show the possibilities for joy in the beautiful monstrosity of self-contesting nature. I conclude by showing the way in such joy aided by levity can make possible gaiety in science, laughter in knowing, and loving life as it is.

As Nietzsche appears to relegate art to the past in HH, he also makes clear that it prepares a disposition that might be taken over by science. This presentation of the role of art appreciates art while looking forward to a time when it will be "a wondrous relic" (HH 223) remembered like other youthful joys. While treating art as preparing the way for the free spirit, its lessons are significant for cultivating the disposition needed for science: "This teaching of art—to have joy [*Lust*] in existence and to regard human life as part of nature" (HH 222). The embrace of life may now be found in science rather than aesthetic joy, Nietzsche claims in HH, but only because art already conditions one for joy in life. The other key aspect of the "teaching of art" expressed in this passage involves regarding human life as part of nature. He praises a disposition cultivated by art for a naturalization of human life that does not allow for a final separation of human capacities from natural processes. Such naturalization prepares the way for science but finds its first manifestations in the teaching of art.

The need to cultivate the disposition suited to science already shows that the perspective of the free spirit works to involve more than positivist science. Ruth Abbey presents HH as involving what she calls an "epistemology-plus" perspective by contrast with those who would describe HH as the work of a positivist stage (2020). She shows the way in which ethical and aesthetic considerations, including the ways that holding ideas will affect the way people will "live, feel, and experience those beliefs," continue to hold importance even as Nietzsche orients his thought toward a kind of enlightenment project (2020: 45). The cultivation of free spiritedness entails such concerns if one aims to account for any commitment to knowledge. In the free spirit works, scientific aims are connected to questions of cultivating free spiritedness, a question beyond the scope of empirical and methodological science. Abbey argues that Nietzsche's scientific lens reveals "the close affinity between art, religion, and traditional metaphysics" (2020: 71). Art's "glorification of philosophical errors" (HH 220) may be a matter for deep sorrow, one that ultimately pits all art against knowledge. Abbey points out that much of Nietzsche's HH treatment of art in "On the Souls of Artists and Writers" seems to establish a sharp dichotomy between art and science (2020: 72). She argues that, contrary to Julian Young, the development of a continued role for art emerges only in the supplemental works of HH II (*Associated Opinions and Maxims* [AOM] and *The Wanderer and His Shadow* [WS]) and not in HH I.[6]

In AOM and WS, Nietzsche's views on art and artists develop, and Abbey has shown the ways in which some art might have a "creative and constructive role in a more enlightened future" (2020: 179).[7] Nietzsche looks to the Greeks for models (AOM 169, 170; WS 140, 214) as he anticipates a future age with "true festivals of joy and freedom"; he acknowledges that they will have no use for "*our* art" (WS 170). In D, Nietzsche continues to indicate a possible role for art in the free spirit project, indicating the way in which it might serve as a gateway to knowledge, prepared by the possibility of taking "joy in reality [*Freude am Wirklichen*]" (D 244). It becomes clear that art can have a role in the enlightenment aims of free-spiritedness.[8] The dynamic between knowledge and art provides an image of the free spirit's liberation as a complex interplay, indicating alternative political possibilities to those that involve limiting state power or preparing the way for philosophical command.[9] While Nietzsche argues in HH that freedom from religion and metaphysics is made possible by a scientific approach to knowing, he moves toward showing the place of art's service to such freedom by the time of GS. In the culminating work of the free spirit period, art is a vital element to love for life.

1. The Future of Laughter

The final work of the free spirit trilogy,[10] GS, includes the goal of forging a new alliance between laughter and wisdom possible only after the "age of tragedy" in which we are still caught. Nietzsche writes of the current "age of tragedy" not as one in which a new birth of the art of tragedy has reshaped culture[11] but as identical to the age of moralities and religions (GS 1). Such "tragedians," Nietzsche explains, have been making attempts to promote the interest and preservation of the species. Taking a more cheerful tone than he does in other places, Nietzsche explains that the effort to do what is "good for the preservation of the human race" has thus far involved efforts to teach "the purpose of existence" (GS 1). His opening treatment of the "teachers of the purpose of existence" notes that there have been many attempts to consider what is beneficial and what is harmful to the preservation of the human race. Such efforts have attempted to divide human beings and ways of life into the "useful and harmful, good and evil" (GS 1), but Nietzsche argues that the division itself does not hold up in a grand accounting. Rather, "we become suspicious of this neat division and finally abandon it" (GS 1). The move beyond good and evil will be no simple reversal, but rather it will look to new modes of preservation.

Presenting the tragedy of ethical systems that have dominated humanity thus far, Nietzsche challenges their role in the preservation of humanity: "All ethical systems so far have been so foolish and anti-natural that humanity would have perished of every one of them if it had gained power over humanity" (GS 1). Following the ethics of self-sacrifice or asceticism to their full extent would have amounted to the very destruction of humanity. These destructive ethical modes result from the efforts of "teachers of the purpose of existence" to posit an aim outside of life. The systems, not humanity, have collapsed, "vanquished by laughter, reason, and nature: the short tragedy always gave way again and returned into the eternal comedy of existence" (GS 1). A comic perspective allows a view of the many small tragedies viewed from sufficient distance to render them laughable, and such laughter offers the more comprehensive view of the nature of existence. With a new consideration of what might serve the species, Nietzsche declares, "Even laughter may yet have a future" (GS 1). As a disposition that can undermine without the direct combat of an effort to erect a moralistic counter-ideal, laughter introduces the possibility of a new alliance and gay science.[12] He reminds us that laughter and the perspective of comedy will not eliminate tragedy but take their place among "necessities of the preservation of the species" (GS 1). A new gay science demands integrating the contesting perspectives offered by the artists of "sublime unreason" (GS 1), rigorous science, and laughter.

2. Beautiful Freedom

The role of the competing perspectives of comedy, tragedy, and science complicates the question of the role of appearances and illusions, which Nietzsche takes up in the express treatment of aesthetic and artistic themes in Part II of GS. He opens GS II addressing realists, describing them as "still far too similar to an artist in love" (GS 57), mocking their belief that reality stood before them "unveiled" and treating their "reality" and themselves as images of Sais.[13] This continues to show art and reality in a conflicting relationship. When Nietzsche turns to a treatment of "the artist in love," he writes in the first-person plural: "When we love a woman, we easily conceive a hatred for nature on account of all the repulsive natural functions to which every woman is subject" (GS 59). The desire to remain at the surface leads such an artist to an aversion to nature, which he associates with repulsive functions, identifying art with pleasing illusions.[14] His aversion to what is "under the skin" will lead the artist to look at nature itself "contemptuously" as an unwelcome reminder of what is beneath beautiful appearances (GS 59).

Nietzsche develops this initial treatment of art within GS II toward *gratitude*, crediting art with shifts in perspective. We have art to thank, not for offering comforting illusions, but for allowing insights that could not be gained otherwise:

> Only artists and especially those of the theatre, have given men eyes and ears to see and hear with some pleasure what each man is himself, experiences himself, desires himself; only they have taught us to esteem the hero that is concealed in everyday characters. (GS 78)

Instead of treating the heroic as a realm of escape, Nietzsche treats images of heroes as a path to self-knowledge. He continues, "Only they have taught us the art of viewing ourselves as heroes—from a distance and, as it were, simplified and transfigured—the art of staging and watching ourselves" (GS 78). Rather than as simply forming illusions and concealing the baser elements of our lives, dramatic heroes provide a means of gaining distance on ourselves. By teaching us to how to view a character from a distance, a perspective in which knowledge of "the base details in ourselves" comes to light (GS 78). Art earns gratitude because it has the capacity to shift perspectives, allowing views beyond the distorted foreground of our immediate drives (GS 78). These possibilities offered in dramatic art provide the beginning of a path toward the liberation of the free spirit project. They allow enjoyment that is combined with a clearer view of human life as it is, pointing the way toward a gay science. While the initial presentation of art seemed to require a denial of nature for anyone to find any joy in it, Nietzsche shows the ways in which it provides the potential for free spirited individuals to see themselves more clearly. As Kathleen Higgins shows, this makes it possible "to take pleasure in what human beings actually are" (2000: 93). As he expresses gratitude for art, Nietzsche begins to show the ways in which joy aligns with knowledge, rather than leaving only deadly truths and comforting illusions.

In a discussion of theatrical and musical art (GS 80), Nietzsche sets beauty against nature, explaining the appeal of both tragedy and modern opera quite differently than he does in *The Birth of Tragedy* (BT). He asserts that the Greeks wished "to hear people speak well" and that they went to the theatre "in order to hear beautiful speeches" (GS 80). While appearing to contrast this with modern operas, for which people wish only to hear the beauty of the music regardless of the "speeches," he ultimately shows the similarity between Greek theater audiences and Italian opera audiences in "the beautiful unnaturalness" of the speeches and the music (GS 80).[15] Instead of treating Greek theater or art more generally as an imitation of nature, Nietzsche claims that it responds to "a need that we cannot satisfy in reality" (GS 80). He suggests that this is a function of human pride that causes us to seek "distinction from nature" and it is for this aim that "man loves art as the expression of lofty, heroic, unnaturalness and convention" (GS 80). With this, he would appear to set aesthetic aspirations to beauty against nature.

Nietzsche rejects Aristotelian mimesis and initially appears to follow his predecessors in the German philosophical aesthetics by identifying beauty with freedom.[16] The suggestion of a realm of freedom accessible through art follows Friedrich Schiller's definition of the beautiful as "an appearance of freedom" (2003 [1793]: 152). Where Nietzsche appears to employ a Kantian dichotomy between nature and freedom, he moves beyond views like Schiller's that would seek to connect aesthetic freedom to moral freedom.[17] Nietzsche's treatment of "beautiful unnaturalness" takes up Schiller's analysis of independent aesthetic experience that finds beauty in speeches so unnatural to a character's circumstances that they thereby offer an appearance of freedom from the passions that could overwhelm them. Nietzsche goes further than his predecessors in in his efforts to separate such aesthetic freedom from moralism by naturalizing the freedom found through art.

Nietzsche's elaboration of the relationship between political, moral, and aesthetic freedom appears in his analysis of Shakespeare's Brutus. In the course of his praise for the greatness of Shakespeare, he introduces the topic of political freedom through the character of Brutus, asking, "Was political freedom only a symbol for something inexpressible?" (GS 98). Declaring that one could not say anything "more beautiful" to praise Shakespeare than describing his capacity to display the virtue of Brutus, Nietzsche claims that "independence of soul" is at stake (GS 98). On Nietzsche's reading, Brutus's "lofty morality" is on display in his efforts to preserve his independence. Shakespeare's presentation of the glory of Julius Caesar, and Brutus's recognition of that greatness, makes the sacrifice all the greater. We can see the character of Brutus as an example of the "beautiful unnaturalness," exhibiting a kind of freedom from mere nature in his deeds as well as his speeches, satisfying the theatrical audiences' demand for beauty seen in an image of freedom.

Nietzsche further praises Shakespeare for "prostrating himself" and "feeling unworthy and remote" before the figure of Brutus (GS 98). He uses the evidence of Brutus's response to the poet in the play. Brutus says of the poet, "What should wars do with those jigging fools?"[18] Nietzsche interprets this to mean that Shakespeare as poet recognizes the superior virtue in the freedom of Brutus. Before such heroic freedom, the poet is a "jigging fool."[19] Yet, Brutus's virtue is tragic, and he does not prostrate himself before Julius Caesar. Brutus's freedom indicates a tragic condition in which his great virtue cannot really stand alone but only shines forth as it follows a course of its own destruction. Poets, "jigging fools" in the eyes of a character like Brutus, see this tragedy more clearly, from a perspective that has sufficient distance from the virtue embodied by Brutus to recognize both its glory and its tragedy. Shakespeare's art, Nietzsche argues, is at its most beautiful when it reveals the greatness of Brutus's virtue as this foundation of his freedom. Yet, rather than understanding the freedom of Brutus as opposition to nature, we can see him as an example of nobility within nature, and we can see in the poet the capacity for distance from himself. Shakespeare's depiction of the tragic freedom of Brutus demonstrates the ability of art, especially the theatre, to see "from a distance" (GS 78). If Shakespeare's Brutus shows us a tragic capacity for distance above natural forces and attachments, Shakespeare exhibits the capacity for comic distance from himself. The value of such distance prepares the way for Nietzsche's treatment of "our ultimate gratitude to art," revealing a crucial role for its levity in the development and liberation of a free spirit.

3. Weight-Bearing Art

When Nietzsche turns to "our ultimate gratitude to art," he shows how its agonistic relationships to truth-seeking ultimately serve knowledge and life-affirmation. Rather than contrasting illusion and knowledge, Nietzsche sets the disposition of art, specifically its "good will to appearance," against the drive of probity (*Redlichkeit*).[20] Nietzsche explains that probity alone will yield only nausea and suicide. In addition to revealing "deadly truths" (BT 5), probity alone would reveal its own grounding in error and illusion. It will not finally yield more accurate knowledge but rather an abysmal awareness of its own unreliable foundations.[21] In this context, art is needed as a condition of health and life. Nietzsche shows probity and art to be counterforces that indicate his agonistic naturalism. The two operate in opposed directions within the same sphere of existence. With this, he eliminates any vestiges of dualism about appearances and substratum that may have lingered in BT[22] and thereby eliminates the earlier appearance of separation between freedom and nature.

Nietzsche's formulation of the role of art in countering the self-destruction of probity reveals an agonistic naturalism at work. He writes, "As an aesthetic phenomenon existence is still *bearable* for us" (GS 107). He uses the word "bearable" to indicate the capacity for an aesthetic view to carry the weight of life as is it revealed by rigorous probity. Herman Siemens and Katia Hay treat the claim that art makes life bearable as a matter of aesthetic justification, which would leave the claim Nietzsche makes in GS identical to the claim he makes in BT that life is *justified* only as an aesthetic phenomenon (BT 5).[23] Yet, there is a crucial difference between the two. The claim that life is justified only as an aesthetic phenomenon entails the assumption that life needs a justification. The claim, "existence is still bearable for us" as an "aesthetic phenomenon," does not include a moral claim about justification (GS 107). It is a descriptive statement. Employing the claim that existence is made bearable by an aesthetic disposition maintains an account of forces and counterforces. The language in which Nietzsche continues involves weight (*Schwere*) and levity. By writing of mutual resisting forces rather than a life of suffering that is justified aesthetically, Nietzsche brings an aesthetic perspective into a naturalistic relationship with probity.

The distinction between moral and naturalistic claims is crucial to interpreting the passage because the capacity to get beyond morality is at stake, and probity remains a moral drive.[24] The overcoming of the morality of probity is crucial because it is self-destructive: "Probity (*Redlichkeit*) would lead to nausea and suicide" (GS 107). For Siemens and Hay, the perspective of laughter yields "a more relaxed *Redlichkeit*" than the self-destructive *Redlichkeit*.[25] Yet, rather than simply providing a path to a sustainable *Redlichkeit* that does not press on to its own logical conclusions, laughter as a counterforce resists the moralism that is inherent in *Redlichkeit*. Only if it is viewed from another perspective can probity come to light as a type of morality. *Redlichkeit* remains a part of the history of moral tragedians who would seek to promote life by supplying a purpose to existence (GS 1). Yet, the morality of *Redlichkeit* fails in this effort like other moralities. It takes a tragic turn in its revelation of its own unsustainability due to its own dependence on error. From an aesthetic perspective above its moralism, probity (*Redlichkeit*) can appear as another product of moral tragedians and part of the "eternal comedy of existence" (GS 1). From a perspective outside that which is driven by relentless probity, probity itself appears as unnecessary and as a moral prejudice. Its self-destructive character becomes comical from a distance, and one need not lament the incapacity of probity to find solid ground once one sees that one's commitment is not necessary.

Our need for the counterforce of art arises, Nietzsche argues, because we are "at bottom grave and serious beings—really more weights than human beings" (GS 107). Because we are heavy (*schwere*), we need what will lift us to heights. A modern scientific perspective shows us to be nothing but weights, to be no different from stones, moved by the basic forces of physics. Pressed by probity, we would see ourselves as a collection of formless forces. From our appearance to ourselves as pieces of matter that are heavy (*schwere*), we may come to appear only as gravity (*Schwere*) or a site of competing forces. Yet, this is what we are at *bottom*, not entirely, what we are in the light of a certain kind of scientific spirit driven by relentless probity. Nietzsche shows us that this perspective is partial.[26] Because scientific probity reveals us only as weights, we also need the levity of an aesthetic perspective, a "fool's cap" and "exuberant, floating, dancing, mocking, childish art" (GS 107). An art of comedy and joyful frivolity provide the levity necessary to provide a sufficient counterforce to probity's weightiness.[27] In contrast to the view of ourselves "at bottom" provided by scientific probity, art allows a perspective that counteracts the one-sided reductionism of science with an elevating perspective. No longer is art simply the deceptive antithesis to science, but the partner to probity that allows for new insights into ourselves and knowledge of life.

Nietzsche describes the freedom supplied by such a floating and dancing perspective as a condition of the freedom "that our ideal demands of us" (GS 107). He appeals to the ideal of the free spirit. The rigors of scientific methodology cannot alone provide the freedom that is the ideal of the free spirit. That approach comes to its nearly tragic denouement in the nausea produced by its awareness of its dependence on error, but art reveals a liberating upward path that is neither crushed by the weight of gravity nor led to its own self-destruction. Free-spiritedness includes the uplifting, floating, and playful as a counterforce to what is burdensome, heavy, and serious. It shows human life to exist between weight (*Schwere*) and levity. The freedom of the free spirit is not one of pure spirit removed from the natural world but rather a capacity to shift perspectives between the two. Such freedom "above things" allows one "to stand above morality" (GS 107). Unlike the unmixed rigors of scientific probity, the playful distancing of art allows genuine distance on morality (including the morality of probity) and thus plays a vital role in the liberation of spirit. As Nietzsche describes, this possibility does not entail only standing above morality "with the anxious stiffness of a man who is afraid he is afraid of slipping and falling any moment" (GS 107). Rather than a simple stance that has conquered morality with certainty, the perspective of art allows one "also to float above it and *play*" (GS 107). It allows freedom of movement beyond morality rather than the continued quest for a resting place. Thus, art and its "good will to appearance" overcome the morality inherent in probity.

The "good will to appearance" is crucial to art's ability to supply the perspective from which this is possible. Art does not involve embracing illusions, but a "good will to appearance" (GS 107). Such an embrace of appearance as appearance is not the denial of reality but rather an acceptance of appearances as part of reality. Art allows us to embrace appearances without mistaking falsehoods for reality or pretending that life is other than it is. To suspend one's disbelief in order to enjoy a work of art is not accepting falsehood or denying the reality of life. One can see colored paints on a flat surface as a multidimensional figure or engage with the actions and emotions of a character played by an actor on stage without mistaking the painting for a window or the actor for a character.

In this way, art is well characterized as making possible a capacity for *play* (*Spiel*).[28] Playful activities involve taking endeavors seriously while maintaining awareness that they do not involve purposes beyond themselves. One can play a game well without suffering under the illusion that the consequences extend beyond the game (*Speil*), and one can craft a work of art with great dedication without believing it is tied to serious purposes beyond itself. One can also enjoy a work of art in the spirit of play without suffering under the illusion that its appearances are a substitute for reality. The combination of probity, which prevents believing the illusion, and levity, which allows temporary suspension of disbelief, makes such play possible. The dynamic interplay between the two makes an aesthetic disposition possible and makes the weight of life bearable.

4. Beautiful Monsters

Nietzsche clarifies in GS IV his departure from a view of aesthetic freedom as a path to moral freedom found in Immanuel Kant and Schiller, and he advances an aesthetics oriented toward overcoming morality, including the morality of probity. Rather than allowing the treatment of "beautiful unnaturalness" in GS II to leave an aesthetic freedom to stand apart from nature, he offers fully naturalized aesthetics in which beauty and monstrosity converge. The departure from an account of aesthetics based in freedom emerges in his famous account of style in GS 290. Nietzsche directly opposes Kant's account of the free play of imagination, pointing to "the constraint of single taste" (GS 290) as the key to giving style in an artistic plan.[29] Describing the strong natures that give style, Nietzsche writes, "Even when they have to build palaces and design gardens, they demur at giving nature freedom" (GS 290). As Gary Shapiro points out, in contrast with Alexander Nehamas, Nietzsche's gardening imagery suggests greater room for growth and change than a literary model of a completed whole than that of a fully ordered literary whole (2016: 158).[30] The "beautiful unnaturalness" (GS 80) to which Nietzsche attributes aesthetic enjoyment earlier in the book now appears to be a result of constraint rather than of freedom. He depicts such restraint as part of nature as he continues to develop gardens as a metaphor for naturalistic self-cultivation.

In his discussion of Genoa, its architecture, and gardens, in the next section, Nietzsche shows the place of building and giving style within a natural dynamic. He notes that as he looks about the peripheries of Genoa, he sees "the faces that belong to past generations," those of "bold and autocratic human beings," "builders" with "violence and conquest in their eyes" (GS 291). Rather than nature or freedom, their gardens give the appearance of conquest. The mountains, sea, and city all appear as things "they want to fit into their plan and ultimately make their possession by making it part of their plan" (GS 291). Even as he sees constraint and conquest, he describes the builders in naturalistic terms: "This whole region is overgrown with this magnificent, insatiable selfishness of the lust for possession and spoils" (GS 291). He treats the builders as part of nature and the products of their lust for possession like they were a field of wildflowers. This description brings the "beautiful unnaturalness" of Genoa's palaces and gardens into the context of an agonistic naturalism. The mutual resistance of wild nature and the builder's insatiable lust provides a "feast for the eyes" (GS 290) in the manifestation of nature that is also opposed to nature. Nietzsche further notes the effects of the sea and the seaside setting in the builders' visions of conquest, envisioning "a human being who knows the sea, adventure, and the Orient" (GS 291). In his eyes, it is a place for the wanderer who seeks conquest, one whose ambitions do not know constraints. The builders' constraints and the open sea offer a parallel with Nietzsche's earlier Apollonian and Dionysian analysis of tragedy. Genoa itself, as he describes it, starts to look like a tragedy, in which the heroic efforts of the builders stand in resistance to the infinite sea and indicate an awareness of the unruly forces beyond their static structures. Like tragedy, the architecture and gardens of Genoa indicate interplay between settled form and infinite variation. In GS, Nietzsche clearly presents both parts of the aesthetic combination as mutually resisting elements of nature. He offers a naturalized vision of the tragic combination, one that reminds his readers that "we speak of nature and forget to include ourselves we ourselves are nature, *quand même*—. It follows that nature is something quite different from what we think of when we speak its name" (WS 327). Nietzsche's artful reminder in GS of the human place within nature brings his agonistic naturalism to fruition in GS IV. Instead of setting freedom against nature, Nietzsche presents nature in opposition to itself, leaving an agonistic account of nature in which human conquest remains a part of nature. Counterforces within nature, rather than beautiful unnaturalness, shape his aesthetic considerations and the view of beautiful monsters that emerges in GS IV.

The structure of Nietzsche's agonistic naturalism appears in relation to his thoughts on building and the sea. While preferring his wandering life to one of home ownership, he writes that if he were to build a house, he would build it "right out into the sea" (GS 240).[31] Such a house would stand at the edge of stability and flux, placing a human project as near as possible to the unruly forces of nature; its "beautiful unnaturalness" resists the sea. Nietzsche explains that such building offers the promise of "sharing a few secrets with this beautiful monster" (GS 240). Resisting the sea entails sharing something with the sea. Naming the sea a beautiful monster appears to present it as a contradiction between a disjunctive combination and a harmonious whole. Yet, Nietzsche finds beauty in the sea's very monstrosity, in its contentious combining of disparate elements. The rising waves provide an image of lofty aspiration while the crashing waves show the fall of the same. The sea emerges as an image of nature in contest with itself. The seaside extends such contest. Waves crashing upon rocks provide an image of perpetual strife in which the contestants mutually shape one another. To build "right into the sea" is to join this agonistic nature. It would make one's own house part of the mutual resistance between stable form and crashing waves.[32] Such a house would resist and imitate the sea at once. Building out into the sea embraces the beautiful monstrosity of the sea by joining it and enjoying the contest of dynamic forces. What resists the sea also subjects itself to its forces, participating like the crest of a wave in the ebb and flow of natural forces.

Nietzsche presents a prose poem in GS 310 that more fully elucidates the significance of his wave imagery. In the passage entitled "Will and Wave," he personifies the waves,[33] attributing to them greed, searching, anticipation, excitement, and savagery. He wonders if they are disappointed or mistrustful. "White with excitement," the crashing waves do not stop in disappointment. After crashing, they rise and dive again driven by a "lust to dig up treasures" (GS 310). He declares, "Thus live waves, thus live we who will" (GS 310), acknowledging the likeness of willing, digging for treasures, seeking hidden knowledge, and the life of waves. The one who seeks knowledge of life shares the nature of the waves, shares the beautiful monstrosity of their relentless rising and falling. From this claim, he turns to address the waves, wondering if "you are angry with me" and again calls them "beautiful monsters" (GS 310). They are a necessary contest of natural forces that he can now find beautiful. No longer wishing to build against the waves, Nietzsche imagines himself in the sea and he describes the waves as a wall, making solid barriers and transient motion into one. He invites them to "carry on as you will," affirming the flux of natural forces he finds himself within as they strive aloft and dive to the depths (GS 310). As he invites them to be what they are, Nietzsche speaks of "your exuberance, roaring with joy and malice [*ihr Übermüthigen, brüllt vor Lust und Bosheit*]" to the waves (GS 310). The waves roar with *Lust*, which bears the sense of joy as well as lust in this context. Carelessly it expresses its dangerous play with exuberance, joyfully rising, lustfully, even maliciously crashing. The waves' *Übermüthigen* express a high-spirited sense of well-being, a joyful expression of life itself, and Nietzsche identifies with this joy in his ode to the waves in which he writes himself swimming.

Waves are moved by both levity and gravity in their perpetual interplay, offering an analogy with the dynamic of life, one Nietzsche writes of experiencing with the waves' own exuberant joy. From this experience and its place in his memory, he becomes able to declare: "Everything suits me, for everything suits you so well [*es ist mir Alles recht, denn Alles steht euch so gut*]" (GS 310). He finds the rise and fall of the waves lovable and with it the rise and fall of "everything [*Alles*]" (GS 310). In this experience he claims knowledge of the waves' secret and most importantly that "you and I" are "of the same kind" (GS 310).[34] Nietzsche embraces union with the fundamental forces of nature. Nature is the interplay of levity and gravity characteristic of waves, and human life entails the same dynamic. The full expression of this play of forces requires the highest aspirations, the probing searches, and the capacity for love that the author brings to the sea. Seeing nature as it is and loving what is are parts of nature and this awareness gives way to a declaration of love. Rather than valorizing art as the opponent of "logical Socratism" (BT) or endorsing science as the opponent of art's deceptions (HH), Nietzsche presents an image in this passage of embracing artful distance and rigorous probity together, bringing laughter and wisdom into alliance. It shows a love for the world as a beautiful monster, one that combines its parts in a perpetual interplay of levity and gravity.

5. Love and Knowledge

Nietzsche expresses a love for the sea that shows an affirmation of life and a love for what is, as he says to the waves, "How could I think of betraying you?," now that he sees that they are "of the same kind" (GS 310). Such love is quite different from that of "the artist in love" (GS 59), which manifests an aversion to nature. Like the lover who wishes to behold the lover and also eliminate all distance from the beloved, life-affirming love requires both the separation for a view of beauty and the unification of immersion. New love launches Part IV of GS and its new year's resolution. In that opening, Nietzsche introduces the principle of *amor fati*, declaring, "Let that be my love henceforth" (GS 276). While there is enormous scholarly commentary on *amor fati* in Nietzsche's thought, it is noteworthy for current purposes that it entails a new way of loving and a new way of seeing beauty: "I want to learn to see as beautiful what is necessary in things" (GS 276). Rather than setting beauty in opposition to necessity or nature, Nietzsche hopes that apprehension of beauty will now align with knowledge of necessity. Only then can unqualified yes-saying become possible (GS 276), the yes-saying that will yield Nietzsche's most life affirming teaching and introduce its teacher. This yes-saying will allow negation only in the form of "looking away" (GS 276) so that all he sees he can find beautiful. Nietzsche proffers the lesson that "moving away from things" to gain distance (GS 299) allows a kind of "looking away" that does not negate but makes possible a more tolerable and complete view. Learning from artists to shift perspective, like the laughter and playfulness that make life bearable (GS 107), provides the levity that serves a dynamic motion of proximity and distance. Intimate engagement and distance, probity and levity, shape the motion of knowledge characteristic of gay science.

Nietzsche's treatment of what knowing means brings to light the vital role for laughter and joy born of it in the new gay science (GS 333). Nietzsche addresses Baruch

Spinoza's "not to laugh, nor to lament, nor to detest, but to understand" (GS 333) by claiming that understanding is not a separate state from these other drives: "Yet in the last analysis what else is this *intelligere* than the form in which we come to feel the other three at once" (GS 333). Where Spinoza presents intelligence as the product of reason that establishes freedom from the passions,[35] Nietzsche describes it as a product of the three drives that Spinoza identifies as passions. Nietzsche's free spirit, unlike Spinoza's, will not be one that operates apart from the drives that constitute human life.[36] The experience of knowing results from a particular combination of the three: "One result of the different and mutually opposed drives to laugh, lament, and curse?" (GS 333). The possibility of experiencing all three at once emerges from opposition itself. According to this account of knowing, a fight among one-sided views precedes knowledge (GS 333). Each view, in its one-sidedness, maintains itself against the others, and when the struggle produces a stable tension, "one finds all three sides right" (GS 333). The conscious thought that all three are right is a product of the calm that results from stabilizing the conflict among the three drives and a "kind of justice and a contract" in which the drives "assert their rights against each other" (GS 333). Laughter provides a vital alternative to the drives of anger and sorrow that would wish the world to be other than it is. It finds delight in things as they are. Understood in the life of politics or in the politics of the self, laughter would challenge the ideals the other drives manifest and allow the play of a dynamic, agonistic relation among drives. By challenging the deadly seriousness of other drives, laughter makes possible a politics that is driven by neither resentment nor anti-natural ideals. As the tonic that makes interaction among the others possible and the disposition that embraces things as they are in the world, laughter serves the justice that makes knowing possible and joyful.

Nietzsche turns to the theme of love from this analysis of competing drives rather than to some dispassionate analytic condition.[37] In this return, he provides a description of love that is not the source of attachment to illusions (GS 334) as it was for the "the artist in love" (GS 59). Nietzsche first uses music to exemplify the phenomenon of a slowly learned love: "First, one has to learn to hear a figure and melody at all, detect and distinguish it, to isolate and delimit it as a separate life" (GS 334). Then, one needs to learn to "tolerate it in spite of its strangeness" (GS 334). This patience allows one to "get used to it" and gives way to feeling it missing, and then, "it continues to compel and enchant us relentlessly until we have become its humble and enraptured lovers who desire nothing better than it and only it" (GS 334). Music provides an example of "how we have learned to love all things that we now love" (GS 334). The melody, like the beloved, becomes enrapturing as its very existence makes the world lovable for the presence of its beauty.[38] Rather than the desire to turn away from nature for the sake of a superficial appearance of the beloved, Nietzsche describes a process of learning love as the source of joy in life. Learned love rewards patience as something strange and new gradually "sheds its veil and turns out to be a new and indescribable beauty" (GS 334). Beyond surfaces, an alliance between love and knowledge allows for learning. Instead of setting beautiful illusions against distasteful truth, the experience of joy in beauty allows for relations of love and growing familiarity, a process of incorporating knowledge into life.

The new place of laughter, love, and joy allows Nietzsche to complete the free spirit trilogy with a new critique of Socrates, the introduction of the most life-affirming teaching, and the debut of its teacher. While BT presented the problem as Socratic optimism, in GS Nietzsche wonders if Socrates was a pessimist (GS 340). The book closes with the introduction of Zarathustra, setting the stage for a new period of Nietzsche's writing and the teaching of eternal return. The heading of the final section in the 1882 edition (GS 342) announces the beginning of tragedy, "*Incipit tragoedia*," as Nietzsche depicts Zarathustra in kinship with the tragic moralists (GS 1), to overcome the error of moralism (EH Destiny 3). In the 1886 preface, Nietzsche refers to Zarathustra's appearance in GS as "*incipit parodia*" and gives us reason to see the 1882 book as the beginning of the parody (GS 342) of moral tragedians (GS 1) that Nietzsche can offer under the new alliance between wisdom and laughter. The introduction of the thought of eternal return as the greatest weight (*Das grösste Schwergewicht*) poses the thought as a problem, question, and experiment. The levity Nietzsche has offered, praised, and explained throughout GS prepares the way for making this greatest weight bearable. Freedom of spirit is not separation from embodied life but instead the natural embodied spirit's capacity for motion like dancing and floating; in resistance to gravity, it entails the capacity to bear the greatest weight. The dynamic interplay of gravity and levity makes it possible to pursue a gay science that incorporates knowing into a joyful life.

Notes

1. Nietzsche established this as a group of works with a notice accompanying the first (1882) edition of *The Gay Science*. See Kaufmann (1974). On defining this period, see Abbey (2000) and Franco (2011). For recent considerations of the period, see Bamford (2015), Meyer (2019), and Fortier (2020). See also Abbey (2020), Ansell-Pearson and Bamford (2021), and Ure (2019) on works in this period.
2. Paul Franco emphasizes the connection between his break with Wagner and the new orientation of the middle period (2011: 9–12), and presents the middle period as the overcoming of Romantic art (2011: 38–44). See Ridley (2007) for the claim that Nietzsche moves from redemption through art to redemption through science. Duncan Large addresses the standard view that the free spirit trilogy lacks an aesthetics by arguing that Nietzsche undertakes a project of self reeducation that ultimately remains dialectically bound to the Romanticism of the early period and colored by ongoing Romanticism (Large 2015: 80).
3. Young (1992), Meyer (2019), and Abbey (2020).
4. See Young (2010: 190–230) for biographical account of Nietzsche's break with Wagner. Julian Young describes HH as a liberation from certain aspects of Schopenhauerianism" that takes a stance, contrary to that of *The Birth of Tragedy*, of the "'theoretical,' 'Socratic,' and 'scientific' (1992: 59). Franco emphasizes the role of the break with Wagner in Nietzsche's rejection of aesthetic aims and delineation of the free spirit period (2011: 1–12). See also Fortier (2020: 41–8) for an account of the break with Wagner and its influence on the free spirit period. Ruth Abbey calls attention to the wide range of artists that Nietzsche treats in HH instead of allowing the generic "artist" to stand in for Wagner (2020: 71).

5. Separating this out as a period leaves some emerging questions about the strict delineation of periods. See Abbey (2020) and Chapter 1 of this volume for an account of the delineation and problems of the periodization first introduced by Lou Salomé. The connection among the free spirit works is nonetheless warranted by the cover of 1882 edition of GS. See Kaufmann (1974: 28) for its reproduction listing HH, WS, D, and GS with the goal of forming "the image and ideal of the free spirit." For an account of the development of HH in AOM and WS, see Abbey (2020). See Meyer (2019) for the argument that Nietzsche's free spirit works are best understood as a single self-consciously constructed *Bildungsroman*.
6. Young (2006); Abbey (2020: 79).
7. Abbey argues that AOM offers "a new view" of the possibility of art in the free spirit project in AOM (2020: 172), shifting from HH I the connection between art and religion. This view emerges through Nietzsche's consideration of particular artists. Abbey tracks this shift toward a place for appropriate arts in a more enlightened future in AOM and WS (2020: 171–82, 210–16).
8. For this development in AOM and WS, see Abbey (2020).
9. See Kirkland (2020c) for a consideration of the ramifications of free-spirited politics and Fortier (2020: 46) on its aim of limiting state power.
10. This chapter treats the free spirit period as ending with the 1882 publication of GS, Parts I–IV.
11. As in the later sections of BT.
12. As Kathleen Higgins argues, the first section of GS shows "that comedy must eventually displace tragedy" (2000: 94). Nietzsche's presentation of comedy takes on the agonistic character of tragedy. I have elaborated elsewhere on the connection between political contest, tragedy (2020b), and "the good European" (2020a). On political contest, laughter, and cheerfulness, see also McNeal (2019a,b).
13. See Schiller (2019). Cf. GS (1886) Preface 5.
14. The gendered language shows Nietzsche taking a male perspective of the "artist in love" for this passage, suggesting a superficiality of a male lover's gaze that resists knowledge of nature. Higgins points out that the "dated" disgust for bodily function plays a role in this passage (2000: 80). She makes clear that the gendered language points to the more general point that the desire "to see the world in a certain way can leave an individual to deny the obvious" (2000: 80). The opposition between art and nature that Nietzsche sets up with this performed superficiality shapes GS II and prepares the way for the more complex relationship revealed in GS 78, GS 107, and GS 334.
15. Commenting on this passage, Higgins shows the way in which even vulgar and base passions can have value when they can sing (2000: 93). Yet, Nietzsche writes of Rossini's "la-la-la-la" as an expression of human freedom. The capacity for song indicates that the singer (or the actor in the case of beautiful speeches) is not overcome by the passion.
16. He distinguishes the aims of art from the Aristotelian presentation of mimesis by highlighting "beautiful unnaturalness" (GS 80). Beautiful images serve as an effort "to counteract the elementary effect of images that might arouse fear and pity" (GS 80). See Aristotle, *Poetics*, XIV. Nietzsche rejects Aristotelian catharsis as the effect of tragedy (BT 7, HH 212). Such effort to free aesthetics from nature has characterized what Jacques Rancière has described as the distinction of the aesthetic regime of art from the mimetic regime of art (2013: 8–19).
17. Rancière has pointed out that this paradox, in which claims for the freedom of art from life, morality, and politics also imply service to freedom in life and morality,

shapes what he calls the aesthetic regime of art (2012: 115–33). The paradox is especially prominent in Schiller's *Aesthetic Education*, which presents the freedom of the aesthetic realm from all other commitments as ultimately serving a political purpose.
18. Shakespeare, *Julius Caesar*, 4.3.135.
19. Franco describes this passage as including some of the most "scathing criticism" of the artist that Nietzsche offers (2011: 125). In light of Nietzsche's subsequent treatment of the need for a fool's cap, the "jigging fool" may not be so disparaging.
20. See GS 110 for Nietzsche's extended treatment of knowledge's dependence on error and the question of incorporation. See Siemens and Hay (2015: 111–34) and Micheson (2015: 139–53).
21. See Siemens and Hay (2015: 120–6) *on Redlichkeit's* self-undermining character. See also Lane (2007).
22. See BT, Attempt 6. Where BT sometimes uses Schopenhauerian language to describe the relationship between Apollonian appearances of fixed forms and Dionysian becoming, at this point in GS Nietzsche is clear in placing appearances and probity in direct tension on the same plane of natural forces.
23. Siemens and Hay (2015: 119). Higgins also notes that this formulation recalls the reasoning of BT without commenting on the difference between justifying life and making life bearable (2000: 94). Matthew Meyer calls attention to the striking reversal of Nietzsche's position from HH in GS 107 while presenting the way in which life is bearable as simply allowing us to "get by" before the more complete aesthetic justification of life offered in GS IV (Meyer 2019: 202).
24. See Siemens and Hay (2015: 125) on *Redlichkeit* becoming aware of itself as morality.
25. Siemens and Hay (2015: 131).
26. Young describes the capacity for artistic distance, lightness, and floating above things as a sort of "forgetting," turning away from the riddle of existence and the results of honest inquiry (1992: 100). For Young, "a life of profound superficiality" can provide a "surrogate" that is suitably healthy for those unable to integrate every element of one's life into an affirmation of eternal recurrence (1992: 116). Rather than such an escape to superficiality, the levity of art is a necessary component of a gay science, a pursuit of knowledge not destroyed by its own reductionism.
27. Siemens and Hay, analyzing this treatment of art, demonstrate the way in which it would require us to "alternate between two perspectives" between the will to knowledge and its opposite (2015: 118).
28. See Schiller (1982 [1794]: 102) for the *Spieltrieb* as the bridge between the drives of reason and sense.
29. See Kant (1987 [1790]: 94) for his treatment of English gardens as an opportunity for imagination to have free play due to their "divorce from any constraint or a rule."
30. While Nehamas makes use of this passage to present literature as the model for giving style to one's character (1985:193), Shapiro points out that the famous passage uses gardening and architectural metaphors rather than literary analogies as the model for self-cultivation. Rebecca Bamford presents gardening as Nietzsche's image for the self-cultivation of the free spirit (Bamford 2015: 87–92).
31. See McIntyre (2012: 24) for the claim that Nietzsche builds his grand politics "right out into the sea."
32. The tension between Apollonian form and Dionysian disintegration.
33. Laurence Lampert argues that GS 310 exhibits "the ultimate understanding" aligned with "profound affirmation" (2017: 232–4).

34. Lampert describes this as a recognition that "the highest form of nature is akin to nature itself" (2017: 234).
35. Spinoza also treats his endeavor as one of "freedom of spirit" and so there is throughout an implicit effort by Nietzsche to contrast his presentation of the free spirit with that which he finds in Spinoza. See Spinoza (2000 [1677]: 232, 260, 310; 2005 [1670]: 4).
36. Nietzsche, of course, treats the other elements as drives (*Triebe*) by contrast with Spinoza's treating them as passive elements of the soul (passions).
37. Cf. Spinoza (2000 [1677]: 308) and TI Skirmishes 23.
38. On the theme of love in Nietzsche in relation to Plato and loving life, see Shepherd (2018).

References

Abbey, Ruth (2000), *Nietzsche Middle Period*, New York: Oxford University Press.
Abbey, Ruth (2020), *Nietzsche's Human, All Too Human*, Edinburgh: Edinburgh University Press.
Ansell-Pearson, Keith, and Rebecca Bamford (2021), Nietzsche's Dawn: Philosphy, *Ethics and the Passion for Knowledge*. Hoboken: John Wiley & Sons.
Bamford, Rebecca (2015), "Introduction," in Nietzsche's *Free Spirit Philosophy*, ed. Rebecca Bamford, 1-9, Lanham, MD: Rowman & Littlefield.
Bamford, Rebecca (2020), "Health and Self-Cultivation in Dawn," in *Nietzsche's Free Spirit Philosophy*, ed. Rebecca Bamford, 85–109, Lanham, MD: Rowman and Littlefield.
Fortier, Jeremy (2020), *The Challenge of Nietzsche: How to Approach His Thought*, Chicago: University of Chicago Press.
Franco, Paul (2011), *Nietzsche's Enlightenment*, Chicago: University of Chicago Press.
Higgins, Kathleen (2000), *Comic Relief: Nietzsche's Gay Science*, New York: Oxford University Press.
Kant, Immanuel (1987 [1790]), *Critique of Judgment*, trans. Werner S. Pluhar, Indianapolis: Hackett.
Kaufmann, Walter (1974), "Introduction" in Friedrich Nietzsche, *The Gay Science*, New York: Vintage.
Kirkland, Paul E. (2020a), "Beyond Boundaries: Contesting Authorities in Nietzsche's Europe," in *European/Supra-European: Cultural Encounters in Nietzsche's Philosophy*, ed. Marco Brusotti, Michael McNeal, Corinna Schubert and Herman Siemens, 183–98, Berlin: de Gruyter Press.
Kirkland, Paul E. (2020b), "Nietzsche, Agonistic Politics, and Spiritual Enmity," *Political Research Quarterly* 73 (1): 3–14.
Kirkland, Paul E. (2020c), "Nietzsche's Good Europeans: Beyond Nationalism and Cosmopolitanism," in *Cosmopolitanism and Its Discontents*, ed. Lee Ward, 109–24, Lanham, MD: Lexington, 2020.
Lane, Melissa (2007), "Honesty as the Best Policy: Nietzsche on *Redlichkeit* and the Contrast between Stoic and Epicurean Strategies of the Self," in *Histories of Postmodernism*, ed. Mark Bevir, Jill Hargis and Sara Rushing, 25–51, New York: Routledge.
Large, Duncan (2015), "The Free Spirit and Aesthetic Re-Education," in *Nietzsche's Free Spirit Philosophy*, ed. Rebecca Bamford, 65–83, Lanham, MD: Rowman & Littlefield.

Lampert, Laurence (2017), *What a Philosopher Is: Becoming Nietzsche*, Chicago: University of Chicago Press.
McIntyre, Alex (2012), *The Sovereignty of Joy*, Toronto: University of Toronto Press.
McNeal, Michael J. (2019a), "Nietzsche on the Pleasure of the Agon and Enticements to War," in *Conflict and Contest in Nietzsche's Philosophy*, ed. Herman Siemens and James Pearson, 147–65, London: Bloomsbury Academic.
McNeal, Michael J. (2019b), "Subversive Joy: Nietzsche's Practice of Life-Enhancing Cheerfulness," *Southwest Philosophy Review* 35 (1): 207–16.
Meyer, Matthew (2019), *Nietzsche's Free Spirit Works: A Dialectical Reading*, New York: Cambridge University Press.
Micheson, Katrina (2015), "The Experiment of Incorporating Unbounded Truth," in *Nietzsche's Free Spirit Philosophy*, ed. Rebecca Bamford, 139–55, Lanham, MD: Rowman & Littlefield.
Nehamas, Alexander (1985), *Nietzsche: Life as Literature*, Cambridge, MA: Harvard University Press.
Rancière, Jacques (2012), "The Aesthetic Revolution and Its Outcomes," in *Dissensus*, trans. Steve Corcoran, 115–33, New York: Continuum.
Rancière, Jacques (2013), *Aisthesis*, trans. Zakir Paul, New York: Verso.
Ridley, Aaron (2007), *Nietzsche on Art*, New York: Routledge.
Shapiro, Gary (2016), *Nietzsche's Earth: Great Events, Great Politics*, Chicago: University of Chicago Press.
Schiller, Friedrich (1982 [1794]), *On the Aesthetic Education of Man*, trans. Elizabeth Wilkinson and L. A. Willoughby, New York: Clarendon.
Schiller, Friedrich (2003 [1793]), "Kallias or Concerning Beauty: Letters to Gottfried Körner," in *Classic and Romantic German Aesthetics*, ed. M. m. Bernstein, New York: Cambridge.
Schiller, Friedrich (2019), "The Veiled Statue at Sais [*Das verschleierte Bild zu Sais*]," in *Complete Poetical Works and Plays of Friedrich Schiller*, New York: Delphi Classics.
Spinoza, Baruch de (2000 [1677]), *Ethics*, trans. G. H. R. Parkinson, New York: Oxford University Press.
Spinoza, Baruch de (2005 [1670]), *A Political Treatise*, trans. Samuel Shirley, Indianapolis: Hackett.
Shepherd, Melanie (2018), "On the Difficult Case of Loving Life: Plato's *Symposium* and Nietzsche's Eternal Recurrence," *British Journal for the History of Philosophy* 26.
Siemens, Herman, and Katia Hay (2015), "*Ridendo Dicere Severum*: On Probity, Laughter, and Self-Critique in Nietzsche's Figure of the Free Spirit," in *Nietzsche's Free Spirit Philosophy*, ed. Rebecca Bamford, 111–34, Lanham, MD: Rowman & Littlefield.
Ure, Michael (2019), *Nietzsche's The Gay Science: An Introduction*, New York: Cambridge.
Young, Julian (1992), *Nietzsche's Philosophy of Art*, New York: Cambridge University Press.
Young, Julian (2006), *Nietzsche's Philosophy of Religion*. New York: Cambridge University Press.
Young, Julian (2010), *Friedrich Nietzsche: A Philosophical Biography*. New York: Cambridge University Press.

Part Two

Nietzsche's Joyful Teachings

3

Nietzsche's *Übermensch*: From Shared Suffering to Shared Joy

Melanie Shepherd

Nietzsche's idea of the *Übermensch* is a goal for a humanity that he thought would overcome myriad features of modernity, but insofar as it is a futural hope, the details of the idea remain imprecise. Yet despite its imprecision in Nietzsche's work, scholars from a wide variety of orientations assume that the *Übermensch* is some sort of ideal type. While for some, the type represents an ideal for individuals who wish to overcome themselves,[1] for others, the goal is better understood as a project for humanity as such.[2] Scholars in the latter camp, however, still tend to describe the *Übermensch* in individualistic terms, either by identifying it with those philosophers of the future who make new values possible for an *übermenschlich* humanity, or by making individual *Übermenschen* the goal of a "great politics."[3] Here, though, I will make the case that we should not limit interpretations of the *Übermensch* to individualistic frameworks construing the concept as a superior individual or improved human type. Instead, I will show that there are some distinct interpretive benefits to understanding the *Übermensch* as a relational concept specifically addressing interpersonal relationships.[4] In particular, this approach will allow for a more integrated and coherent account of the roles of joy and pity in *Thus Spoke Zarathustra* (Z).

Although joy and pity are frequent themes in Z, they are nevertheless seldom integrated tightly into interpretations of the more dominant themes in the work. While several scholars have noted the importance of pity for Book IV, given Zarathustra's overcoming of it there as his final sin, Nietzsche himself is careful to remind readers that the theme's prevalence in Part IV is not isolated, prefacing the section with an epigraph from "On the Pitying," in Book II. Nor is Nietzsche's concern with pity isolated to that section that calls it by name. In fact, Z begins with the problem of pity, and Zarathustra's initial reaction to it provides the context wherein central themes of Z are established. The first person that Zarathustra meets upon descending from his cave is the saint, and they speak about how one ought to relate to human beings. Zarathustra brings human beings a gift, while the saint recommends giving alms (Z I Prologue)—a paradigmatic act of pity (Z IV Ugliest Man). Thus, the book quite literally begins with the problem of pity and ends with joy, first in Part III as the willing of eternal recurrence, and again in Part IV as Zarathustra's song of joy ends with the overcoming of pity. While some scholars have argued that the ideas of eternal recurrence and

Übermensch are contradictory or that eternal recurrence replaces Übermensch as Zarathustra's concern,[5] I join the scholars who think that they must be understood together even (or especially) if there is a tension between them. Zarathustra teaches both, and his affirmation of eternal recurrence is the demonstration of a joy that has overcome pity. Such an affirmation of life seems to be precisely what Nietzsche intends to usher in as Übermensch.

Joy and pity, though, are thoroughly interpersonal in nature, and in observing a more essential link between the Übermensch and joy as an overcoming of pity, we are also able to explore the possibility of an inter-relational conception of the Übermensch. In this chapter, I hope to show several ways in which interpretations that take the ultimate aim of Nietzsche's thoughts of self-overcoming and Übermensch to be an individualized expression of power are limited. Instead, I will argue, the problem of humanity that most concerns Zarathustra is relational. Turning in particular to Part IV of Z, I will show that Nietzsche's anxieties about pity in Zarathustra's final temptation do not primarily consist in pity's danger for the individual *qua* individual but rather in the way in which it degrades the quality of human relationships.[6] I will then argue that Nietzsche's calls for joy aim beyond the individual and toward a new relational framework that overcomes the life-denying relations arising from the morality of pity.

1. *Mitleid* as the Basis of Morality

A number of scholars have shown that Nietzsche's aversion to pity grows out of an effort to distance himself from Arthur Schopenhauer, for whom compassion forms the basis of moral interpersonal relations (Schopenhauer 2005).[7] Indeed, Schopenhauer's distinct privileging of *Mitleid* offers some needed context for understanding Nietzsche's curious vehemence toward what seems like basic human feeling, and Nietzsche's distaste for Schopenhauer's morality of compassion is likely as much a reaction to what he thinks Schopenhauer gets right as to what he gets wrong. Daniel Harris astutely notes a passage in which Ida Overbeck remembers Nietzsche in 1878–9. She writes,

> A bad chapter of Schopenhauer affected Nietzsche especially strongly, the idea that man is not constituted to share joy, and can be interested in another person's misfortune or well-being only temporarily by the detour of former participation in misfortune; that well-being, on the contrary, is suited to arouse envy; wherefore he concluded also from other premises, that hardship is the real positive condition of the human race, and that only pity can be the real well-spring of morality. Nietzsche's disgust rebelled against this; he was indignant. (Gilman and Parent 1987: 110)

Overbeck's comments indicate that Nietzsche was deeply affected by the possibility that human beings are constituted to relate to one another primarily through suffering in a way that precludes a genuine experience of shared joy. Harris shows that Nietzsche's passages on *Mitfreude* in *Human, All Too Human* (HH) are better understood in light of Overbeck's remarks and that Nietzsche's thought of friendship as shared joy is his response to the Schopenhauerian claim that we share others' suffering while, for the most part, only envying their joy (2015: 199–201). Nietzsche replaces the centrality of suffering in ethical relationships with joy when he says, "Fellow rejoicing [*Mitfreude*], not fellow suffering [*Mitleiden*] makes the friend" (HH 499). The goal of overcoming the morality of pity seems to include the goal of shared joy.[8]

As Harris notes, however, Nietzsche says that such *Mitfreude* is so rare that "there have been philosophers who have denied the existence of joying with" (AOM 62). If *Mitfreude* is, as Harris argues, a fundamental conception for Nietzsche's ethics, then we must understand "ethics" in a distinctly Nietzschean way: neither as an account of the foundations for ethical life nor as a set of normative principles guiding action but, rather, as a possibility for a form of life. As possibility, *Mitfreude* is, on the one hand, "accessible only to the choicest exemplars" (AOM 62) and, on the other, a potential opening to an unknown future for humanity more generally. In order to understand that possibility, however, we need to clarify the problem with the disgust-inducing morality of pity.

Z opens with the problem of how one ought to relate to human beings, particularly when one has something to offer humanity. Zarathustra has been in his cave for ten years when he decides that he will descend to the social world. Before he meets the social world, however, he runs into a fellow creature of solitude, the old saint, in the woods. Zarathustra expresses his love for humanity, and the saint replies by saying that he loves God because loving human beings would kill him. The saint gives alms instead. His particular brand of pity, then, is a survival strategy in the face of some danger presented by human relationships. Zarathustra wonders, however, at the saint's replacement of love for human beings with love for God, since God is dead. Later, we find that God has died of his *pity* for human beings. Therefore, the saint's use of pity as a survival strategy might strike us as odd. That which killed God presumably allows the saint to survive. Yet, on closer inspection, we see that God's pity is also love. God has died of some combination of love and pity for human beings. Zarathustra suggests that pity is "'the cross on which he is nailed who loves man'" (Z I Prologue 3). This contrast between the saint's pity and the cross indicates that pity is only deadly when one is a lover, and the saint's almsgiving strategy becomes clearer. Rather than risk a love that might entrap him in pity, the saint practices a detached and loveless pity. He is safe in his love for the dead. Zarathustra, having stated early on his love for humanity, responds to the saint with "Did I speak of love? [*Was sprach ich von Liebe!*]" (Z I Prologue), and he corrects himself with "I bring men a gift [*Ich bringe den Menschen ein Geschenk*]" (Z I Prologue 2). In this ambiguous disavowal, Zarathustra does not renounce his love for humanity, but instead perceives a need for a new way of speaking. The saint expresses a conception of love that is tied to the cross, and Zarathustra realizes that he will need new vocabulary for a love that gives gifts not motivated by pity. Upon leaving the saint and encountering people, he says, "*I teach you the overman*" (Z I Prologue 3). This prefacing conversation with the saint indicates that the gift that Zarathustra gives in his teaching of *Übermensch* will offer a correction of petty and loveless almsgiving. Thus, the teaching of the *Übermensch* first arises in the context of a decision to relate to human beings, a question concerning how to best relate to human beings, and a rejection of pity as an appropriate relation.

2. The Morality of Pity

The juxtaposition of pity and joy in Z indicates that Zarathustra's action over the course of the work is the replacement of pity with joy. Pity and joy are affects, and while Nietzsche might be said in a general way to seek the replacement of pitying affects with joyful ones, his efforts are aimed at the overcoming of pity as a relational structure—as a dominant set of affects, tendencies, and interpersonal practices that make up the background social framework. Supporting and intertwined with such a structure is a system of value—what Nietzsche refers to as the morality of pity. The morality of pity takes several distinct forms. While many of his examples of pitying relations in Z allude to Christianity, Nietzsche's critique of the morality of pity extends to post-Christian value systems—most notably, utilitarianism, positivist meliorism, and Schopenhauerian resignation. The central feature uniting Christian and modern post-Christian systems of value is a repeated failure to find an affirmative response to suffering.

Christianity

In *On the Genealogy of Morality* (GM), Nietzsche shows that pervasive suffering has commanded a great deal of energy and resources from human existence, and Christianity has been a way of accounting for and giving a meaning to this phenomenon that seems to make life objectionable. But Nietzsche shows that the various attempts to handle and manage suffering have in fact only multiplied the forms it can take. Suffering takes more intense and more subterranean forms the more that human beings focus on solutions for it. But Nietzsche's insight concerning these solutions is that we don't actually object to suffering and that we will do it readily if only it can have a meaning (GM III 28). While this demonstrates an undeniable creativity of the human will, Nietzsche thinks that the creativity renders a suffering that pervades an entire life form. He does not think, however, that the act of will creates the suffering life form. As he notes in several places, the madness of will that is Christianity is evidence of a life that was already suffering, and that suffering life itself became creative and gave birth to values. The values created by this suffering life-form enable an economy in which suffering is the primary currency. Nietzsche notes that slaves are tyrannical in their demand that suffering be acknowledged: "Their copious, *hidden* suffering makes them furious at the noble taste that seems to *deny* suffering" (BGE 46). The ubiquity of suffering is thus a presupposition of this morality, as is its undesirability. Life must be understood as necessarily and systematically pervaded by undesirable suffering. This suffering, however, receives a meaning as a *punishment* for the sufferer's own sinful nature, and this explanation in turn produces *more* suffering in the form of guilt (GM III 15–16). As a kind of self-cruelty, though, guilt also induces a form of pleasure in the sufferer, who is able to experience himself both as sufferer and as inflictor. Moreover, as punishment, it receives a meaning within a larger narrative of salvation. In suffering and guilt, the sufferer is also assured of his relative goodness. Indebted to God, he joins the earthly community of the good and the just and anticipates another life beyond his earthly one, free of suffering. Suffering, then, remains an evil for the human being understood as natural, but it also gains a meaning that allows the human being to become a part of an economy that exceeds nature. The ability to enjoy it as meaningful is predicated upon the condemnation of the entire earthly realm in which it occurs, constituting a condemnation of life by a sick will. The energy spent avoiding the suffering brought on by meaninglessness multiplies and intensifies suffering, denying the world in which one must nevertheless still live by creating an inaccessible world beyond it in which to house its meaning. More importantly, though, this strategy of abolishing meaninglessness shifts suffering of all kinds to the center of collective life. One acts toward the other *as* sufferer, seeking to share and relieve a piece of that universal condition from the other. Rather than relieving suffering, these relationships of pity simply reinforce suffering as the universal feature of life. In this way, the elaborate creations of an already suffering life preserve and proliferate that kind of life by establishing interpretive norms that assume and esteem it.

Enlightenment, Positivism, Utilitarianism

It is not only Christianity, however, that Nietzsche understands to promote a morality of pity. In the wake of the death of God, Christian morality has remained entrenched despite the decline in Christian dogma:

> The more one liberated oneself from the dogmas, the more one sought as it were a *justification* of this liberation in a cult of philanthropy: not to fall short of the Christian ideal in this, but where possible to outdo it, was a secret spur with all the French freethinkers from Voltaire up to Auguste Comte: and the latter did in fact, with his moral formula *vivre pour autrui*, out-christian Christianity. (D 132)

Despite giving up Christian dogmas, the various shapes of enlightened human beings promote an unhealthy aversion to suffering:

> If you, who adhere to this religion [of pity], have the same attitude toward yourselves that you have toward your fellow men; if you refuse to let your own suffering lie upon you even for an hour and you constantly try to prevent and forestall all possible distress way ahead of time; if you experience suffering and displeasure as evil, hateful, worthy of annihilation, and as a defect of existence, then it is clear that besides your religion of pity you also harbor another religion in your heart that is perhaps the mother of the religion of pity: the *religion of comfortableness*. (GS 338)

These more enlightened moralities of pity no longer seek a spiritual meaning for suffering but instead take the optimistic approach of eliminating it through progress. Nietzsche sees in this pursuit of comfort a "weakening and abolition of the *individual*" (D 132), as the human being is reduced to an animal species and human tasks are construed as collective social actions. Yet, more important than their collective nature for Nietzsche is the socioeconomic understanding of what constitutes the collective human project in the first place. Echoing the Wagnerian concern about the role of commerce in modern society, Nietzsche notes that social goods are increasingly understood "according to the needs of the consumer" (D 175). At times, however, Nietzsche goes further. In *Beyond Good and Evil* (BGE), he pairs his critique of the modern leveling of the human being with an explicitly positive evaluation of suffering: "*Your* pity is aimed at the 'creature in humans,' at what needs to be molded, broken, forged, torn, burnt, seared and purified,—at what necessarily needs to *suffer* and *should* suffer" (BGE 225). While Christian morality creates more suffering in its avoidance of meaningless suffering, the moralities that follow it are so averse to suffering that, in their attempts to abolish it, they reduce the human being to an undifferentiated sentience and passivity. Thus, Nietzsche's challenges to the morality of pity also point toward the necessity of a revaluation of suffering.

Schopenhauerian *Mitleid*

In Dawn 132, Nietzsche includes Schopenhauer among the post-Christian moralists of pity, yet Schopenhauer's morality of pity also drives Nietzsche's critique in a unique way. Schopenhauer's morality of pity is central for Nietzsche because it is grounded in certain insights concerning the meaning of suffering that Nietzsche thinks are correct. Schopenhauer, unlike Christians and the gamut of post-Enlightenment moralists of pity, abandons all hope of either meaning or progress when it comes to suffering. His unsentimental account of life's pervasive and unredeemed suffering is for Nietzsche compelling and accurate. Yet Schopenhauer's unflinching assessment also embeds suffering in a metaphysical reality in a way that overdetermines human relational possibilities. Suffering is the binding force between human beings, making *Mitleid* the foundation for any substantive human relationships. Therefore, Nietzsche is especially responsive to Schopenhauer because Schopenhauer's morality of pity proscribes joyful human relational possibilities while also recognizing meaningless suffering in a way that other moralists have failed to. Nietzsche upholds Schopenhauerian insights concerning suffering while resisting Schopenhauer's conclusions about the necessity of shared suffering as a relational foundation.

Schopenhauer says that in *Mitleid*, "the wall of partition" that separates individual beings is "broken down, and the non-ego to a certain extent identified with the ego" (2005: 86). For Schopenhauer, this affective experience is rooted in the metaphysical reality of a shared will. Suffering is the very nature of the will as a constant, unfulfilled desire (Schopenhauer 1969: 363). The other's suffering triggers a recognition of my own fundamental reality, which is the same suffering will that manifests itself in the other. To the extent that I identify with the other's suffering, I also break down the illusion of my own ego and become the undifferentiated reality of universal will. The moment of *Mitleid*, then, is a moment in which self and other experience a unity rooted in the structure of a shared reality concealed by everyday illusion.

Nietzsche departs from Schopenhauer both in the positive evaluation of this disindividuating experience of shared suffering and in the notion that such disindividuation accurately describes the everyday experience of *Mitleid*. As we will see, Nietzsche does recognize a *Mitleid* of the type described by Schopenhauer, but he thinks that it is rare, whereas pity is typically petty and not a profound phenomenon. Furthermore, as we have seen, Nietzsche is critical of Schopenhauer's claim that "direct sympathy with another is limited to his sufferings, and is not immediately awakened by his well-being." Schopenhauer adds, "The sight of success and enjoyment, purely as such, is very apt to raise the envy, to which every man is prone" (2005: 87). It is unclear from Schopenhauer's metaphysics why this should be so. As Michael Ure points out, "if Schopenhauer is correct about the ontological identity of all individuals, then it should also be possible for one person to participate directly in another's *pleasures* or *joys*" (Ure 2006: 73–4). Indeed, Nietzsche's idea that pity is in most cases an expression of power would lead much more readily than Schopenhauer's account to the deflating conclusion that the basic relationship to the other is a game of petty power struggles. Therefore, while Schopenhauer's morality of pity reflects an acceptance of meaningless suffering that distinguishes Schopenhauer from other moralists of pity, Nietzsche objects to the gloomy notion that shared suffering must necessarily be the foundation for positive human relationships.

3. Pity as a Relational Structure

While the morality of pity arises from a failure of will in the face of meaningless suffering, its effects are relational in nature. Nietzsche does not provide just one account of pity, however. While he does recognize the possibility of a pity like the one described by Schopenhauer, in which the walls of the ego dissolve and one feels the other's pain, Nietzsche also describes a more familiar relation of pity, following a logic completely contrary to that described by Schopenhauer. Still, both of these relations establish and reinforce a tie between suffering and shame that degrades humanity by publicizing suffering in a way that both increases suffering and also eliminates its potential benefits.

Distinguishing among Pities: God, Man, Zarathustra

Through the eyes of the ugliest man, Nietzsche describes three distinct types of pity.[9] Zarathustra first recognizes the ugliest man as the murderer of God through his own experience of pity: "*Pity seized him*; and he sank down all at once, like an oak tree that has long resisted many woodcutters" (Z IV Ugliest Man). Zarathustra's visceral pity is so overwhelming that it threatens his own well-being. Like the pity that felled the murdered God, it is rooted in recognition. The ugliest man says that God had to die, for "he saw with eyes that saw everything; he saw man's depths and ultimate grounds, all his concealed disgrace and ugliness" (Z IV Ugliest Man). Likewise, Zarathustra immediately guesses the ugliest man's riddle, telling him, "'I recognize you well'" (Z IV Ugliest Man). Yet, while this recognition is a catalyst for his debilitating reaction, it is also a significant factor in Zarathustra's immediate redirection of his pity, whereby he honors the ugliest man with his silence and his shame. In this way, Zarathustra acts neither as God, nor as a man, but in a new way that allows the ugliest man to recognize him as Zarathustra.

The ugliest man describes the pity of both God and man as obtrusive. God, like Zarathustra, recognizes the ugliest man, but his recognition takes him into the depths of the ugliest man's suffering. In the preceding conversation with the retired pope, Zarathustra says that the old God "saw how *man* hung on the cross," and, unable to bear it, "his love of man became his hell, and in the end his death" (Z IV Retired). The pitying God loves humanity, and, unable to bear the sight of human suffering, he takes it on himself to the point of his own annihilation. Zarathustra tells the pope that "when gods die, they always die several kinds of death," and indeed, the ugliest man tells a slightly different story, explaining that God did not merely drown in pity for humanity but, rather, that his immersion in humanity's suffering was the cause of his violent death at humanity's hands. Nietzsche suggests in these two stories that pity is not only ruinous for the one who pities but also undesired by at least some who receive pity. Thus, Nietzsche recognizes the possibility for a pity that eliminates the boundaries of self as described by Schopenhauer, but he reserves it for gods and profound types like Zarathustra. Furthermore, he demonstrates that despite the spiritual depth involved in such pity, it is ultimately harmful to the profound one while doing further damage to the one pitied, making it a waste of energy with life-negating results on both sides. Nietzsche thus shows that such pity is a temptation for lovers of humanity, and while Zarathustra is susceptible to such pity, he resists it.

This God's pity is markedly different from Nietzsche's more human descriptions of pity. The ugliest man complains that everyone else is an alms thrower, and this expression of *Mitleid* remains obtrusive. The human expression of pity, however, unlike God's, does not seek to take on the suffering of the sufferer or to alleviate it in any substantive way. Rather, it acknowledges the suffering and capitalizes on it as an opportunity for a sublimated expression of power. In Part II, Zarathustra notes that the "merciful who feel blessed in their pity" lack shame (Z II Pitying). They recognize the individual only as sufferer, eclipsing his individuality with a universal condition. Against this universality, pitiers pull themselves out of the universal condition of suffering and enjoy a moment of an individuality built upon negation. In D, Nietzsche writes,

> In every case in which we *can* avoid the sight of the person suffering, perishing, or complaining: we decide *not* to do so if we can present ourselves as the more powerful and as a helper, if we are certain of applause, if we want to feel how fortunate we are in contrast, or hope that the sight will relieve our boredom. It is misleading to call the *Leid* (suffering) we may experience at such a sight, and which can be of various kinds, *Mit-Leid* (pity), for it is under all circumstances a suffering which he who is suffering in our presence is *free* of: it is our own, as the suffering he feels is his own. But it is *only this suffering of our own* which we get rid of when we perform deeds of pity. (D 133)

In this more common form of pity, the enjoyment of power in the elevation of the pitier above his own suffering and boredom comes at the expense of the sufferer for whom the pitying action is purportedly undertaken. Thus, in this more human version of *Mitleid*, the pitier gains a feeling of power by performing a helpfulness that exposes the sufferer without relieving his suffering. Even those who seek pity, Nietzsche observes, only want the pleasure of possessing *"the power to hurt"* (HH 50). Attracting pity does not relieve suffering but simply makes more total suffering in order to spice the sufferer's pain with a bit of pleasure. Yet as we have seen, it is only rarely, in the case of a profound nature, that a pain with any depth is felt. Instead, the pitier expressing some pain also gains the pleasure of power in his pity, and if the one seeking pity enjoys the petty pleasure of his ability to hurt, he also exposes himself to further shame.

Suffering and Shame

Relations of pity tie suffering to shame by insisting that suffering be public and that it draw a public. Almsgiving is a public ritual of seeing the sufferer *as* sufferer. The response of alms—currency—is the universal response to a universal condition, singling the sufferer out merely as an example of the universal. Zarathustra's objection to such displays is primarily an aesthetic revulsion to gestures of pity: "Therefore I wash the hand that helped the sufferer; therefore too I wipe even my soul" (Z II Pitying). That his revulsion is to his own gesture and not to suffering itself is clear when he says that he "was ashamed for the sake of his shame; and when I helped him I transgressed grievously against his pride" (Z II Pitying). The violation caused by almsgiving pity is rooted in its refusal of the sufferer's individuality. While suffering is indeed universally human, its effects are singularizing. The morality of pity insists upon making this universal condition visible, but because suffering is a universal condition attached to what is essentially private and undergone individually, it exposes the sufferer without being able to offer any relief of the burden. Nietzsche writes that "whenever people *notice* that we suffer, they interpret our suffering superficially. It is the very essence of the emotion of pity that it strips away from the suffering of others whatever is distinctly personal" (GS 338). Thus, the suffering remains unknown and unshared as it becomes the center of a spectacle that makes "our worth and will smaller" (GS 338). In promoting the sharing of suffering, pity presents what is most personal and singularizing as the universally human, misinterpreting it while also insisting that it be visible. In this way, relations of pity tie suffering to shame.

Zarathustra aims to break this tie. The noble response to human suffering, he suggests, is to impose shame upon oneself rather than to shame another. His admonition to take shame on ourselves rather than imposing it is, at the same time, a call to feel shame properly by allowing what must be done by the solitary individual to be done privately.[10] Interestingly, then, Zarathustra is proposing measures that seem akin to pity in order to effect its overcoming: self-sacrificial action intended to alleviate the other's suffering.[11] Zarathustra's reversal of shame from the sufferer to the obtrusive viewer then opens a space for a new and reevaluated experience of suffering. His cave represents, among other things, a support system for solitary suffering, as he tells the ugliest man that he can find many hiding places there (Z IV Ugliest Man).

Nietzsche's emphasis on removing suffering from the public eye is complemented by an exhortation to engage with suffering more profoundly. In BGE, he laments the shortsightedness of the morality of pity, calling instead for "the discipline of suffering, of *great* suffering," which "has been the sole cause of every enhancement in humanity so far" (BGE 225). He continues, "In human beings, *creature* and *creator* are combined," contrasting a pity of his own—a pity for the creator—with the "pity aimed at the 'creature in humans,' at what needs to be molded, broken, forged, torn, burnt, seared and purified,—at what necessarily needs to *suffer* and *should* suffer" (BGE 225). Pity aims at the creature in human beings because it relates to the other in a way that *evokes* the creature. Nietzsche is critical of the way in which the morality of pity produces a subjectivity in which creaturely passivity is heightened, suppressing creativity and self-experimentation. Acting against his own temptation to pity, then, Zarathustra puts the creator in the human being in a better position to receive what Nietzsche calls "the gifts of suffering" (BGE 225). Such an engagement with suffering is precisely what is necessary for the task by which Zarathustra ushers in joy—that of willing eternal recurrence.

4. Eternal Recurrence: The Path to Shared Joy

The consistent juxtaposition of *Mitleid* and joy[12] and Nietzsche's effort to move from the former to the latter in Z might not immediately suggest Nietzsche's concern with human relationships, were it not for the fact that he also exhorts readers to *share* joy rather than suffering in several places: "I want to teach them what is understood by so few today, least of all by these preachers of pity: *to share not suffering but joy* [*Ich will sie Das lehren, was jetzt so Wenige verstehen und jene Prediger des Mitleidens am wenigsten:—die Mitfreude!*]" (GS 338). If it is uncommon to share joy, that is likely due to the fact that, as Zarathustra says, we have felt too little of it (Z II Pitying). However, if Nietzsche means that we share joy too little because we feel too little joy, then a more singularized experience of suffering that ties it to joy rather than seeking ways to eliminate it might allow us to feel "better joys." Furthermore, if pity wastes energy on the general problem of suffering in order to avoid one's own suffering, turning to what is one's own enables one to become the sort of developed, particular self who can then relate to another as a particularity. In other words, engaging the particularity of suffering might cultivate the kind of self who is capable of friendship. Thus, the possibility of bringing joy to the fore of experience and human relationships more generally requires a transformation of the human relationship to suffering.

Joy appears in Z as an inclination to life: "All joy [*Lust*] wants the eternity of *all* things" (Z IV "Drunken Song"). Nietzsche does not indicate that this life-affirming *Lust* is shareable in the context of eternal recurrence. Zarathustra's joy is decidedly private in scope, and several of his proclamations concerning joy in this song would seem to refute the idea that Nietzsche understands joy to be fundamentally relational: "Joy [*Lust*], however, does not want heirs, or children—joy wants itself, wants eternity, wants recurrence, wants everything eternally the same" (Z IV "Drunken Song"). This passage's solipsistic self-delight reflects an important dimension of Nietzsche's presentation of his highest thought of affirmation. We could perhaps read Zarathustra's journey among and away from others as culminating finally in the moment of affirmation that is solely his own, thereby taking Nietzsche to promote an affirmation of sameness indifferent to social and political life. In fact, even interpretations making a case for Nietzsche's broad political aims have emphasized the way in which a class of liberated individuals is the ultimate end for any politics promoted by Nietzsche.[13] However, there are several reasons to resist reducing relationships to an instrumental role and to avoid an individualistic interpretation of Nietzsche's conceptions of joy and affirmation.[14] Given that the thought of eternal recurrence brings joy and suffering together in order to allow for a novel engagement with suffering, we might instead think of eternal recurrence as instrumental in producing the conditions for the possibility of joyful relationality. The joy cultivated by eternal recurrence is accessible through a singular engagement with suffering. As I will show, Nietzsche envisions the joy arising through an engagement with suffering as the affective root of a new relational structure.

Zarathustra celebrates with the higher men, but upon waking on the morning after the Ass Festival, he decides that they are not his proper companions. Upon leaving them sleeping in his cave, he comes to understand that he has pitied them, and this has been his final sin. Proclaiming himself rid of that pity, he then announces his intention to get on with his work. Paul Loeb has shown persuasively that Part IV is an analeptic satyr play situated chronologically somewhere toward the end of the events of Part III, which is the chronological ending (Loeb 2010: 85–99). This reading would make sense of the work left for Zarathustra to do as that of willing eternal recurrence. Yet if we take seriously the idea that one of the aims of willing eternal recurrence is a transformation of the way in which suffering takes place in a culture mired in the morality of pity, then this engagement with what Nietzsche sees as a major problem of modernity means that the willing of eternal recurrence has an aim beyond the individualized joyful affect that wants only itself. The sign indicating the coming of his children at the end of Part IV is clearly of consequence to Zarathustra:

> About all this Zarathustra spoke but a single sentence: "*My children are near my children.*" Then he became entirely silent. But his heart was loosed, and tears dropped from his eyes and fell on his hands. And he no longer heeded anything and sat there motionless without warding off the animals anymore. (Z IV Sign)

The fact that Zarathustra's moment of clarity develops directly following his contemplation of the sign of his children suggests that his belief in their proximity enables his insight concerning his final temptation. This is especially noteworthy since it occurs almost directly following "The Drunken Song," in which joy is said *not* to want children. The willing of eternal recurrence would thus seem to require indifference concerning whether the children come, yet the sign that the children are near also somehow frees Zarathustra to break away from his pitying relationship to the higher men and to get on with his work. Part IV's parodic references to the final moments of Christ in the gospels indicate that there are structural similarities between Christ's work on the cross and Zarathustra's work of willing eternal recurrence. The children, then, offer the promise of a new humanity brought about by Zarathustra's willing eternal recurrence, overcoming the form of humanity engendered by Christ's death on the cross.

It is significant, however, that Zarathustra determines that the higher men are not his proper companions prior to his renunciation of his pity for them. The moment in which Zarathustra realizes his own pity is described as transformative: "'*Pity! Pity for the higher men!*' he cried out, and his face changed to bronze" (Z IV Sign). That he pities them seems to be his own failure rather than theirs. Perhaps, then, when Zarathustra finally announces that his children and his hour have come (Z IV Sign), the children who are near are the ones still asleep in his cave.[15] Zarathustra is waiting not for a new type who will subsequently create new values as a result of its superior physiology, but rather the transformed values of a new relational framework. Zarathustra's act of willing eternal recurrence initiates a new value framework through a transformed relationship to suffering.

Zarathustra is like Christ in that he is capable of genuine *Mitleid*, taking on others' burdens as his own in a way that erases the boundaries between self and other. But Christ's self-sacrifice on behalf of the suffering symbolizes and encourages a proliferation of suffering life. While Nietzsche enumerates the forms of suffering in Christian conscience in detail throughout his corpus, the morality of pity seems to be the principal dimension of Christian consciousness to which Zarathustra as parodic repetition of Christ offers an alternative. The fact that Zarathustra must overcome pity as his final sin signals the centrality of pity as the decisive hurdle to be overcome if Zarathustra's work of willing eternal recurrence is to be possible. As a profound nature and lover of humanity in the same deep way that Christ is, Zarathustra experiences pity for all of humankind in pitying the higher men. But to indulge that pity would only repeat and reinforce the morality of pity. Thus, Zarathustra walks away and undergoes his own suffering in a cave, joined only by his animals. Taking the suffering of humankind on his shoulders in an intensified form in his thought of the small man's eternal recurrence,[16] he then responds with the affirmative, joyful will and in doing so sets a new precedent for both the manner and the meaning of human suffering. While this joy contains an undeniably affective character, then, it is an affective response to a specific content—that of suffering without meaning. Therefore, rather than a simple affect that comes, goes, and spreads on a contingent basis, a joy that would emerge in a confrontation with the problem of suffering would constitute the more stable phenomenon of a complex affective network. This more substantial learning "to feel differently" (D 103) would constitute a new evaluative and relational structure.

5. The Relational *Übermensch*

If Nietzsche was affected strongly by that passage of Schopenhauer, it is likely because he endorsed the accuracy of Schopenhauer's observation that human beings are poorly constituted to share joy abundantly and habitually and that we are easily drawn to envy and petty varieties of pity. To transform this tendency would mean becoming *übermenschlich*. But the transformation of this tendency demands a more direct confrontation with suffering and a reinterpretation of its meaning. Zarathustra's willing of eternal recurrence is a revaluation of suffering that overcomes the morality of pity. Rather than an invitation to individual nascent *Übermenschen* to become what they are, Zarathustra's willing is directed toward the goal of *Übermensch* understood as a way of relating to others and of sharing the earth.[17]

That Nietzsche's efforts in Z are aimed at human relationality is implied by the way in which Zarathustra advises against *Mitleid*. While a godlike nature such as Zarathustra needs to reject pity on grounds of self-preservation since pity saps his strength, it is unclear why it would be important for human beings to overcome the morality of pity if the strength and power of individuals has ultimate priority for Nietzsche. The more human variety of pity *increases* the feeling of power in the pitier. If the suffering one is already suffering, why is it important not to increase that suffering for the sake of my own power? Or rather, how might we explain the problem with such a strategy without being moralistic?

One possible response to this question would still allow for an ultimately egoistic reading of Nietzsche. Pity, we might say, is an undesirable route to power because engaging the suffering of another for power is a one-shot deal, offering a stimulus, but no resistance. Perhaps this is why Zarathustra instead teaches the friend, in whom "one should have one's best enemy" (Z I Friend). Power as Nietzsche envisions it is not a feeling but rather a kind of expansion that is only possible through engaging and overcoming resistance.[18] Thus, we could see the warning against petty human pity as an encouragement to seek the resistance that will allow for self-improvement rather than being lured into a complacent and stagnant feeling of power.

But in fact, Zarathustra recommends an alternative to almsgiving pity that turns the suffering of the sufferer into resistance when he suggests the discipline of taking shame upon oneself instead of heaping it onto the sufferer. Such a strategy would enable the cultivation of an expanded power insofar as it takes on the burden that is genuinely heavier, rather than merely providing the superficial appearance of having shared a burden. It would engage the suffering of the other as a kind of resistance, solving the problem introduced by the pettier variety of *Mitleid*. Yet Zarathustra insists on going further than changing our engagement with suffering and says that this superior manner of dealing with the sufferer is a mere means to a still better way of engaging suffering: that of "learning to feel better joy [*lernen wir besser uns freuen*]" (Z II Pitying). Moreover, Zarathustra makes the treatment of the other paramount in his call to joy, saying, "And learning better to feel joy, we learn best not to hurt others or to plan hurts for them" (Z II Pitying). It would seem that beyond the aim of cultivating resistance and acting nobly for purposes of self-overcoming, Zarathustra is also explicitly concerned with the effects that one's own dispositions have on the flourishing of others. Thus, overcoming the morality of pity has aims beyond the avoidance of a danger for the profound soul, as Zarathustra expresses a desire for the dignity of the sufferer. Nor is it plausible, given Nietzsche's attitudes toward suffering and toward utility, that Nietzsche merely seeks to reduce the overall amount of suffering. The problem with pity is in the relation itself, as the thing that is shared by the parties freezes the avenues to continued open engagement.

In calling for joy instead, Zarathustra does not stop at his own more subdued approach to the sufferer, but instead suggests a more radical opening of the relation to the other rooted in joy.[19] Thus, Zarathustra's teaching of the friend over the neighbor opens new possibilities for addressing suffering through a transformed way of relating to others. If we can learn to feel better joys, then we are better equipped to provide a resistance that affirms the other.[20] Harris writes, "The second self of the friend is not one thing reflecting back, but an opening onto the numberless possibility of growing out of ourselves into something new" (2015: 219). This still leaves unresolved, though, the question of whether relationality is ultimately instrumental for Nietzsche, since he would understand this mutual affirming resistance as an integral component for a better self. Robert Gooding-Williams, for instance, says that for Nietzsche, closeness to another is valuable "only if it prompts a person to love the farthest and thus overcome himself" (2001: 144). But if, as I have argued, joy and friendship are for Nietzsche the ethos that overcomes *Mitleid* and the neighbor, then friendship cannot have a merely instrumental relation to self-overcoming because it is the relation constitutive of that overcoming. This is not to say that self-overcoming means indiscriminately being a friend, but rather that one is disposed toward sharing joy as the primary relation to the other. Such a disposition would still be consistent with discriminating among those for whom one expends the energy of friendship, but life under the sign of eternal recurrence might have, Nietzsche imagines, an abundance that overflows and shares, instinctively shunning petty pleasures from the sufferings and failures of others. Robert Guay, who also argues that relationality is of fundamental and not merely instrumental importance to Nietzsche, distinguishes between culture as a forum for mutual engagement and belonging and the particular relationships that arise against that background, arguing that Nietzsche hopes for "a culture that allows for a range of other human relationships, and itself provides a source of value" (Guay 2016: 377). We might then speak of a *culture* of friendship, promoting a variety of relationships beyond friendship itself in a forum of engagement anchored by joyful abundance and valuing shared joy. Such a culture of overflowing abundance would constitute a transformed humanity: *Übermensch*.

When Zarathustra overcomes his pity for the higher men, he overcomes the dominant form of moral relation to the other. I have shown that in overcoming pity and willing eternal recurrence, Zarathustra aims to initiate a relational structure rooted in shared joy. While Nietzsche leaves only clues concerning more concrete aims and expectations of this *übermenschlich* relationality, and the coming children who do not arrive leave uncertainty concerning Nietzsche's vision for the future, several passages at the end of Book V of *The Gay Science* (GS) provide a direction for thinking about what might be achieved in a transformed relational structure.[21] Nietzsche speaks there to a group of homeless (GS 377) and as yet nameless (382) friends, calling them together on the basis of a dissatisfaction with the current state of humanity and temptation by a superhuman (*übermenschlich*) ideal (GS 382). Calling the task of this new ideal the beginning of "the great seriousness," in the penultimate section of the work, Nietzsche seeks to correct this "gloomy question mark at the end" in the final one (GS 383). He imagines the spirits of his own book attacking him and delivering a speech ending in "No! Not such tones! Let us strike up more agreeable, more joyous tones [*Sondern lasst uns angehmehre anstimmen und freudenvollere*]!" (GS 383). Not only does Nietzsche suggest joy as the end toward which the superhuman ideal aims, but he also offers in this formulation a very distinct image of that joy. In this clear reference to Beethoven's "Hymn to Joy," we are reminded of an earlier reference to the same work in *The Birth of Tragedy* (BT), where Nietzsche tells us to imagine Beethoven's hymn as a painting, at which point we will approach the Dionysian (BT 1). Dionysian joy is a joy for its own sake. This is consistent with Nietzsche's description of the superhuman ideal as that of "a spirit who plays naively" (GS 382). While Nietzsche seeks a transformed evaluative and relational structure, the aim of such a structure might simply be the more joyous affects created in such a structure. To be joyful in more than just a passing sense is to find oneself generous, wanting to share more joy. Nietzsche is not merely concerned with the way in which this produces stronger subjects, but seems to care about the relation itself. The joyful sharing of joy is a relation as its own end—it is play. By understanding the *Übermensch* relationally, we are reminded that what Nietzsche often characterizes as a weighty and serious task is all for naught without joy. Calling up more joyous tones among friends, he points to a goal above power, something higher and more useless, that, like play itself, expands as it is shared.

Notes

1. This includes Kaufmann (1974), Nehamas (1985), and Reginster (2009).
2. See, for instance, Loeb (2010).
3. See, e.g., Drochon (2016).
4. There is precedent in the scholarship for this type of interpretation as well. Daniel Conway writes that Nietzsche's *Übermensch* "could be realized in a community, a discourse, a confluence of traditions, a network of social institutions, a constellation of cultural practices, an unanticipated mutation in the human phenotype—perhaps even a cyborg mechanism" (1997a: 26), thus opening the *Übermensch* to more relational interpretations. Conway focuses ultimately, though, on the convergence of these networks in the individual in his perfectionist interpretation of the concept. Similarly, numerous scholars have related the *übermenschlich* to self-overcoming and revaluation, which makes *Übermensch* a dynamic concept, but the dynamism still tends to be focused around a self. Robert Gooding-Williams suggests that creating overman "would be to become a new-values creator in his own right and to inspire others (his companions; later, his children) to become new-values creators" (2001: 273). Birte Loschenkohl describes overman as "a *call for continuous transformation*" (2020: 27). This has a collective and political dimension for her, but I will argue for more determinate content.
5. See, e.g., Lampert (1986), Clark (1991), and Meyer (2019).
6. Robert Guay argues that Nietzsche is explicitly concerned with interpersonal relations as important in their own right (2016: 351–83).
7. For the relationship between Schopenhauer and Nietzsche's critique of pity, see Cartwright (1993), Frazer (2006), Ure (2006), and Harris (2015).
8. Compare, e.g., with Keith Ansell-Pearson who argues that Nietzsche wishes to replace the morality of compassion with care of the self (2011: 199).
9. Very few attempts exist in the literature to develop an account of the enormous differences in the phenomena that Nietzsche criticizes as *Mitleid*. One exception is Frazer (2006).
10. Jean-Paul Sartre's classic account of shame under the Other's gaze in *Being and Nothingness* is instructive here, since the shame is felt not by the person inside but by the one looking through the peephole. In other words, the most obvious candidate for the experience of shame is not the one whose privacy is violated but rather the one apprehending himself as the violator of the private (1984: 347–54).

11. Bernard Reginster (2009: 185) notes that Nietzsche rejects the morality of compassion on altruistic grounds in EH I: 4.
12. *Freude* and *Lust* are both translated sometimes as joy, sometimes as pleasure, and they are in the same family of affects for Nietzsche. He uses *Lust* consistently in Zarathustra's songs of eternal recurrence, but shared joy is consistently *Mitfreude*.
13. Hugo Drochon (2016), for instance, understands the point of institutions for Nietzsche to be the support of a certain *type* of life, understood in heavily physiological terms. Jeffrey Church (2012), on the other hand, argues that Nietzsche's goal of the sovereign individual is ultimately directed toward the redemption of the community.
14. Both Ure (2006) and Harris (2015) give accounts of friendship that make relationality central to Nietzsche's conception of self-overcoming.
15. Conway (1997b: 166) argues that Zarathustra's real children are his various disciples, and that the higher men of Part IV may actually fulfill the prophecy he claims to honor, but Zarathustra misinterprets the signs.
16. Unlike Deleuze (1962) and Loeb (2010), I think that willing the recurrence of the small man remains essential. For a nuanced interpretation of this part of the thought as one of its conflicting demands, see Gooding-Williams (2001).
17. Willow Verkerk (2014: 279–91) also highlights issues of relationality and friendship in her account of the Overhuman. For Verkerk, the Overhuman provides a symbol of superior traits for friends pushing one another toward greater *Redlichkeit*, rather than the relational mode itself.
18. See Reginster (2009: 126–7).
19. Paul Kirkland (2009: 215–70) argues that pity is overcome by laughter in Z, tying pity and laughter to the dramatic forms of tragedy and comedy and making the context in which the emotions arise the relation between spectator and spectacle, the subject and himself, reader, and text.
20. Nietzsche's expressed desire to replace shared suffering with shared joy would be facile if understood as a simple replacement. A friendship worthy of the name surely shares sufferings in some form. It is a question of the transformation of the dominant affect structuring human connection. Nietzsche says that our suffering is incomprehensible to *almost* everyone (GS 338), intimating that there could be someone—the friend—who could comprehend the personal and thus share suffering appropriately. Referring to this passage, Harris argues that attention to the suffering of others can sometimes be called for (2017: 254). Robert Miner (2010) also points out that Nietzsche distinguishes between *Mitleid* and *Mitgefühl*.
21. Conway (1997b: 165–70) argues that Zarathustra's real children are the motley crew that he collects in Books I–III and that Nietzsche's "real readers, like the higher men who are drawn to Zarathustra, faithfully reflect the depleted vitality of the age."
On my reading, the potential transformation in eternal recurrence introduces the possibility of transformed relationality, while Conway argues Zarathustra's failure to acknowledge his real children is an unresolved chronic failure.

References

Ansell-Pearson, K. (2011), "Beyond Compassion: On Nietzsche's Moral Therapy in *Dawn*," *Continental Philosophy Review* 44: 179–204.
Cartwright, D. (1993), "The Last Temptation of Zarathustra," *Journal of the History of Philosophy* 31 (1): 49–69.

Church, J. (2012), *Infinite Autonomy: The Divided Individual in the Political Thought of G.W.F. Hegel and Friedrich Nietzsche*, University Park: Penn State University Press.

Clark, M. (1991), *Nietzsche on Truth and Philosophy*, Cambridge: Cambridge University Press.

Conway, D. W. (1997a), *Nietzsche and the Political*, New York: Routledge.

Conway, D. W. (1997b), *Nietzsche's Dangerous Game*, Cambridge: Cambridge University Press.

Deleuze, Gilles (1962), *Nietzsche and Philosophy*, New York: Columbia University Press.

Drochon, H. (2016), *Nietzsche's Great Politics*, Princeton, NJ: Princeton University Press.

Frazer, M. L. (2006), "The Compassion of Zarathustra: Nietzsche on Sympathy and Strength," *Review of Politics* 68: 49–78.

Gilman, S. L., and D. J. Parent, eds. (1987), *Conversations with Nietzsche*, Oxford: Oxford University Press.

Gooding-Williams, R. (2001), *Zarathustra's Dionysian Modernism*, Stanford: Stanford University Press.

Guay, R. (2016), "Ethics as Social Philosophy: Nietzsche on Mutuality," *Journal of Nietzsche Studies* 47 (3): 351–83.

Harris, Daniel I. (2015), "Friendship as Shared Joy in Nietzsche," *Symposium: Canadian Journal of Continental Philosophy* 19 (1): 199–221.

Harris, Daniel I. (2017), "Nietzsche and Aristotle on Friendship and Self-Knowledge," *Journal of Nietzsche Studies* 48 (2): 245–60.

Kaufmann, W. (1974), *Nietzsche: Philosopher, Psychologist, Antichrist*, Princeton, NJ: Princeton University Press.

Kirkland, P. E. (2009), *Nietzsche's Noble Aims: Affirming Life, Contesting Modernity*, Lanham, MD: Lexington Books.

Lampert, L. (1986), *Nietzsche's Teaching*, New Haven, CT: Yale University Press.

Loeb, P. (2010), *The Death of Nietzsche's Zarathustra*, Cambridge: Cambridge University Press.

Loschenkohl, B. (2020), "Nietzsche's 'Great Politics' and Zarathustra's New Peoples," *Journal of Nietzsche Studies* 51 (1): 21–45.

Meyer, M. (2019), *Nietzsche's Free Spirit Works: A Dialectical Reading*, Cambridge: Cambridge University Press.

Miner, R. C. (2010), "Nietzsche on Friendship," *Journal of Nietzsche Studies* 40: 47–69.

Nehamas, A (1985), *Nietzsche: Life as Literature*, Cambridge, MA: Harvard University Press.

Reginster, B. (2009), *The Affirmation of Life*, Cambridge, MA: Harvard University Press.

Sartre, J.P. (1984), *Being and Nothingness*, New York: Washington Square Press.

Schopenhauer, A. (1969), *The World as Will and Representation I*, trans. E. F. J. Payne, New York: Dover.

Schopenhauer, A. (2005), *On the Basis of Morality*, Mineola, NY: Dover.

Ure, M. (2006), "Nietzsche contra Schopenhauer and Rousseau," *Journal of Nietzsche Studies* 32: 68–91.

Verkerk, W. (2014), "Nietzsche's Goal of Friendship," *Journal of Nietzsche Studies* 45 (3): 279–91.

4

"Is the Sea Not Full of Verdant Islands?": Zarathustra on Passing by the Great City

Peter S. Groff

Thus Spoke Zarathustra (henceforth cited as Z in text) presents us with the first, and perhaps most forceful, expression of the political Platonism that will characterize Nietzsche's later thought: the philosopher-type steps forth as commander and legislator, replete with prophetic trappings, and offers up a new table of values by which humanity will live.[1] Indeed, one might say that Zarathustra's descent back into the cities of human beings represents the culmination of what Nietzsche will elsewhere call "great politics": the revaluation of values, the creation of new world-interpretations, meanings and goals, and the cultivation or "perfection" of the human being.[2] Yet in spite of Zarathustra's grandiose task, one can find in his story a reassertion of the ancient tension between philosophy and the city—and even a recognition of its indissolubility. Indeed, the book might be read as an extended, if interstitial, argument against the grand political ambitions of philosophy.[3] This chapter considers Zarathustra's own joyful relinquishment of the political life of the city and his continual deferral, if not ultimate abandonment, of the attempt to fix humanity.

I begin by reconstructing the initial ebb and flow of Zarathustra's great politics and then focus on one speech in particular, "On Passing By." This speech, delivered at the gates of "the *great city*" to an ignoble figure simply named Zarathustra's ape, suggests that the best response to the life-denying morality of custom is not critique and supersession, but rather withdrawal and disregard.[4] "Where one can no longer love," Zarathustra counsels, "there one must—*pass by!*—" (Z III Passing By).[5] As it turns out, this teaching applies more generally to Zarathustra's own great politics, inasmuch as he can no longer convince himself that he loves humanity. So when the prophet withdraws from the political realm for the third and final time, he does not return. Yet, I argue that the seemingly quietistic teaching of "passing by" contains within it the germ of a more powerful yea-saying orientation toward the world that leads us up the ladder of love toward more radically affirmative doctrines such as *amor fati* and eternal recurrence—suprapolitical teachings suitable for anchorites or small isolated friendship communities, but not the city.

1. Descent and Withdrawal

The book begins with Zarathustra's impending descent from his isolated mountain world. We are told that when the prophet was thirty years old, "he abandoned his home and the lake of his home and went into the mountains," where "he enjoyed his spirit and his solitude and for ten years did not tire of them" (Z I Prologue 1). Interestingly, no further explanation is given for Zarathustra's original retreat from the human world a decade before, but a few salient details can be cobbled together. First, earlier drafts and sources for this initial speech indicate that his home—which at first glance might seem rustic and pastoral—was in fact a city.[6] Second, the saint in the forest who he passes on the way back down recollects having seen him "carrying [his] ashes to the mountains" a decade before, suggesting that the nascent philosophical legislator came to experience the customs, opinions, and practices of the city as spiritually exhausting (Z I Prologue 2). Finally, Zarathustra's subsequent speeches make clear the emancipatory function of withdrawal as an ascetic practice—albeit one arguably shorn of any religio-metaphysical significance or stable, preestablished goal.[7] Solitude enables us to bracket the inherited values of the city, provides leisure for contemplation and self-exploration, and opens up a feeling of height, distance, and freedom in which new values and ways of life can emerge. It is no surprise, then, that Zarathustra repeatedly valorizes the desert and forest—archetypal symbols of ascetic withdrawal and solitude—as sanctuaries from human political life and potential places of self-overcoming, transfiguration, and creation.

Now, after a decade of anchoretic self-cultivation, Zarathustra is overburdened by his accumulated wisdom and wants to share it with those below. And so he goes back down into the cities of human beings to disseminate his transformative teaching.[8] His initial attempt at great politics goes badly: in the first town he encounters, he indiscriminately presents his doctrine of the superhuman to the vulgar multitude in the market place and is met with derision and hostility (Z I Prologue 3–8).[9] Zarathustra quickly recalibrates, however, and decides to seek out a smaller, select group of "companions" and "fellow creators," whom he finds in a city called the Motley Cow (Z I Prologue 9; Z I Transformations).[10] The second transmission of Zarathustra's teaching takes place there and seems to go more successfully, but by the end of the First Part of the book, the prophet has once again retreated into his mountain solitude, this time ostensibly for the sake of his companions: he wants to give them space to "lose" him and "find" themselves, and to give his teachings time to take root and come to fruition (Z I Bestowing; Z II Child).

Zarathustra's second solitude, which lasts for several years, is marred by loneliness, concern, and impatience. Eventually spurred to action by a prophetic dream, he rejoins his companions, who have now abandoned the Motley Cow and regrouped as an insulated colony of sorts on the "Blessed Isles" (*glückseligen Inseln*) (Z II Child).[11] The establishment of this community can be understood as a continuation and intensification of the legislator's rhetorical shift from the many to the few: just as Zarathustra by the end of the Prologue chooses to reserve his message for a select group of friends and cocreators recruited in the archetypal city, the Blessed Isles represent the eventual withdrawal of that elite few from the city itself.

As suggested by Zarathustra's earlier teaching, this isolation is necessary for their proper cultivation. Yet, instead of each disciple retreating individually to the wilderness, they opt for a small, tightly knit friendship community—a hidden cloister of free spirits, as it were.[12] Its placement on a cluster of islands seems particularly significant in this respect: it is far away, sequestered and secure, cut off from the demands of political life.[13] Zarathustra himself must travel over "distant seas" to find it.[14] At the same time, the Isles' location evokes the sea symbolism that looms so large in the middle period works immediately preceding Z, alternately representing (1) "the great silence" that allows us momentarily to forget the city and the stifling provinciality of anthropocentric life, (2) an uncharted and seemingly infinite horizon for free-spirited exploration in a newly de-deified world, and (3) a dehumanized new vision of nature as will to power.[15] Finally, the Isles themselves provide a "soft greensward" for Zarathustra's teaching, a paradisiacal halfway house of sorts between everyday political life and the unadulterated solitude of the desert, forest, or mountain cave.[16] In short, the Blessed Isles represent the possibility of a shared philosophical life freed from the tyranny of the city—a sanctuary that provides the necessary distance and leisure for contemplation, self-cultivation and individual creativity while still permitting a selective, upbuilding sociality. In this respect we might think of them as a naturalized version of the mythic Isles of the Blessed (after which it is loosely named) or even a new Epicurean Garden.[17]

The Blessed Isles would seem to be the ideal place for a transformative philosophical reeducation and Zarathustra's small, transplanted community of fellow creators would appear to be ideal pupils. Accordingly, his third transmission is more nuanced and advanced than his first two. Yet by the end of the Second Part, he has taken leave of them again. Zarathustra's third and final withdrawal is harder to make sense of than the previous two, for he provides different reasons at different moments. On the one hand, his departure is prompted by pivotal challenges from less sympathetic audiences (e.g., the soothsayer, the "cripples and beggars")—challenges that reveal the existential incompleteness of his teaching, test his mettle as a philosophical legislator, and make him doubt his ability to command.[18] But at the very beginning of the Third Part, we find another reason: here he observes that the "protection" afforded by the Blessed Isles has made him "sickly" (Z III Wanderer), suggesting that the sheltered life of a philosophical friendship community will eventually become dogmatic, self-indulgent, and enfeebling. This point is further developed in a subsequent speech, where he recognizes that his own work of self-cultivation is not yet done: he still needs to "perfect himself" for the sake of his children and for the "greater perfection of all things" (Z III Blissfulness). In short, he must articulate, wrestle with, and ultimately affirm his most difficult abysmal thought, the eternal recurrence—and this is something that he can only do alone, through a final *anachōrēsis*. Yet before he even left, he had observed (in a speech notably delivered only to himself) that his role as legislative gift-giver was making him increasingly isolated and lonely, and he yearned for the solitude of his mountain retreat (Z II Night Song, cf. III Return Home). This, of course, was the very task that brought him back down to humanity in the first place and one that the saint in the forest had preemptively warned him against (Z I Prologue 2).[19] Curiously, by the time he returns home to the mountains, this last reason has completely overshadowed the other two (Z III Return Home). We might say, then, that Zarathustra's third and final withdrawal is overdetermined: he doubts his abilities as commander and legislator, he senses that his work on himself and his teaching are not yet complete, he feels that even the limited and selective sociality of the friendship community has become counterproductive, he seeks silence and solitude, and he seems increasingly conflicted about—one might even say less concerned with—his "gift" to humanity.

In Zarathustra's farewell speech to his friends, he appears troubled and weeps inconsolably (Z II Hour). Yet within a day of his departure, he is again savoring his solitude, almost as though he has awakened from the malaise of a sad dream (Z III Blissfulness). The way home is long and winding: his ship journey takes several days and upon reaching the distant shore Zarathustra decides not to return directly to his cave. Rather, he takes the scenic route, wandering at leisure through the various cities that lie between the sea and the mountains in order "to experience what had happened to humanity in the meantime" (Z III Virtue). It is at this point that Zarathustra delivers his speech "On Passing By."

2. Disgust and Revenge in the Great City

"On Passing By" is the prophet's penultimate public address before finally arriving home at his mountain retreat. It is delivered at the gate of "the *great city*"—no other name is given—to a figure simply called "Zarathustra's ape."[20] Zarathustra seems not to be visiting this place deliberately; he is described as having stumbled upon it "suddenly" or "unexpectedly" (*unversehens*).[21] At that very moment, he is confronted by a degraded imitation of himself:

> Here a frothing fool with hands outspread leaped before him and barred his way. But this was the same fool that people called "Zarathustra's ape": for he had gathered something of the phrasing and cadences of Zarathustra's speech and also liked to borrow from the treasure of his wisdom. (Z III Passing By)[22]

The ape warns Zarathustra away from the city, launching into a joyless and obsessive critique overstuffed with gruesome images: great thoughts being "boiled alive" and "cooked down small," "slaughterhouses and soup-kitchens of the spirit," souls hanging like "limp and filthy rags." A grotesque parade of caricatures is trotted out: money-grubbing shopkeepers, grasping beggars, war-mongering pseudo-patriots, venal princes, and so forth. In the ape's feverish imagination, the whole city seems to be awash in a deluge of swill, vomit, spittle, blood, and sewerage. His central practical teaching, repeated several times, is to "spit upon the city and turn back." The entire speech is essentially a crude caricature of Zarathustra's own teachings, appropriating and regurgitating vulgarized fragments from some of the prophet's earlier speeches.[23]

Zarathustra finally interrupts the ape's tedious harangue by putting a hand over his "frothing" mouth. His counter-speech unmasks the base, ignoble sentiments that have animated this condemnation of the city: the ape despises it and yet remains within it to curse it and wage war against it—a choice that has made him as small and loathsome as the place he despises. Zarathustra presses the ape on this point and, in one of the few gentle moments of his response, asks him why he hasn't simply left:

> "Why did you live for so long in the swamp that you yourself had to become a frog and a toad?
> Does a putrid and spumy swamp blood not now flow through your own veins, that you have learned to croak and blaspheme such?
> Why did you not go into the forest? Or plough the earth? Is the sea not full of verdant islands?"

Now, the ape was initially described as a frothing fool who is simply imitating Zarathustra's words without understanding. But Zarathustra's interrogation here implies that there is perhaps more to him than his present state might suggest. So let us assume for the moment that the ape, despite his failings, is still a philosopher—or at least aspires to be one. Zarathustra says that he *became* a frog and a toad from living in a swamp for so long. His virulent disgust toward the city is thus not an essential aspect of his character, but rather has been acquired circumstantially. He experiences first hand on a daily basis the tension between what the human being is in his petty society and what it could be. His own attempt to reorder the regime of his soul and self-legislate healthy values is incessantly disrupted by the feverish city in which he lives. That is to say, the great city is a monster against which he perpetually struggles. But as Nietzsche elsewhere counsels, "whoever fights monsters should see to it that in the process he does not become a monster" (BGE 146).[24]

Zarathustra is thus reiterating a familiar point: if the philosopher's way of life is irreducibly at odds with the opinions and practices of the city, there are other extra-political options: the life of the renunciant or anchorite (the forest, or by extension, the desert or mountain cave), the life of the agrarian primitivist recluse (the self-sufficient farm), the life of the philosophical friend (the Epicurean Garden or Blessed Isle). All of these are examples of withdrawal.[25] The final option here, however, provides the most striking juxtaposition of the three: over against the fetid, gloomy, claustrophobic swamp of the ape's great city we envision a small cluster of green islands far away in the midst of a vast ocean, with fresh air blown in by trade winds.[26] Over against the ignorant masses, avaricious merchants, and fanatical ideologues we envision a small, self-selected community of philosophical companions and fellow creators. Over against the oppressive heteronomous customs, petty gossip, and screaming headlines of traditional political life we envision the possibility of contemplation, self-cultivation, and the exploration of new shapes of life. One wonders whether this idyllic alternative is really available to the ape; Zarathustra himself is confident that such islands are hidden everywhere.[27] Whether or not this is true, we see here, in spite of Zarathustra's own recent abandonment of the Blessed Isles, a residual acknowledgement of their abiding importance for nascent free spirits and higher types. If nothing else, his initial reply to the ape makes it clear that, wherever the appropriate place of the philosopher may ultimately be, it is *not* locked in a perpetual *agon* with the monstrous city.

The ape's insistence on remaining in the great city in order to critique it in some ways recalls Nietzsche's great antipode, Socrates. But the ape is no Socrates in the marketplace: he lacks the ironic distance, the dialectical finesse and the gentle humor. We might even say that he is Socrates's ape just as much as Zarathustra's. Indeed, if there is a philosophical type under which the ape can be subsumed, it is the Cynic: a kind of vulgarized, dogmatic, and implacably combative Socrates. The Cynic despises the conventional morality of the city, relentlessly exposing its hypocrisies and transgressing them in as shocking a manner as possible. Yet this still requires an audience of the good and righteous before whom one can perform such indictments. In this respect, the Cynic remains dialectically bound up with the customs and values he is rejecting. As Nietzsche points out elsewhere, in committing himself to the continual critique of his fellow citizens' opinions and desires, the Cynic merely negates them without ever managing to raise himself above them and free himself from them.[28] In effect, the dog-philosopher defines himself reactively in opposition to that which he hates and thus allows himself to remain inversely conditioned and determined by it. This is the ape-philosopher's conundrum as well. Perhaps that is why Zarathustra accuses him of secretly wanting recognition from his fellow citizens: "What was it then that made you begin grunting? That no one has *flattered* you enough:—therefore you sat yourself down in this filth, that you might have grounds for such grunting—that you might have grounds for much *revenge!* For revenge, you vain fool, is what all your frothing is" (Z III Passing By, cf. II Wise Men).

At the same time, Zarathustra acknowledges the dangerously close kinship between the ape's diatribes and his own previous teachings: "But your words harm *me*," he says, "even when you are right! And if Zarathustra's words *were* even a hundred times right, by my words you always—*do* wrong!" This is because the ape's words are rooted in resentment and the spirit of revenge rather than love and great longing.[29] That at least is what Zarathustra claims, but his own response to the ape's speech seems residually bound up with feelings of repulsion and the need for vengeance: he admits that he is "disgusted" by the ape and claims to "despise [his] despising."[30] And when he finally looks at the great city—recall that he came upon it unexpectantly and was initially distracted by the ape's performance at its gates—he sighs and then, after a long reflective silence, confesses that he too is disgusted by it. He even indulges himself at this point in a vengeful prophecy of Biblical proportions: "Woe unto this great city!— And would that I might already see the pillar of fire in which it will be consumed! For such pillars of fire must precede the Great Midday. Yet this has its own time and its own fate." Is this yet another illustration of the infectious nature of resentment? One wonders whether Zarathustra's unexpected exposure to the ape and the great city has rekindled the smoldering embers of his basest and most reactive sentiments— or whether Zarathustra's great politics too have been fueled by the spirit of revenge all along.

3. Zarathustra's Lesson

It is at this point, however, that Zarathustra leaves the ape with a parting gift, which leavens and perhaps even redeems the pervasive ugliness of their exchange: "Where one can no longer love, there one should—*pass by!*—" This teaching is not without its antecedents: consider, for instance, the saint's initial warning to Zarathustra *not* to bring humanity a gift (Z I Prologue 2), or Zarathustra's subsequent advice to his disciples to pass by priests quietly with a sleeping sword, lest they "besmirch" themselves in attacking their kin (Z II Priests). But something new is coalescing here.[31]

There is an odd symmetry between the ape's speech and Zarathustra's. The ape urges us to "turn back" (*kehre um*) from the city because it is despicable; Zarathustra counsels us to "*pass by*" (*vorübergehn*) because it cannot be loved. Consider the difference: the ape's orientation is essentially one of recoiling and sheer negation. It blocks the way and does not allow us any recourse to move forward.[32] We are, in effect, returned to our previous square and prohibited from continuing along our way (whether deliberately chosen or merely stumbled upon). The city thus continues to stand before us as that which defeated our plans. It remains an object of regret, resentment, and imagined revenge even after we have ostensibly abandoned it. What, then, is Zarathustra's orientation? It too involves negation, but it is of a more nuanced and indirect sort. He doesn't encourage us to "spit" on the city, as the ape does. Yet he can't bring himself to "bless" it either—a noteworthy fact, given the increasing prevalence and significance of that gesture in the latter part of the book.[33] Similarly, while he doesn't advise us to retreat from the city as the ape does, neither does he encourage us to confront it and overcome it, as an earlier (and more agonistic or hyper-volitional) version of himself might have (Z I Transformations, II Self-Overcoming). Zarathustra's counsel is to pass *by* the great city, not to pass *through* it. On the face of it, this teaching of evasion appears unexpectedly quietist and apolitical. It may even sound like an admission of defeat, an abdication not only of the philosopher's zetetic responsibility to the city, but of the task of great politics itself. Yet Zarathustra's apparent disregard here contains within it the seed of a more affirmative teaching. And it is not just a remedial lesson intended for the ape. Zarathustra subsequently repeats it to himself—as a vital insight that he too has gained—two more times throughout the remainder of the Third Part.

The first is when he has returned to his mountain world for the third and final time. This is a pivotal moment in the narrative and, notwithstanding his concluding songs in celebration of eternal recurrence, arguably the most unadulterated expression of joy to be found in the book. He reflects on the superiority of solitude to lonely sociality, of free and honest private discourse with oneself to public dissimulation or even prudent silence among others, of communing with worldly things instead of attempting to manipulate and control them:

> "Here the words and word-shrines of all being spring open for me: all being wants to become word here, all becoming wants to learn from me how to talk.
>
> "Down there however—there all talking is in vain! There forgetting and passing by are the best wisdom: *that*—I have now learned!
>
> "Whoever wanted to grasp [*begreifen*] everything about human beings would have to grapple with [*angreifen*, i.e., attack, assail] everything. But for that my hands are too clean." (Z III Return)

It is wisest to pass by and forget the city because engagement with it is ultimately fruitless—it will not be improved—and contending with it only soils and infects the philosopher-legislator (cf. Z II Priests).[34] He goes on to juxtapose the pure air and blessed stillness of his mountain retreat with the foul smells and empty chatter of political life, celebrating the fact that his "greatest danger"—humankind—now "lies behind" him. One gets the sense here that Zarathustra is weary of encountering things to which he must say no, among them humanity itself. Forgetting and passing by are the best wisdom at this juncture because they prepare the ground for new experiences to which one can finally say yes.

Zarathustra articulates the doctrine of "passing by" one final time in "On Old and New Tablets," a lengthy speech in which he recapitulates all his various teachings:

> "I love those who are brave: but it is not enough to be an old swordsman—one must also know how and whom to fight!
>
> "And there is often more bravery in restraining oneself and passing by: so that one might save oneself for a worthier enemy!" (Z III Tablets 21)

Zarathustra develops the point at some length, reminding himself to "keep your eyes clear" of the contentions of unworthy enemies, since whoever "looks on" such things merely becomes angry. Zarathustra here seems to be recollecting his own visceral disgust and desire for revenge when he finally looked upon the great city. He sums up his lesson with the dictum: "Go *your* ways! And let folk and people go theirs!" The overall point is clear: one shows greater valor by choosing one's enemies carefully and not indiscriminately squandering one's forces with petty skirmishes. Whether the "worthier enemy" here is the eternal recurrence or Zarathustra himself as object of self-overcoming, he no longer seeks to contend with imperfectible humanity.

As a formula of selective affirmation, Zarathustra's teaching on "passing by" anticipates the book's culminating doctrine: eternal recurrence.[35] That chief concept has already begun to emerge at this point in the narrative, and we might even say it hovers in the background of the three speeches above, although Zarathustra has not yet adequately articulated it, let alone managed to affirm it himself. To appreciate the relation between these two teachings (one fairly modest, the other almost impossibly ambitious), we need to turn to an intermediate doctrine which does not explicitly appear in Z, but which might nonetheless be said to pervade the entire book: *amor fati*, or 'love of fate'. It is first presented in *The Gay Science* (GS), as Nietzsche's own personal New Year's Day "wish" and "dearest thought." In full it reads,

> I want to learn more and more to see as beautiful what is necessary in things; then I shall be one of those who make things beautiful. *Amor fati*: let that be my love henceforth! I do not want to wage war against what is ugly. I do not want to accuse; I do not even want to accuse those who accuse. *Looking away* shall be my only negation. And all in all and on the whole: someday I wish only to be a Yes-sayer. (GS 276)

In the first and last parts of this passage, one can certainly see the germ of Zarathustra's climactic doctrine: the desire "to see as beautiful what is necessary in things," to "make things beautiful" through one's love and someday "to only be a Yes-sayer" anticipates the will to affirm all things—not only every joy and pain of one's individual life but the totality of natural history itself—and indeed to will their eternal recurrence.[36] We might say that these desires point toward the ideal of unadulterated and indiscriminate love. The middle three sentences, however, offer a provisional and slightly tempered teaching that may help illuminate Zarathustra's parting gift to the ape, so let us focus on those.[37]

"I do not want to wage war against what is ugly": is this not precisely what the ape does in the great city? We might say as well that it is the error into which Zarathustra himself too often falls when he attempts to transform and redeem humanity. So it is no small matter that the prophet congratulates himself on having escaped this temptation at the beginning of his final solitude. Yet Nietzsche's own wish in GS 276 makes it clear that he still feels the pull of such conflict. However far the sphere of necessity extends, *not everything* is beautiful for the author of this wish.[38] The world still unfortunately contains for him much that is ugly and bad and even painful. He cannot love it yet, but at least he will endeavor not to organize his life around attacking it.

"I do not want to accuse; I do not even want to accuse those who accuse": he no longer wants to degrade the world for its ostensible imperfections and disappointments or to reproach the base and lowly. Of course, this is easier said than done: the ugly aspects of the world do not just sit there passively allowing themselves to be observed, they often actively reach out to us and assault us. But we should be careful not to respond in kind. Here we might be tempted to replace "accuse" with "injure" or "harm," and this would certainly capture the aforementioned point about fighting monsters. But having enemies or even hurting another is by no means incompatible with this teaching: for better or worse, Nietzsche and Zarathustra both praise the "swordsman." Nietzsche's resolution is not a commitment to nonviolence or "turning the other cheek" but rather an attempt to twist free of the infectious and self-replicating nature of reactive sentiments like resentment, the spirit of revenge, or the need to punish.

"*Looking away* [*Wegsehen*] shall be my only negation": after contemplating the lofty but seemingly impossible ideal, we arrive at the strategic compromise. Nietzsche is not yet capable of universal affirmation; *some* form of denial is inescapable. But there are different sorts of practical negation. One might negate something by actively trying to annihilate it or irreparably damage it. One could hate something but not have the power to combat it and thus be perpetually wounded or haunted or paralyzed by it, passively suffering from the existence of that which is irredeemably painful or ugly or unlovable. One could negate something by insisting on its unreality, demoting it to a dreamlike or merely illusory status. One could negate something by accusing it or reproaching it. One could negate something by assigning blame or guilt and punishing it. One could even negate something by trying to change it or improve it. Or one could negate something *only insofar as one chooses not to acknowledge or recognize it*: that is to say, one could simply "look away" or "pass by."[39]

This last strategy points toward the "pathos of distance," a sentiment that Nietzsche will elsewhere associate with the emergence of noble moralities and the phenomenon of rank-ordering: the noble look down from afar on the lowly and base, not hating them, not dwelling on them, not unduly amplifying their significance.[40] Their self-affirmation and embrace of comparably good things is the fundamental evaluative act; their negative evaluation of the bad a mere afterthought.[41] Similarly, the doctrine of passing by, despite its evasive and nonconfrontational overtones, insists on the primacy of affirmation and the parasitic or at least merely reactive nature of negation. If we cannot yet say yes to everything, we can at least minimize and decentralize our nay-saying so that it does not sap our joy, degrade us, poison our highest ideals, or distract us from cultivating our own gardens.[42] In passing by that which we cannot love, in looking away from that which we cannot see as beautiful, we break its spell over us, move beyond it, and open up the possibility of finding that which we *can* affirm. Modest as it seems, it is thus a crucial stepping stone in the process of learning to say yes to everything, a process that reaches its apotheosis in the teaching of eternal recurrence.[43]

4. Farewell to Great Politics

Let us return, then, to the question of Zarathustra's great politics. The book began with the philosophical legislator's ambitious descent from his mountain solitude into political life, bearing the gift of a radical new affirmative teaching that would transform humanity and thereby redeem the world. But Zarathustra's own education, it turned out, was not yet entirely complete. As he absorbed his final lessons, his teaching evolved. At the same time, his intended audience increasingly narrowed. An indiscriminate speech to the vulgar multitude in the marketplace soon gave way to more advanced discourses reserved for friends and fellow creators in the cosmopolitan Motley Cow, and they in turn gave way to more nuanced exchanges shared with a select and isolated hermetic friendship community. Now, by the Third Part of the book, Zarathustra is once again alone, his speeches directed only to himself, or solitude, or his animals, or life, or eternity.[44] It is in this "blissful stillness" that he will articulate and affirm his culminating doctrine of eternal recurrence (Z III Return Home).

The climactic events that unfold during Zarathustra's third and final solitude are often framed by commentators as preparation for one final descent back into humanity, by means of which Zarathustra will triumphantly disseminate his completed teaching.[45] This is not an unreasonable assumption: there are indeed moments when he expresses a desire to return to humankind once more (Z III Tablets 1, IV Honey, Sign). And of course, his previous two withdrawals were both undertaken with an eye to his eventual return. Yet Zarathustra never actually undertakes this last descent. The Third Part (the original conclusion of the book) ends with the prophet singing his affirmation of eternal recurrence. The subsequently appended Fourth and Final Part, more satirical in mood and distributed only to a small circle of friends, finds an aged Zarathustra still enjoying his mountain solitude before awkwardly navigating a surprise visit from the higher humans.[46] One again finds occasional promissory gestures toward a final dramatic descent—he claims to be waiting for a sign to return, abruptly anticipates an imminent reunion with his children, and even emerges dramatically from his cave as the sun rises at the very end, prophesying the arrival of the Great Midday.⁴⁷ But we never actually see Zarathustra return to humanity, and indeed the rhetoric of going "down" and "under" one last time is belied by both the history of his own formative experiences and the content of his completed teaching.⁴⁸

Consider the first: Zarathustra's experiences in the human world have been almost invariably disappointing. What is it that brought him down from his mountain retreat in the first place? Zarathustra speaks of being "overburdened" with his wisdom, of wanting to "overflow" and "distribute" it to humanity (Z I Prologue 1). Mid-descent, he tells the saint in the forest, "I love human beings": that is his very first moment of intersubjective communication after ten years of solitude (Z I Prologue 2). But when the saint observes that human beings are "too incomplete an affair" for him to love, the prophet quickly corrects himself: "What did I say of love! I bring human beings a gift." Zarathustra also sees the human being as too incomplete an affair and envisions its transfiguration into something higher and more perfect, something more capable of affirmation.⁴⁹ That in a sense is his gift: a new teaching, a new table of values, a new way of life, a new mode of being in the world. He even characterizes himself as a sculptor of sorts, freeing human potentiality from the natural-historical prison in which it finds itself (Z II Blessed Isles). Yet as his task unfolds, he seems to have an ever-lower estimation of the raw materials upon which he is working.⁵⁰ What draws him toward humanity is ultimately the same thing that repels him: its incompleteness or imperfection. He is of course also repeatedly frustrated and discouraged by what we might call the problem of prophetic misunderstanding: if there is one constant in the book, it is the incapacity of those audiences to whom Zarathustra addresses himself fully to apprehend the radical import of his gradually developing doctrines.⁵¹ Even among his elite inner circle, he is reduced to fending off misunderstanding through dissimulation and silence.⁵² It is perhaps for these two reasons that Zarathustra finds little joy in the midst of human sociality. He struggles to breathe, think, and create in cities, finds even the friendship community of the Blessed Isles lonely and stultifying, and quickly chafes at the company of higher humans who visit his mountain abode.⁵³ One wonders *why* he would want to go back down again: what would be different this time?

On the other hand, he thrives and seems genuinely happy during his anchoretic periods. At the very beginning of the story, we are simply told that Zarathustra "enjoyed" his spirit and solitude. Admittedly, its value at that stage lay first and foremost in its *utility* for the task of great politics: after all, the greatest events are our stillest hours and "thoughts that come on doves' feet direct the world" (Z II Great Events, cf. I Flies, II Hour). But this begins to shift as we see Zarathustra repeatedly flounder in the midst of community; he increasingly longs for withdrawal. When he finally returns to his mountain retreat, it is a profoundly cathartic and even ecstatic moment. He calls solitude his "home" and his "mother" (Z III Return Home). Withdrawal is at that moment no longer just a means to great politics; it is an end in itself. It should come as no surprise, then, that Zarathustra associates joy almost exclusively with withdrawal and solitude and never with descent or dissemination.⁵⁴ One might say that the apex of his existence, far from being a *vita activa* of great politics, turns out to a kind of post-metaphysical *vita contemplativa*.

Now consider the evolutionary logic of Zarathustra's own teachings. The first two parts of the book are heavily freighted with doctrines of ambitious striving and the pressing need for radical transformation: the ideal of the superhuman, the legislation of new this-worldly values, the liberatory capacity of creativity, will to power, self-overcoming. But by the Third Part, the wheel has turned and we sense a nascent fatalism (Z II Redemption). The abysmal thought of eternal recurrence is gradually emerging, a thought that will unmoor or at least radically reframe his previous teachings. I have argued above that Zarathustra's teaching of passing by is a crucial step on the way to this highest formula of affirmation. The philosophical legislator recognizes that he is incapable of loving humanity, just as the ape is incapable of loving the city, and so instead of grappling with it—accusing it, critiquing it, trying to improve it—he has decided to pass it by, or in the words of Nietzsche's *amor fati* resolution, to "look away." He has been redeemed from his world-redeeming ambitions. The Third Part might then be read as the story of Zarathustra withdrawing from the realm of human affairs altogether and with it, the grand political project of epochal human transfiguration, to embrace a kind of blissful, self-sufficient, divine solitude.[55]

And yet, this still misses something important. The doctrine of passing by remains a teaching of selective affirmation—of deliberately limited horizons—and as such is too weak for Zarathustra's final experience of the world. The noble pathos of distance must ultimately be superseded by an even more powerful, healthy, and joyfully indiscriminate embrace of all things. At first this ascent up the Nietzschean ladder of love might seem to reenergize the task of great politics: Zarathustra has learned to see as beautiful what is necessary in all things—among them human beings—and thus no longer need pass them by or look away. But as has often been pointed out, the circular temporality of eternal recurrence disrupts the residually teleological and millenarian underpinnings of Zarathustra's project.[56] In any case, his affirmation of that epiphany requires him to accept and embrace humanity's incompleteness. It is no longer simply a question of "not ... accus[ing] those who accuse" but of affirming those who cannot affirm or—bearing in mind its profoundly un-Christian spirit—loving those incapable of genuine love. This means: no nausea over the recurrence of the small human being (Z III Convalescent), no pity for the higher humans (Z IV Sign), and presumably, no further need to transform or redeem humanity. Nor does it permit the paternalistic cultivation of a select coterie, that is, his fellow creators or "children."[57] As Zarathustra makes clear in his final presentation of the eternal recurrence teaching, "joy does not want heirs, nor children—joy wants itself, wants eternity, wants recurrence, wants everything eternally the same" (Z IV Sleepwalker). One might say that the joyful philosophical doctrines of eternal recurrence and *amor fati* are excessive teachings that cannot be subsumed or implemented within the traditional sphere of politics. They cannot even be accommodated by Zarathustra's great politics, which is always returning us to the question of what we *ought* to become and aiming at our completion or perfection.[58] They are suprapolitical teachings, insofar as they accept and affirm the human being as it is.[59] As such, they have no place in the cities of humanity. They are doctrines for the forest, the desert, the mountains—or perhaps, at most, for verdant islands.

Notes

1. I characterize Nietzsche's political philosophy as "Platonic" insofar as it envisions the ideal coincidence of philosophical wisdom and political power, epitomized by the philosopher "king" (Plato, *Republic* 473c–e and Books VI–VII *passim*; cf. *Laws* 712a, 713e *ff* and *Seventh Letter* 326a–b, 328a). On Nietzsche's insistence that genuine philosophers are "*commanders and legislators*," see BGE 211, as well as 61–2, 203, 208, 212; cf. KSA 11:26[407], 35[47], 37[8], 38[13]. This idea is anticipated by Z: see, e.g., Z I Flies, Goals; Z II Self-Overcoming, Events, Hour; and Z III Tablets. Nietzsche himself is keenly aware of his prophet's proximity to Plato: in a letter to his friend Overbeck, he confesses amazement at "*how much* Zarathustra *platōnizei*" (KSB 6:469). On Nietzsche's political Platonism, see Strauss (1983), Zuckert (1985), Ottman (1987: 239–65, 276–81), Picht (1988: 226–41), Rosen (1995: vii–xvii), Lampert (1996: 117–28; 2004: 205–19), McIntyre (1997: 74–99), Hutter (2006: 1–8), Groff (2006), and Drochon (2016: 36–48).
2. Although Nietzsche's own peculiar notion of great politics is not articulated as such until *Beyond Good and Evil* (1886), one might say that Z (1883–5) exemplifies it and in doing so offers the richest portrait of this task in all of Nietzsche's corpus; on this, see Loschenkohl (2020). Paul Loeb (2019) argues that Nietzsche's elevated and demanding conception of the genuine philosopher is in fact fulfilled *only* by Zarathustra. On the import and parameters of Nietzsche's great politics, see Ottman (1987: 239–81), Ansell-Pearson (1991: 200–24), Conway (1997: 1–27, 61–5), McIntyre (1997: 74–99), Siemens (2008), Lemm (2014), Shapiro (2016: 1–22), Drochon (2016), and Groff (2020b).
3. This is how Plato's *Republic* has itself sometimes been read: as a critique of the *bios politikos* and defense of the *bios philosophos* or *theōrētikos*; see, e.g., Strauss (1964: 50–138, esp. 65), Carter (1986: 155–86), and Lampert (2013: 19–20). I have explored these themes relative to Z in Groff 2020a and Groff 2021.
4. I adapt here Nietzsche's expression from *Dawn* (D 16), the "morality of custom" (*Sittlichkeit der Sitte*), to represent the hegemony of received or inherited values in traditional political life.
5. All quotations of the text are from Graham Parkes's translation of Z, with occasional alterations.
6. Cf. Z I Prologue 1 with the previously published version in GS 342, the initial sketch in Notebook M-III-1 (KSA 9:11[195]) and the source in Hellwald (1874: 128): the original Persian prophet was born in the city of Urmia (i.e., Orūmīyeh, situated in the northwesternmost province of modern-day Iran).
7. The ascetic practice of withdrawal or retreat (*anachōrēsis*) is typically associated with the Desert Fathers and Christian monastic communities but has older and deeper roots in Greek philosophy and Mazdayasna, as well as much older Brahminical texts. On withdrawal as an ascetic strategy, see Ware (1995). Nietzsche himself interprets such ascetic strategies not as moralistic renunciations of this-worldly existence but rather as "bridges to *independence*" (GM III 7) and "the most appropriate and natural conditions of their best existence, their fairest fruitfulness" (GM III 8); cf. D 9 and 14, which consider the ways in which they can be used as masks for overcoming the morality of custom and legislating new values or ways of life.
8. Zarathustra's language of descent (*untergehen*) evokes the motif of *katabasis* in Plato's *Republic* 327a, 516c–517a and 618e; on which, see Gooding-Williams (2001: 50–64) and Woodruff (2007).

9. The narrator describes this as "the nearest town [*Stadt*], which lay on the edge of the forest" (Z I Prologue 3). *Stadt* can refer either to a town or a city, and Parkes's translation opts—rightly, I think—for the former. The location of Zarathustra's first destination ("on the edge of the forest"), the provincial character of its denizens, and their instinctive distrust of strangers all suggest that it is a smaller town.
10. The Motley Cow is also simply referred to as a *Stadt*, and Parkes renders this again as "town." But this second locale seems more of a city, at least in part because of its implied cosmopolitanism and selective receptivity to Zarathustra's teachings. The name *die bunte Kuh* (the "colorful," "variegated," or "gaudy" cow; cf. the imagery in Z II Culture) additionally suggests a likeness to the democratic polis envisioned by Plato, which prioritizes freedom over all other values, manifests a striking diversity of ways of life, and is receptive to novelty (*Rep.* 557c-d). It would seem that for both Plato and Nietzsche, the democratic city, despite being feverish and spiritually complacent, is a charming and fertile breeding ground for philosophers.
11. Although it is not made clear at the beginning of the Second Part, it seems that the Blessed Isles friendship community involves a smaller subset of the companions and fellow creators that Zarathustra originally recruited in the Motley Cow. This becomes clear in Z III Apostates, when the prophet revisits that city on his final journey home from the Blessed Isles and reencounters some of his "believers," who have now "become pious again."
12. On Nietzsche's own transformative experiment with a small friendship community during his 1876-7 sabbatical in Sorrento, see D'Iorio (2016: 37–43). As Nietzsche later confessed to Peter Gast, the concrete inspiration for the Blessed Isles was the Isle of Ischia in the Gulf of Naples, which he first encountered during this period (Letter to Heinrich Köselitz, August 16, 1883 [KSB 6:452]); see D'Iorio (2016: 79–88) and Groff (2021).
13. Nietzsche's middle period works are saturated with critiques of spirit-flattening political life in the city, often set side by side with portraits of productive withdrawal and solitude; see e.g. HH 438 and D 174–9.
14. The Blessed Isles' considerable distance from mainland Europe is stated outright in Z II Child and suggested again in Z III Vision, Blissfulness, and Sunrise—all of which take place on his long journey back to the mainland.
15. See respectively D 423 and 483 (cf. Z I Prologue 2); D 575, GS 124, 289, 343 (cf. II Wise Men, and III Tablets 5, 16, 28); and GS 310 (cf. Z II Priests, and III Wanderer). See also Z I Prologue 3 for an image of the sea as that which is great enough to absorb the "polluted stream" of the human without itself becoming "unclean."
16. Zarathustra in fact juxtaposes his own withdrawal into "lonely mountains" and the "harsh desert" with the "soft greensward" of the Blessed Isles (Z II Child), suggesting that his companions are perhaps not yet ready for the more severe demands of complete withdrawal and solitude; cf. the retroactive description of Zarathustra's children as "trees" who must for now stand together as a grove (Z III Blissfulness).
17. On the Isles of the Blessed (*makarōn nēsoi*) of Greek myth, see Rohde (1925: 55–87); for their relevance to *Zarathustra*, see Bishop (2017: 2–4) and Groff (2020a). On Zarathustra's Blessed Isles as representing a late modern Epicurean Garden, see Groff (2021).
18. Z II Soothsayer, Redemption, and Hour.
19. This is the second time the saint has been proved right; cf. his warning that human beings are suspicious of solitaries, and it is better to remain in the forest, counsel borne out by the prophet's failed first transmission in Z I Prologue 3–8.

20. The great city is *not* the Motley Cow, a detail that is made clear in the subsequent section (Z III Apostates). The Motley Cow is the final city Zarathustra revisits before returning to his mountain retreat.
21. Carl Jung is the only commentator who acknowledges this detail as noteworthy. Emphasizing the vehemence with which Zarathustra excoriates the small people of the previous city he had visited (Z III Virtue), he suggests that, like the moralist who is secretly obsessed with the lurid, there is something that unconsciously draws the prophet to the great city even as he is repulsed by it (1988: II: 1389).
22. The image of the ape recurs throughout Nietzsche texts, variously representing the human being's coming into being and "shameful origins," as well as superficial mimicry and imitation; see Groff (2004).
23. Cf. Z I Prologue 3–5, Idol, Flies, Chastity, II Rabble, and III Virtue.
24. Cf. the "great dragon" in Z I Transformations.
25. On the forest, see Z I Prologue 2, 8–10, I Flies, Chastity, II Dance-Song, III Passing By, Return Home, and IV Kings. On the desert, see Z I Prologue 2, Z I Transformations, and Z II Wise Men. The mountain is of course Zarathustra's own choice for solitary political sanctuary. The third option (the "verdant islands") evokes the afore-mentioned Blessed Isles (Z II *passim*; see Z II Child, and III Blissfulness, for descriptions of them as green), but also one might say the cloister or monastery. On this again, see D'Iorio (2016) and Groff (2021). Interestingly, Zarathustra's second suggestion—that the ape might "plow the earth"—does not seem to point back to real options explored elsewhere in the text in the way the forest or island possibilities do, unless we consider Z I Prologue 8. Whether or not this is first time the life of agrarian retreat is broached in *Zarathustra*, it has a long history as a response to sick cities and has at times been taken up as a philosophical life-strategy; see, e.g., Carter (1986: 76–98) and Graham (1989: 53–72). The image of the plow, as breaking up, turning over and resuscitating the compacted, exhausted soil of received traditions was also a crucial one in Nietzsche's thought. The working title of *Human, All Too Human*, his first middle period work, was *Die Pflugschar*, or "The Plowshare" (D'Iorio 2016: 47).
26. For comparable juxtapositions, see Z I Prologue 3 and II Poets.
27. For instance, he speaks eloquently at the end of the First Part of "a thousand healths and hidden islands of life," which are as yet "unexhausted and undiscovered" (Z I Bestowing). The intended sense here is predominantly metaphorical, but the passage also invokes the hope that one can still find physical spaces in the world not territorialized by the morality of custom. In a similar vein, when the soothsayer tells Zarathustra that the Blessed Isles are no more, Zarathustra grows angry and insists that such places still exist (Z IV Cry of Need).
28. Nietzsche compares the Cynic to the more promising Epicurean philosopher, who "uses his higher culture to make himself independent of prevailing opinions [and] rais[ing] himself above them" (HH 275, cf. 291).
29. As Robert Gooding-Williams points out, his speech captures "the spirit but not the letter of Zarathustra's teaching" (2001: 243). Laurence Lampert suggests that "what Zarathustra hears in the fool's abuse and vituperation is his own teaching of contempt for the last man unrelieved by the great longing for something higher; he hears what can be made of his teaching by imitators moved only by vengeance or envy" (1986: 165). I have elsewhere read this passage as articulating an existential notion of truth as subjectivity: there are true propositions that in the mouths of certain people become untruth, inasmuch as truth is something be lived (Groff 2004: 24–5).

30. As some commentators have pointed out, the ape's vulgarization is a bit too close for comfort. Stanley Rosen observes that "the fool is a grotesque caricature of Zarathustra, but the caricature has some bite; Zarathustra's own rhetoric is sufficiently perfervid to give rise to this sort of imitation" (1995: 191–2). Thomas Seung sees even more bite in the caricature than Rosen does: on his account, the ape's speech hardly differs at all from Zarathustra's in either content or motivating spirit (2005: 143–45).
31. In warning Zarathustra against sharing his teaching in the cities of human beings, the saint is urging him to "stay in the forest" (Z I Prologue 2) and Zarathustra dissuades his disciples from picking fights with priests because, despite the fact that Zarathustra considers them his "enemies," their blood is related—i.e., he too is still "pious," or working in the lineage of the ascetic ideal even as he overcomes it (Z II Priests, cf. GS 344 and GM III: *passim*).
32. Cf. D 49.
33. See, e.g., Z III Blissfulness, Sunrise, Tablets 3, and Convalescent; cf. Z I Prologue 1, and Bestowing, for anticipations.
34. Nietzsche frequently insists on forgetting as a necessary condition for the possibility of life and health. Its pairing here with passing by (and elsewhere with looking away) suggests the necessary selectivity and even falsification involved in such strategies (truth being inimical to life).
35. Nietzsche characterizes the eternal recurrence doctrine as the "fundamental conception" of Z and "the highest formula of affirmation that is at all attainable" (EH Books Z 1, cf. BT 2).
36. In Nietzsche's final formulation of *amor fati*, the first and last parts are in fact all that are emphasized and indeed are amplified to the point where it seems almost indiscernible from eternal recurrence: "My formula for greatness in a human being is *amor fati*: that one wants nothing to be different, not forward, not backward not in all eternity. Not merely bear what is necessary, still less conceal it … but *love* it" (EH Clever 10, cf. Books CW 4). The experimental tentativeness, modesty, and hopefulness of the original formulation (Nietzsche's "I wish" and "I want" indicate that this is an ideal that stands above him) are lost in the less nuanced bombast of the late period.
37. The following discussion is an attempt to shed further light on Z III Passing By, by means of GS 276. For more detailed and comprehensive readings of this pivotal section, see Higgins (2000: 146–50), and Ure (2019: 160–73).
38. The realm of necessity remains an open interpretive question in Nietzsche's texts. In GS itself, one finds a range of possible positions, from the idea that "one thing is needful" (GS 289) to the claim that "there are only necessities" (GS 109).
39. This theme recurs throughout the remainder of GS IV; see especially GS 290 (which reflects on the necessity of attaining satisfaction with oneself, lest we become the kind of people who seek revenge and hurt others by forcing them to gaze upon our ugliness and gloominess) and GS 321 (which examines the often unproductive and self-injurious ways in which we punish, reproach, and attempt to improve others, counseling instead self-perfection, "step[ping] aside" and "look[ing] away").
40. The first explicit mentions of this phrase occur in KSA 12:1[7], 1[10], and 2[13]. However, the idea had already effectively emerged during the composition of Zarathustra; see Letter to Heinrich Köselitz, August 3, 1883, where Nietzsche speaks of the "*affect [Affekt] of distance*" in the context of hygienic withdrawal into the friendship community of the Blessed Isles.
41. BGE 257, GM I 2 and GM III 14.

42. Reframing the teaching in terms of vision and proximity introduces a middle option between seeing as beautiful that which is necessary and "looking away" from that which is not: provisionally adopting a sufficiently distant perspective that allows one to find some beauty in the phenomenon (D 485; GS 15, 299); for discussion, see Higgins (2000: 147–8).
43. See Schacht (1995: 244–45).
44. Z III Return Home, *ff*. The one possible exception to this is Z III Tablets.
45. See e.g. Lampert (1986), Seung (2005), and Loeb (2010). Higgins (1987), Conway (1988), Pippin (1988), Rosen (1995), and Gooding-Williams (2001) take ironic or deflationary approaches to the text that, while still sometimes entertaining the possibility of a final descent, are more sensitive to the failure or at least limitations of Zarathustra's ambitions.
46. On the question of whether to include Z IV as an integral part of Z (and if so, how to understand its relation to the previous three parts), see, e.g., Lampert (1986: 287–311), Higgins (1987: 203–32), Gooding-Williams (2001: 269–304), Seung (2005: 241–359), and Loeb (2010: 85–91). For the purposes of the present discussion, it does not matter.
47. Z IV Honey, Welcome, Sign.
48. See Groff (2020a, 2021).
49. Z II Isles, Redemption, III Blissfulness, IV Midday. In these last two speeches, Zarathustra recognizes the residual need to perfect himself and the world. Cf. Z I Afterwordly, which critiques the afterworldly for seeing the world as eternally imperfect.
50. Z I P 5, 9, II Isles, Redemption, Prudence, Z III Return Home, Z IV *passim*.
51. See, e.g., the popular crowd in the marketplace (Z I Prologue 3–6), the soothsayer (Z II Soothsayer, IV Cry of Need), the "cripples and beggars" (Z II Redemption), the dwarf (Z III Vision), the ape (Z III Passing By), his animals (Z III Convalescent), the higher humans (Z IV *passim*), and even his own disciples (Z II Child, Soothsayer, III Wanderer, Apostles).
52. See, e.g., Z II Night-Song, Soothsayer, Redemption, Prudence, Hour; cf. Z III Return Home.
53. Z I Prologue 9, Idol, Flies, Friend, II Rabble, Wise Men, Events, III Virtue, Passing By, Return Home, IV Welcome, Melancholy 1, Awakening, Festival, Sign.
54. As mentioned previously, Zarathustra is initially described as having "enjoyed" (*genoss*, i.e., savored or relished) his solitude (Z I Prologue 1), a detail repeated in IV Midday, just before he experiences the world becoming perfect. The language of joy (*Lust*) is however primarily concentrated in four speeches. Z II Rabble describes life as a "well-spring of joy," which is however poisoned by the rabble; in order to discover its source and drink from pure waters, Zarathustra says he had to fly to the "highest heights"—an expression that here evokes both his mountain world and the austere solitude of the anchorite. The next two take place in said solitude: Z III Tablets 5 characterizes joy in terms of epistemological exploration (the open seas trope), while Z III Dance-Song constitutes Zarathustra's climactic celebration of life, concluding with the motif: "all joy wants Eternity – / – wants deep, deep Eternity!" Z IV Sleepwalker, is ostensibly addressed to the higher humans, although Zarathustra himself seems to be dreaming or in a trance. Arguably the most powerful and extensive expression of the eternal recurrence teaching in the book, it reprises and expands upon the conclusion of Z III Dance-Song, with multiple expressions of the idea that "joy wants the eternity of all things," even those that are sorrowful and

painful and unjust (see esp. 10–12). The word *Freude* itself surprisingly never actually occurs in Zarathustra; one finds the occasional adjectival form (*froh*), although it is rarely employed in any philosophically substantive sense (see, however, Z II Pitying, which celebrates the ability to enjoy oneself [*sich freuen*]). An investigation of comparable words—*Glücke*, *Seligkeit*, and their variants—yields wider and less consistent usage, but the substantive, non-ironic or non-disparaging mentions of such terms again occur almost invariably in the context of Zarathustra's solitude.

55. In this respect, he is rather like the Epicurean gods, who are unconcerned with the affairs of human beings and experience no need to intervene or correct their errors. As Nietzsche explicitly admits, he himself is incapable of such divine detachment, let alone the affirmation of incompleteness ultimately required by eternal recurrence (BGE 62); hence, his own insistence on the need for *Zucht* and *Züchtung*. For discussion, see Groff (forthcoming).
56. See, e.g., Löwith (1997), which shows its conflict with the will to power. Robert Pippin (1988) notes its tension with the future ideal of the superhuman, and Rosen (1995) sees it as at odds with the need for transformation and redemption.
57. The middle period works often emphasize privatized experimental aesthetic self-cultivation among a small select group; a more modest project than the great politics broached in this book. For discussion, see Groff (2020b).
58. Conway (1997: 3, 9).
59. Cf. Paul van Tongeren, who argues that Nietzsche is ultimately an *Über-politischer Denker*, insofar as his thought goes beyond the political by universalizing war and multiplicity and thus problematizing the very idea of unified, stable political actors (van Tongeren 2008). However, I mean that Zarathustra's doctrines overturn the meaningfulness of normative prescriptions (the "ought" of the question "*what ought we to become?*"). I set aside the question of how exactly this reading of *Zarathustra* applies to Nietzsche, i.e., whether he himself twists free of the temptation to great politics.

References

Ansell-Pearson, Keith (1991), *Nietzsche Contra Rousseau: A Study of Nietzsche's Moral and Political Thought*, Cambridge: Cambridge University Press.

Bishop, Paul (2017), *On the Blissful Islands with Nietzsche and Jung: In the Shadow of the Superman*, London: Routledge.

Carter, L. B. (1986), *The Quiet Athenian*, Oxford: Clarendon Press.

Conway, Daniel W. (1988), "Solving the Problem of Socrates: Nietzsche's *Zarathustra* as Political Irony," *Political Theory* 16 (2): 257–80.

Conway, Daniel W. (1997), *Nietzsche and the Political*, London: Routledge.

D'Iorio, Paolo (2016), *Nietzsche's Journey to Sorrento: Genesis of the Philosophy of the Free Spirit*, trans. Sylvia Mae Gorlick, Chicago: University of Chicago Press.

Drochon, Hugo (2016), *Nietzsche's Great Politics*, Princeton, NJ: Princeton University Press.

Graham, A. C. (1989), *Disputers of the Tao*, Chicago: Open Court.

Groff, Peter S. (2004), "Who is Zarathustra's Ape?," in *A Nietzschean Bestiary: Animality Beyond Docile and Brutal*, ed. Christa and Ralph Acampora, 17–31, Lanham, MD: Rowman & Littlefield.

Groff, Peter S. (2006), "Wisdom and Violence: The Legacy of Platonic Political Philosophy in al-Fārābī and Nietzsche," in *Comparative Philosophy in Times of Terror*, ed. Douglas Allen, 65–81, Lanham, MD: Lexington Books.
Groff, Peter S. (2020a), "Cultivating Weeds: The Place of Solitude in the Political Philosophies of Ibn Bājja and Nietzsche," *Philosophy East and West* 70 (2): 699–739.
Groff, Peter S. (2020b), "Great Politics and the Unnoticed Life: Nietzsche and Epicurus on the Boundaries of Cultivation," in *Nietzsche and Epicurus*, Ryan Johnson and Vinod Acharya, 172–85, London: Bloomsbury Academic.
Groff, Peter S. (2021), "Zarathustra's Blessed Isles: Before and After Great Politics," *Journal of Nietzsche Studies* 52 (1): 135–63.
Groff, Peter S. (forthcoming), "The Return of the Epicurean Gods," in *Nietzsche's Gods: Critical and Constructive Perspectives*, ed. Russell Re Manning, Carlotta Santini, and Isabelle Wienand, Berlin: De Gruyter.
Hellwald, Friedrich von (1874), *Culturgeschichte in ihrer natürlichen Entstehung*, Augsburg: Lampert.
Higgins, Kathleen (1987), *Nietzsche's Zarathustra*, Philadelphia, PA: Temple University Press.
Higgins, Kathleen (2000), *Comic Relief: Nietzsche's Gay Science*, Oxford: Oxford University Press.
Hutter, Horst (2006), *Shaping the Future: Nietzsche's New Regime of the Soul and Its Ascetic Practices*, Lanham, MD: Lexington Books.
Jung, Carl G. (1988), *Nietzsche's Zarathustra: Notes of the Seminar Given in 1934-1939*, ed. James L. Jarrett, 2 vols., Princeton, NJ: Princeton University Press.
Lampert, Laurence (1986), *Nietzsche's Teaching: An Interpretation of* Thus Spoke Zarathustra, New Haven, CT: Yale University Press.
Lampert, Laurence (1996), *Leo Strauss and Nietzsche*, Chicago: University of Chicago Press.
Lampert, Laurence (2004), "Nietzsche on Plato," in *Nietzsche and Antiquity: His Reaction and Response to the Classical Tradition*, ed. Paul Bishop, 205–19, Suffolk, UK: Camden House.
Lampert, Laurence (2013), *The Enduring Importance of Leo Strauss*, Chicago: University of Chicago Press.
Lemm, Vanessa (2014), "Nietzsche's Great Politics of the Event," in *Nietzsche and the Political*, ed. Keith Ansell-Pearson, 179–96, London: Bloomsbury.
Loeb, Paul S. (2010), *The Death of Nietzsche's Zarathustra*, Cambridge: Cambridge University Press.
Loeb, Paul S. (2019), "Genuine Philosophers, Value-Creation, and Will to Power: An Exegesis of Nietzsche's *Beyond Good and Evil* §211," in *Nietzsche's Metaphilosophy: The Nature, Methods and Aims of Philosophy*, ed. Paul S. Loeb and Matthew Myer, 83–105, Cambridge: Cambridge University Press.
Loschenkohl, Birte (2020), "Nietzsche's 'Great Politics' and Zarathustra's New Peoples," *Journal of Nietzsche Studies* 51(1): 21–45.
Löwith, Karl (1997), *Nietzsche's Philosophy of the Eternal Recurrence of the Same*, trans. J. Harvey Lomax, Berkeley: University of California Press.
McIntyre, Alex (1997), *The Sovereignty of Joy: Nietzsche's Vision of Grand Politics*, Toronto: University of Toronto Press.
Ottman, Henning (1987), *Philosophie und Politik bei Nietzsche, Monographieren und Texte zu Nietzsche Forschung 17*, Berlin: de Gruyter.
Picht, Georg (1988), *Nietzsche*, Stuttgart: Klett-Cotta.

Pippin, Robert (1988), "Irony and Affirmation in Nietzsche's *Thus Spoke Zarathustra*," in *Nietzsche's New Seas: Explorations in Philosophy, Aesthetics and Politics*, ed. Michael Allen Gillespie and Tracy B. Strong, 45–71, Chicago: University of Chicago Press.

Rohde, Erwin (1925), *Psyche: The Cult of Souls and Belief in Immortality among the Ancient Greeks*, trans. W. B. Hillis, London: Kegan Paul.

Rosen, Stanley (1995), *The Mask of Enlightenment: Nietzsche's Zarathustra*, Cambridge: Cambridge University Press.

Schacht, Richard (1995), "Zarathustra/*Zarathustra* as Educator," in *Nietzsche: A Critical Reader*, ed. Peter R. Sedgwick, 222–49, Oxford: Blackwell.

Seung, T. K. (2005), *Nietzsche's Epic of the Soul: Thus Spoke Zarathustra*, Lanham, MD: Lexington Books.

Shapiro, Gary (2016), *Nietzsche's Earth: Great Events, Great Politics*, Chicago: Chicago University Press.

Siemens, Herman (2008), "Yes, No, Maybe So … Nietzsche's Equivocations on the Relation between Democracy and 'Grosse Politik'," in *Nietzsche, Power and Politics: Rethinking Nietzsche's Legacy to Political Thought*, ed. Herman W. Siemens and Vasti Roodt, 231–68, Berlin: De Gruyter.

Strauss, Leo (1964), *The Philosopher and the City*, Chicago: Chicago University Press.

Strauss, Leo (1983), "Note on the Plan of Nietzsche's *Beyond Good and Evil*," in *Studies in Platonic Political Philosophy*, 174–91, Chicago: University of Chicago Press.

Ure, Michael (2019), *Nietzsche's Gay Science: An Introduction*, Cambridge: Cambridge University Press.

Van Tongeren, Paul (2008), "Nietzsche as 'Über-Politischer Denker'," in *Nietzsche, Power and Politics: Rethinking Nietzsche's Legacy for Political Thought*, ed. Herman W. Siemens and Vasti Roodt, 69–83, Berlin: De Gruyter.

Ware, Kallistos (1995), "The Way of the Ascetics: Negative or Affirmative?," in *Asceticism*, ed. Vincent L. Wimbush and Richard Valantasis, 3–15, Oxford: Oxford University Press.

Woodruff, Martha Kendall (2007), "*Untergang* und *Übergang*: The Tragic Descent of Socrates and Zarathustra," *Journal of Nietzsche Studies* 34: 61–78.

Zuckert, Catherine (1985), "Nietzsche's Rereading of Plato," *Political Theory* 13 (2): 213–38.

5

Why "All Joy Wills Eternity" for Nietzsche

Richard J. Elliott

Joy of a certain kind has an important affective role in demonstrating the overcoming of nihilism for Nietzsche. In this chapter I explore how one might arrive at a point where they too can give voice to Zarathustra's proclamation that "all joy wills eternity." There are consistent references to eternity and infinitude in passages of Nietzsche's discussing nihilism. This is most obviously borne out in Nietzsche scholarship with reference to discussions of eternal recurrence. But eternal recurrence does not have a monopoly for denoting Nietzsche's employment of the motifs of eternity and infinitude. Eternal recurrence and its affirmation, I argue, is only a kind of end point for a process of overcoming nihilism.[1]

Nietzsche doesn't offer any hard distinction between the two concepts, which obviously intertwine in many senses. My concern here is the manner in which Nietzsche employs these motifs to track three different stages related to nihilism. The first stage demonstrates an affective response of initial disorientation, which aims to engender a realization by the "marketplace atheists" that humanity must undergo the phenomenon of nihilism. The second stage documents an active confrontation with this phenomenon, which in turn offers deeper, more terrifying yet also more positive consequences of this realization, ones proffering new forms of freedom. The third stage is the constructive use to which Nietzsche sets these motifs in the service of life-affirmation, of which eternal recurrence plays an integral part. I examine several important passages using these motifs in Nietzsche's mature writings, particularly from *The Gay Science* (GS) and *Thus Spoke Zarathustra* (Z), to claim that they inform a developmental process concerning the realization of nihilism and its overcoming.

First, I establish context by discussing Nietzsche's claim that humans are meaning-seeking animals. This bears upon an ambiguity Nietzsche demonstrates about Christianity, amid all of his claims that it denies life. This relates to the so-called problem of meaning as it is identified at various points in the mature works. Though most prominent in the third essay of *On the Genealogy of Morality* (GM), it elsewhere underscores the problem of nihilism.

I then demonstrate how Nietzsche frames the crisis of meaning by invoking the motifs of the eternal and the infinite. I argue that his use of these motifs tracks his conception of nihilism as a developmental phenomenon. Analysis of key passages from GS and Z will demonstrate that these motifs accord with each of three broad stages.

The first stage looks at the "infinite nothing" associated with the death of God. This indicates the affective disorientation that comes as an initial reaction to the first exposure to nihilism in GS 125. The second stage looks at Nietzsche's claims about the infinitude of potential interpretations as an acknowledgement of a new "horizon." Here, infinity tracks the promise that might be available through some humans recognizing their new freedom to experiment with values. Awe is possible in response to this openness, but not exaltation—the "sea" is open but may not be bright, Nietzsche writes. The third stage affectively delineates arriving at a new form of life-affirmation—Nietzsche's ascription of eternal recurrence, and a joy in "willing eternity." Eternity and infinity in this third context denote the affirmative praxis of the self-legislator, who creates their own values. A sense of eternity is "incorporated," as an internal measure of life-affirmation. It is in this context that Zarathustra identifies a specific sort of joy as the proper disposition toward eternity, as a recognition of having overcome nihilism. I conclude by claiming that the motifs of eternity and infinitude's employment at each of these three stages mirrors the substance of the "Three Metamorphoses of the Spirit" section in Z.

1. Christianity as Expressing the Impulse toward Human Meaning

Nietzsche's critical stance toward Christianity is one of the most obvious aspects of his work. It is for good reason that he is offered up as the representative atheist bogeyman in many a philosophy of religion seminar. Nietzsche's various criticisms of Christianity are diverse in tenor. Sometimes the critique takes a more anthropological inclination. For example, in *Dawn* (D), Nietzsche draws the claim that the fruitfulness of Christianity in "saints and desert solitaries" does nothing to prove itself, owing to its role in filling Jerusalem's "vast madhouses for abortive saints" (D 14). Sometimes these criticisms are focused on Christianity's negative effects; sometimes they are directed toward the values Christianity inherently expresses. Indeed, these two aspects of Nietzsche's critique often feature within the same passage and are often run so closely together that they get conflated.[2] For example, in the closing section of *The Antichrist* (A), Nietzsche both describes Christianity as the "the greatest corruption conceivable" that "has not left anything untouched by its corruption", as well as expressing "an art of self-violation, a will to lie at any cost, a disgust, a hatred of all good and honest instincts!" (A 62).[3]

Similar versions of these criticisms appear throughout Nietzsche's works. Their prominence, however, does not preclude Nietzsche's later works from wishing to explore the impulses that drive humans toward religious belief. This exploration is not a staple throughout each of the periodic shifts that take place in Nietzsche's works. It doesn't seem present during the so-called positivist phase, for example. The Nietzsche of *Human, All Too Human* (HH) often speaks as if the kind of impulses toward the transcendent, which motivate the adoption of Christianity in the first instance, are something contingent and possible to dismiss, and that it would be right to dismiss them. Nietzsche approvingly echoes his one-time closest friend

Paul Rée, of "taking an axe to the root of metaphysical need" about religion and the impulses that motivate it (HH 37).[4]

But a shift occurs for Nietzsche by the early 1880s. Thereafter, he is no longer best read as dismissing all of the impulses which motivate the religious disposition. Indeed, some of Nietzsche's most famous pronouncements in the mature works wouldn't make sense, if taking an axe to this root remained either possible or effective for him. The vacuum left in the wake of religious belief is one Nietzsche takes seriously. The death of God demands a compensatory response, rather than refutation alone settling the matter. From GS on, Nietzsche considers humans to be the animals possessing a will to meaning, arguably innately so, of which Christianity is a nihilistic expression. There is a dimension of Nietzsche's critique against the "will to lie at any cost" built into Christianity. But more central is a focus on how the normative injunctions of Christianity poorly fit with human instincts. Christianity demands unwieldy psychic repressions and obstructs human self-cultivation by means of the free expression of our deeply engrained drives.[5] This is not to mean Nietzsche is undermining the importance of the search itself. On a more nuanced reading, Nietzsche's works from the 1880s onward explore the problem of meaning and its status as a feature of human motivation. This concern forms the backbone argument, in particular, of the third essay of GM. There, Nietzsche analyses how the values in-built to the Christian belief system arose and came to be sustained, in relation to those psychological needs they aim to fulfill. The Christian schema was adopted for the reasons of providing a meaning to suffering, justifying it. In this sense, particular human impulses were positioned within a framework of meaning, even if that resulted in denying their expression.

It is not for nothing that the "shadow of God" is so lingering for Nietzsche (GS 108). Human life has been provided an entire interpretive framework of meaning by adopting Christianity. A particular standard of value has been provided for two millennia, with a metaphysical story to support it. Despite Nietzsche's contention that Christian belief is itself a form of nihilism (i.e., that it is antithetical to the particular values the adoption of which Nietzsche considers genuinely life-affirming), GM III argues that a nihilistic standard of value, as evinced in the 'will to nothingness' of the ascetic ideal, has been preferred to no standard of value ('no will') at all (GM III 28).[6] This "will" expresses a particular answer to this search for meaning. Despite his contention that it is a life-denying expression, it has served as the only game in town in this justificatory search for two millennia.[7]

Part of what makes Nietzsche's critique of Christianity more interesting than the garden variety atheism (including arguably his own in HH) is his emphasis on its far-reaching consequences. If the metaphysical claims that buttress Christian belief are no longer acceptable, then there's no way to sustain the Christian brand of morality, of the kind he sees as pervasive in Western life. Nietzsche is not just casting off Christianity but is being honest about the consequences of its demise, and the ramifications of what humanity will have to work through, as a result. As he says later in *Twilight of the Idols* (TI), "when you give up Christian faith, you pull the rug out from under your right to Christian morality as well," and that Christian morality "has truth only if God is the truth,—it stands or falls along with belief in God" (TI Skirmishes 5).

2. Nietzsche's Use of the Motifs of Infinitude and Eternity

Christian belief has offered a network of conceptual and affective relations between human impulses and provided justifications for them. This is done via injunctions stemming from Christianity's metaphysical commitments, specifically the Judeo-Christian conception of God, which is a conception bound up with the attribute of infinitude: infinite goodness, infinite wisdom, infinite power, and an infinite ground. These attributes are discussed by many in diverse philosophical contexts, from Schelling to Tillich, and many points in between.[8] Each use of these associations gains traction from a common grasp of the Christian tradition's conceptual apparatus.

Likewise, eternity is intrinsic to the Judeo-Christian concept of God. Just as God is taken to be an infinite ground, so too is he an eternal ground (Rom. 1:20). But the most prominent Biblical verses discussing eternity focus on the eternal life guaranteed by accepting Salvation (cf. Jn 3:16; 5:11, 24; 6:51; and 10:27–28). A passage from the Old Testament too states God has "set eternity in the human heart" (Eccl. 3:11).[9] The inverse of this sentiment has the consequence of eternal punishment, which comes from unrighteous deeds or from rejection of God (cf. Thess. 1:9; Mt. 25:46).

This foray gives the requisite context for why Nietzsche employs these concepts of infinity and eternity, in passages where he discusses nihilism at its various stages. A significant reason for his doing so is that the Judeo-Christian tradition has established a familiar heritage to these concepts. Nietzsche in his own way sees his own project as tied to recognizing and indeed encouraging the demise of this tradition. Thus, it is fitting that he utilizes the conceptual heritage of these motifs in his own idiosyncratic manner.

This Judeo-Christian backdrop is familiar to the readership, which Nietzsche can exploit to radically revise the concepts involved in what he argues it means to affirm a life. As Brian Leiter has argued in another context, employing a term from Charles Stevenson, Nietzsche frequently uses "persuasive definitions" in service of similar purposes.[10] While Leiter identifies concepts such as "soul," "power," "will," and "freedom" for this (Leiter 2019: 152), something like this also holds true for Nietzsche's invocation of eternity and infinitude.[11]

Nietzsche uses these motifs to assess the developmental stages of nihilism and plot the terrain of the affective dispositions coinciding with them. The sense of magnitude they are meant to instill in each stage denotes a range of dispositions, to accord with the development of a revised conception of life-affirmation, *through* nihilism, rather than merely avoiding it. Nietzsche uses them at various stages to both describe and facilitate a range of affects—first, a sense of deep initial disorientation; then, a sense of awe at the possibilities that nihilism exposes as possible within the human scope; and finally, a positive sense of exaltation, with the affirmation of life being magnified by association with eternity and infinitude.[12]

It is again worth reiterating that there are good reasons for thinking that Nietzsche offers no explicit conceptual delineation between "eternal" and "infinite" in the texts I explore throughout this chapter. He appears to use each of the motifs to similar ends, and though he sometimes appears to identify the infinite more in relation to perspectives, he usually conflates the content of the two concepts. Conceptions of the eternal are framed as something unending and limitless in time within the tradition of cosmology, while conceptions of the infinite are usually considered as various forms of innumerability or boundlessness, in relation to space, time and quantity, often in contrast to human temporality. But Nietzsche uses them with no great exclusivity from each other. What matters is that Nietzsche utilises each motif, sometimes both together, to denote an affectively loaded sense of scope and magnitude. A good example of this comes in one of the unpublished notes Nietzsche describes as having been "thrown onto paper" in August 1881 (EH Books Z 1), after first being confronted by the great stone at Lake Silvaplana. One of the notes reads,

> 5. The new *heavy weight: the eternal recurrence of the same*. Infinite importance of our knowing, erring, our habits, ways of living for all that is to come. What shall we do with the rest of our lives—we who have spent the majority of our lives in the most profound ignorance? We shall *teach the doctrine*—it is the most powerful means of *incorporating* it in ourselves. Our kind of beatitude, as teachers of the greatest doctrine. (KGW V 2. 11[141])

I discuss the specific ways eternal recurrence instantiates these motifs in Section 5, but this note demonstrates Nietzsche is not sticking to a commonplace use of these concepts, while exploiting their Judeo-Christian heritage. Instead, he carves out space to employ them for his own uses, and to demonstrate their role in fostering a new disposition of life-affirmation, for "our kind of beatitude."

Whether Nietzsche is entitled to equivocate eternity and infinity in this way is beside the point. I simply point out that he does so. Perhaps this interchange is intentional on Nietzsche's part: perhaps it is the case that for him, any firm distinction is lost as a result of nihilism. A consequence of the death of God is the death of the possibility of the absolutely eternal, and the possibility of comprehending infinitude independently of the context of human experience. As such, I shall argue that in these passages, Nietzsche uses the terms "eternal" and "infinite" pretty much interchangeably Whether this interchange is erroneous or not, I maintain that it is his reasons for using these concepts in this way that are more interesting.

3. Plunging into an Infinite Nothing: The Death of God

Nietzsche stuffs the "death of God" passage chock-full with Christian imagery. The madman of the GS 125 passage is in the first instance seeking God, employing the same rhetoric as injunctions found in both the Old and New Testament, as evinced in 1 Chr. 22:19, to "set your mind and heart to seek the Lord your God." Then, the madman changes rhetorical tack and proclaims God's death. The effects of this are then described by the madman in many affectively loaded metaphors: the wiping away of the horizon, the unchaining of the sun, and the need for bright lanterns in the morning—rhetoric emphasizing the catastrophe that the death of God is for the post-Christian, secular sensibilities of modern European society.

It is notable that Nietzsche has the madman ask his onlookers—representative of the atheistic Germans of the nineteenth-century "marketplace" of ideas—if they have strayed into an "infinite nothing." This infinite nothing is described as a continual plunging in any and all directions, suggesting an affective sense of heightened disorientation, to accompany the cognitive inertia that follows from the end of God's being believed. This disorientation offers a rhetorical juxtaposition, between God's provision of an infinite ground and this infinite nothing once we become aware of God's death. Some, most prominently Bernard Reginster, have argued that the disorientation suggested in this passage is itself the phenomenon of nihilism.[13] But it likelier suggests the disorientation is that affective state that facilitates a journey into and through nihilism, into recognizing its multifaceted aspects, and becoming more aware of how it has seeped into the dominant ideological frameworks of Europe over the past two millennia. I develop this point further, below.

Returning to the death of God passage: when he is ignored by the astonished and confused atheists in the marketplace, the madman forces his way into a number of churches, and therein strikes up "his *requiem aeternam deo*" (GS 125), the eternal requiem for the old Christian God. This has the rhetorical effect of demonstrating the magnitude of the crisis that the madman pronounces—God remains dead, eternally.

In response to this crisis, the madman asks, must we become Gods ourselves, to become worthy of His death? This passage in Nietzsche has long been emphasized as important for any positive, post-Christian enterprise he might proffer. Martin Heidegger, in his notorious Rectoral Address, described Nietzsche as a "great passionate seeker after God" (Heidegger [1933] 1990: 7). There is an important double entendre here. As well as being a seeker for a new kind of redemption after Christianity ceases to provide meaning, the description also tracks something like a fervent religiosity in Nietzsche's search.[14] But what exactly does this claim of becoming akin to Gods ourselves amount to? It has commonly and rightly been taken to involve values—their experimentation and creation. However, there might also be a level at which the assumption of the same status of a God, "becoming a god oneself," is to provide one's own ground, just as God (infinitely) did before his "death." Alternatively, it may be an injunction to do without a ground: this would fit Nietzsche's claims elsewhere about shirking the spirit of gravity, and with the imagery of birds escaping their cages. Maybe this is a difference in terminology and it is wholly possible to reconcile these two points. Either way, it is within this context that Nietzsche moves to using the motifs of infinity and eternity in a more positive fashion.

4. The Promise of Nihilism, In the Horizon of the Infinite

The death of God passage at GS 125 is often taken in isolation as the summa of Nietzsche's claims about nihilism. But is a bad habit of a lot of Nietzsche scholarship to take passages out of their intended context. With the exception, arguably, of GM, it is GS above all other works of Nietzsche's where the context and ordering of passages matters most. When taken within its wider context, GS 125 is importantly caveated by the passage that precedes it. Immediately before this passage, at GS 124, Nietzsche returns to speculations made at the very end of D 575 when he writes the following:

> *In the horizon of the infinite.*—We have forsaken the land and gone to sea! We have destroyed the bridge behind us—more so, we have demolished the land behind us! Now, little ship, look out! Beside you is the ocean; it is true, it does not always roar, and at times it lies there like silk and gold and dreams of goodness. But there will be hours <u>when you realize it is infinite and that there is nothing more awesome than infinity</u>. Oh, the poor bird that has felt free and now strikes against the walls of this cage! Woe, when homesickness for the land overcomes you, as if there had been more *freedom* there – and there is no more 'land'! (GS 124; underlining mine)

Nietzsche sets the passages up in succession, so that GS 124 might act to contextualize the nihilistic pronouncement in GS 125, for those of the proper disposition. Read alone, the "death of God" offers a destructive pronouncement of a coming crisis and without fleshing out how the imperative of being alike to Gods ourselves might work. But read in the context of GS 124, it reads as a necessary inroad, the undertaking required to begin the development through nihilism. God's death is a stage, the first stage of this development.[15]

Two things are interesting in this context. The first is that the metaphor of the sea is obviously meant to delineate the recognition of being *in* nihilism. The second is that although the sea is said to perhaps sometimes "roar," and Nietzsche gives heed to the "little boat," there is nothing to suggest that this voyage remains an intrinsically disoriented one. Indeed, the disorientation was something felt on the "land," which the recognition of nihilism has now destroyed. This gives further credence to the notion that the disorientation of the "infinite nothing" was an affect that got the ball rolling. But we should beware of thinking that it is disorientation that encapsulates Nietzsche's fundamental claims about the phenomenon of nihilism.[16]

What we find in GS 124 is a disposition of awe at the possibilities available to those who manage to cast off the axiological tenets of Christianity. This is most often narrowly framed as a rejection of Christian morality, and for good reason, since it is this that Nietzsche talks of the most. But it is broader than this—it is a rejection of the motivational norms that Christianity argues ought to determine human behavior. The disposition spoken of in GS 124 is one of an adventurer or inquirer, who has followed Nietzsche in this rejection (cf. GS 344). Its adoption involves new possibilities and a specific sense of freedom to pursue them. This is not the same as an exercise in full-blooded value creation or self-legislation, which Nietzsche takes to be a mature development available to some out of this disposition. What is significant here is his revision of the idea of the infinite with its own positive valence in this passage. It explicitly contrasts with the motif of the "infinite nothing" in the passage following it, at GS 125. But though the motif is here revised to fit a positive purpose, infinitude is again used to denote a great magnitude, to highlight the significance of one's change of disposition.

While the crisis of the death of God is considered a turning point in Nietzsche's oeuvre that instigates a central concern of his later works, this important context has to my knowledge been overlooked in the secondary literature. Nietzsche's placement of these two passages demonstrates his concern with the prospect of offering tools for actively confronting nihilism, by reframing the motif of the infinite into one of positive valence. GS 124 enjoins his desired readers to embrace the fear and awe that this new "infinite" freedom induces, as a means of facing nihilism diagnosed by the madman, in the immediately ensuing passage at GS 125. Built into this is the link between Nietzsche's imagery of the horizon, infinitude, and the availability of new perspectives on or interpretations of life. A revision of our relation to this motif is one that facilitates recognizing that our hitherto held interpretations of life are no longer the only game in town, which causes terror and awe. Yet integral to that is the potential to foster a shift to a more affirmative disposition. Although Nietzsche does not use the term "perspectives" explicitly in GS 124, he does so in a section that similarly discusses this theme. In the fifth book added to GS in 1887, he supplements these motifs already present in the 1882 edition. Giving passage 374 the heading, "Our New Infinite," he writes,

> How far the perspective character of existence extends, or indeed whether existence has any other character than this … it is a hopeless curiosity that wants to know what other kinds of intellects and perspectives there *might* be. … I should think that today we are at least far from the ridiculous immodesty that would be involved in decreeing from our corner that perspectives are permitted only from this corner. Rather, the world has once again become "infinite" to us: insofar as we cannot dismiss the possibility that it includes infinite interpretations. Once more the great horror seizes us—but who again would desire immediately to deify in the old manner *this* monster of an unknown world? And to worship from this time on the unknown thing as the "unknown one" in future? Alas, too many ungodly possibilities of interpretation are included in this unknown; too much devilry, stupidity and foolishness of interpretation,—our own human, all too human interpretation itself, which we know. (GS 374)

Here Nietzsche shifts tack, away from conceiving of the infinite in terms of God's grounding. GS 374 reconceives the infinite in terms of the multiplicity of human interpretations and the competing ways in which one might evaluate life. He discusses the lack of an absolute, singular, and monolithic perspective on values. The "great horror" that arises in us is the new recognition of this potential infinitude of human interpretations—as if one were disposed to view it as the "infinite nothing" of GS 125. But Nietzsche immediately counters the notion of returning to the Christian value system as being unthinkable. We are already *within* nihilism: the death of God is a Rubicon of values. He identifies this "monster of an unknown world" as something that doesn't lend itself to the narrow prism through which the Christian perspective might frame it. There are "too many ungodly possibilities" requisite in interpreting the world in this new sense—our perspectives can no longer be trammelled by Christian-moral constraints.

Nietzsche suggests that overcoming the death of God involves drawing upon a multiplicity of interpretations and assessing their aptitude for the promotion of genuine flourishing, rather than resorting back to the prior, "deified" conceptions of the infinite.[17] These new perspectives are the lanterns in the morning, of the kind the madman claims are needed in GS 125. The metaphor of the sea as offering a "freedom" is not contrasted with the land having been left—rather, for Nietzsche, there is no more "land" (GS 124). The land was the ground that nihilism swept up when God was pronounced dead.

This metaphor from the passage in Book Three of the 1882 edition is utilized again at passage 343 from 1887's Book Five. There, Nietzsche writes of the sea being open, even if it is not bright. This freedom offered by the sea is the reason for "our cheerfulness" at the advent of God's death. But more significantly, Nietzsche invokes awe in the face of the sense of infinitude offered by this open sea one passage before the madman's discussing the prospect of an "infinite nothing" (GS 125). It is in this context that the passage at GS 343 describes "horizon" alongside the open sea. Rather than, for example, Heidegger's quasi-idealistic usage of the term "horizon" to show the limits of human meaning, Nietzsche uses it as what happens when a hitherto limiting boundary is thrown open, as a result of engaging with the practical consequences of nihilism. A horizon can show us not only the going down of the sun but also its rising. Nietzsche, no doubt cognizant of this double meaning, aims to encapsulate that just as one value system passes into dusk, we open up the possibility of a new, ascendant value system, or systems. It is in this respect that the scope of human meaning is expanded, as a result of casting the old boundary aside. This exacts as a cost the grounding to human meaning as its price, in some sense, as that which was provided by the Judeo-Christian god. But in another sense, Nietzsche wants to abandon thinking of a ground of human meaning in the manner conceived by this old Judeo-Christian framework. This gets to the heart of his discussion of the bird as a poor animal, whose conception of freedom is limited to "this cage." Nietzsche at GS 124 uses the imagery of the bird to refer to those who misapprehend their capacity for freedom while labouring under Christian morality. Not only did this old morality offer a false sense of freedom, but there can also be no return to it. That doesn't mean getting rid of freedom. Nietzsche explicitly invokes again the motif of infinity to describe this new sense of freedom, in a poem, "Towards New Seas," from *The Songs of Prince Vogelfrei* passage added in 1887 to the close of the book.[18] Without plan, Nietzsche's "ship" heads out into the vast open sea. Nietzsche writes, "Only *your* eye—monstrously, Stares at me, infinity!" A question remains about who Nietzsche is addressing when he uses the inclusive "our" in "our new infinite" (GS 374). The rhetoric around these passages suggests Nietzsche realized that GS 125 would be read as a deep, irresolvable crisis to most. It would only be those predisposed with the requisite favourable conditions who might come to possess a flourishing affective response to it.[19] It is the demandingness of this injunction of becoming alike to gods ourselves which carries over to Nietzsche's most studied use of the motifs of eternity and infinity.

5. The Possibility for Joy through Willing the Eternal Recurrence

The most commonly cited passage from Nietzsche's involving these motifs is GS 341, the first positive invocation of eternal recurrence. Up until now, infinity and eternity have been used to first expose the disorientation recognized at the advent of nihilism, and then to denote a kind of awe at the openness that active engagements with nihilism present. How eternal recurrence differs from these two uses will be the focus of this section. If a "new infinite" involves rethinking our interpretation of life's meaning, and that a measure of the life-affirmation of this interpretation would be Nietzsche's test for successfully overcoming nihilism, there is no stronger example of such a test as the thought that he considered to be his most fundamental.[20]

GS 341 offers eternal recurrence as an existentially significant hypothetical test. It is employed as a measure of whether the individual in question's disposition towards life could be one of full-blooded affirmation. Confronting someone with the thought of eternal recurrence is supposed to act as a gauge for the strength of the interpretation, that which evaluatively guides the actions of that individual. Setting aside the myriad interpretive questions surrounding the status and successfulness of eternal recurrence in its context, with eternal recurrence, these central motifs are employed to probe whether one might be able to justifiably embody a joyous disposition to life, as a final consequence of engaging with nihilism.

The hypothesis, as Nietzsche presents it at GS 341, invokes several examples of the eternal and the infinite. The thought centrally involves the prospect of eternally repeating one's life. Nietzsche speaks of the "eternal hourglass of existence," which "will ever *be turned over again and again, and you with it, speck of dust!*" When the positive response to the eternal recurrence is couched in the language of divinity ("*Or have you once experienced a tremendous moment when you have answered: 'You are a God, and never did I hear anything so divine!'*"), the passage closes with the question of how well disposed to life one would have to be "to long for nothing more fervently *than this ultimate eternal confirmation and seal.*"

Through eternal recurrence, one's value-interpretation of life is measured. But the manner in which Nietzsche views eternal recurrence as a thought to be "incorporated" by the would-be life affirmer is also important. Reconsidering the Lake Silvaplana notes from August 1881, eternal recurrence is framed in terms of the "infinite importance of our knowing, erring, our habits, ways of living for all that is to come," as well as how we might find the best way of "*incorporating* [eternal recurrence] in ourselves" (KGW V 2.11[141]).

Much more needs to be said of the metaphor of incorporation and how Nietzsche uses it more broadly.[21] But its application here shows a kind of internalization of one's own meaning. In one sense, this returns to a form of the value scheme featured, in a more primitive fashion, in the nobles of GM I. It is "slavish," by contrast, to always seek meaning in what is external to oneself. But whereas the nobles were unreflectively expressing their value-commitments, the affirmer of eternal recurrence is a cognitive and affective alignment to the proposition, "what if this all occurred eternally?" It is possible to will eternal recurrence by virtue of having incorporated it into oneself. Now, this runs the risk of sounding like an appeal to the transcendent to affirm life. Perhaps this is superficially true about even the passages discussed earlier, denoting the awe in the horizon of the infinite. If so, this would clash with Nietzsche's wish elsewhere to naturalize the impulses associated with appeals to the transcendent, as they are in religious belief (BGE 230). But incorporation is used here as a way of making eternity immanent. Rather than

God, whom it is claimed "set[s] eternity in the human heart" (Eccl. 3:11), Nietzsche does not see eternal recurrence as securing an exalted perspective upon life at the expense of the immanent. The eternal recurrence confronts the individual with the injunction to see immanent phenomena as imbued with eternal significance (TI Ancients 4–5). To again invoke Leiter's idea that Nietzsche is using these motifs as what Stevenson calls "persuasive definitions," what value these motifs had on earlier transcendent models have been *revalued*. It may be argued that Nietzsche's developmental story aims to revalue eternity and infinity, by inverting the notion that they invoke some otherworldly beyond. Rather, they are affective tools to heighten one's relation to this world, while avoiding metaphysics in the fulfillment of a basic human need. By Nietzsche's lights, Judeo-Christian theodicy—which claims this world is finite, while the world beyond is eternal and infinite—got it exactly the wrong way round. Nietzsche is flipping that on its head. Christianity and Christians are finite; the world, so perceived by the experimenter, and then the value-creating life-affirmer, is eternal and infinite.

Here Nietzsche does something arguably similar to the sentiment encapsulated in the opening stanza of William Blake's "Auguries of Innocence":

To see a World in a Grain of Sand
And a Heaven in a Wild Flower
Hold Infinity in the palm of your hand
And Eternity in an hour

To have incorporated an eternal perspective on the immanent as such would lend itself to being able to joyously will it so. Being able to describe the eternal recurrence as nothing matched in its divinity expresses its own kind of exalted disposition, which Nietzsche ties to a form of joy. This seems rather more than the commonplace variety of joy that can be felt at a football game result, or the feeling that follows the laughter at a joke's punch line. Consistent with the earlier claims about Nietzsche's "persuasive definitions" in how he employs certain concepts, arguably this is at work in his talk of this form of joy, too. It is this joy which is the appropriate affect once one can totally affirm their disposition towards life. Nietzsche sees it as the response arrived at after overcoming nihilism, by means of longing the eternal confirmation and seal of the immanent world (GS 341). There remains a further interpretive question as to whether Nietzsche views this disposition of joy as a fundamentally epiphenomenal state, through which we might recognize one's status as a genuine affirmer; or whether the joy itself is efficacious in promoting this life-affirming disposition, by virtue of willing eternity; or whether it may be both. As how Nietzsche arguably sees *ressentiment* as both a product and a cause of psychic corrosion, this special affective joy might be positioned as, inversely, a stimulant to affirm life, as well as a state arising from that stimulation. Whatever the case, this joyful willing of eternity delineates a special kind of affect, as well as perhaps the willing of eternity being the target of this affect.[22]

In a piece of characteristically bad poetry in Z by Nietzsche, the repetition of the motif of eternity is held up by Zarathustra as something both appetitively desired and loved: "Oh, how could I not be ardent for Eternity, and for the marriage-ring of rings—the ring of the recurrence? ... I love thee, O Eternity! For I love thee, O Eternity!" (Z III Seven Seals). Zarathustra is willing not the incipience of "the ring of recurrence" but an immersion into it, since his disposition runs in joyful consonance with it. It is in "On the Vision and the Riddle" that the shepherd (inferably a version of Zarathustra himself) is described as becoming an overjoyed, transfigured being who laughed as "never on earth laughed a man" (Z III Riddle).

Whether or not this would ultimately collapse back into a kind of transcendent perspective for Nietzsche is a matter of interpretive debate.[23] One thing in Nietzsche's favour on this front is that his reconceptions of the eternal and the infinite make no appeal to Providence and its consolations. As he writes at GS 109, "When will we have completely de-deified nature? When may we begin to *naturalize* humanity with a pure, newly discovered, newly redeemed nature?" In line with this, eternal recurrence is intended to redeem life by means of giving a new, exalted meaning to it. But this meaning is secured by means of being able to joyfully will the eternal recurrence of the immanent, rather than by falling back into the nihilistic baggage of Christianity.[24] Indeed, the confrontation with nihilism has led to this new means of life-affirmation, as a consequential boon unavailable beforehand. Nihilism, then, has instrumentally facilitated a new kind of meaning to life, by means of eternal recurrence.

In a famous passage in *Beyond Good and Evil* (BGE), Nietzsche speaks of the process to undertake thinking pessimism in its depths. Only by going one step beyond Arthur Schopenhauer, in a deepening of pessimism, to overcome morality can one arrive at an "opposite ideal." The most world-negating perspective thus allows one to arrive at

> the ideal of the most high-spirited, lively, world-affirming human being who has learned not just to accept and go along with what was and what is, but who wants it again *just as it is and was* through all eternity, insatiably shouting *da capo*, not just to himself but to the whole play and performance, and not just to a performance, but rather, fundamentally, to the one who needs precisely this performance—and makes it necessary: because again and again he needs himself—and makes himself necessary—What? And wouldn't this then be—*circulus vitiosus deus*? (BGE 56)

This last notion of a God being a "vicious circle" confirms the intended similarity here with the eternal recurrence motif. But it also tracks the developmental process through nihilism, so as to overcome it. Notable is Nietzsche's claim that morality's overcoming is something which inhibited Schopenhauer from undertaking this process. This passage ties together the notion that nihilism is developmental, and that its final stage includes a desire for viewing a life as willable in an eternal magnitude.[25]

Conclusion

This chapter has examined three ways Nietzsche uses the motifs of eternity and infinity to track three developmental stages of nihilism's inception and its overcoming. In Z, Nietzsche offers another passage where he talks of three stages of development: the

"Three Metamorphoses of the Spirit." There is little explicit textual evidence to support the claim that these two developmental processes are the same. But there is great conceptual overlap—enough, I argue, to draw a link.

The first stage of the "infinite nothing" describes a disposition of disorientation, in reaction to the death of God. Built into GS 125 is the idea that those marketplace atheists remain Christian in their morality. Schopenhauer falls into this camp, just as he remained unable to think pessimism in its depths in BGE 56. This camp is therefore confronted with a crisis of meaning while remaining burdened by an inability to freely develop their own disposition towards nihilism—the camel, the first metamorphosis of spirit.

For those who start to unburden themselves, the prospect of an infinite horizon comes to the fore (GS 124, 343, 371). This horizon is characterized by a new sense of freedom to experiment with values and combat the old morality which hitherto constrained that freedom. The lion, the second metamorphosis of spirit, is described as capturing its own freedom, and gaining its own lordship from the wilderness of its own perspective. It combats the great dragon "Thou-shalt" through its will. Those who undertake the new perspectival experimentation amidst infinite interpretations are metaphorically captured as the lion, destructive of the old morality and experimental in its wake.

However, Zarathustra is clear that the lion is not yet a creator of values. Rather, it facilitates the freedom that constitutes the conditions for creativity at a later stage. Nietzsche's allusions to the great dragon and later the eternal recurrence as a sleeping, dormant *Wurm* bear affinity with Wagner's Siegfried in combat with Fafner in his guise as the lizard-like serpent-worm, or *Schlangenwurm*.[26] But note that whereas Siegfried slays Fafner, the lion metamorphosis can only combat but not slay the great dragon by means of his freedom. Extending the comparison, this is because Siegfried wields the sword named *Nothung*, or "Child Born of Need." Whereas the one in awe of the infinite that is opened up after the death of God could experiment with values and interpretations, the affirmer of eternal recurrence is a self-legislator, a genuine creator. This final use of the motif of eternity, the joyful disposition toward the eternal recurrence, is synonymous with the value creating child, the third metamorphosis. Nietzsche describes the child as "innocence ... and forgetfulness, a new beginning, a game, a self-rolling wheel ... a holy Yea. Aye, for the game of creating ... there is needed a holy Yea unto life: its *own* will willeth now the spirit" (Z I Metamorphoses).[27]

What of the kind of joy embodied by the affirmer of eternal recurrence? In the penultimate passage before the "Epilogue" from GS V, Nietzsche invokes the image of a coming "spirit that plays naively, i.e. not deliberately but from overflowing abundance and power, with everything that was hitherto called holy, good, untouchable, divine" (GS 382). Hearkening to the great task of overcoming nihilism, Nietzsche continues, "It is perhaps only with it that *the great seriousness* really emerges; that the real question mark is posed for the first time; that the destiny of the soul changes; the hand of the clock moves forward." Invoking imagery of sailing and seas, these "argonauts of the ideal" embark on a great journey, one Nietzsche thinks has consequences for all humanity. Through this journey, one sets out to traverse enough perspectives upon life to be able to arrive at an interpretation of this life which one could desire as eternally recurring. Nietzsche hopes the eternal recurrence thought will provide this "eternal confirmation and seal" (GS 341) for all actions, as Zarathustra proclaims in his Roundelay, "*alle Lust will Ewigheit*," or "all joy wills eternity."[28]

Notes

1. It might count as one end point among others, for Nietzsche. In the fourth book of *Thus Spoke Zarathustra*, some evidence suggests that eternal recurrence is Zarathustra's own idiosyncratic means of achieving life-affirmation. See Johnson (2019: 189–91). However, Nietzsche elsewhere refers to eternal recurrence as the fundamental thought of *Zarathustra* the *text*, not just Zarathustra the *figure* (EH Books Zarathustra 1). Nietzsche also refers to himself as the teacher of the eternal recurrence (TI Ancients 5).
2. Huddleston (2015) delineates the important difference between these, and why the negative effects of Christianity alone are insufficient to explain the grounds for Nietzsche's critique.
3. There is an underappreciated aspect of Nietzsche's claims about Christianity that demonstrate how it might facilitate kinds of instrumentally positive consequences— see Huddleston (2015) again, Huddleston (2019: 60–70), and Neuhouser (2014).
4. Nietzsche quotes this passage again at EH Books HH 6, where after a decade, he arguably offers some critical distance from its sentiment.
5. See Elliott (2020: esp. 73–7) for a detailed discussion of this and how it squares with Nietzsche's claims about the possibility to remove and eliminate certain other drives in the service of self-cultivation. While never being goods in themselves, I, however, also take it that Nietzsche sees repressions as having instrumentally led to the formation of new, interesting, and unforeseeable aspects of human psychology. This is most prescient in GM II. The life-affirming speculations Nietzsche offers there as a result of the formation of these aspects remains an understudied topic in Nietzsche scholarship.
6. Whether "no will" at all, construed as the complete absence of a will to meaning, is even possible is contentious, since Nietzsche's closest apparent candidate, the "last man" figure, still possesses a meaning, albeit a narrow, parochial one (Z P 5).
7. Although Nietzsche is obviously aware of the fact that other cultures have had ideals, Judeo-Christianity is novel in offering a kind of justificatory ideal in its answer to the will to meaning, rather than an embodied affirmation. He thinks the virtues of Greco-Roman culture (for one) were primarily *expressed* by its adherents, rather than conscientiously extolled.
8. In a move away from what he took to be the unacceptable determinism of Spinozism, Schelling claims that that which makes the world intelligible and grounded "is not God seen absolutely, i.e. insofar as He exists; for it is only the ground of His existence, it is *nature* in God; an essence which is inseparable from God, but different from Him" (1856–61 I/7: 358, as quoted in Bowie 1993: 95). The idea of God as the 'ground of Being' is a central concept in Tillich's work; Cornelius de Deugd (1968) provided a treatment of this concept in Tillich, in relation to Spinozism.
9. Tom Hanauer helpfully observed that the original Hebrew commonly translated here as "eternity" (*olam*) could also be interpreted as "world." In Hebrew, if you conjoin the word "for" and "world," you get "eternity" (*le'olam*) but the more accurate translation would be "forever." "Eternity" is usually translated from the Hebrew *net'zach*, which

interestingly shares the root for the Hebrew word for "victory": the eternal is the victorious. I wonder what Nietzsche with his philologist's cap on would have made of that.
10. As Stevenson puts it, "a 'persuasive' definition is one which gives a new conceptual meaning to a familiar word without substantially changing its emotive meaning, and which is used with the conscious or unconscious purpose of changing, by this means, the direction of people's interests" (1938: 331).
11. Similarly, it would repay further consideration to think of Nietzsche as utilizing the heritage of concepts in a manner akin to Gricean implicatures: a kind of productive misleading of the reader, by articulating familiar concepts to conversationally imply new, rhetorically subversive meanings to them. Cf. Grice (1989).
12. Dirk R. Johnson has intimated that eternity's scope is broader than just eternal recurrence, for Nietzsche. In his account of Z, he writes that the eternal recurrence "is less crucial to the text as a whole than the feeling of eternity that the work attempts to convey" (2019: 175). Johnson's account also rightly notes Nietzsche's "strategy of intimate, delicate persuasion" (2019: 175) to engage his ideal readers, similar points by Stevenson and Grice made above. However, Johnson's discussion fails to sufficiently explain how eternity functions, either as something that informs a disposition Zarathustra arrives at, as something distinct from the usual claims made about eternal recurrence as a regulative thought-experiment, or as a general motif used by Nietzsche. Though drafts of this chapter were produced before Johnson's piece appeared, one of my intentions here is to clearly explicate this point, among others, and provide context for the philosophical significance of Nietzsche's use of this motif, in addition to infinity.
13. Reginster (2006) provides the most prominent account of nihilism's features as disorientation and despair, though some argue that it doesn't adequately attend the affective dimension of nihilism: see Gemes (2008) and Creasy (2020). I take the disorientation at GS 125 as possessing an affective character: our affects are jumbled up, owing to how our feelings do not cohere with the madman's revelation of God's death. Indeed, that we do not feel we know what we ought to feel about our newly realized malaise may comprise a meta-affectual quandary.
14. Cf. Heller (1988: 11).
15. Some might argue that following the linear ordering of the passages themselves would be neater, and thus, the condition described in GS 124 precedes the condition described in GS 125. However, Nietzsche's linear ordering of texts frequently breaks with the developmental stages of various ideals they have in focus. GM II 2 is a helpful counterexample here: the sovereign individual denotes the developmental culmination into a new and refined ideal, before Nietzsche tells the story through the rest of GM II of the sickness that made this exemplar of greater health possible. Nietzsche offers the often-cryptic image of the Overman early in the preface to Z, but does not expound upon it until later in the book. We also get intimations of eternal recurrence far earlier than any concrete analysis of what affirming it amounts to or would require of us. In other words, GS 124 and 125 are best understood like those places where Nietzsche asserts an ideal *before* explaining how it comes to pass. Thanks to James Mollison for pressing this alternative.
16. What gives GS 125 its force is that those in the marketplace, including some of those who might count as candidates for Nietzschean ideals, have no idea what has just hit them—they were totally unprepared. Would the death of God be that shocking to one already in the process of realizing their engagement with nihilism, construed as

re-engagement with values, as in GS 124? Viewing it so would likely undermine what gives the death of God passage its critical dimension, since value experimentation is only possible after feeling the full shocking force of GS 125.
17. Cf. also BGE 211 and GM III 12.
18. In his translation of GS Walter Kaufmann points out that this poem echoes the motifs of GS 124.
19. There are residual questions about these conditions under which one might be so disposed. To put some questions for Nietzsche on the table; is this a conscious effort to become better disposed? Is it wholly or largely unconscious? Is it something we can make a habit of, to engrain into ourselves? Is the fostering of such a disposition completely unavailable to some? If so, how tenable is his task of experimenting with values, as facilitating human flourishing, if only a few superlative cases might be able to even come close to it? What about the rest of us? These important questions are beyond the scope of this paper but should be pressing to any discussion of what might broadly be called Nietzsche's positive ethical account.
20. EH Books Z 1.
21. See Elliott (2021) for a discussion of incorporation in the context of Nietzsche's claims about the psychological faculty of active forgetting.
22. Whether Nietzsche can account for the difference between what might be called "proximate willing" of events close to one's life (e.g., the success that follows turning down one job to secure another, etc.) versus "distant willing," things that we have a hard time making any connection at all with one's life (e.g. the extinction or flourishing of a bug in some far-flung ecosystem, whose existence I know nothing of) is another story. Sometimes he intimates that there is no real distinction between them, as all things are connected. This difficult matter cannot be answered here.
23. May helpfully considers whether Nietzsche remains in thrall to an ideology of life-denial by seeking to justify life through total affirmation, rather than overcoming the need to do so (2011: 86–98). There are other problems with practical injunctions of eternal recurrence, including the notion of the creative will turning an "it was" into a "thus I willed it" (Z II Redemption), as one intractably grounded in a form of self-deception, rather than honesty about one's life. I address this problem in a forthcoming paper.
24. We can reasonably question whether all forms of Christianity are precluded from something like the Nietzschean picture here. Romantic poetry such as Wordsworth's "Lines Composed a Few Miles above Tintern Abbey" (1798) arguably illustrates this, where the joyful mood he describes feeling towards the immanence of Nature is no doubt inspired by his own Christian belief.
25. BGE 56 notably conceives of eternal recurrence as an ideal which a life-affirming individual can will more stably, rather than just for a single tremendous moment, as implied at GS 341. Although Z III Vision frontloads the imagery of the "Moment," Zarathustra there suggests that recognition of this moment will make lasting changes to one's soul. See too the aforementioned injunction to "incorporate" eternal recurrence, which suggests more than some momentary change.
26. See Loeb (2010: 148–52). Nietzsche's emulation of Wagner's imagery of the *Schlangenwurm* was the same imagery that inspired one of Schopenhauer's objections to Wagner's *Ring*, in his copy of the book sent to him by Wagner, which he read over the winter of 1854–5. Pencil in hand, he was prone to mocking Wagner's stylistic choices and strange phrasings in the margins.

27. See Loeb (2010: 220): "Zarathustra begins by predicting a culminating spiritual metamorphosis into a child's creative freedom whereby the will wills its own will, and Zarathustra's later speeches show how eternal recurrence is the key to this metamorphosis."
28. Drafts of this chapter were presented at the British Society for Philosophy of Religion (2017), the Friedrich Nietzsche Society (2017), and as a keynote at the Religion & Culture conference in Warsaw (2018). I am grateful to Jessica Berry, Eva Cybulska, Samuel Hughes, Paul Kirkland, T. J. Mawson, Michael McNeal, Allison Merrick, William Parkhurst, Russell Re Manning, Mikołaj Sławkowski-Rode, and Ralph Weir for their comments. I am also indebted to Tom Hanauer and James Mollison for detailed feedback on this chapter.

References

Bowie, Andrew (1993), *Schelling and Modern European Philosophy: An Introduction*, London: Routledge.

Creasy, Kaitlyn (2020), *The Problem of Affective Nihilism in Nietzsche: Thinking Differently, Feeling Differently*, Basingstoke: Palgrave Macmillan.

de Deugd, Cornelius (1968), "Old Wine in New Bottles? Tillich and Spinoza," *Royal Institute of Philosophy Lectures* 2: 133–51.

Elliott, Richard (2020), "The Role of Removal and Elimination in Nietzsche's Model of Self-Cultivation," *Inquiry* 63 (1): 65–84.

Elliott, Richard (2021), "What Is 'Active' Forgetting in Nietzsche's *Genealogy* II, 1?," in *Nietzsche on Memory and History*, ed. Anthony K. Jensen and Carlotta Santini, pp. 113–28, Berlin: De Gruyter.

Elliott, Richard, "Eternal Recurrence, 'On Redemption' and the Risk of Self-Deception" (forthcoming).

Gemes, Ken (2008), "Nihilism and the Affirmation of Life: A Review of and Dialogue with Bernard Reginster," *European Journal of Philosophy* 16 (3): 459–66.

Grice, Paul (1989), "Logic and Conversation," reprinted in *Studies in the Way of Words*, Cambridge, MA: Harvard University Press.

Heidegger, Martin ([1933] 1990), "The Self-Assertion of the German University," in *Martin Heidegger and National Socialism*, ed. Gunther Neske and Emil Kettering, 5–13, New York: Paragon House.

Heller, Erich (1988), *The Importance of Nietzsche: Ten Essays*, Chicago: Chicago University Press.

Huddleston, Andrew (2015), "What Is Enshrined in Morality? Understanding the Grounds for Nietzsche's Critique," *Inquiry* 58 (3) 281–307.

Huddleston, Andrew (2019), *Nietzsche on the Decadence and Flourishing of Culture*, Oxford: Oxford University Press.

Johnson, Dirk R. (2019), "*Zarathustra*: Nietzsche's Rendezvous with Eternity," in *The New Cambridge Companion to Nietzsche*, ed. Tom Stern, 173–94.

Leiter, Brian (2019), *Moral Psychology with Nietzsche*, Oxford: Oxford University Press.

Loeb, Paul S. (2010), *The Death of Nietzsche's Zarathustra*, Cambridge: Cambridge University Press

May, Simon (2011), "Why Nietzsche Is Still in the Morality Game," in *Nietzsche's* On the Genealogy of Morality: *A Critical Guide*, ed. S. May, 78–99, Cambridge: Cambridge University Press.
Neuhouser, Frederick (2014), "Nietzsche on Spiritual Illness and Its Promise," *Journal of Nietzsche Studies* 45 (3): 293–314.
Reginster, Bernard (2006), *The Affirmation of Life: Nietzsche on Overcoming Nihilism*, Cambridge, MA: Harvard University Press.
Schelling, Friedrich Wilhelm Joseph (1856–61), *Sämmtliche Werke*, ed. K.F.A.Schelling, I Abtheilung vols. 1–10, II Abtheilung vols. 1–4, Stuttgart: Cotta.
Stevenson, Charles (1938), "Persuasive Definitions," *Mind* 47: 331–50.

Part Three

Predecessors and Heirs

6

"What Do I Matter!": Nietzsche on Pascal, Self-Obsession, and Good Cheer

Jamie Parr

Incongruity of Affect

The phrase "*Was liegt an mir*" or "What do I matter" (hereafter WM) appears several times in Nietzsche's corpus and illuminates his concept of cheerfulness. However, with the exception of Marco Brusotti (1997) and Matthew Meyer (2019), this phrase has received little scholarly attention.[1] The most important use of WM in Nietzsche's published texts is in *Dawn* (D 547). Here Nietzsche discusses the arrogance of previous philosophers who sought to "arrive at the end of knowledge" within their lifetimes. Hitherto the pursuit of knowledge usually involved discarding all "the small individual questions and experiments" into knowledge in favor of intellectual shortcuts that aimed to "compress the problem of the world" into a riddle one often believed one had solved. This behavior requires the conceit that the world is amenable to being known by humans in this manner and produces an intense experience of self-centered pleasure at feeling oneself to be the practitioner of such knowing: "The boundless ambition and jubilation of being the 'unriddler of the world' were the stuff of the thinker's dreams." In contrast to this hubristic simplicity, Nietzsche claims that future philosophers will cultivate a very different relationship both to knowledge and their own lives. Hitherto,

> philosophy was … a sort of supreme struggle for the tyrannical rulership of the spirit—that such a rule was intended and reserved for some such very fortunate, subtle, ingenious, bold, powerful person—a single individual!—this no one doubted, and several, most recently Schopenhauer, have fancied themselves this very individual.—From which it follows that the quest for knowledge, by and large, has been held back by the *moral narrow-mindedness* of its disciples and that in the future it must be pursued with a higher and *more magnanimous* basic feeling. "What do I matter!" stands over the door of the future thinker. (D 547)

Without qualification, WM suggests an experience of desperation, akin to Pascal's "What is a man in the infinite?" (S 230), which is uttered in response to our physical insignificance before the material universe.[2] Yet in D 547, WM expresses the *Grundempfindung* of the future thinker's practice of knowledge. This practice not only appears to proceed from a (complex) positive attitude, but Nietzsche also depicts WM as fixed over the threshold of the future thinker's abode as a signal to others.[3]

Given the conditions of existence of the future thinker in a world unable any longer to enjoy the transfiguring effect of the Judeo-Christian God, WM denotes an apparent incongruity of affect.[4] Nietzsche is well aware of this fact, asking at GS 343 why it is that, though we know the catastrophic effects of the death of God that must now ensue for humanity, we experience *cheerfulness* at God's demise. Nihilism cannot now be avoided; why do we then "look forward to the approaching gloom without any real sense of involvement and above all without any worry and fear for *ourselves*?" This is an important question. Even if one feels relief at the removal of limitations to the practice of knowledge following God's death, how is it possible to be cheerful under such conditions, given the "monstrous logic of terror" (GS 343) that death supposedly brings? Deeper still, WM seems to cut against what Nietzsche elsewhere recognizes as our fundamental need for our lives *to* matter (GS 1). Do we no longer matter? If so, why is this a reason for happiness?

In this chapter I argue that WM vocalizes the passion of knowledge and concisely articulates its self-understanding. As a drive competing with our long-standing need for our lives to possess transcendent significance, the passion of knowledge alters our experience of ourselves and accounts for the incongruousness of Nietzschean good cheer. In WM we may discern the tensile nature of Nietzsche's contemporary thinker, "in whom the impulse for truth and [the] life-preserving errors clash for their first fight" (GS 110). Accordingly, in my first section I consider Nietzsche's thinking of Christianity in terms of our habitual understanding of our lives as possessing a particular value and importance; for Nietzsche, this understanding allows us to experience a type of existential comfort that fosters cowardice and personal vanity. To illustrate this problem and explore some changes that individuals must undergo to make WM an expression of their fundamental attitude toward life and knowledge, I consider Nietzsche's reading of Pascal. For Nietzsche, Pascal is a tragic figure, a natively courageous individual destroyed by a faith that bred in him a pernicious self-obsession; essential to his tragedy is his *inability* to utter WM. Finally, in my third section I use the case of Nietzsche's Pascal to explore the nature of those who *can* say WM. I unpack the self-consecration and self-sacrifice contained within that phrase to reveal Nietzsche's positive concept of a life once more rescued from despair by a transfiguring vision of existence. However, while this vision confronts life's tragedy, it resists becoming one more iteration of "the tragic," for it is practiced by those capable of the noble and affirmative art of *laughing* at themselves.

1. Nietzsche on Christian Good Cheer

A major psychological consequence of the failure of Christianity is the loss of a particular sort of confidence. The following moment from the Roman Catholic *Book of Blessings* (Catholic Church 1989: 22) is instructive: "Whether God blessed the people himself or through the ministry of those who acted in his name, his blessing was always a promise of divine help, a proclamation of his favor, a reassurance of his faithfulness to the covenant he had made with his people." The meaning and power of this sentence lies in the horror in which it is steeped and the transfiguration it allows one to enjoy. Without divine help, life is a problem without definitive solution. To feel ourselves favored is to resist the conclusion that we mean nothing to the universe, which everywhere the natural world suggests. In a world of ceaseless flux, to be convinced of God's faithfulness binds one to a ground of permanence that is also the ultimate protective power.[5]

For Nietzsche, a major portion of the problem of living is that the conditions of our existence deny us the existential meaning and purpose we have come to crave (GS 1). There is no intrinsic meaning to things. To know this fact is to court despair. Yet with Christianity we enjoyed the ability to transfigure the problem of reality; it enabled us to "cloak an execrable reality in the mantle of justice, virtue, and godliness" (KSA 13:14[123]). Naturally, this did not abolish life's suffering, but one knew *why* one suffered. The Christian perspective spared us the agony of meaningless pain (GM III 28), allowing us to hold fast to a supernatural ground of restitution, rescue, and love. "I write these things to you who believe in the name of the Son of God," declares the Johannine author,

> so that you may know that you have eternal life. And this is the boldness we have in him, that if we ask anything according to his will, he hears us. And if we know that he hears us in whatever we ask, we know that we have obtained the requests made of him. ... We know that we are God's children. (1 Jn 5:13-15, 19)[6]

Nietzsche views the Christian as confident because he enjoys "the delusion that he is protected by a god" (KSA 13:11[285]). This delusion eases what Nietzsche believes is the average Christian's inherent cowardice, which, like all cowardice, is rooted in impotence.[7] While there are singular exceptions—such as Pascal—as a rule the Christian is a weak person whose faith is "completely out of touch with reality" (A 15) for the good reason that he struggles to cope with it. The Christian's hatred of reality is born of resentment; unable to feel strong and important in life, he seeks that feeling "behind" life, in the web of imaginary experiences manufactured by Christian theologians. Such people are Christians because it falsifies reality to their advantage, providing an "escape" from life, in life. "Who are the only people motivated to *lie their way out of* reality? People who *suffer* from it" (A 15). In Christianity, therefore, is self-esteem of a kind (KSA 12:7[3]), and at its self-serving core is the "enormous lie of personal immortality":

> That as immortal souls, everyone is on the same level as everyone else, that in the commonality of all beings, the "salvation" of *each* individual lays claim to an eternal significance ... you cannot heap enough contempt on this, every type of selfishness increasing *shamelessly* to the point of infinity. And yet Christianity owes its *victory* to *this* miserable flattery of personal vanity[.] ... "Salvation of the soul"—in plain language: "the world revolves around *me*." (A 43)

Confident in God's favor, the Christian's trust in life rests on his belief in the "crude nonsense" of the idea of "the eternally continued existence" of his own person (KSA 13:11[279]). For the believer, his essence is "something immortal, something 'divine', a 'soul'!," a claim enabling him "to attach an absurd amount of importance to himself" (KSA 13:15[30]). Now he is a temple and locus of the Spirit's action (1 Cor. 3:16); now Christ's transfiguration (Mt. 17:1-2; Mk 9:2-3; Lk. 9:28-29) portends the eventual completion of the believer's own supernatural metamorphosis into the "image" of Christ (2 Cor. 3:18). According to Nietzsche, this conception of the human amounts to "the most extreme form of *self-absorption* [*Verselbstung*]" (KSA 13:11[226]): to make one's personal salvation the sole criterion by which all existence is valued and meaning in life found is to grossly overinflate the desire of the individual to feel that they matter. It produces "nothing but absurdly self-important souls, terribly anxious about themselves" (KSA 13:11[226]). This anxiety arises from a profound hedonism that mollifies cowardice and indulges vanity, especially the frustrated desire to experience the power one lacks in reality. As Kathleen Higgins points out, not only does the doctrine of personal immortality offer believers a way to deny the reality of death, by insisting that death is merely the occasion for a quickened form of life, but Christianity also provides believers with an escape from the problem of themselves, "by assuring them that one can lose oneself in God[.]" However small they may be in life, the Christian always has access to the sop of "a vicarious sense of power by virtue of his or her relationship to God" (Higgins 2010: 33, 34). In every case, faith allows one to avoid a lucid connection to the reality of existence; at each moment one is turned inward, toward the pleasure of the problem of oneself.

With God's will discernible in all things (1 Thess. 5:16-18), Christian good cheer was possible. The believer trusted in the promise of salvation from death and the recompense of her suffering. In the face of the "trifling and accidental role" she in fact plays "in the stream of becoming and passing away" (KSA 12:5[71]), the believer asserted her own essential value for God. With the death of God and the deconsecration of the Christian world, this form of existential insulation becomes impossible. "The trust in life is gone: life itself has become a *problem*" (GS Preface 3). However, preempting his own conception of cheerfulness, Nietzsche immediately cautions that "one should not jump to the conclusion that this necessarily makes one gloomy. Even love of life is still possible, only one loves differently. ... We know a new happiness" (GS Preface 3). The nature of this "new happiness" and its connection to WM is the subject of the third section of this chapter. In order to reach that point, we must consider Nietzsche's thinking of Pascal.

2. Nietzsche's Pascal

The following notebook entry is essential to any attempt to understand Nietzsche's use of WM:

> The idea that we are chained to something terrifying colours all our feelings. Or: to be an exiled god, or to settle the debts of earlier times. All these frightening secrets

of ours make us very interesting to ourselves! but so egotistical! One *could* not and *should* not look *away* from oneself! To lose this passionate interest in ourselves and turn it away from ourselves, toward things (science) is now possible. What do I matter! Pascal could not have said that. (KSA 9:7[158])

Pascal could not look away from himself, because he took far too much pleasure in what he saw, and he believed he should not look away because he was too afraid of the consequences. Nietzsche regards Pascal as a richly instructive exception to the average Christian. Abandoning his scientific career, Pascal allied himself to the so-called Jansenist sect of Catholicism, which held a bleak and uncompromising view of salvation: requiring supernatural assistance for every good act, all humans deserve damnation; Christ died only for a tiny number of elected persons, and once given, his grace is not infrequently withdrawn, returning the individual to the damned mass.[8] While framing life in such terms maximizes the ecstasy of grace, it also infuses life with unassuageable fear. Only strong, singular individuals were attracted to and could incorporate such a worldview. Yet this is the problem. In Nietzsche's view, while Christianity is often attractive to the strong because of its engagement with the problem of life, to live seriously the facile nature of the Christian response is ruinous, and there is no more tragic example of such ruin than that of Pascal, "Christianity's most instructive victim" (EH Clever 3). By placing his personal strength in the service of the Christian conception of reality, Pascal exposed the inimical nature of that conception for all natively powerful, self-confident individuals (see KSA 13:11[55]).[9]

Pascal occupies a unique position in Nietzsche's project, central to which is his thinking of Pascal's laughter.[10] Nietzsche refers to Pascal's brilliant satire of Jesuitism, his *Provincial Letters*, when he notes, "The ecclesiastical pressure of millennia has created a magnificent *tension* of the bow ... Pascal is the glorious sign of that terrible tension: he laughed the Jesuits *to death*" (KSA 11:34[163]). And, in accord with the metamorphic effect of all spiritual practices—Christianity itself understood as such a practice, on the grandest of scales—Pascal is not only a sign of the accumulated "spiritual" power of European humanity, but in his *Pensées* (ironically, an apology for Christianity) he portends the future collapse of the faith (D 68). This collapse will come about not only through the cultivation of intellectual honesty (KSA 12:2[123]) but also the destructive power of laughter: "In Pascal, for the first time in France, *a sinister and tragic mocking,—'comedy and tragedy combined.'* Of the *Provincials*" (KSA 11:26[443]).[11]

In the event, despite portending the end of Christianity, Pascal remained a Christian, out of fear (KSA 13:15[94]). What is thereby lost, in Nietzsche's view, is a laughter that, had Pascal only lived thirty years more, would have seen him "laugh to scorn Christianity itself, out of his magnificent, wicked soul, as he had done earlier in his youth to the Jesuits" (KSA 11:34[148]).[12] His example is therefore negative (a laughter that failed to break from service to Christ and which recedes almost entirely by the end; an intellectual honesty that sides against itself) but no less instructive for it. The remainder of this section therefore presents a concise survey of key aspects of Nietzsche's Pascal that allow us to understand why he was unable to utter WM.

Ecstasy

Nietzsche's marginalia in his personal copy of Pascal's works show a repeated interest in texts which speak of an exclusive relationship with God.[13] A striking example of such texts are those concerning the supposed miracle by which Pascal's niece was cured of a lacrimal fistula through "devotion to the Holy Thorn" (Pascal 1910: 365). Pascal was convinced this event was intended by God not only to heal his niece but also to fortify the faith of the persons involved, including Pascal himself (Pascal 1962: 47). He is most revealing on this topic in the following text, which Nietzsche marked in several places; the approximate span of his marginal strokes is indicated by curled brackets:

> {If God uncovered himself continually for men, there would be no merit in believing in him; and if he never uncovered himself, there would be little faith. But he conceals himself ordinarily and discovers himself rarely to those whom}[14] he wishes to engage in his service. ... Heretical Christians have recognized him through his humanity and adored Jesus Christ God and man. But to recognize him under the species of bread is peculiar to Catholics alone: none but us are thus enlightened by God. ... {All things cover some mystery; all things are veils that cover God. Christians ought to recognize him in everything.}[15] ... Let us give [God] infinite thanks that, having concealed himself in all things for others, he has uncovered himself in all things and in so many ways for us.[16]

It is hard not to see pride and exultation in this text: God has broken cover to engage precisely *us* in his service.[17] As Pascal and his sister Jacqueline put it in an earlier letter, without the light of grace, those living in the prison of the world can neither see nor read the instructions in material things which speak of our liberator. While all humans are justly confined in this prison, by grace the Pascals have been rescued from this nothingness and given a place in the universe. From this vantage point they can and must combat their sinfulness and strive to grow in Christian perfection (Pascal 1865: 1.27–31).

Nietzsche's view of such ecstatic gratitude accords with his remark that Christians arrogantly regard "the laws of nature" as being "constantly *broken* for their sake" (A 43). The Jansenist preoccupation with damnation ensures that Pascal's religious experience turns around a thoroughgoing self-obsession that unfolds in terms of a permanently overexcited emotional register: "All these saints are egoists, and how could one not be when threatened with Hell! It goes beyond all strength and reason to think of others in such a situation!" (KSA 9:7[106]). While Pascal views himself as a sinner empowered by grace, Nietzsche sees an individual reveling in the difficulty of the Jansenist interpretation of existence and exulting in the distance he feels between himself and all those not so empowered: "Pascal's state is a passion that has all the signs and consequences of happiness, misery, and the deepest, abiding seriousness. Thus it is actually laughable to see him so proudly countering passion— [in him] it is a type of love that despises every other kind and pities those who lack it" (KSA 9:7[234]). Such is the self-deluding position in which Pascal finds himself: to enjoy his own power without also believing himself sinful, he ascribes his power to God and all other experiences to himself. Thinking himself aided by God feeds his sense of personal distinction: out of the damned mass God has chosen *him* for enlightenment.

However, if *all* things are "veils that cover God," the good cheer of the evangel must be discoverable in life's negative experiences, too: in death and suffering. Nietzsche's view of Pascal's response to these experiences demonstrates the self-obsession that made WM a fearful impossibility for him.

Horror

The deepest point of convergence between Nietzsche and Pascal is their understanding that the problem of existence requires transfiguration. Without transfiguration, we may merely endure suffering and are prone to despair. The sharpest divergence between the two men, however, turns on the nature of the transfiguration they privilege. For Nietzsche, transfiguration is wholly intra-worldly, whether it is one's own act of creativity or one's experience of an event (such as a work of art or falling in love). For Pascal, however, transfiguration may come only through grace. Further, it is an experience we may be empowered to participate in but which ultimately we do not and cannot control.

I want to briefly examine two texts in which Pascal seeks to transfigure threats to his experience of Christian good cheer. The first is Pascal's letter to his sister Gilberte, following their father's death.

Pascal's letter provides his response to the primary features of death: his father's absence from the world and the decomposition of his body. Absence suggests annihilation; decomposition means rot. Untransformed, these features break Pascal's trust in his personal relationship to God. He therefore counters these features with the claim that death is not a natural event. Rather, as the necessary penalty for and expiation of sin, death for Christians must be an occasion for joy. It is proper to *love* death "when it separates a holy soul from an impure body" (Pascal 1910: 342). The life of the Christian is a perpetual sacrifice, completed by death, "in which the soul … achieves its immolation and is received in the bosom of God" (1910: 340). In dying, "the will of God is accomplished" in their father, whose will "is absorbed in God" (1910: 340). It is an error to trust the evidence of the senses on this point; nature lies and must be ignored. In dying, their father is more alive. "Let us no longer regard his soul as perished and reduced to nothingness, but as quickened and united to the sovereign life" (1910: 341). The same approach is taken to bodily decay. "Let us no longer regard a corpse as putrid carrion, because deceitful natures figures it thus, but as the inviolable and eternal temple of the Holy Spirit, as faith teaches" (1910: 340). Nietzsche marked both of these sentences (Pascal 1865: 1.45), as well as this: "Without Jesus Christ, [death] is horrible, detestable, the horror of nature. In Jesus Christ it is altogether different: it is benign, holy, the joy of the faithful. Everything is sweet in Jesus Christ" (Pascal 1865: 1.41; 1910: 338).

In this way, Pascal opposed despair with joy: "Let us … consider the greatness of our blessings in the greatness of our ills and let the excess of our grief be in proportion to that of our joy" (1910: 344). Yet Nietzsche regards this joy as gained at unacceptable cost. First, it requires the falsification of reality; only by dethroning his intellect (KSA

9:7[34]) can Pascal believe that death is unnatural.[18] Second, Pascal demonstrates Christianity's needless exaggeration of life's problems, including the significance of death, to the point of inventing nonexistent sources of fear (KSA 9:7[184, 185]). Finally, the desire to separate the "truth" of human life from its material conditions is seen as rooted in the desire to maintain a sense of one's own importance. In this case, presumably, Pascal cannot allow his eventual death and decomposition to diminish his self-regard. Therefore, as "God has not abandoned his elect" to the "caprice" of nature, Pascal claims, we must regard death "not in itself and apart from God, but apart from itself and in the inmost part of the will of God" (1910: 336). For Nietzsche, this is simply self-interested delusion: "You must lie to yourself about things as so not to lose your feelings of power and greatness!" (KSA 9:7[174]). The upshot is a response to death that affirms the self-obsession at the core of Pascal's Christian good cheer.

Sacrifice

The second text is Pascal's *Prayer to Ask of God the Proper Use of Illnesses*. Pascal's final years saw an intensification of disabilities he had lived with for much of his adult life; according to Gilberte, it was in this period that he composed the *Prayer* (Pascal 1962: 54). Here I want to consider two aspects of this text; read from Nietzsche's position, they illustrate both the egoism that meant Pascal *could* not look away from himself (KSA 9:7[158]) and the fear that led him to believe that he *should* not do so.

The first aspect is Pascal's anxiety at his struggle to respond to his pain in the manner expected of him:

> Lord, whose spirit is so good and so gentle in all things, and who is so merciful that not only the prosperity but the very disgrace that befalls your elect is the effect of your mercy, grant me the favour not to act towards me as towards a heathen in the condition to which your justice has reduced me; that like a true Christian I may recognise you for my Father and my God, in whatever condition I may find myself, since the change of my condition brings none to yours; as you are always the same, however subject I may be to change, and as you are none the less God when you afflict and punish than when you comfort and are indulgent. (1910: 370)[19]

As a Jansenist, Pascal's experience of grace was inherently unstable. For him, it was a complex feeling he believed was due to an external power over which he had no influence. Essential to that experience was a feeling of resolve and efficacy of will; its waning, in the manner of all affects, immediately raised the suspicion that grace may be diminishing in him, perhaps to the point of withdrawal. Such is the crisis of the *Prayer*: the terror that his struggle to respond appropriately to his suffering is due to God's gradual abandonment of him. This is the negative side of the egoistic belief in an immortal soul, namely, an immortal soul whose eternal damnation God allows.

Wracked by illness, Pascal is struggling to maintain his hold on the transfiguring joy of the evangel. His pain is producing impious emotions whose existence only increases the fear that grace is receding. He begs God for the power to control himself: "Move my heart to repent of my faults, [Lord], since without this internal sorrow the external ills with which you afflict my body will be to me a new occasion of sin" (1910: 373). He asks not to be "abandoned to the sorrows of nature"—mere nature, devoid of hope, filled with rotting flesh—without the transfiguring consolations of grace (1910: 375).

Under these circumstances, it is impossible to look away from oneself, as one's self is not only the nub of the problem but, as the ecstatic close of the *Prayer* demonstrates, also essential to its resolution:

> Unite me to you [Lord]; fill me with yourself and with your Holy Spirit. Enter into my heart and soul, to bear in them my sufferings and to continue to endure in me what remains to you to suffer of your passion, that you may complete in your members even the perfect consummation of your body, so that being full of you, it may no longer be that I live and suffer, but that it may be you that lives and suffers in me, O my Saviour; and that thus having some small part in your sufferings, you will fill me entirely with the glory that they have acquired for you, in which you will live with the Father and the Holy Spirit through ages upon ages. Amen. (1910: 378)

This is the second aspect of the *Prayer* that illustrates Nietzsche's claim that Pascal could never look away from himself. Like any lover, he burned with the desire to suffer and even sacrifice himself for his lover. Thus, Pascal offers his body to God as a site for Christ's ongoing Passion.[20] For Nietzsche, the self-effacement of this move is merely apparent and demonstrates the extent of the self-delusion Pascal's faith requires. His experience of "grace" is simply his own strength of will: "To say like Pascal, 'It is God who does this in us,' is not to make the human nothing and put God in its place: rather, the grace he invokes is the *greatest exertion of human nature*. ... He calls 'God' that which he feels to be exalted and pure in himself" (KSA 9:7[271]).[21] While he can only misunderstand himself on this point, nonetheless Pascal *enjoys* these acts of mortifying self-overcoming (cf. BGE 46, 229; KSA 9:7[208, 254], and 12:10[128]).[22] Further, this cryptic self-indulgence is compounded by the egoism of the *Prayer*'s act of "sacrifice," which demonstrates the Christian's demand for an absurd degree of self-importance (KSA 13:11[226]). To be filled with Christ is not only to be saved by him and filled with his glory—hardly a minor ambition—but to enjoy a crucial place within the one process in the entire universe which truly matters: hosting within oneself the cosmic work of redemption that is the purpose of the continued existence of the world (S 690). The self-sacrifice of the *Prayer* thereby vastly magnifies Pascal's personal importance, aligning him with the ultimate source of power. Nietzsche argues that those who indulge in such acts of "piety" and the feeling of being "at one" with God are thoroughly disingenuous: "You feast on the feeling of his power, which has once again just been confirmed by a sacrifice. In truth, you only *seem* to sacrifice yourselves; instead, in your thoughts you transform yourselves to gods and take pleasure in yourselves as such" (D 215).

For the weak, Christian good cheer is a boon. For the strong, it weakens. Pascal's idea of grace distanced him from his own will, convincing him of his helplessness and leaving him terrified at the natural fluctuations in his feeling of power (D 86). Believing his damnation to be a constant likelihood, eventually he became too afraid to pursue the apostasy of which he was capable. Maintaining his Christian good cheer was his true self-abnegation (KSA 13:15[94]), robbing him of his self-confidence and sense of humor. In Pascal, Nietzsche saw the honesty that would lead to the passion of knowledge; in the event, the Frenchman was a "sublime abortion" (BGE 62).

3. The New Human Comportment

Nietzsche's concept of a new human comportment depends on a fundamental change in our erotic economy. For those in whom the passion for knowledge has arisen it is now possible to turn our interest in ourselves "away from ourselves, toward things (science)" (KSA 9:7[158]).[23] This redirection of passion is the condition of possibility for new experiences of love and consecration, new consolations, and new forms of self-sacrifice. As the *Grundempfindung* of this comportment (D 547), WM is "the expression of true passion, it is in the utmost degree to *be beyond oneself*" (KSA 9:7[45]). Though capable of it in principle, in practice, Pascal could not redirect his passion in this way—the apostasy that was required was too great a risk. Yet even for those of us who do not struggle so tragically with a binding faith, it is important to underline the challenge posed by Nietzsche's concept of the human being. We live now in the "interregnum" (D 453) between the old morality and the future of our species. As Keith Ansell-Pearson notes (2018: 123), as we practice our humanity in this space, we must strive to "become equal" both to the event of God's death and the task of thinking through anew what it means to be human.

While the passion of knowledge drives those in its thrall toward the problems of life, the ugliness of truth makes despair a continual risk. Yet to feel that our lives are *consecrated* to knowledge (D 195) affords us a measure of protection—more so if we consider ourselves *destined* to such a life. Here, too, we see that WM is the concise expression of this pathos. Chronically ill for much of his adult life, Nietzsche learned from the Stoics the value of saying WM during periods of distress (KSA 9:15[59]); declaring WM, he claims, is "the way to *encourage* me" (KSB 6:58; cf. 6:60). The contrast here with Pascal—also chronically ill—is striking. Pascal offers himself to Christ, hoping thereby both for salvation and magnification; Nietzsche's letters echo Zarathustra's final words: "My suffering and my pity—what do they matter [*was liegt daran*]! Do I strive for *happiness*? I strive for my *work*!" (Z IV The Sign).[24] And immediately after writing of the consecration of his life by pursuit of his passion of knowledge, Nietzsche makes plain the Stoic root of WM with a quotation from Cleanthes: "Fate, I *follow* you! And were it not my wish / I'd *have* to nonetheless and take along my sighs!" (Z IV The Sign). Here and elsewhere Nietzsche transforms the Stoic understanding of destiny into "a passionate and self-sacrificing fatalism" in which he feels his own dominant passion as the fate ruling over him (Brusotti 1997: 207); he embraces his own nature as an organism that lives to know (1997: 208; cf. GS 110).

WM therefore indicates Nietzsche's view of the proper relation between the individual and the whole to which she is subject. At the heart of this relation is a particular kind of *trust*. In *Twilight of the Idols* (TI), Nietzsche praises Goethe's conception of a "strong, highly educated, self-respecting human being" who, having "*become free*[,] stands in the middle of the world with a cheerful and trusting fatalism" (TI Skirmishes 49). Essential to this trust is "the highest of all possible beliefs," namely the Dionysian belief that "only the individual is reprehensible [or, "only *what* is individual is reprehensible," "*dass nur das Einzelne verwerflich ist*"], that everything is redeemed and affirmed in the whole" (TI Skirmishes 49). The Dionysian perspective of the whole includes and affirms everything; while the disciplined cultivation of the individual is essential, it is no less the case that to assert the value and worth of the individual over and against the totality is "reprehensible." Ironically, on this view, the Christian view of the unique value of the individual reveals a fundamental *distrust* of the nature of "natural" existence—a clear example being Pascal's insistence that death is unnatural. In fact, Pascal's efforts to rescue his father from the reality of bodily decay illustrate Christianity's magnification of the worth of each individual to the point of terror. As steward of an immortal soul, everything in life *matters* terribly; for the Christian, "*one* is always one, something first and last and tremendous" (GS 1). To this perspective Nietzsche juxtaposes what Henry Staten (1990: 11) has termed the "limit point" of the "potlatch economy," the Dionysian perspective of the maximal view of the whole, in which the waste inherent to the "grand economy" (1990: 10) of life is revealed. Even the most robust hubris cannot resist this point of view, in which one's "boundless, fly-like, froglike wretchedness" (GS 1) is laid bare. Yet it is precisely at this point of awareness that Nietzsche refers to a particular kind of laughter:

> To laugh at oneself as one would have to laugh in order to laugh *out of the whole truth*—to do that even the best so far lacked sufficient sense for the truth, and the most gifted had too little genius for that. Even laughter may yet have a future. I mean, when the proposition "the species is everything, *one* is always none" has become part of humanity, and this ultimate liberation and irresponsibility has become accessible to all at all times. (GS 1)

As Staten puts it, "the grand economy is not afraid to squander, and what it squanders is individuals. Therefore, what do *I* matter? '*One* is always none.' This is the insight that releases laughter, laughter at oneself" (1990: 11).

I shall return to this point shortly. For now, it must be noted that both Nietzsche's use of WM as an encouraging refrain, and that refrain's link to the Dionysian view of the relation of the individual to the totality, hinge on the abandonment of the concept of an immortal soul. Previously, Nietzsche wrote,

> The salvation of poor "eternal souls" depended on the extent of their knowledge during a short lifetime; they had to *make a decision* overnight—"knowledge" took on a dreadful importance! We have seized once again the good courage to make mistakes, attempts to take things provisionally—everything is less important!— and precisely for this reason individuals and generations can set their sights on undertakings of a grandeur that would have appeared to earlier ages as insanity and a toying with heaven and hell. (D 501)

The loss of the immortal soul produces a change in the lived economy of the human. The world is no longer the self-obsessed drama of the interval between hell and heaven (S 185). For those accustomed to view the world in the old way, the negative psychological impact of this insight is profound (KSA 13:11[99]). Yet those who view the discarding of the immortal soul as a positive development also face a significant problem, precisely because in being increasingly comprehended the world has seen its solemnity decrease—and with it, a certain kind of charm (D 551). However it is here that knowledge as a *passion*, and the decrease in the personal relevance of knowledge to the knower, is essential. As knowledge of the world now has no relevance to the salvation of one's soul, a *freer* relationship to knowledge is possible: "Now every trial and self-experiment is open to the knower" (Brusotti 1997: 282). At the same time, Nietzsche understands that it is of the nature of passion to drive those it grips to risk and, ultimately, sacrifice themselves (Brusotti 1997: 282). In this way, therefore, WM becomes the expression of "true passion" (KSA 9:7[45]), because it denotes the joyous offering of oneself as an apostle and instrument of knowledge. The world—and we ourselves—may be less "important" in the old sense, but the increase in our passion to know the world drives us toward it once more in an attitude of questing and self-offering. As such, just as WM articulates the "higher and *more magnanimous*" basic feeling of the thinker (D 547), so the thinker's "most beautiful virtue" is "the magnanimity with which he ... often with sublime mockery and smiling—offers himself and his life in sacrifice" (D 459). In Nietzsche's view, the nature of this sacrifice differs sharply from its Christian variant. As Meyer observes (2019: 177), "the consecration of one's life to knowledge ... is not a flight from a hated self that Nietzsche associates with Pascal, but rather comes from a self well disposed toward itself." This is an important point: the self-offering practiced by Nietzsche's future thinker is possible only on the basis of a counterbalancing *consecration* of one's self. Again, as Meyer notes, arises the distinction between Nietzsche and Pascal: not an offering of the self in which the self is ablated by the god, but an offering made out of one's cultivated abundance. Zarathustra's *untergang*, for example, begins only after he has become so full that he *wants* to overflow (Z Prologue 1). Nietzschean selfishness is "ideal" when its practice leads one to give oneself away: 'This is the proper *ideal selfishness*: always to care for the soul ... so that our fructification *comes to a beautiful conclusion*!' (D 552).

The death of God may have broken the trust we enjoyed regarding the problem of our existence, making the old means of transfiguring that problem redundant, but Nietzsche also understands this event to be an opportunity for us to cultivate a new spiritual maturity. While the good cheer of this new comportment is incongruous when contrasted with the established view of our nature, Nietzsche believes it allows for the development of a new form of laughter. However, we must tread carefully. The passion of knowledge presses us inexorably into life's tragedy. This is its *leidenschaftlich* nature: our deepest joys lie in the discovery of truths that often terrify us. Although we will counterbalance our pursuit of knowledge with our aesthetic transfiguration of existence—transfiguration being the essential human task (KSA 12:1[127])—still we must avoid falling prey to the kind of existential exhaustion that would cause us to resent life. As noted, there is consolation in knowing that our lives are consecrated to knowledge (D 195); we may also incorporate the idea that, however ugly truths may be, "knowledge even of the ugliest reality is itself beautiful" (D 550; cf. Meyer 2019: 176). Yet still another way, at least as effective, is to learn to laugh at ourselves precisely as the passionate, serious seekers of knowledge that we are

> at times we need a rest from ourselves by looking upon, by looking *down* upon, ourselves and, from an artistic distance, laughing *over* ourselves or weeping *over* ourselves. We must discover the *hero* no less than the *fool* in our passion for knowledge; we must occasionally find pleasure in our folly, or we cannot continue to find pleasure in our wisdom. Precisely because we are at bottom grave and serious human beings—really, more weights than human beings—nothing does us as much good as a *fool's cap*: we need it in relation to ourselves. (GS 107)

The artistic "distancing" Nietzsche describes here is a practice of self-overcoming of which few are capable. Our passion may now be turned away from ourselves toward the world, but we do not thereby disappear; on the contrary, the more we know, the more our "flylike, froglike wretchedness" (GS 1) is apparent. In response to this view, however, WM releases *laughter* at ourselves (Staten 1990: 11). Such a thing is possible only for those capable of overcoming their pity at the sight of their own wretchedness. We must assume an "artistic" point of view "above" ourselves and from this point of vantage laugh at (as well as, on occasion, cry over) ourselves. We are challenged to hold both the comedy and tragedy of our lives, our heroism and foolishness, together in tension, *but* with the comedic able to surmount and accept the irreconcilable nature of the tragedy of one's life. As Paul Kirkland shows (2009: 215–44), this feat requires that, for as long as the comic stance is maintained, one sufficiently frees oneself from the negative emotions of one's situation to be able to master them: "As courage overcomes fear, laughter overcomes pity, and in each case the relevant sentiment is not eliminated, rather it is ruled" (2009: 218). In this manner, laughter transfigures existence. Pity, sympathy for our agony, is present but controlled, affording the individual a view of their existence that is not vitiated by personal suffering. One occupies a perspective of existential lucidity unencumbered by emotions that could cause resentment. This enables a transformation of existential vision, as Kirkland explains:

> While Nietzsche appears to embrace the tragic view that all wisdom comes from suffering, he denies the conclusion that wisdom must *remain* suffering. Laughter emerges precisely where sympathy is present, but one stands apart from suffering. … Laughter allows one to *accept* the conditions of human life, providing a model for the affirmative disposition toward life, one that neither flees into comforting illusions nor allows itself to be crushed by despair. (2009: 218, my emphases)

To practice our humanity in this way is to begin to unlearn the pernicious self-obsession and moral certainty Nietzsche sees exemplified by Pascal. Nietzschean good cheer is informed by the "glad tidings" of science (D 450), which cultivate an animal that is passionate, brave, and capable of transfiguring laughter in the face of suffering. With its energies redirected toward the challenge of the world, the character of this new comportment is antithetical to the narrowness of all forms of fanaticism and partisanship, whether philosophical, religious, or political. This provocative new practice of the human stands in stark contrast to a contemporary sociopolitical landscape scarred by the polarizing effects of rage, populism, selfishness, and self-righteousness.

For those of us raised with contrary ideas, Nietzsche's assertions that no one is favored by a god, that death is a mere reality of life, and that supernatural aid is an illusion, are deeply shocking. But—what do *we* matter?

Notes

1. Reference to WM may also be found in Bertram (2009: 256–7) and in Higgins (2010: 35). WM appears eighteen times in Nietzsche's corpus: three times in published works (D and GS), twice in drafts for D 488 and D 539 (see KSA 14:224 and 226), ten times in the *Nachlaß*, and three times in Nietzsche's letters. "*Was liegt an mir*" is strongly context dependent in German, the verb *liegen* possessing a range of connotations, including the bearing of both responsibility and fault (that which "lays upon" a person). Any comprehensive examination of "*Was liegt an mir*" should include consideration of the phrases "*Was liegt an dir*" ("What do you matter") and "*Was liegt daran*" ("What does it matter"). *Was liegt an dir* appears four times: twice in the *Nachlaß* and twice in print, in GS 332 and Z II Stillest Hour. The two *Nachlaß* references are preparatory variations on the Zarathustra text. References to *Was liegt daran* are more numerous (31 in total: 6 in letters, 10 in the *Nachlaß*, 15 in print). Those relevant to the meaning of WM appear in book Z IV Higher Man (14, 15 and 20), Awakening 1, Sleepwalker 1, Sign.
2. Texts of Pascal's *Pensées* use the translation by Roger Ariew (2004). Ariew's edition follows Philippe Sellier's arrangement of the fragments, hence the siglum "S" (e.g., "S 230").
3. In D 96, Nietzsche wonders how the collapse of Judeo-Christian morality might be accelerated and a new intellectual culture brought about. "There exist today perhaps ten to twenty million people among the different countries of Europe who no longer 'believe in God'—is it too much to ask that they *give a sign* to one another?" Placing a statement above one's front door is a significant act. Such display may be a form of consecration ("I believe and value X"), a sense that reveals a parallel with a form of Christian piety often referred to as "chalking the door":

> Many traditions and genuine manifestations of popular piety have been developed in relation to the Solemnity of the Lord's Epiphany[.] … [For example,] the blessing of homes, on whose lentils [sic] are inscribed the Cross of salvation, together with the indication of the year and the initials of the three wise men (C+M+B [traditionally taken to be Caspar, Melchior and Balthasar]), which can also be interpreted to mean *Christus mansionem benedicat* ["Christ bless this house"], written in blessed chalk[.] (Congregation for Divine Worship and the Discipline of the Sacraments 2002: 92–3)

This practice was common in Germany. If Nietzsche meant to associate the lintel display of WM with this practice, it would be consistent with his subversive engagement with Christian thought and expression. He may also have wished to

suggest the ancient use of apotropaic magical symbols and charms, commonly affixed to buildings and doorways to ward off evil.
4. A construct of psychiatry, incongruity of affect "refers to the objective impression that the displayed affect is not consistent with the current thoughts or actions (e.g. laughing while discussing traumatic experiences)" (Semple et al. 2005: 94).
5. The *Book of Blessings* (Catholic Church 1989) demonstrates the remarkable range of events, groups, and items sanctified by Catholic Christianity, including marriage (54–72), childbirth (110–24), the sick (163–76), libraries (327–34), gymnasia (365–70), and means of transportation (371–82). Catholicism considers blessings to be

> sacred signs by which, somewhat after the manner of the sacraments, effects of a spiritual nature, especially, are symbolised and are obtained through the Church's intercession. By them, people are made ready to receive the much greater effect of the sacraments, and various occasions in life are rendered holy. ... There is scarcely any proper use of material things which cannot ... be directed toward people's sanctification and the praise of God. (Vatican Council and Austin Flannery 1996: 139)

6. All Bible quotations use the New Revised Standard Version (Catholic edition).
7. At A 45, Nietzsche quotes Paul:

> Has not God made foolish the wisdom of the world? For since, in the wisdom of God, the world did not know God through wisdom, God decided, through the foolishness of our proclamation, to save those who believe. Not many of you were wise by human standards ... But God chose ... what is low and despised in the world, things that are not, to reduce to nothing things that are, so that no one might boast in the presence of God (1 Cor. 1.20–1, 26–9).

Nietzsche considers this text "a first-rate testimony of ... a Chandala morality born of *ressentiment* and impotent revenge" and is the last of a slew of scripture quotations he considers representative "samples of what these petty people fill their heads with" (A 45).
8. The "Jansenist" group was named after Dutch theologian Cornelius Jansenius (1585–1638), whose posthumous work *Augustinus* was its major theological inspiration. In practical terms the group was just as influenced by the spirituality and guidance of Jansenius's close friend, Jean Duvergier de Hauranne (1581–1643).
9. For Nietzsche's remarks concerning Pascal's strength, see KSA 9:7[262]; 11:44[7]; 12:2[144]; 12:5[35]; 12:7[6]; 13:11[55]; and BGE 62, A 5.
10. I deal with Pascal's importance for Nietzsche at length in my forthcoming book, *Nietzsche and Pascal: Transfiguration, Despair and the Problem of Existence* (London: Bloomsbury Academic).
11. A truncated reference to a remark by Ximénès Doudan (1878: 586): "C'est dans Pascal que vous trouverez pour la première fois en France la raillerie sinistre et tragique aiguisée et affilée comme un poignard: c'est la comédie et la tragédie tout ensemble." For an excellent study of the role of the comedic in Pascal, see Russell (1977). A number of insightful studies of the Nietzsche–Pascal relation have appeared fairly recently, but the field remains sparse; in English language Nietzsche scholarship, the only book-length treatment of the relationship is that of Natoli (1985). See also Donnellan (1982 and 1985), Williams (1952), and Voegelin (1999: 251–303). The works of Vivarelli (1998), Vioulac (2011), and Lebreton (2017) are particularly notable.

12. At Z I Free Death, Nietzsche makes the same claim about Christ.
13. For a codified list of Nietzsche's marginalia, see Campioni et al. (2003: 430–1). Nietzsche owned *Pascal's Gedanken, Fragmente und Briefe*, translated and edited by C. F. Schwartz (Pascal 1865).
14. Pascal (1865: 1.57).
15. Pascal (1865: 1.58).
16. Translation adapted from De Certeau (2015: 196–7). Nietzsche refers to this event at KSA 9:7[260]. Also seemingly concerning experiences of intimacy between Pascal and God, Nietzsche places marginal strokes against Pascal's reference to Jn 17:25 at S 742 (Pascal 1865: 1.230), and to 1 Kgs 19:18 at S 597 (Pascal 1865: 2.276).
17. This is not to claim that the Jansenists were not permanently liable to anxiety about the loss of their supposed favor. While they believed it was impossible to know with certainty whether one was of the elect, the psychological need every Jansenist had for reassurance on this point is consistently evident. For example, the letters of Duvergier de Hauranne (the group's original spiritual director) are littered with his efforts to achieve an edificatory balance between his commitment to the ultimate unknowability in life of the fate of one's soul and his desire to buoy the confidence of his directees, many of whom were in charge of conventicle bodies of Christians. "If you are to him as he is to his elect," Saint-Cyran soothes in one letter, "you are safe" and must not be afraid; fear is for those who do not enjoy the "eternal regard" of God, nor the "incomparable favours" of professing a Christian life, which is a sign of God's love (Duvergier De Hauranne 1962: 105–6). For Pascal's own anxiety on the same topic, see Pascal (1865: 1.60–1); Nietzsche places a marginal stroke against this passage.
18. For Nietzsche's remarks concerning the ruining of Pascal's intellect by his faith, see, e.g., BGE 45, 46, A 5. D 68 juxtaposes Pascal's intellectual honesty with the mendacity of Paul; see also D 91 and 192.
19. I have made minor adaptations to this translation to modernise the language.
20. Pascal speaks of Christ's "continual and uninterrupted sacrifice" (Pascal 1910: 338); see also S 749: "Jesus will be in agony until the end of world." Pascal's thinking of himself as a locus for the salvific sufferings of Christ has several scriptural connections, chief of which is Col. 1:24: "I am now rejoicing in my sufferings for your sake, and in my flesh I am completing what is lacking in Christ's afflictions for the sake of his body, that is, the church"; cf. 1 Cor. 3:16 and 6:17; Rom. 8:17; Gal. 2:20; Phil. 3:10-11; 1 Pet. 4:12-13.
21. In the next note Nietzsche illustrates this idea with a truncated quote from the fifth *Provincial Letter*: "'To withdraw the soul from the world, make it die to itself, and bind it solely and immovably to God—that is only possible by an omnipotent hand.' Pascal" (KSA 9:7[272]; see Pascal 1988: 78). This concern for Pascal's preoccupation with and misunderstanding of experiences of power is likely behind the two firm marginal strokes Nietzsche places against the following text:

> It is not shameful for man to yield to pain, but it is shameful for him to yield to pleasure. ... [This] is because it is not pain that tempts and attracts us. It is we ourselves who choose it voluntarily and want it to prevail over us, so that we are masters of the situation; and in this, man yields to himself. But in pleasure it is man who yields to pleasure. Now mastery and control alone bring glory, and subjection alone brings shame. (S 648)

22. Nietzsche's marginal stroke beside the following text illustrates this point:

> None would ever quit the pleasures of the world to embrace the cross of Jesus Christ, did he not find more enjoyment in contempt, in poverty, in destitution, and in the scorn of men, than in the delights of sin. And thus, says Tertullian, *it must not be supposed that the Christian's life is a life of sadness. We forsake pleasures only for others which are greater.* (Pascal 1910: 360; Pascal to Charlotte de Roannez, beginning of December 1656. The reference is to Tertullian's *De Spectaculis*, §29)

23. In the next entry he writes, "I want to bring things to the point where one needs a *heroic temper* to *devote* oneself *to science!*" (KSA 9:7[159]). The facsimile of this page makes plain the continuity between this note and entry 158 (see http://www.nietzschesource.org/DFGA/N-V-6,49); Nietzsche clearly is thinking still of Pascal as a negative case.
24. Cf. 9, 7[126]: "This path is so dangerous! I dare not call to myself, just as a sleepwalker strolling on the rooftops has a sacred right not to be called by name. 'What do I matter!' is the only comforting voice I want to hear." The connection of WM to Stoicism is noted by both Brusotti (1997: 206–9) and Meyer (2019: 177).

References

Ansell-Pearson, Keith (2018), *Nietzsche's Search for Philosophy: On the Middle Writings*, London: Bloomsbury Academic.

Bertram, Ernst (2009), *Nietzsche: Attempt at a Mythology*, Chicago: University of Illinois Press.

Brusotti, Marco (1997), *Die Leidenschaft der Erkenntnis. Philosophie und ästhetische Lebensgestaltung bei Nietzsche von* Morgenröthe *bis* Also sprach Zarathustra, Berlin: Walter de Gruyter.

Campioni, Giuliano, Paolo D'Iorio, Maria Christina Fornari, Francesco Fronterotta, Andrea Orsucci, and Renate Müller-Buck (2003), *Nietzsches persönliche Bibliothek*, Supplementa Nietzscheana 6, Berlin: Walter de Gruyter.

Catholic Church (1989), *Book of Blessings: Approved for Use in the Dioceses of the United States of America by the National Conference of Catholic Bishops and Confirmed by the Apostolic See*, New York: Catholic Book Publishing.

Congregation for Divine Worship and the Discipline of the Sacraments (2002), *Directory on Popular Piety and the Liturgy. Principles and Guidelines*, Strathfield, NSW: St Pauls.

De Certeau, Michel (2015), *The Mystic Fable. Volume Two: The Sixteenth and Seventeenth Centuries*, ed. L. Giard, trans. M. B. Smith, Chicago: University of Chicago Press.

Donnellan, Brendan (1982), *Nietzsche and the French Moralists*, Bonn: Bouvier.

Donnellan, Brendan (1985), "'The Only Logical Christian', Nietzsche's Critique of Pascal," in *Studies in Nietzsche and the Judaeo-Christian Tradition*, ed. J. C. O'Flaherty, T. F. Sellner, R. M. Helm, 161–76, Chapel Hill: University of North Carolina Press.

Doudan, Ximénès (1878), *Mélanges et Lettres*, Tome II, Paris: Calmann Lévy.

Duvergier de Hauranne, Jean (1962), *Lettres inédits de Jean Duvergier de Hauranne, Abbé de Saint-Cyran: Le manuscrit de Munich (Cod. Gall. 691) et la Vie D'Abraham*, édités avec notes et commentaires par Annie Barnes, Les Origines Du Jansenisme IV, Paris: J. Vrin.

Higgins, Kathleen Marie (2010), *Nietzsche's Zarathustra*, rev. ed., Lanham, MD: Lexington Books.
Kirkland, Paul E. (2009), *Nietzsche's Noble Aims: Affirming Life, Contesting Modernity*, Lanham, MD: Lexington Books.
Lebreton, Lucie (2017), "Nietzsche, Lecteur de Pascal: 'Le Seul Chrétin *Logique*,'" *Revue philosophique de la France et l'étranger* 142 (2): 175–94.
Meyer, Matthew (2019), *Nietzsche's Free Spirit Works: A Dialectical Reading*, Cambridge: Cambridge University Press.
Natoli, Charles (1985), *Nietzsche and Pascal on Christianity*, New York: Peter Lang.
Pascal, Blaise (1865), *Pascal's Gedanken, Fragmente und Briefe*, Aus dem Französischen nach der mit vielen uneditirten Abschnitten vermehrten Ausgabe P. Faugère's, Deutsch von Dr. C. F. Schwartz, zweite Auflage, in zwei Theilen, Leipzig: Otto Wigand.
Pascal, Blaise (1910), *Thoughts, Letters and Minor Works*, The Harvard Classics, vol. 48, trans. C. W. Eliot, ed., W. F. Trotter, M. L. Booth, and O. W. Wight, New York: P. F. Collier & Son.
Pascal, Blaise (1962), *Pascal's* Pensées, trans., with an introduction by Martin Turnell, London: Harvill Press.
Pascal, Blaise (1988), *The Provincial Letters*, trans. A. J. Krailsheimer, London: Penguin.
Pascal, Blaise (2004), *Pensées*, ed. and trans. Roger Ariew, Indianapolis: Hackett.
Russell, Olga Wester (1977), *Humor in Pascal: An Examination of the Comic Humor of the French Philosopher Pascal*, North Quincy, MA: Christopher Publishing House.
Semple, David, Roger Smyth, Jonathan Burns, Rajan Darjee, and Andrew McIntosh (2005), *Oxford Handbook of Psychiatry*, New York: Oxford University Press.
Staten, Henry (1990), *Nietzsche's Voice*, Ithaca: Cornell University Press.
Vatican Council, and Austin Flannery (1996), *Vatican Council II: Constitutions, Decrees, Declarations*, Northport, NY: Dominican Publications.
Vioulac, Jean (2011), "Nietzsche et Pascal: Le Crépuscule Nihiliste et la Question du Divin," *Les Études philosophiques* 96 (1): 19–39.
Vivarelli, Vivetta (1998), *Nietzsche und die Masken des freien Geistes: Montaigne, Pascal and Sterne*, Würzburg: Königshausen & Neumann.
Voegelin, Eric (1999), *Collected Works of Eric Voegelin, Volume 25*, in *History of Political Ideas* Vol. VII: *The New Order and Last Orientation*, ed. Jürgen Gebhardt and Thomas A. Hollweck, 251–303, Columbia, MO: University of Missouri Press.
Williams, W. D. (1952), *Nietzsche and the French: A Study of the Influence of Nietzsche's French Reading on His Thought and Writing*, Oxford: Basil Blackwell.

7

Schopenhauer's Jokes and Nietzsche's Riddles: Toward a Morphology of Laughter

Glen Baier

More than three decades ago, Lawrence Hatab rightly declared "Nietzsche is funny" and noted that "Nietzsche's humor is not accidental or incidental to his message" (1988: 74). Scholarly questions, however, persist as to the scope and nature of Nietzsche's comedic intent.[1] In this chapter, I look to address some of these questions by drawing connections between Nietzsche's *Thus Spoke Zarathustra* (Z) and Schopenhauer's treatment of laughter in *The World as Will and Representation* (WWR). The position I forward is that a reading of Z benefits from an overview of Schopenhauer's delineation of irony and humor in relation to jokes, which is part of his overall analysis of laughter. In what follows, I introduce the fundamentals of this analysis as a way of situating Nietzsche's deployment of riddles in Z. I propose that in Z, Nietzsche utilizes riddles that fit easily within the parameters Schopenhauer establishes for jokes and how they facilitate irony and humor.

In making such an argument, I do not go as far as to conclude that Nietzsche consciously appropriates Schopenhauer's thought on this front. I merely demonstrate there are ample grounds for taking Nietzsche's preoccupation with riddles to be a continuation of what is found in Schopenhauer's diagnosis of laughter. Nevertheless, as I explore the commonalities in their views, I articulate a substantial difference, namely that Nietzsche finds in laughter a true measure of the quality of a human life. In this regard, he departs from Schopenhauer, in that Schopenhauer merely identifies laughter as a genuinely human capacity without attaching further existential significance to it. In the end, I show that in Z, Nietzsche champions a view of laughter rooted in a robust conception of human existence that has the power to upset and unseat Schopenhauer's nihilistic pessimism. Hence an examination of Nietzsche's riddles shows that they are vital to his understanding of our psychology and our condition. Riddles, for Nietzsche, are definitive of our being and invite a knowing laughter. As such, they are at the heart of the philosophical teaching in Z.

To begin, I should note the reading of Nietzsche I offer appears to be at odds with Nietzsche's own estimation of his supposed "liberation" from Schopenhauer, particularly as expressed in the preface appended to *The Birth of Tragedy* (BT) in 1886. There Nietzsche laments, in "*An Attempt at Self-Criticism*," that his first major work is mired in "Schopenhauerian formulations" that "obscured and ruined" its most genuine insights. He comes "to regret very much" lacking the strength or audacity to use a language of his own, and "labouring instead to express strange and new evaluations" in a vocabulary borrowed primarily from Schopenhauer (BT 10). However, Nietzsche's frustration is due to his overarching worry that Schopenhauer has nothing to offer a theory of the tragic.[2] The criticism directed at Schopenhauer, on this front, contains no mention of his remarks on the nature of the comic. So, even if Nietzsche rejects Schopenhauer's assessment of tragedy, that does not entail they disagree on what should count as comedic.[3]

From Nietzsche's perspective, Schopenhauer's failure to appreciate tragedy is a consequence of his unrelenting pessimism. Nietzsche espies in this pessimism a form of nihilistic moralizing which he finds particularly distasteful. Nietzsche thus binds the denial of the value of life, indicative of Schopenhauer's pessimism, to conventional morality. "Morality itself—might it not be a 'will to negate life,' a secret instinct for annihilation, a principle of decay, belittlement, calumny, the beginning of the end?" (BT 9). This dread of suffering, which fuels the hatred of life, is taken to be the core of such moral teachings. Nietzsche, in this context, goes on to counsel his readers on how to live without denigrating life. He asserts, "You should first learn the art of comfort *in this world*, you should learn to *laugh*" (BT 12). This edict is followed by "the words of that Dionysiac monster who bears the name of *Zarathustra*" (BT 12), from the Fourth and Final Part of Z,[4] where Zarathustra announces he has "sanctified" laughter. Thus, what begins as an acknowledgment of the profound significance of tragedy ends as a commendation of laughter.[5] In this respect, laughter is elevated in terms of its overall import. Nietzsche, in the process, finds in laughter the means necessary to defeat Schopenhauerian pessimism,[6] but as I argue, Nietzsche's approach to laughter has much in common with that of Schopenhauer. As such, we find, in Schopenhauer's treatment of jokes, ideas that Nietzsche, in essence, uses against him.[7]

1. Schopenhauer on Jokes and the Nature of the Ludicrous

Jokes, for Schopenhauer, are deliberate undertakings, purposeful attempts to trigger laughter. Schopenhauer's willingness to see jokes as a matter of choice adds a regulative dimension to his account in that he introduces criteria for judging what qualifies as successful performance of a joke. In this regard, he stipulates that a joke must contain an obvious moment of contradiction. The emphasis on contradiction here leads to the standard designation of his position as a specimen of "incongruity theory."[8] According to incongruity theory, a joke yields laughter because it exposes and exploits incompatibilities. Hence, a joke turns on a fundamental inconsistency. Later, in connection to Nietzsche, I show that his conception of a riddle makes it a paradigm case of the kind of contradiction Schopenhauer stresses, namely the coming together of factors which are complete contraries.[9] Indeed, the lure riddles have for Nietzsche rests in their power to combine contraries, because riddles, so construed, mirror the description he gives of human beings. In this respect, the riddle serves as an access point to conclusions Nietzsche draws regarding the human circumstance, especially on the level of psychology. Furthermore, when it comes to matters of psychology, Nietzsche is quick to point out the advantages of his method, one that he exclaims to be a proper exercise in "morphology." Subsequently, I will indicate that Schopenhauer's treatment of comedic laughter is offered as a psychological account,[10] one that anticipates themes Nietzsche makes explicit through his recourse to morphology. This convergence in their thought, I argue, is not entirely coincidental, given the similarities in their preoccupations. The opening for Nietzsche's psychology, on this level, is discernible in Schopenhauer's investigation of laughter.

Schopenhauer introduces his thoughts on jokes and laughter when he turns his attention to what he calls the "ludicrous." The ludicrous, for Schopenhauer, is designated as a by-product of the interplay of reason and perception. The ludicrous, as a category, marks the "incongruity of knowledge from perception and abstract knowledge" (WWR I 59). Such a divide is illustrated by a variety of examples, including the case of "an experienced billiard-player" who "can have a perfect knowledge of the laws of impact of elastic bodies on one another, merely in the understanding, merely from immediate perception" even though "only the man who is versed in the science of mechanics … has a real rational knowledge" of these laws in their abstract form (WWR I 56). Thus, the billiard player does not know the laws of motion and does not need to in order to excel in billiards. Schopenhauer, at this stage, concludes there is no clear or easy transition from perception to reason. If, in keeping with his example, the billiard player relies on reason, rather than perception, such "passage through reflection" interrupts the process and makes things "uncertain, since it divides the attention, and confuses the executioner" (WWR I 56). The problem encountered rests in the "rigidity and sharp delineation" of concepts that "however finely they may be split by closer definition are always incapable of reaching the fine modifications of perception" (WWR I 57). Reason, as the means for abstract knowledge, is unable to unseat perception because it cannot do justice to perception. As a result, concepts cannot capture or match the richness of perceptual experience.

The limitation inherent in concepts, as described here, does not discredit abstract knowledge entirely. The point is not that perception is all that is needed for knowledge; rather, the contention is that purely conceptual understanding cannot substitute for perception. Perception, however, has limits of its own. For example, a builder can ascertain "from perception, directly and completely the mode of operation of a lever, a block and tackle, a cog-wheel, the support of an arch, and so on," but this knowledge "is not sufficient for constructing machines and buildings." At that moment "reason must put in an appearance" (WWR I 53). Reason, so denoted, provides awareness of the relationships between things that is not available in the immediacy of perception. Therefore, both reason and perception factor into human knowledge, but the difference in their functions introduces an irresolvable tension. Each has its assigned role, yet as we move from one mode of knowing to the other, the transition is never smooth. Something is always left behind, whether it is the fine detail of perception or the completeness of comprehension supplied by reason.

For Schopenhauer, the idea of the ludicrous proves relevant to his overall epistemology because it is a consequence of the gap existing between concepts and objects. Concepts are found in the domain of abstraction and objects are the particulars that constitute reality. Since there is a separation between concepts and objects, there is always the chance of mistaken classification. If there is no guarantee that the move from object to concept or concept to object can be seamless and continuous, then errors can occur. Assuming that concepts allow us to generate sets, the possibility of encountering the ludicrous resides in the fact we may arrive at problematic set allocations. For Schopenhauer, there are two basic "species" of the ludicrous. The first arises when "we have previously known two or more very different real objects … and arbitrarily identified them through the unity of a concept embracing both" (WWR I 59). In other words, the shift from objects to concept fails because the things under consideration are not fully commensurate, yet they are treated as if this is the case. The set is suspect because the items placed in it lack genuine commonality. For instance, I may think a coffee cup and a rock share a nature merely because they are both things I can touch. However, this feature, which they do share, is not sufficient to deem they belong together necessarily. To stress this feature as definitive is to convert a superficial aspect into a determining factor, which is more of an arbitrary imposition upon these objects than it is the detection of a real and decided commonality.

The second species of the ludicrous comes into play when "the concept first of all exists in knowledge, and from it we pass to reality and to operation on reality, to action" (WWR I 59). In this movement from concept to action, the one relying on reason imprudently assumes all things grouped under a basic concept will be equivalent in ways not designated directly by that concept, and this hasty generalization gives rise to conspicuous absurdities: "Objects in other respects fundamentally different, but thought in that concept, are now regarded and treated in the same way, until, to the astonishment of the person acting, their great difference in other respects stands out" (WWR I 59–60). Supposing, for example, a domesticated housecat and a feral racoon are to be dealt with in the same manner merely because they both fit in the set of mammals has obviously distressing results. I cannot act on the supposition they are equivalent, even if they find a ready home within the same general set. Their differences betray whatever generic commonality they may have.

In summary, the first variety of the ludicrous is engendered through the unwarranted imposition of a concept on perceived objects and the second is due to the erroneous inference that the sameness of perceived objects exceeds the confines of the concept which groups them together initially. These two species of the ludicrous are labeled by Schopenhauer in a manner meant to convey their comic potential. The first he calls "wit" and the second he calls "folly" (WWR I 59–60). He later expands on these categories and supplies examples.[11] In reference to wit, he shares

> the well-known anecdote of the Gascon at whom the king laughed when seeing him in the depth of winter in light summer clothes, and who said to the king: "If your Majesty had put on what I have put on, you would find it very warm"; then to the question what he had put on, replied "My whole wardrobe." (WWR II 92–3)

This story, as an instantiation of the first form of the ludicrous, speaks to the mirth arising when two remotely similar circumstances are treated as interchangeable. "Whole wardrobe" is a concept that, in this situation, unites two fundamentally opposing circumstances and thus enables them to be viewed as commensurate when they clearly are not. Employing the term "whole wardrobe" to refer to that of a pauper and that of a king at the same time is to force extremes together under a single heading. As for folly, Schopenhauer cites the story of a man who, when stating he likes to walk alone, receives the reply from someone who exclaims, "You like to walk alone; so do I; then we can walk together" (WWR II 96). In this scenario, the folly is a matter of assuming that the concept of "walking alone" accommodates particulars that exclude each other entirely. In both instances, the clash is a result of contradiction. Their ludicrousness issues from the incongruity evident in the forcing together of irreconcilable contraries.

I am not, at this point, interested in contesting Schopenhauer's definitions or the aptness of his examples.[12] Instead, I wish to draw two lessons from his examination of the ludicrous. First is his grounding of irony and humor in the dynamics of wit and folly. Second is his perspective on how the ludicrous leads him to assert that its recognition, and our responses to it, are distinctly human. In short, the proper reaction to moments of the ludicrous is laughter, and only human beings are said to be capable of laughter. Human beings are the only creatures who laugh because "the phenomenon of laughter always signifies the sudden apprehension of an incongruity" that exists between "a concept and the real object thought through it" (WWR II 91). It is this assumption, that laughter is properly human, that I argue finds a parallel in Nietzsche's Z.

Near the end of his overview of the ludicrous, Schopenhauer asserts, "The *intentionally* ludicrous is the *joke*" (WWR II 99). This claim adds to the prior discussion of wit and folly. Wit, as made evident in the anecdote of the Gascon, is unintentional to the extent that it does not have to be planned in advance. The king's remark allows the Gascon the chance for a quick and spontaneous retort. A joke, in contrast, requires prior calculation. Likewise, the folly of the fellow inviting another to walk alone with him is not staged, not plotted beforehand. The immediacy operative in these examples is absent in the case of a joke, which, again, is an intentional undertaking. Thus, in his initial foray into the ludicrous, Schopenhauer speaks of wit occurring as "a flash" and folly as evident in "a foolish action" (WWR I 60), implying that neither depends on forethought or scheming. He then augments these basic forms of the ludicrous to extend the idea to jokes, and to demonstrate they are consistent with wit and folly, in that jokes depend on incongruity and result in a tangible disconnect between concept and object. However, Schopenhauer thinks there is more to a joke than this gap. He sees a joke as an attempt to challenge the thought or experience of the individual selected as the purported target of the joke. As Schopenhauer puts it, the joke is the result of an "effort to bring about a discrepancy between another's concepts and reality by displacing one of the two" (WWR II 99). In other words, a joke calls for an incongruity that is made explicit by the one responsible for the joke, and the joke succeeds by unsettling its victim's supposed assuredness regarding the compatibility of their concepts and perceptual reality. In this manner, the joke itself brings about incongruity, deliberately and with a specific aim.

Schopenhauer further characterizes the joke as having its own prior opposite. A joke is possible only if there is "seriousness" that is interrupted by the joke. Seriousness is the disposition active when concept and objects are assumed to be congruous, and so it welcomes "the exact suitability" of concept and objects as that "which is at any rate striven after" (WWR II 99). Less abstractly, seriousness is evident when an individual assumes the movement from concept to object or object to concept can occur unimpeded. The joke is the negation of such a state of confidence; it is the willful disturbance of seriousness. This contrasting of the joke with seriousness allows for two variations in the form of the joke. The first is irony. "If the joke is concealed behind seriousness, the result is irony" (WWR II 99). To be ironic then is to feign serious in one's presentation of a joke. It is to act as if one is serious when one is not. It can take the form of giving "assent to opinions of another which are the opposite of our own and pretend to share them" (WWR II 99). Schopenhauer notes that this is "the attitude of Socrates" in his dealings with his interlocutors. In what comes later, I indicate how Nietzsche adopts this strategy of "mock seriousness" in his writing of Z.[13] Since irony, so defined, is a function of disposition, of attitude, I will highlight how Nietzsche is ironic in relation to the work as a whole. Z is presented as serious for the sake of displacing seriousness.

The second form of the joke, according to Schopenhauer, is humor. The dynamic attributed to humor is the reverse of that at play in irony. Humor is the "seriousness concealed behind a joke" that "might be called the double counterpoint of irony" (WWR II 100). Humor is that which first challenges seriousness by seeming comedic, but, by the end, seriousness is reinstated as the dominant disposition. So, humor is a matter of being ironic about one's irony. As Schopenhauer describes it, in humor "the impression of the intentionally ludicrous, and of the joke, arises, and yet behind this the deepest seriousness is concealed and shines through" (WWR II 100). He then succinctly captures the contrast of irony and humor. "Irony begins with a serious air and ends with a smile; in humour it is the reverse" (WWR II 100). In relation to my reading of Z, I relate it directly to this definition of humor. The irony directing the work continually lapses into the seriousness informing humor. Nietzsche is being ironic about his irony in order to reinstate the seriousness of that which he finds comedic.[14]

There is an obvious obstacle to my application of Schopenhauerian considerations to Nietzsche's text. As it stands, I seem to endorse a contradiction. I am arguing that what Schopenhauer circumscribes as a matter of contrasting opposites is indicative of Z as a whole. It is, at the same time, irony and humor, and as a result the distinction Schopenhauer articulates collapses or is lost. However, there are clear ways around this difficulty. Z, after all, is a work that calls for the embracing of contradiction.[15] As well, Schopenhauer himself mitigates this apparent contradiction through another binary coupling. He holds that "irony is objective and so is aimed at another; but humour is subjective, and thus exists primarily for one's own self" (WWR II 100). Irony, on this level, emerges through the provocation of another because it is aimed at the seriousness of the other. Humor, in comparison, is aimed at one's own seriousness and does not presuppose the presence of the other. In this regard, the contrast between the two is directional,[16] a matter of *whom* is the focus. Therefore, I can be ironic in my engagement with others, and humorous in relation to myself. The contradiction between the two dissipates somewhat, perhaps entirely, in that one can be ironic and humorous at the same moment. The shift that defines each is still a matter of contradistinction, but there is no reason to suggest one cannot be both ironic and humorous at the same time, especially if each has its own separate target.

Schopenhauer here, oddly enough, seems to anticipate what I identify as Nietzsche's simultaneous recourse to irony and humor. In his contrasting of these modes of comedic expression, Schopenhauer notes, "We find the masterpieces of irony among the ancients, of humour among the moderns" (WWR II 100). He thinks this judgment is vindicated by the preference for "objectivity" among the ancients and the favouring of "subjectivity" among the moderns. Nietzsche is curious, in this regard, because he seems to be a thinker who combines the ancient and the modern. In respect to Z, it is possible to see it as a retrieval of ancient ideals.[17] Nevertheless, it is meant to speak to the modern audience. Nietzsche is not an "antiquarian,"[18] looking to preserve or reinstate the past. He seeks means for addressing his times and thus ensconces what he takes from the ancients in a thoroughly modern work.[19] Hence the disruption of seriousness on both fronts, the objective and the subjective, infuses Z with ancient and modern elements.

The interpretation that I am developing of Nietzsche, nevertheless, is not completely in keeping with all that Schopenhauer proffers in respect to comedy.[20] This departure is most visible in respect to the standard designation of Z as parody. Nietzsche deploys irony, very much in the manner defined by Schopenhauer, to parody specific individuals and their works, including those of Goethe and Wagner. T. K. Seung (2006) goes as far as to cast Zarathustra as "a parody of Richard Wagner's *The Ring of the Nibelung*" (2006: xiv).[21] Higgins points to the conspicuous parodying of Plato in Z, especially when it comes to the "Myth of the Cave" (Higgins 2010: 42).[22] Schopenhauer, in contrast, is not so enamored with parody. Sander Gilman (1976) attributes Schopenhauer's dissatisfaction with parody to it being "one of the least subtle forms of the comic" (1976: 13). There is an obviousness to parody in the manner in which it manages incongruity. As Gilman observes, "the more heterogeneous the incongruity between the universal and the real, the more marked (and cruder) the effect" (1976: 13). So, the contradiction of the concept and particulars, which instantiates incongruity, depends on differences thought to be too blatant. There is a lack of subtly in parody that appeals to "coarser" instincts and for this reason, Schopenhauer views "parody as a demeaning of the noble" (Gilman 1976: 14). Nevertheless, Gilman thinks there is nothing in Schopenhauer's disdain for parody which discourages Nietzsche from exploring its philosophical potential. My intent at this point is to add to Gilman's trenchant analysis by showing that in Nietzsche's hands Schopenhauer's models of irony and humor enrich parody.

Schopenhauer's dismissal of parody mirrors his contempt for what he sees as lowly forms of the comic. In particular, he strives to disentangle his conception of humor from more mundane indulgences. He bemoans, "that at the present day 'humorous' is generally used in German literature in the sense of 'comic' arises from the miserable mania for giving things a more distinguished name than belongs to them, and hence the name of a class standing above them" (WWR II 101). For clarification, he adds that his use of the word "humour" has been "borrowed from the English, in order to single out and denote a quite peculiar species of the ludicrous" and "it is not meant to be used as a title for any jest and buffoonery" (WWR II 101). For Schopenhauer, humor results in laughter but not merely because something funny happens, so jest and buffoonery are not to be confused with humor. Humor finds its ground in the ludicrous in a fashion unavailable to simpler and simplistic forms of comic amusement.[23]

Schopenhauer goes on to stipulate that "the origin of the ludicrous is always the paradoxical, and thus unexpected, subsumption of an object under a concept that is in other respects heterogeneous to it" (WWR II 91). Along with this stipulation comes another, which sets out the proper conditions for laughter. He asserts, as noted earlier, "the phenomenon of laughter always signifies the sudden apprehension of an incongruity between such a concept and the real object thought through it, and hence between what is abstract and what is perceptive" (WWR II 91). The enjoyment of laughter is said, by Schopenhauer, to be found in the experience of a conflict between reason and perception. Reason, as we have seen, is an intellectual operation concerned with abstraction, whereas perception is an engagement with the reality of particulars. The tension between the two is due to their fundamental incompatibility. As aforementioned, concepts cannot take the place of perception or capture all that is revealed through perception. In the end, however, Schopenhauer holds that perception will win out and this is where enjoyment is found.

> In the case of the suddenly appearing contrast between the perceived and the conceived, the perceived is always undoubtedly in the right, for it is no way subject to error, and needs no confirmation from the outside, but is its own advocate. Its conflict with what is thought springs ultimately from the fact that the latter, with its abstract concepts, cannot come down to the infinite multifariousness and fine shades of what is perceived. This triumph of knowledge over thought gives us pleasure. (WWR II 98)

As for the causal mechanism operative in this account, Schopenhauer draws a link between perceptual knowledge and the will, which is, after all, his designation for the entirety of existence.

> For perception is the original kind of knowledge, inseparable from animal nature, in which everything that gives immediate satisfaction to the will presents itself. It is the medium of the present, of enjoyment and cheerfulness, and moreover it is not associated with any exertion. (WWR II 98)

The pleasure of laughing, thus, is tied to some very basic capacities. Its root in animal nature explains why "children and uneducated people laugh at the most trifling things" (WWR II 98) in that they are the ones most proximate to animals. In this light, the failings of parody, and of jest and buffoonery, are made clear. Their shortcomings are not due to an absence of incongruity but result from the manner in which incongruity is realized. If laughter comes through the limited of abstract thinking, and does not require mental exertion, then such laughter comes too easily. The preoccupation some may have with "the most trifling things" precludes the opportunity for more rewarding encounters with the ludicrous, those which are "too subtle and too elevated" for the general public (WWR II 101).

In his own way, Schopenhauer appears to be deriding those who find satisfaction in what we would now call "cheap laughs," jokes that require little intellect or effort on behalf of all those involved. Those who pander to audiences in this way "endeavour to make everything flat and vulgar" (WWR II 101). In this regard, it is clear that there is an evaluative dimension to Schopenhauer's ranking of jokes. There are "better" jokes, superior forms of the comic, which are to be preferred, simply because they are more reliant on what is proper to our intellect. Since laughter is a function of encountering the incongruity between reason and perception, it cannot reside in animal nature alone. Indeed, laughter is unavailable to animals. "Because of the lack of the faculty of reason, and thus of the lack of universal concepts, the animal is incapable of laughter" (WWR II 98). If laughter is exclusive to human beings, then the deficiencies of lower forms of comedy reflect a lack of intellect, a dearth of reason. In the end, Schopenhauer's hierarchal measure of the quality of humor conveys the weight he places on what is specifically human. Nietzsche, I hold, shares the view of laughter as uniquely human. He, however, adds the idea that it is definitive of human beings, and as such, can be the means by which we can measure, not only the adequacy of a joke, but a human life.[24]

Schopenhauer and Nietzsche on the Psychology of Laughter

All that Schopenhauer tells us about laughter and the ludicrous is offered as a replacement for failed attempts to give a "psychological explanation of laughter" (WWR II 91). This claim needs to be acknowledged because it entails that an analysis of laughter cannot be strictly epistemological or metaphysical.[25] Schopenhauer's goal, in part, is to show that other theorists are unable to explain why human beings laugh, and the fault lies in their flawed psychological models. If laughter is uniquely human, that is because of how our thinking operates. While any such account will include reference to what we can know or what we are, the phenomenon of laughter is not merely an aspect of our knowledge or a direct manifestation of our being. It instead is a consequence of how we think and process experiences. In this regard, explaining laughter is not a purely philosophical task. It is not a matter of logically deriving conclusions about laughter from the definitions of concepts alone. It is, rather, the formulation of generalizations based on observational insights, the endeavour to tell us what it means to laugh and why we laugh when we do. On this level, Schopenhauer supposes that he surpasses other thinkers who have attempted to provide a psychology of human laughter.

Schopenhauer's recourse to psychology proves relevant to my approach to Nietzsche since Nietzsche repeatedly gives himself the appellation of "psychologist." Indeed, the tactics he endorses for making sense of human activity are those of the psychologist. In *On the Genealogy of Morality* (GM), he addresses his readers as "us psychologists" (GM 99) and "we psychologists" (GM 101). In *Beyond Good and Evil* (BGE), he demarcates his undertaking as that of "a born, inevitable psychologist and unriddler of souls" (BGE 164). In keeping with the themes of this paper, it is telling that the task of the psychologist is equated with the solving of riddles, and that it entails riddles are of special interest to the genuine psychologist. In both BGE and GM, Nietzsche goes on to issue calls for this "true" psychologist. All prior attempts at psychology he thinks are "stuck in moral prejudices and fears" (BGE 23) and psychology is "shipwrecked" because "it had put itself under the dominance of morality" (BGE 46). This specific observation comes during a search for an answer to the question "what is noble?" Pity, as that which proves to be the undoing of the noble, is also that which can waylay the psychologist. In GM, the power of psychologists to do their jobs is restricted by the fact they "are probably still the victims" of the "moralized taste of the times" (GM 101). In both works, the risks presented to psychologists are associated with the fundamentals of ordinary morality. The psychologist "*needs* hardness and cheerfulness more than anyone else" to avoid the trap of pity (BGE 164). Nietzsche, in this respect, casts his project in terms of an exercise in "morphology," as a means for countering those psychologies that take their lead from morality. He contends the hold "moral prejudices and fears" have on psychology is due to it having "not ventured into the depths." The novelty of his work lies in its provision of "depth," which in itself is the arena of morphology. "To grasp psychology as morphology and the *doctrine of the development of the will to power,* which I have done—nobody has ever come close to this" (BGE 23).

Morphology, as the proper concern of psychology, is supposed to take us "into the depths." What, then, counts as the "depths" in this context? Christian Emden sheds light on this matter by noting that what Nietzsche "had in mind was a 'genuine physio-psychology' that is, a morphology of mental forms and intellectual configurations, which is already linked to the material world since it is embedded in the body" (Emden 2014: 40). A morphology, so conceived, exposes that which lies behind or beyond the "surface" of ordinary consciousness. Psychologists, operating within ordinary paradigms, make superficial appraisals of human intentions. They find, through their interpretation of human behavior, nothing more than what Nietzsche takes to be the re-instantiation of commonplace moral prejudices, including the disdain for life that flavors the morality of pity and inspires life-negating pessimism. A "new" psychology, as morphology, allows us to overcome existing methodologies and to craft a "physio-psychological" explanation of our behaviours.

Clearly the scope of Nietzsche's psychology is extensive. For our purposes, we need only comment on two phases of it. First is the focus on diagnostic aspects, the isolation of those factors said to give rise to dominant human dispositions. For example, the link between dread of suffering and hatred of life itself, which fuels Schopenhauer's pessimism, is said to be a symptom of fatigue and disappointment, resulting in "a secret instinct for annihilation" (BT 9). Second there is a curative dimension to Nietzschean psychology. The "sanctifying" of laughter I mentioned earlier is viewed as a means for surmounting pessimism. Nietzsche's recourse to morphology is intended to foster health, a "physio-psychological" strength, to counter the denigration of life. The final portion of the last sentence of the passage from Z, included at the end of the preface of 1886 of BT, makes this evident. It reads, "You higher men, *learn* to laugh, I beseech you!" (BT 12). The message here is simple. The remedies for the ills of humanity, its "physio-psychological" ailments, are to be found in laughter. In this regard, the positive role assigned to "sanctified" laughter pits it against the pessimism fostered by moralizing pity. Nietzsche, thus, promotes cheerfulness, a finding of joy in life in the face of suffering.

To this end, in Z, cheerfulness is conspicuous in the teachings of its main character. Zarathustra urges us to take joy even in that which strikes us as the most tragic, as that for which pity may appear the more appropriate response. There is no more direct indication of this point than when Zarathustra exclaims "Life is a well of joy" (Z III Tablets 16). This joy, however, is threatened by those unable to "drink" from the well, because "they have such ruined stomachs" and "their spirit is a ruined stomach: *it* recommends death!" (Z III Tablets 16). The alternatives are clear: either we find salvation in joy or we long for death. However, the joy we seek is not that which comes without suffering. As we learn later, "Pain says 'Refrain! Away, you pain!' But everything that suffers wants to live, to become ripe and joyful and longing" (Z IV Sleepwalker Song 8). The willingness to still seek joy and welcome life, despite the inevitability of pain and suffering, is definitive of cheerfulness, that which is fostered through proper laughter. My contention is this cheerfulness is facilitated and sustained through the mechanisms of irony and humor, in a mode consistent with Schopenhauer's description of them, and which are the chief dispositions informing his understanding of jokes.

2. Nietzsche, Riddles, and Human Betterment

The prescription for cheerfulness, which guides Nietzsche's work, is, as noted, meant to reflect the findings of morphology. Morphology acknowledges our psychological complexity in that we are not merely as we are manifest on the "surface." In GM, Nietzsche links this complexity to the cruelty and asceticism that have shaped us as a species. The human being is "an *interesting animal*" to the extent its "soul" came to "acquire *depth* in a higher sense" (GM 16). However, given that this depth is a product of what we have done to ourselves, it is a contingency. Our status as "interesting animals" is not a direct outcome of an enduring essence or a natural biological predisposition. As such, it is an achievement, something we have arrived at through our own collective doing. In the remainder of this chapter, I connect the complexity Nietzsche attributes to us to our capacity to concoct riddles. Given Nietzsche's preoccupation with psychology, it is safe to conclude he sees riddles as more than just amusements; they are testimonials in that they reveal something fundamental about our circumstance and they prove to be curative in that they enable us to laugh at our situation.

Riddles, as I mentioned earlier, satisfy the conditions Schopenhauer sets for jokes in that they are a function of incongruity. According to Archer Taylor, "the riddle in the strict sense compares an object to an entirely different object" (1943: 129). The juxtaposition operative in a riddle thus involves the coming together of fundamental incompatibilities, as, for example, in the case of things that cannot be grouped together under the same concept. Moreover, riddles issue an "expressed or implied demand for a solution" and as such qualify as "verbal puzzles" (1943: 129). Nietzsche clearly operates within these parameters.[26] He gives us problems that exploit incongruity and which "demand a solution." As we consider Nietzsche's riddles going forward, we need to keep in mind that they will, in the words of Taylor, "contain some discordant detail to put the hearer on his guard and suggest the correct answer" (1943: 129).

At the centre of my argument is Nietzsche's presentation of riddles in Z. In relation to the work as a whole, the invocation of riddles is a clue to understanding the nature of the text itself. This contention is grounded in a pivotal claim made by Zarathustra, namely "And how could I bear to be a human being if mankind were not also creator and solver of riddles and redeemer of accidents?" (Z II On Redemption 110). In keeping with Nietzsche's assertion that our psychological complexity is rooted in contingency, in "accidents," it is safe to argue that the creating and solving of riddles is definitive of what human beings have become. Our capacity to generate and understand riddles is an ability we have gained; it is not an expression or consequence of something innate and timeless. Moreover, the attempts we can make to psychologically "unriddle" ourselves are exercises in morphology. We can "unpack" ourselves and our condition in a fashion similar to the treatment of a riddle, but the riddle itself is one we give ourselves. We are not treating the human condition then as the extension of some grand "cosmic riddle" that needs to be fathomed.[27] We are, rather, approaching ourselves as a riddle we have generated, and which we can address. However, since a riddle presupposes incongruity, its solution is not dependent on the cancellation or erasure of contradiction. In a riddle we find a contradiction which must be contemplated. In this regard, Sarah Kofman's declaration that Z gives us a philosophy which "deletes all oppositions with one great burst of laughter" (1993: 5) seems somewhat misplaced since a riddle presupposes the persistence of incongruity. Such incongruity is not erased when the riddle is "solved"; instead, the incongruity is cemented and sustained through reflection on its meaning. A riddle is a unity of its own which depends on paradox, as irresolvable contradiction. The solution of the riddle acknowledges the contraries it combines but does so in a way that sustains tensions. To think these tensions disappear when a solution is reached is to deny of them the efficacy that makes the riddle possible in the first place.

On this reading, we can take Z, as a whole, to be a kind of riddle. Its subtitle—*A Book for All and None*—sounds very much like a riddle. It gives us as a sort of verbal puzzle to ponder, as it contains a conspicuous contradiction. On the surface, it makes no sense to claim a book is for everyone and for no one. As a particular, it belongs to the set of books. How can it then stand apart from the remainder of this set? What gives it a special status? Moreover, to claim it is simultaneously a book for all and for none yields incongruity, comparable to that which informs Schopenhauer's ideal of a joke. Nevertheless, as the text unfolds, we find a response to this riddle. Zarathustra's efforts to locate an audience for his teachings alert us to the perpetual possibility of his failure. In this way, it may be that the text remains a "book for none," but it is also a "book for all" given that it contains no intrinsic limits on whom may read it. On this level, we "solve" the riddle of the text by reading it in a manner receptive to its content. The task for the reader, then, is established. The reader must come to terms with the riddle of the text, which, in part, requires awareness of the riddles within the text.

In terms of my overview of Schopenhauer, we find as well, in Z, a case of irony.[28] Recall that according to Schopenhauer's definition, irony starts with seriousness and it is this seriousness that is disrupted by a joke. Furthermore, irony is meant to challenge the seriousness with which others hold their beliefs.[29] In this light, we can see the riddles in Nietzsche's text as willful attempts to disrupt the readers' seriousness, which, in broader terms, reflects the seriousness of their culture. Hence the targets of Nietzsche's parody are individuals granted an exalted place in the minds of his readers. Even though the tone of Z is undeniably "sombre," in that it mimics that of important thinkers such as Plato and Goethe, it is meant to give rise to laughter. Thus, the primacy of riddles in Nietzsche's work belies its apparent seriousness. Nowhere is this more visible than in the section entitled "On the Vision and the Riddle." There we are told of Zarathustra's encounter with a vexatious dwarf whom Zarathustra names "the spirit of gravity" (Z III Vision 2). The reference to gravity in this context is telling in that it denotes a kind of seriousness, a *gravitas*, that Zarathustra looks to overcome. It also is important to note the story of the encounter with the dwarf is directed toward Zarathustra's presumed audience, namely "bold searchers, researchers and whoever put to terrible seas with cunning sails" (Z III Vision 1). Nietzsche, in this respect, uses the tropes of an adventure tale to frame an intellectual puzzle. His audience is not expected to take to the seas. Instead, they need to reckon with a philosophical problem that is presented as a riddle. This point is made abundantly clear when he tells these "searchers and researchers" that they are "the riddle-drunk" (Z III Vision 1). Not surprisingly, the remainder of the story recounts how Zarathustra defeated "the spirit of gravity" through the interpretation of a riddle.

In a chapter of this length, I cannot provide an exhaustive treatment of this riddle. It is a puzzle regarding the status of the present in relation to the future and the past, and it raises questions beyond the scope of what can be covered here. I am citing it merely to reinforce points I have already made. It does, I hold, meet the requirements for a joke as established by Schopenhauer. It involves an incongruity in that Zarathustra must confront how a moment of time, namely the present, can stand in relation to the eternity of past and future. The present, as a particular unit of finite time, seems incompatible with the concept of eternity, yet it must in some way be part of it. As well, the eternities of past and future are incompatible with each other because they extend in opposite directions from the present. Such apparent contradictions trouble us in a manner consistent with what Schopenhauer outlines as the experience of the "ludicrous" in that we cannot reconcile fully reason and perception. Even though we grasp, conceptually, the idea of the eternal, we cannot make it completely congruent with our lived experience of temporality. In the end, if we see Zarathustra as gaining the upper hand in the "struggle" against the "spirit of gravity"[30] through the "solving of the riddle," then it succeeds in facilitating irony in the Schopenhauerian sense. It is a joke used as a deliberate challenge to the seriousness with which Zarathustra's "opponent" holds onto his beliefs.

Similar observations regarding Z can be garnered in respect to what Schopenhauer calls humor. Humor, as noted previously, is distinct from irony in that humor commences with the start of a joke. However, in the unfolding of the joke, there is the "return" of seriousness, the cancellation of irony. As such, Schopenhauer thinks humor allows us to recognize the significance of those things about which we make jokes. Unlike buffoonery or jest, humor speaks to the properly "elevated" concerns of the human being. In relation to Z, there is no better example of humor than the Fourth Part. In this concluding section of the text, added by Nietzsche several years after the completion of the first three parts, there is ample evidence of Nietzsche finding humor in Zarathustra's situation. Even though there are a variety of ways of reading this final section, and its overarching intent can be debated,[31] it is clear Nietzsche is having fun at his own expense. He is mocking some of the most serious aspects of his own project, primarily his apparent search for followers.[32] A wonderful example of this foray into humor is the section entitled "*The Ass Festival*." There Zarathustra is seen scolding his "followers," the "higher men," who think they have best understood his teachings. They have made Zarathustra into an object of worship and as a result have obscured his lessons on cheerfulness. "'They've all gone *pious* again, there are *praying*, they're mad'—he said and he was amazed beyond measure" (Z IV Awakening 2). However, as Zarathustra learns of their motives, he finds, within their explanations, reasons for supposing that they have not truly lost touch with his summoning of cheerfulness. "And once again Zarathustra began to speak. 'Oh my new friends, he said—you strange, you higher men, how well I like you now—since you have become gay again!'" (Z IV Festival 3). The twist, in the end, is that these "higher men" had "worshipped" a jackass who represented Zarathustra in their festival. Zarathustra is not dismayed by their choice of a jackass; rather, he is upset by their dispositions, their willingness to worship him. His realization that there is a playfulness underlying their "solemn" festival allows him to properly appreciate what they have done.

The "ass festival" is, in itself, a joke in the Schopenhauerian sense. It is a case of incongruity in that it treats a lowly animal as deserving of divine reverence. The jackass, as a particular, does not fit in the set of beings properly considered "holy." In this regard, Nietzsche uses a joke as a way of undoing his own seriousness. He parodies his own text, to ensure that his dedication to cheerfulness does not wane. However, this lampooning is meant to underscore the seriousness of his thought and the significance of his text. Thus, as the book draws to a conclusion, Zarathustra reflects on his teachings and how they have been received. At one point, after having "laughed scornfully at his own words," he "became immersed in himself." This reflection eventually gives rise to his final assessment of his circumstance. He states, "My suffering and my pity— what do they matter! Do I strive for *happiness*? I strive for my *work*!' (Z IV Sign). The point is that Nietzsche does not equate the "success" of Z with simple happiness; the cheerfulness of which he speaks is not meant to be the result of pleasure and satisfaction devoid of suffering. Zarathustra thus exemplifies what Nietzsche sees as the curative power of laughter, but it is a laughter that must return us to seriousness, namely through the recognition of the unavoidable suffering that defines our lives.

In connection to Schopenhauer's view of the comic, Nietzsche's text serves as a clear example of humor, because it is a case of a joke giving way to seriousness and it also is a case of making fun of oneself, of highlighting the "subjective" through the deliberate upsetting of one's own pretenses. Nevertheless, the fact that Zarathustra can laugh at himself does not mitigate the seriousness of his work. Laughter, in this regard, is to be won through effort and dedication.[33] It does not come easy or depend on individual happiness. It thus counts as a "serious" achievement. If Zarathustra's challenge is to teach us to laugh properly, then we cannot rest content with the belief that laughter is a function of our basic dispositions alone. We need to learn to laugh properly and at the right things. Schopenhauer can only take us partway down this path. He recognizes that we laugh best when we laugh at clever jokes, those which correctly utilize intellect. For Nietzsche, there must be more to laughter; it must enable the overcoming of life-denying pessimism and must reflect a genuinely cheerful attitude toward life. As such, it requires struggle, very much like how Zarathustra strives to vanquish the "spirit of gravity." In this regard, Nietzsche assigns a redemptive power to laughter which is unavailable within Schopenhauer's philosophy. Proper laughter, for Nietzsche, is transformative in that it enables us to be more than pessimists. He thinks such laughter requires that we accept the seriousness of our suffering and struggle yet find within all this seriousness the means for joyfully embracing life.

Conclusion

In this chapter I have introduced Nietzsche's riddles and his version of the comic in relation to Schopenhauer's work on the "ludicrous." At the heart of Schopenhauer's incongruity theory is the idea of contradiction. A joke, for Schopenhauer, counts as a specimen of the ludicrous to the extent that it plays with conspicuous incompatibilities. This aspect, I have claimed, carries over into Nietzsche's use of riddles in Z. On my reading, these philosophers think that laughter depends on incongruity and that human beings are creatures defined by the capacity to laugh at such contradictions. Indeed, for both, it is a matter of finding a psychological dimension within laughter that not only reveals truths about us but also allows for a ranking of laughter in terms of what is more "noble," more proper to the human being. However, it seems Nietzsche takes this position to the extreme. His view is consistent with Schopenhauer's contention that human beings are the only beings capable of laughter and that one should only laugh at that which is worthwhile, yet Nietzsche turns these insights into a kind of overarching imperative. Since laughter is specific to us, it should be made definitive of us. In this regard, his work exceeds Schopenhauer's when it comes to setting the domain of laughter, and this aspect, as a prescription for cheerfulness, serves as a rejoinder to Schopenhauer's pessimism. The "sanctifying" of laughter in Z depends on a number of complex psychological maneuvers, made evident through Nietzsche's exercises in morphology. To laugh in a fashion appropriate to our circumstance is difficult, yet it opens up the possibility for a rewarding response to our plight. In riddles, we find the means for realizing what it means to be human, but the full force of that realization depends on recognizing how funny things actually are. In the end, it is a matter of writing good jokes.

Notes

1. See the second chapter of Gilman (1976), and Lippitt (1992).
2. In answer to his own question "What, after all, did Schopenhauer think about tragedy?," Nietzsche asserts that Schopenhauer sees it in terms of a "whole philosophy of resignation" (BT 10). So, in this light, Nietzsche thinks his book suffers because its reliance on Schopenhauer betrays the Greek vision of the tragic which it is meant to illuminate. For more on Nietzsche's criticism of Schopenhauer's approach to tragedy, see Nussbaum (1999).

3. If we take Nietzsche at his word, his later philosophy should be rid of conspicuous reliance on Schopenhauer. However, as James Porter suggests, "Nietzsche's emancipation" from "Schopenhauer can be found overstated in Nietzsche himself" (2000: 25). Similar concerns are raised by Janaway (2003).
4. In this context, Zarathustra is addressing the "higher men," those most suited for his teachings. The status of the higher men in relation to laughter will be discussed later in this paper.
5. This point is underscored in the *Preface* to the second edition of *The Gay Science* (GS). There Nietzsche writes, "*Incipit Tragoedia*, we read at the end of this suspiciously innocent book. Beware something utterly wicked and mischievous is being announced here: *incipit parodia*, no doubt" (GS 4). On this front, see Kress (2008) for an overview of *GS*, which attributes to it some of the same features I will highlight in respect to Z. This passage also will prove relevant later in this paper in connection to the discussion of Z as parody.
6. Hay offers a reading of Nietzsche's 1886 preface which emphasizes the connections between BT and Z to "show that Nietzsche's analysis of tragedy cannot be understood as a *tragic* or a pessimistic interpretation, but as one that emerges from the experience of the *comic*" (2011: 243, Hay's italics). Hatab (2008) makes a similar move when he stresses how important the figure of the satyr in BT is for Nietzsche's overarching ideal of the "tragicomic."
7. Rampley provides an overview of where Nietzsche and Schopenhauer differ in terms of the significance of comedy. His point is that Nietzsche finds a value in comedy which is unavailable to Schopenhauer due to his pessimism. My position is compatible with this interpretation. The commonality I find between Schopenhauer and Nietzsche is on the level of the "devices" used to generate laughter, but I agree with Rampley that they differ in terms of what they take to be the overall lessons of laughter (2000: 103–8).
8. Swift (1995) connects Nietzsche's reliance on incongruity theory to Schopenhauer and Kant. Weeks (2004), as well, situates Nietzsche's view of laughter in a discussion of Kant and Schopenhauer. See Lewis (2005) for a full overview of Schopenhauer's incongruity theory.
9. Nicholas Pappas contends that "Nietzsche's humour does not take the form of outright jokes" and "it might better to speak of *gags* like the ones that a stand-up comic would tell" (2005: 54). However, when Pappas gives an example of a gag, it very much sounds like an example of what I, following Schopenhauer, call a joke. Pappas cites a Groucho Marx quip: "Outside of a dog a book is man's best friend. Inside of a dog, it is too dark to read" (2005: 54). This is a clear example of an incongruity, so whether we call it a "joke" or a "gag" does not matter to my position.
10. See Lewis (2005) for more on the psychological dimension of Schopenhauer's analysis of laughter.
11. In typical Schopenauerian fashion, he begrudgingly gives examples even though, in Volume I, he observes it "is so simple and easy to understand" what he is saying that it does not need them (WWR I 59). In the supplements constituting Volume II, he volunteers examples "to come to the aid of the mental inertness of those readers who always prefer to remain in a passive state" (WWR II 92).
12. Lewis (2005), Weeks (2004), and Gunter (1968) raise questions regarding the plausibility of Schopenhauer's position.
13. Here I disagree with Higgins's assessment of Z. She remarks, "*Zarathustra*, often ironic in its context …, nonetheless reflects in its tone the almost deadly seriousness with which Nietzsche approached questions of suffering and the nature of human life"

(2010: 9). In this context, Lippitt's differentiation of "seriousness" and "solemnity" proves valuable. He contends that "solemnity … is a mood fundamentally at odds with the mood appropriate to laughter" but seriousness, in contrast, "represents an overall attitude toward something … which is perfectly compatible with laughter" (1999: 110).

14. In Laurence Lampert we find the designation of Nietzschean jokes as requiring both "gravity" and "levity." This way of describing Nietzsche's attempts at humor I think is consistent with the point I am making here (1999: 75). Note, as well, the importance of the idea of "gravity" for Nietzsche, which will resurface in my subsequent discussion of Zarathustra's dealings with the "spirit of gravity."
15. In *Ecce Homo*, Nietzsche says explicitly of the character Zarathustra that "this most affirmative of all spirits contradicts with every word he speaks; all oppositions are combined into a new unity with in him" (EH Books Zarathustra 6).
16. Lewis makes this aspect of Schopenhauer's analysis an explicit feature of his definition of laughter (2005: 37).
17. Nietzsche seems to propose this interpretation in *Ecce Homo* when he declares that Zarathustra embodies "*the concept of Dionysus himself*" (EH Books Zarathustra 6). So he seems, at least on this level, to welcome the "return" of something associated with the ancient world.
18. In "On the Uses and Disadvantages of History for Life," Nietzsche warns against a purely "antiquarian" approach to history that "no longer conserves life but mummifies it" (UM 75).
19. Robert Gooding-Williams (2001) goes as far as to frame Zarathustra as a "modernist" narrative. See especially the chapter "Introduction to Zarathustra's Dionysian Modernism."
20. As Michael Ure rightly points out, "Schopenhauer maintains that the comic genres express the way the interest of the species dupes individuals into believing they are pursuing their own interests when in fact they are realizing the species' interests to their own detriment" (2013: 29–30). Schopenhauer thus converts comedy into a supplement for tragedy. Comedy merely reminds us of the "pointlessness" of our existence and in this regard, Schopenhauer renders comedy redundant. It has no higher function than reinforcing pessimism. In Nietzsche, as I am arguing, we find a connection between comedy and the affirmation of life, contra Schopenhauer.
21. I agree with Seung's general assessment of Z but do not think Nietzsche is bound by a specific etymological rendering of the term "parody." Seung falls back on the origins of "this word as derived from the parody mass of the Renaissance, a solemn and reverent imitation of the Roman Catholic Mass" (2006: xv). For Seung, this rendering of the meaning of the word is meant to forestall the modern reduction of parody to "satire and derision." I contend that Nietzsche is more than happy to embrace this modern conception of parody, as the laughter inspired by Zarathustra comes through mockery of the "solemn and reverent" or as we found in my overview of Schopenhauer, that irony or humor must come at the expense of someone. There must be the upsetting of "seriousness" so that we can laugh eventually at that which is most serious, namely our circumstance as human beings. As for Nietzsche's reliance on satire, Douglas Burnham and Martin Jesinghausen (2010: 32-4) give a nice overview of the possible inspirations for Nietzsche's use of satire in Z.
22. Gooding-Williams thinks that Nietzsche also targets the Bible and Plato's *Timaeus* (2001: 50–61). Also, what More says about Nietzschean satire in *Ecce Homo* applies

equally to Z: "Many satires involve a protagonist who makes a hazardous journey to fantastical lands" (2014: 49–50).

23. Lewis observes that Schopenhauer is decidedly narrow in his conception of humor and notes, "Schopenhauer wishes to restrict the scope of humor and comedy to forms of art that have an underlying serious intent. But it is plausible to think that most, if not all, jokes and witticisms play a similar role in everyday life of keeping us 'in a good mood.'" As a result, Schopenhauer's analysis does nothing to address pessimism, and in fact "adds a diabolical dimension to it in that it closes off in advance the possibility of laughter which renders us cheerful" (2005: 50).

24. Lampert identifies a category of Nietzschean joke that he refers to as "human jokes." He holds these "are all rooted in our ways, the ways of our kind and have fun with us as the laughable species" (1999: 65). On my reading our ability to laugh at ourselves indicates how human we actually are.

25. For more on the metaphysics underlying Schopenhauer's view of laughter, see Lewis (2005: 42–6).

26. It is possible to contend that Nietzsche utilizes what Malcolm Davies identifies as "existential riddles" that derive from "a primeval pattern in folk-tale," which he believes can be linked to "Greek Pessimism." On this level, finds within existential riddles an awareness of "an utterly basic perception" of "a fundamental shared by and basic to all human beings, the states of existence and non-existence" (2015: 455).

27. The pronouncement of the "death of God" in GS ends the search for some overarching meaning for existence. As per the opening sections of Book Three that anticipate this declaration, we are to think of "the world" as "for all eternity chaos, not in the sense of a lack of necessity but of a lack of order, organization, form, beauty, wisdom and whatever else our aesthetic anthropomorphisms are called" (GS 109).

28. Nietzsche's relationship with irony is complicated and somewhat ambivalent, so it is difficult to claim he explicitly designates his work as ironic. My point is more that what he does in Z qualifies as ironic. Ernst Behler offers an explanation for this hesitancy: "Nietzsche usually avoided the term 'irony,' which for his tastes had too much romanticism in it and preferred the classical notion of dissimulation which he translated as 'mask'" (1998: 17). Despite his misgivings regarding the term itself, it is still reasonable to propose that Nietzsche is being ironic in Z.

29. In *Human, All Too Human* (HH), Nietzsche asserts that irony's "objective is humiliation, making ashamed," and it should only be used as "a pedagogic tool" by which a teacher "awakens good resolutions" in the pupil. Its over use, however, "spoils the character to which it gradually lends the quality of a malicious and jeering superiority" (HH 146–7). It is safe to take this as a hint as to what Nietzsche eventually produces in Z, namely a controlled and careful use of irony intended to educate the reader, as if they were a "pupil." Irony then is a "tool," a means to an end and not an end in itself.

30. It is common to point out that the overcoming of the "spirit of gravity" is not immediate. Hence Zarathustra's solution to the riddle must be worked out in detail before he comes to grasp his victory. See Lampert (1986: 160–81), or Rosen (1995: 177–89).

31. For more on questions surrounding this section of the text, see Higgins (2010: 131–52); Loeb (2010: 85–118), and Lampert (1986: 287–311).

32. The Fourth and Final Part begins with Zarathustra thinking he needs to cease to be a hermit of sorts and find a human audience because he is "a raiser, a cultivator and a taskmaster" (Z IV Sacrifice).
33. It could be argued that such labor is necessary when one is the "creator and solver" of riddles.

References

Behler, Ernst (1998), "Nietzsche's Conception of Irony," in *Nietzsche, Philosophy and the Arts*, Salim Kemal, ed. Ivan Gaskell and Daniel W. Conway, 1–35, Cambridge: Cambridge University Press.

Burnham, Douglas, and Martin Jesinghausen (2010), *Nietzsche's Thus Spoke Zarathustra*, Indianapolis: University of Indiana Press.

Davies, Malcolm (2015), "'All' and 'Nothing': Existential Riddles and Cosmic Pessimism in Ancient Greek Literature and Shakespeare," *Gaia* 18: 455–69.

Emden, Christian J. (2014), *Nietzsche's Naturalism: Philosophy and the Life Sciences in the Nineteenth Century*, Cambridge: Cambridge University Press.

Gilman, Sander L. (1976), *Nietzschean Parody: An Introduction to Reading Nietzsche*, Aurora, CO: The Davies Group.

Gooding-Williams, Robert (2001), *Zarathustra's Dionysian Modernism*, Stanford, California: Stanford University Press.

Gunter, Peter A. (1968), "Nietzschean Laughter," *The Sewanee Review* 76 (3): 493–506.

Hatab, Lawrence J. (1988), "Laughter in Nietzsche's Thought: A Philosophical Tragicomedy," *International Studies in Philosophy* 20 (2): 67–79.

Hatab, Lawrence J. (2008), "To Laugh Out of the Whole Truth: Nietzsche as Tragicomic Satyr," in *Reading Nietzsche at the Margins*, ed. Steven V. Hicks and Alan Rosenberg, 73–85, West Lafayette, IN: Purdue University Press.

Hay, Katia (2011), "Zarathustra's Laughter or the *Birth of Tragedy* from the Experience of the Comic," in *Nietzsche on Instinct and Language*, ed. Joao Constancio and Maria Joao Mayer Branco, 243–58, Berlin: De Gruyter.

Higgins, Kathleen (2010), *Nietzsche's Zarathustra*, Plymouth, UK: Lexington Books.

Janaway, Christopher (2003), "Schopenhauer as Nietzsche's Educator," in *Nietzsche and the German Tradition*, ed. Nicholas Martin, 155–85, Bern: Peter Lang.

Kofman, Sarah (1993), *Nietzsche and Metaphor*, trans. Duncan Large, Stanford: Stanford University Press.

Kress, John (2008), "The Alliance of Laughter and Wisdom: Nietzsche's Gay Science," *Soundings: An Interdisciplinary Journal* 91 (1): 109–32.

Lampert, Laurence (1986), *Nietzsche's Teaching: An Interpretation of Thus Spoke Zarathustra*, New Haven, CT: Yale University Press.

Lampert, Laurence (1999), "Nietzsche's Best Jokes," in *Nietzsche's Futures*, ed. John Lippitt, 82–98, London: Macmillan Books.

Lewis, Peter B. (2005), "Schopenhauer's Laughter," *The Monist* 88 (1): 36–51.

Lippitt, John (1992), "Nietzsche, Zarathustra and the Status of Laughter," *British Journal of Aesthetics* 32 (1): 39–49.

Lippitt, John (1999), "Laughter: A Tool in Moral Perfectionism?," in *Nietzsche's Futures*, ed. John Lippitt, 99–125, London: Macmillan Books.

Loeb, Paul S. (2010), *The Death of Nietzsche's Zarathustra*, Cambridge: Cambridge University Press.

More, Nicholas D. (2014), *Nietzsche's Last Laugh: Ecce Homo as Satire*, Cambridge: Cambridge University Press.

Nussbaum, Martha (1999), "Nietzsche, Schopenhauer and Dionysus," in *The Cambridge Companion to Schopenhauer*, 344–74, Cambridge: Cambridge University Press.

Pappas, Nickolas (2005), "Morality Gags," *The Monist* 88 (1): 52–71.

Porter, James (2000), *The Invention of Dionysus: An Essay on The Birth of Tragedy*, Stanford: Stanford University Press.

Rampley, Matthew (2000), *Nietzsche, Aesthetics and Modernity*, Cambridge: Cambridge University Press.

Rosen, Stanley (1995), *The Mask of Enlightenment: Nietzsche's Zarathustra*, Cambridge: Cambridge University Press.

Schopenhauer, Arthur (1958), *The World as Will and Representation*, vol. I (WWR I), trans. E. F. J Payne, New York: Dover Publications.

Schopenhauer, Arthur (1958), *The World as Will and Representation*, vol. II (WWR II), trans. E. F. J Payne, New York: Dover Publications.

Seung, T. K. (2006), *Goethe, Nietzsche and Wagner: Their Spinozan Epics of Love and Power*, Oxford: Lexington Books.

Swift, Paul (1995), "In-Jestion: Intestinal Laughter in Kant and Nietzsche," *International Studies in Philosophy XXVII* (1): 97–103.

Taylor, Archer (1943), "The Riddle," *California Folklore Quarterly* 2: 129–47.

Ure, Michael (2013), "Nietzsche's Schadenfreude," *Journal of Nietzsche Studies* 44 (1): 25–48.

Weeks, Mark (2004), "Nietzsche and the Birth of 'Super-Laughter,'" *Journal of Nietzsche Studies* 27: 1–17.

8

Subversive Playfulness in Nietzsche and Dada

Philip Mills

In the second decade of the twentieth century, visual artists inspired by Nietzsche founded an influential movement oriented against the self-destructive war convulsing Europe and the world. Working just a decade-and-a-half after Nietzsche's death, these aesthetic provocateurs—labeling their movement "Dada" and themselves "Dadaists" in a humorous acknowledgment of the absurdity and ultimate meaninglessness of existence—employed Nietzsche's ideas to highlight the tragicomic nature of modern European life. Their aesthetic adoption of Nietzsche's critique of language to protest the decadence of their age reconceived art and influenced its course over the twentieth century.[1]

How did the Dadaists take up the challenges Nietzsche expected his free spirits to pose to the decadent values of their age, particularly in their adoption of his critique of language, and how were those challenges radically life-affirming? I begin this chapter by offering an overview of Nietzsche's influence on key figures of Dadaism, showing how the philosopher served as a major inspiration to the latter's creative production. In the second section I focus on critical aspects of these influences, particularly the Dadaist's criticism of language. I set this assessment in the broader context of the war Dada arose in response to, as well as the critical attitude toward conventional language and the dissipative tradition they took it to represent, a stance they shared with Nietzsche. In the third section I show how the Dadaists' efforts to undermine language constituted an initial step toward the construction of a new one. This novel language would bring poets and philosophers into relation with the task of destruction through subversive playfulness. Acting on Nietzsche's advocacy of laughter, parody, and play, the Dadaists interpreted the dichotomy between creation and destruction in terms of mischievous humor. Their provocative artworks gave expression to this insight as an aesthetic means of combating Europe's decadence and nihilism.

1. Dada: Playing Nietzsche

In *Dada Siegt! Ein Bilanz des Dadaismus*, Richard Huelsenbeck acknowledges the importance of Nietzsche in the intellectual and artistic development of the Dadaists:

> As strange as this might sound, we had all read Nietzsche, including the foreigners, and above all Ball whose entire life problem revolved around the tension between

the brutal naivety of Nietzsche's ideal human and a Catholic-sentimental moral theology which he tried to escape. (1920: 12)[2]

This influence has been explored from various perspectives—artistic, cultural, and political, respectively. For instance, Christine Battersby (2013) considers the buffoon imagery of Dada as being influenced by Nietzsche's *Ecce Homo* (EH), Tim J. Berard (1999) relates the Dadaists' conception of culture to Nietzsche's own, and Seth Taylor (1990) retraces Nietzsche's political influence on German avant-garde movements, including Dada. These scholars have provided perspectives highlighting themes and ideas that can be found both in Nietzsche and the Dadaists. Another crucial connection relies on the parodic dimension of some of Nietzsche's texts—especially EH—that the Dadaists took a step further. Two intertwined aspects of Dada's artistic gesture are essential for comprehending Nietzsche's influence on the movement: first, the Dadaists appropriated many of Nietzsche's philosophical ideas, as my discussion of Tristan Tzara's *Dada Manifesto* will illustrate; second, these Nietzsche's philosophical ideas were incorporated into their artistic gesture, as exemplified by Hugo Ball's veritable impersonation of him.

Tzara's 1918 *Dada Manifesto* contains numerous elements indicating Nietzsche's influence, but three intertwined ones are especially significant to this inquiry: perspectivism, the rejection of the absolute, and the embrace of chaos. Perspectivism appears in Tzara's definition of philosophy:

> Philosophy is the question: from which angle to start looking at life, god, ideas, or anything else. Everything we look at is false. I don't think the relative result is any more important than the choice of patisserie or cherries for dessert. The way of looking quickly at the opposite side of things, in order to impose one's opinion indirectly, is called dialectic, in other words, heads I win and tails you lose, dressed up to look scholarly. (Danchev 2011: 140)

Tzara defines philosophy as a matter of point of view: the central question is how to look at things. However, he does not take any interest at all in the results to which a perspective can lead: insofar as everything is relative in the sense that it depends on the way one looks at it and as "everything we look at is false," it is impossible to judge which point of view is better; there is no best point of view. It is only a matter of choice and Tzara's gastronomic reference seems to indicate that it is a matter of taste. In other words, Tzara reenacts Nietzsche's famous conclusion to *Beyond Good and Evil* (BGE 22): "And given that he too is just interpreting—and you'll be eager to raise that objection, won't you?—then, all the better." Much has been said about this "all the better," and Tzara pushes the provocation one step further by relating it to a choice of dessert.

This shift from a metaphysical or epistemological ground to a choice of dessert underscores the Dadaists' efforts to employ subversive playfulness to undermine traditional categories of thought. This playfulness is further embraced in the idea that philosophy *qua* perspectivism becomes a game of "heads I win and tails you lose."

If most of what is called "true" is context dependent and perspectively determined, or relative, there can be no absolute, transcendent truth:

There is no ultimate Truth. Dialectics is an amusing machine that leads us (in banal fashion) to the opinions which we would have held in any case. Do people really think that, by the meticulous subtlety of logic, they have demonstrated the truth and established the accuracy of their opinions? Even if logic were confirmed by the senses it would still be an organic disease. (Danchev 2011: 141)

By denying the existence of any "ultimate truth" and criticizing dialectics as an "amusing machine," Tzara continues the abovementioned playful subversion exemplified by the "heads and tails" view. However, he extends this criticism to logic, which he characterizes as an "organic disease." Tzara pursues Nietzsche's critiques of logic and truth as a matter of evaluation—that is, Nietzsche criticizes the value we attribute to logic and truth rather than logic and truth themselves—by playing with this evaluation, by ridiculing logic and truth, by making them part of the game of dialectics, which is just emptiness "dressed up to look scholarly."

This rejection of dialectics brings Tzara to a two-step appreciation of chaos. First, he shares with Nietzsche his rejection of systems: "I am against systems; the most acceptable system is that of having on principle none" (Danchev 2011: 141). Once again, Tzara is ridiculing the notion of system by bringing it to a form of playful self-contradiction. This quote from his *Manifesto* reminds us of Nietzsche's aphorism in *Twilight of the Idols* (TI): "I mistrust all systematists and avoid them. The will to system is a lack of integrity" (TI Arrows 26). Chaos cannot be ordered through systematicity. If we relate it to Nietzsche, we can see that this critique of system also has a moral dimension: the mistrust toward systematists is rooted in their "lack of integrity."

Second, this rejection of systematicity brings Tzara to acknowledge the chaos that constitutes the human and to criticize two historical attempts to put order into this chaos:

How can one expect to put order into the chaos that constitutes that infinite and shapeless variation: man? The principle: "love thy neighbour" is a hypocrisy. "Know thyself" is utopian but more acceptable, for it embraces wickedness. No pity. After the carnage we still retain the hope of a purified mankind. (Danchev 2011: 138)

Insofar as the human is an infinite and shapeless variation, there is no possibility to put order into the chaos. He thus criticizes the Christian religion with its charity principle ("Love thy neighbour") and the Socratic philosophical ideal of self-knowledge ("Know thyself") as two attempts to establish such an order. The charity principle aims at establishing order among humans and the Socratic ideal aims at fostering order within oneself.

These criticisms reveal a Nietzschean vein as Christianity and Socrates are main targets for Nietzsche's attacks. The idea of chaos reminds us of Nietzsche's substitution of God by chaos in rewriting Spinoza's proposition: "*Chaos sive Natura.*" However, and like with Nietzsche, Tzara does not only remain at the critical level but also suggests that this critique has a positive outcome, that there is something better to build on the ruins of the old culture, a "better humanity to come," which might relate to Nietzsche's idea of the *Übermensch*. Although this notion is subject to many interpretations and the "positive" dimension of Nietzsche's philosophy is hard to precisely locate, we will see that this constructive aspect as expressed in his discussion of creation is best understood in relation to language: therein lies the possibility to create new words and meanings which, in turn, create new values.

The notion of value is of central importance for Nietzsche and usually understood within the framework of his philosophical task of "revaluation of all values," a task that Ball precisely aims to pursue in his work. Ball pushes Tzara's appropriation of Nietzsche further by impersonating Nietzsche in a short text on Kandinsky from 1917:

> God is dead. A world has collapsed. I am dynamite. World history breaks into two parts. There is a time before me. And a time after me. Religion, science, morality—phenomena that have arisen from the anxiety of primitive people. ... There is no more perspective in the moral world. Up is down, down is up. Revaluation of all values has taken place.[3] (Ball 1917)

In this short paragraph, perspectivism and the acknowledgement of chaos that we have seen in Tzara find a new expression, one which uses the Nietzschean term of revaluation of all values. However, Ball does not only mention themes from Nietzsche's philosophy such as the death of God or the revaluation of values, he also adopts the same posture—"I am dynamite"—and the same critical stance toward the culture of his times: religion, science, and morality. Nietzsche indeed states "I am dynamite" in various 1888 letters[4] and in EH Destiny 1 where he further distinguishes this "explosive" philosophical stance from what he perceives to be a negative academic stance:

> How I understand the philosopher, as a fearful explosive material from which everything is in danger, how I remove my concept "philosopher" miles away from a concept which includes in it even a Kant, not to speak of the academic "ruminants" and other professors of philosophy. (EH Books UM 3)

Nietzsche compares two philosophical attitudes that represent two concepts of the philosopher: the academic philosopher is a ruminant in the negative sense that she only chews on old ideas,[5] whereas Nietzsche's concept of the genuine philosopher endangers everything. By comparing the authentic philosopher to an explosive, Nietzsche indicates that the philosopher must not stay distant from the world but must have an impact on it. Correlatively to the endangering of everything, the philosopher must take risks: as an explosive, she puts her life at stake to have an impact.

Ball's text is almost a parody or pastiche of Nietzsche; Ball plays to be Nietzsche and, by doing so, shows an ambivalent relation to him. On the one hand, there is admiration, insofar as Nietzsche pointed out elements that are central to Ball's critique of culture; on the other hand, there is criticism in the allegation that Nietzsche's philosophy is just an attitude that lacks concrete effects. It is one thing to say, "I am dynamite"; it is another to really be dynamite. In his imitation of Nietzsche, Ball suggests that he is going a step further than Nietzsche, that he is pursuing his project, and this can be seen in the last sentence of the paragraph: "Revaluation of all values has taken place." Here lies an essential difference between Ball and Nietzsche: whereas Nietzsche attributes the task of revaluating values to the free spirits, Ball considers it to have already taken place. Ball's impersonation of Nietzsche can therefore be understood as if Ball was Nietzsche's successor, as if he had to deal with the situation which arose from the free spirits' revaluation of values. In that sense, the Dadaists would take up the task Nietzsche attributes to the philosopher of the future; they not only would be Nietzsche's heirs but also would actualize Nietzsche's philosophy.

2. From Destruction to Subversive Creation

"We had lost confidence in our 'culture,'" writes Marcel Janco, explaining the feeling that gave rise to Dada in a retrospective text from 1966 (Lippard 1971: 36). In it he distinguishes between two "speeds" of Dada: a destructive and a constructive one. This loss of confidence is understandable when we consider that Dada was born at the height of the First World War, a slaughter that represented the failure of the reigning system of values. Not all of Europe shared the identical values, of course, but the major-power security alliances, combined with the growing nationalist spirit that animated European peoples, led to the war. Despite their national differences, the Dadaists were united in their opposition to this toxic nationalist spirit. Janco continues, "Everything had to be demolished. We would begin again after the *tabula rasa*. At the Cabaret Voltaire we began by shocking the bourgeois, demolishing his idea of art, attacking common sense, public opinion, education institutions, museums, good taste, in short the whole prevailing order" (Lippard 1971: 36). Interestingly, the Dadaist's response to the actual war is coined in a vocabulary of destruction. Through this violent response, the Dadaists play the role of Nietzsche's free spirits who are "a living declaration of war" (AC 13). For the Dadaists, the only way to prevent the ongoing slaughter from repeating itself is to destroy the foundations upon which it arose and transform the conditions that led divisive nationalisms to thrive. However, this bellicose vocabulary is only one part of Nietzsche's rhetorical strategy, as he also suggests that the philosopher is a physician.

The metaphor of the artist as a warrior is therefore balanced in Nietzsche's works by the metaphor of the philosopher as a physician who treats sicknesses.[6] To diagnose this sickness (decadence), the physician must observe its symptoms, one of which, according to Nietzsche, is the lack of great art. While focusing on Greek tragedy, Nietzsche's thought in *The Birth of Tragedy* (BT) extends to his contemporary concerns as he believes that the study of the birth and death of tragedy can be of use for a rebirth of tragedy, and that such a rebirth is necessary to cure the nihilism and pessimism of his modern world. Similarly, in response to the ongoing massacre in the countries surrounding Switzerland, the Dadaists turn to art. Jean Arp explains,

> In Zurich in 1915 [*sic*], losing interest in the slaughterhouses of the world war, we turned to the Fine Arts. While the thunder of the batteries rumbled in the distance, we pasted, we recited, we versified, we sang with all our soul. We searched for an

elementary art that would, we thought, save mankind from the furious folly of these times. (Lippard 1971: 23–24)

The Dadaists, akin to the Nietzschean physician, attempt to save humanity from repeating the bloodshed. As we will see, it is by cheerfully playing with the absurdity of their surrounding world that the Dadaists aims to cure nihilism.

The decline of Greek tragedy represents for Nietzsche the decline of the whole Greek way of life. Nietzsche thus turns an aesthetic question into an existential one:

> The reader will have guessed at which point I had placed the great question mark over the value of existence. Is pessimism necessarily a sign of decline, decay, malformation, of tired and debilitated instincts—as was the case amongst the Indians and appears to be the case amongst us "modern men" and Europeans? Is there a pessimism of *strength*? (BT Attempt 1)

To study the value of existence in his times, Nietzsche returns to the Greeks and their view of life, which seems quite contrary to that of "modern men and Europeans." For Nietzsche, whereas "modern men" consider pessimism as a sign of decline, the Greeks did not. This shift in evaluation reveals the central question of value: must the value given to pessimism necessarily be a negative one? Is pessimism really a sign of decline? Or, to the contrary, isn't our negative attitude toward pessimism—that is, our inability to deal with it constructively—a symptom of decline? Nietzsche links the latter and the decline of European culture to the Greeks' turn to optimism and logic. By turning to logic and reason as their only guides—therefore abandoning the whole Dionysian dimension—the Greeks and the tradition that followed was weakening and fostered decadence. By extension, our modern culture, which inherited this ethos, weakens life rather than enhancing it.

This critique of logic and its classification is, as we have seen, a strong element of Tzara's *Dada Manifesto*. Because of this rejection of truth and logic, Tzara rejects theory as a unifying force: "And so Dada was born of a need for independence, of a distrust towards unity. Those who are with us preserve their freedom. We recognize no theory" (Danchev 2011: 138). As with Janco quoted above, Tzara also considers that

> there is a great negative work of destruction to be accomplished. We must sweep and clean. Affirm the cleanliness of the individual after the state of madness, aggressive complete madness of a world abandoned to the hands of bandits, who rend one another and destroy the centuries. Without aim or design, without organization: indomitable madness, decomposition. Those who are strong in words or force will survive, for they are quick in defence, the agility of limbs and sentiments flames on their faceted flanks. (Danchev 2011: 143)

In Nietzschean terms, Tzara aims at a revaluation of values: the rejection of reason for instance calls for a reintegration of madness in the thought process. Against the idea that madness is something essentially negative that must be eliminated, Tzara considers it to be part of life and hence valuable. The rejection of madness is the consequence of the overvaluation of rationality and logic, values that need revaluation.[7] Insofar as this revaluation aims to destroy an established system of values, it necessarily entails forms of violence.

However, unlike the violence and destruction occurring elsewhere across Europe, the Dadaists' violence does not aim at endangering individuals but at reforming the system of values that somehow allowed the war to happen. While we might argue that the rejection of systematicity that Nietzsche and Tzara advocate would lead to a complete anarchy of values and hence a form of nihilism (in which nothing has meaning nor value), both Nietzsche and the Dadaists offer a positive and affirming response, commending new values upon which to build. By considering that "those strong in words will survive," Tzara places the work to be done on the field of language. In this context, the critique of unity becomes a critique of the "word," which bears similarities with Nietzsche's critique of "concept" in *On Truth and Lie in a Nonmoral Sense*, a matter I will explore in the next section. "Each thing has its word," says Ball,

> but the word has become a thing by itself. Why shouldn't I find it? Why can't a tree be called a Pluplusch, and a Pluplubasch when it has been raining? The word, the word, the word outside your domain, your stuffiness, this laughable impotence, your stupendous smugness, outside all the parrotry of your self-evident limitedness. The word, gentlemen, is a public concern of the first importance. (Danchev 2011: 128–9)

The word is a concern of first importance in a twofold way: first, it is—with the language containing those words—one of the Dadaists' (but also Nietzsche's) main targets of criticism; second, because it is only with language (and therefore with words) that one can elaborate a response to the decline of culture. Language is of first importance because it is both a symptom and a cure for decadence and nihilism. For Ball and the Dadaists, the way to overcome the nihilism of meaninglessness is to embrace meaninglessness even further and disrupt the categories of thought that are established in language.

In order to undertake a revaluation of all values, Nietzsche rejects our faith in traditional language and the moral value judgments it is built upon. This rejection is related to his diagnosis of European culture as nihilistic. Nietzsche's use of nihilism has been explored and discussed extensively,[8] and I will only point out three aspects of nihilism that are relevant to its relation to Dada and that relate to a certain philosophical and moral tradition, which has, as we have seen, led to the supposed decline of European culture. First, Nietzsche distinguishes between—at least—two forms of nihilism: "meaninglessness" and "moral value judgments";[9] second, these two forms of nihilism are closely related to one another insofar as "moral value judgments" fail to bring meaning to life; third, one of the causes of nihilism is the belief in the categories of reason, the value of which we attribute to rationality.[10]

For Nietzsche, one of the fields in which such a belief is most visible is language because of the prejudices it is built upon: "Language and the prejudices upon which language is based are a manifold hindrance to us when we want to explain inner processes and drives" (D 115). The Dadaists also see language as a constraint to thinking, and as such a contributing source of cultural decadence. Ball's suspicion of words brings him to reject traditional language:

> It's a question of connections, and of loosening them up a bit to start with. I don't want words that other people have invented. All the words are other people's inventions. I want my own stuff, my own rhythm, and vowels and consonants too, matching the rhythm, and all my own. If this pulsation is seven yards long, I want words for it that are seven yards long. Mr Schulz's words are only two and a half centimetres long. (Danchev 2011: 128)

Against other people's words that have becomes tainted by decadence and nihilism, Ball is looking for new and "innocent" words.

Ball's criticism of words somewhat mirrors Nietzsche's theory of language—if it can be said that Nietzsche has such a "theory"—which is aptly summarized in BGE:

> Words are acoustic signs for concepts; concepts, however, are more or less precise figurative signs for frequently recurring and simultaneous sensations, for groups of sensations. Using the same words is not enough to ensure mutual understanding: we must also use the same words for the same category of inner experiences; ultimately, we must have the same experience in *common*. (BGE 268)

This idea—that words are acoustic signs for concepts—reframes and reconceptualizes Nietzsche's early text on language, *On Truth and Lie*. In this early text, he considers words and concepts to be residues of metaphors, to be dead metaphors. The relation between word and world is mediated through a series of metaphors: first a nerve stimulus into an image, then an image into a sound, then a sound into a word, then a word into a concept.

In BGE 268, Nietzsche returns to this idea of the mediation between the sensation and the word but insists on the "common" character of words, that is, the social and cultural dimension that does not appear in *On Truth and Lie*. Language is therefore a social construct, which in turn limits our possibilities for inner experiences. There is a correlation between what we can feel and think and our language. Nietzsche uncovers here the subtle relation between the social and the individual through language. It is precisely this relation that Dadaists aim to subvert, which echoes Nietzsche's assertions at GS 58: "We can destroy only as creators. —But let us not forget this either: it is enough to create new names and estimations and probabilities in order to create in the long run new 'things.'" Creating new names amounts to creating new things or new experiences. However, Nietzsche argues that this creation of new words, things, experiences, cannot happen without destruction. Not only can we only destroy as creators, but we can also only create as destructors. Creation and destruction are intimately related, and Dada embraces this idea play of destruction and creation.

In order to escape decadence and nihilism, the Dadaists suggest reinventing language, but how can this revolution in language occur? As we have seen, paradoxically, when destruction surrounds it, Dada's first step toward reinventing language is to attack the categories of thought on which tradition and the language that supports it are built. To do so, the Dadaists attack the social hierarchy in a comic and playful way:

> I destroy the drawers of the brain and of social organization: spread demoralization wherever I go and cast my hand from heaven to hell, my eyes from hell to heaven, restore the fecund wheel of a universal circus to objective forces and the imagination of every individual. (Danchev 2011: 140)

The destruction of traditional language goes therefore much further than the mere boundaries of language: it involves the whole social worldview, our way to relate to the world and to one another. This great negative work is however not the only one that needs to be undertaken—and perhaps not the most important one. As aforementioned in quoting Janco, Dada has two "speeds," a destructive and a constructive one. While the destruction of the established order—the old values—is a necessary one, it must not remain mere destruction but bring to creation through a play with perspectives.

3. Philosophers, Poets, Players

Destruction and creation coalesce in the play of perspectives, insofar as "*we can destroy only as creators.*" This perspectival shift is epitomized in the work of Marcel Duchamp, another Dadaist. By placing a urinal in a museum, he reveals that any object can gain special significance under certain circumstances. Describing his work *Fountain*, he writes, "He [Richard Mutt, the signature in Duchamp's *Fountain*] took an ordinary article of life, placed it so that its useful significance disappeared under the new title and point of view—created a new thought for that object" (Lippard 1971: 143). This play of perspectives creates new meanings but also destroy old ones as the urinal loses its original function.

Through this shifting in perspective, the Dadaists aim to uncloak things, as Huelsenbeck notes:

> Dadaism for the first time has ceased to take an aesthetic attitude towards life, and this it accomplishes by tearing all the slogans of ethics, culture and inwardness, which are merely cloaks for weak muscles, into their components. (Danchev 2011: 146–7)

For the Dadaists, life is not something which must be looked at as an object of aesthetic appreciation, it must be taken as it is, that is neither beautiful nor ugly. This idea seems to go against Nietzsche's statement in BT that the "justification of the world [is] an aesthetic phenomenon" (BT 24).

However, two conceptions of the aesthetic are competing here: on the one hand, Nietzsche uses "aesthetic" in its etymological sense of sensation, focusing on the pleasure that art—music in this case—can produce; on the other hand, Huelsenbeck's use of "aesthetic" refers to the notion of beauty. Nietzsche probably agrees with Huelsenbeck's rejection of the aesthetic *qua* the beautiful as he suggests at GS 290: "Whether this taste was good or bad is less important than one might suppose, if only it was a single taste!" The importance is therefore not on the evaluation but on the feeling itself. In the same aphorism, Nietzsche coins the importance of this taste as style. This stylization through art is what makes life tolerable: "To 'give style' to one's character—a great and rare art. ... For one thing is needful: that a human being should *attain* satisfaction with himself, whether it be by means of this or that poetry and art; only then is a human being at all tolerable to behold" (GS 290). In addition to making life tolerable, the Dadaists aim to bring the spectator, often through laughter and comic effects, to experience the world differently. To do so, they play with perspectives by generating a tension between elements—be it between the urinal and the situation in a museum for Duchamp's *Fountain*, between the various objects used in a collage, or between the words (or sounds) used in a poem. In doing so, they aim to realize that things are not always as simple as they seem, that we do not live, as Nietzsche says, "entirely in the spell of that perspective which makes what is closest at hand and most vulgar appear as if it were vast, and reality itself" (GS 78).

In their rejection of the "aesthetic attitude towards life," the Dadaists embrace this Nietzschean trend by "tearing down all the slogans of ethics, culture and inwardness" in order to offer new perspectives on the world, to give style to the world. Whereas decadent perspectives like Christianity negate life, Nietzsche and the Dadaists are looking for perspectives that enhance life, as Tzara says, "Freedom: DADA DADA DADA, a roaring of tense colours, and interlacing of opposites and of all contradictions, grotesques, inconsistencies: LIFE" (Danchev 2011: 144). In other words, the Dadaists freely create new meanings, in an attempt to overcome the nihilistic hegemony of the meaningless by embracing meaninglessness. It is through this paradoxical and subversive play with language that the Dadaists intend to escape the traps of traditional culture. The creation of perspectives is a way of broadening a culture toward the enhancement of the life it sustains.

The Dadaists therefore offer a subversive and playful response to Nietzsche's call for revaluation of values. The Dadaists embrace Nietzsche's play with perspectives and emphasize the subversive and playful dimension of this enterprise. In other words, by focusing on a certain aspect of Nietzsche's philosophy, that is, its play with parody (as in EH, for instance), the Dadaists offer a response that allows for the creative, that is, the destructive *qua* subversive playfulness, to thrive. The meaninglessness and absurdity that Dadaists play with might not be, and most probably is not, an exact rendering of what Nietzsche intended in his revaluation of all values, but it is an interpretation that precisely attempts to bring out a subversive playfulness from reading Nietzsche. Such a reading of Nietzsche also is both creative and destructive, and indicates the uses that the Dadaists generally agreed could be made of Nietzsche's thought in their era. Respectively, this creative reading of the world is what Nietzsche considers to be the task of artists and what we can learn from them: "For with [artists] this subtle power usually comes to an end where art ends and life begins; but we want to be poets of our life—first of all in the smallest, most everyday matters" (GS 299). Whereas art usually ends when life begins, following the idea that art and life are somehow distinct from one another, Nietzsche argues that we can overcome this distinction, by giving "style to one's character," by becoming poets of our lives.

This notion of "poets of our lives" involves two intertwined aspects: play and creation. Indeed, the Dadaists' embrace of meaninglessness and absurdity as a play for its own sake might seem at first quite distant from Nietzsche "serious play" that involves establishing new values. As Nietzsche argues in BGE, there must be seriousness in play: "A man's maturity: having rediscovered the seriousness that he had as a child, at play" (BGE 94). For Nietzsche, the children are taking play seriously and maturity is reached when such seriousness at play is rediscovered. Indeed, Aaron Harper explains the reason why play is a serious matter for Nietzsche: "Through play, individuals take part in activities that offer new sources of value, purpose, and identity" (2016: 313). For Nietzsche, play is therefore not a vain activity but a crucial one that involves the creation of new values and the affirmation of life, as the third and final transformation of the spirit in *Thus Spoke Zarathustra* suggests.[11] However, it is not because the play is taken seriously that it must look serious. On the contrary, play will always look as play from the outside. It is only from within that one can take playing seriously. In this sense, the Dadaists' artworks and performances might look nonsensical and nonserious but they in fact are a serious attempt at playful creation.

Following the etymology of poetry (*poiesis*), to be poets of our lives means that we are creators. To be creators requires us to shift perspective and abandon the traditional conception of language and the order established thereupon.

> The *ascertaining of* "*true*" versus "*untrue*, "in general the *ascertaining* of facts, differs fundamentally from creative *positing*, from the forming, shaping, overwhelming, *willing*, which is of the essence of *philosophy*. *Putting in a meaning*—this task still remains *to be done* whatever happens, assuming there *isn't a meaning* already *there*. Thus it is with sounds, as well as with the destinies of peoples: they are *capable* of very different interpretations and of being directed toward *different goals*. The still higher stage is to *posit goals* and mould reality accordingly; thus, the *interpretation of the deed* and not merely its conceptual rewriting. (KSA 12:9[48])

Nietzsche shifts from a representative or mimetic form of operating with the world—"The ascertaining of 'true' versus 'untrue'"—to a creative and expressive shaping of the world. That is, Nietzsche argues, the 'essence of *philosophy*.'

Creating values is the task Nietzsche ascribes to the philosopher of the future in contrast to the philosophical worker in BGE: "I must insist that we finally stop mistaking philosophical workers or learned people in general for philosophers. … The task itself calls for something else—it calls for [the philosopher] to *create values*" (BGE 211). In contrast to the workers of philosophy who "merely rewrite [the deed] in a different form,"[12] the philosopher of the future, poet of her own life, is capable of *putting in meaning* where there is none, of interpreting in the positive sense of creating values rather than merely repeating what has already been said. The positing of goals and the creation of values are ways of shaping the world. This shaping of reality occurs primarily through creative uses of language, through the naming of things which in turn creates new things, as Nietzsche suggests in GS 58. This creation of new things by means of language is not only the task Nietzsche assigns to the philosopher of the future, but the task the Dadaists undertook in their artistic enterprise.

In a short text entitled "Dada Skating," André Breton describes the poet's task as creating words as well:

> We pass for poets in the most general sense of the word because we target the worst conventions in language. You can be terribly familiar with the word "hello" and still say "goodbye" to the woman you've just met up with again after being away for a year. (Danchev 2011: 175)

The poets are those who have the power to modify completely the meaning of words by using them in a different—often contradictory—fashion. So, like Nietzsche's philosopher, Breton's poet is a creator of words. Philosophers and poets—Nietzsche and Dada—therefore have a similar task.

The task of poems is, Ball argues, "to dispense with conventional language, no less, and to have done with it" (Danchev 2011: 128). Poets manage to clean up language and achieve the task Tzara proclaimed: "to sweep and clean." To do so, Ball goes back to the origins of language and shows that poetry—because of its focus on sound and rhythm rather than meaning and reference—can avoid the downfalls of conventional language: "A line of poetry is a chance to get rid of all the filth that clings to this accursed language as if put there by stockbrokers' hands, hands worn smooth by coins. I want the word where it ends and begins. Dada is the heart of words" (Danchev 2011: 128).

Yet what does a renewal of language do? How is it important to escape decadence? The main idea is that conventional language only gives one point of view on the world, only one perspective. Nietzsche's perspectivism calls for a plurality of perspectives, which calls, in turn, for a plurality of means of expression. Nietzsche describes his "art of style" similarly:

> At the same time I'll say something about my art of style in general. Communicating a state, an inner tension of pathos through signs, including the tempo of these signs—that is the point of every style; and considering that in my case the multiplicity of inner states is extraordinary, in my case there are many stylistic possibilities—altogether the most multifarious art of style anyone has ever had at their disposal. (EH Books 4)

To reflect the multiplicity of inner states, the drive perspectivism,[13] Nietzsche develops a "multifarious art of style." This multiplicity of perspectives, and the experiencing of many perspectives, opens the possibility of escaping the decadent perspective of our culture. Tzara also believes that this multiplicity must be taken into account: "We observe, we regard from one or more points of view, we choose them among the millions that exist" (Danchev 2011: 141). There are myriad points of view, each one providing a different perspective on the world and of the things in it.

Conclusion

The Dadaists agreed with Nietzsche that it is not merely the poet's task to imitate, but to create words and perspectives, and thus imbue meaning into life. However, this creative task is intimately linked to a destructive one as new perspectives, words, and meanings destroy old ones. New uses of words and new meanings might in time take old meanings out of use. However, we cannot destroy meanings without offering new ones. Creation and destruction are hence inseparable; their relation goes two ways: destruction is needed for creation; creation is needed for destruction. The revaluation of values Nietzsche calls for aims at the destruction of decadent values and the creation of life-affirming ones. While Nietzsche looked back at the Greeks in order to find answers to the problems of his times, the attitude that he inspired in the Dadaists provided a provocative response to the prevailing crisis of their times. That response was both playful and subversive—thus pursuing two important aspects of Nietzsche's line of thought—in its attempt to create a culture which could answer the central crisis of that era. Such creation cannot exist without destruction, but this destruction must be understood as subversive playfulness. To what extent can the Dadaists' reading of Nietzsche help us?

The Dadaists' interpretation of Nietzsche shows the importance of play and its relation to subversiveness, both in their artistic work and in Nietzsche's philosophy, as well as in our way of being in the world. To be the poets of our lives, to embrace and overcome the meaninglessness of our world, we must be able to play with values and take this play seriously. This play is therefore never in vain, nor is it innocent. Rather, as a remaking of the world it is subversive, dangerous, and explosive. To be the poets of our lives means to return to our childhood seriousness, to take the meaninglessness of existence seriously in order to bestow value in the world. From the Dadaists' realization of destabilizing potentials in Nietzsche's philosophy we see that subversive playfulness is key to creating new values. Their example may therefore be useful as a means of addressing various crises of our time, by prompting us to embrace the meaninglessness of existence, rather than merely rejecting it, in order to overcome it. As the Dadaists' demonstrated, this creative playfulness requires free spirited poets of their own lives to be able to laugh at, sublimate, and transfigure the meaninglessness that surrounds them.

Notes

1. For their help and comments on various drafts of this chapter, I thank Isabelle Wienand, Florian Häubi, Tessa de Vet, and the editors of this volume.
2. My translation: "So komisch das klingt, wir hatten alle Nietzsche gelesen, auch die Ausländer, vor allem aber Ball, dessen ganzes Lebensproblem sich zwischen der brutalen Naivität des Nietzscheschen Idealmenschen und einer katholisch-sentimentalen Moraltheologie, der er durch die Tat immer zu entgehen suchte—abspielt."
3. My translation.
4. In a letter to Paul Deussen dated November 26, 1888, Nietzsche claims, "I am more dynamite than man." In a letter to Georg Brandes from early December 1888, he asserts, "I am the most terrible dynamite there is," and in another letter to Helen Zimmer from December 17, 1888, "I am no man, I am dynamite."

5. Nietzsche uses here the term "ruminant" in a negative sense, whereas he considers it to be a necessary and positive feature of his readers in the foreword to the *On the Genealogy of Morality*.
6. At least two types of therapy are operative in Nietzsche: a therapy of the soul and a therapy of culture. The latter is of particular interest with respect to this chapter. On that topic see, e.g., Ahern (1995) and Wotling (1995).
7. Michel Foucault famously analyses the relationship between madness and reason in his *Civilization and Madness*. He especially criticizes Descartes's rational doubt which consists in "the great exorcism of madness" (Foucault 1973: 108). On the role of madness, one cannot forget Nietzsche's madman announcing the death of God in GS 125. His witnesses (society) fail to understand and take him seriously.
8. On the nature of nihilism, see Reginster (2006: 21–53) on the distinction between the two aforementioned forms of nihilism, whereas Clark contests this distinction (2019).
9. See KSA 12:2[127].
10. See KSA 13:11[99].
11. I have argued elsewhere that the child has two central roles in *Thus Spoke Zarathustra*: a narrative one that structures the story and a philosophical one as it appears as a poetic figure of creative affirmation (Mills 2019: 209).
12. "*What we lack is the philosopher*, one who interprets the deed and does *not* merely rewrite it in a different form" (KSA 12:9[44]).
13. Pierre Klossowski observed that our drives also operate perspectivally (1997: 44). Paul Katsafanas suggests that the interpretation of our drives is necessarily perspectival because of its constitution (2016: 53–54).

References

Ahern, Daniel R. (1995), *Nietzsche as Cultural Physician*, University Park: Pennsylvania State University Press.

Ball, Hugo (1917), "Kandinsky," *Schriften zum Theater, zur Kunst und Philosophie 1909-1926*. Available online: http://www.textlog.de/ball-manifeste.html (accessed November 29, 2020).

Battersby, Christine (2013), "'Behold the Buffoon': Dada, Nietzsche's Ecce Homo and the Sublime," in *The Art of the Sublime*, ed. Nigel Llewellyn and Christine Riding. Available online: https://www.tate.org.uk/art/research-publications/the-sublime/christine-battersby-behold-the-buffoon-dada-nietzsches-ecce-homo-and-the-sublime-r1136833 (accessed November 29, 2020).

Berard, Tim J. (1999), "Dada between Nietzsche's Birth of Tragedy and Bourdieu's Distinction: Existenz and Conflict in Cultural Analysis," *Theory, Culture & Society* 16 (1): 141–65.

Clark, Maudemarie (2019), "Nietzsche's Nihilism," *The Monist* 102 (3): 369–85.

Danchev, Alex, ed. (2011), *100 Artists' Manifestoes*, London: Penguin.

Foucault, Michel (1973), *Madness and Civilization: A History of Insanity in the Age of Reason*, trans. Richard Howard, New York: Random House.

Harper, Aaron (2016), "Playing, Valuing, and Living: Examining Nietzsche's Playful Response to Nihilism," *Journal of Value Inquiry* 50 (2): 305–23.

Huelsenbeck, Richard (1920), *Dada Siegt! Ein Bilanz des Dadaismus*, Berlin: Der Malik Verlag.

Katsafanas, Paul (2016), *The Nietzschean Self: Moral Psychology, Agency, and the Unconscious. The Nietzschean Self*, Oxford: Oxford University Press

Klossowski, Pierre (1997), *Nietzsche and the Vicious Circle*, trans. Daniel W. Smith, Chicago: University of Chicago Press.

Lippard, Lucy R., ed. (1971), *Dadas on Art. Tzara, Arp, Duchamp and Others*, Mineola, NY: Dover.

Mann, Philip (1987), *Hugo Ball. An Intellectual Biography*, London: University of London Institute of Germanic Studies.

Mills, Philip (2019), "L'enfant de Zarathoustra: Figure poétique de l'affirmation créatrice," in *Nietzsche, penseur de l'affirmation. Relecture d'Ainsi parlait Zarathoustra*, ed. Clément Bertot, Jean Leclercq, Nicolas Monseu, and Patrick Wotling, 209–18, Louvain-la-Neuve: Presses universitaires de Louvain.

Reginster, Bernard (2006), *The Affirmation of Life: Nietzsche on Overcoming Nihilism*, Cambridge, MA: Harvard University Press.

Taylor, Seth (1990), *Left-Wing Nietzscheans: The Politics of German Expressionism 1910–1920*, Berlin: De Gruyter.

Wotling, Patrick (1995), *Nietzsche et le problème de la civilisation*, Paris, PUF.

Part Four

Perspectives on Laughter

9

On Nietzsche's "Teachings" about Learning to Laugh at Oneself: A Critical Approach*

Katia Hay

> Oh Zarathustra: whoever wants to kill most thoroughly, laughs.
>
> (Z Festival 1)

The tension between democracy and comedy is probably as old as democracy itself.[1] The origin of the idea that laughter can be dangerous, on the other hand, is not so easy to locate.[2] Still, one might be tempted to say that Nietzsche's formula that "from time to time the human species will ever again decree: "There is something one is absolutely forbidden henceforth to laugh at" (GS 1, KSA 3:372) is not only valid for the present and future but also for the past of humanity. In other words, that morality and valuation has always involved in one way or other the prohibition that we laugh at the values we adhere to, that is, that we scorn, undermine, mock them. Since we cannot live without values and without taking them seriously, it seems we will always be involved in the "prohibition" of some form of laughter. But, compelling as it may seem, this would fall short of accounting for the differences, not only between polytheistic and monotheistic cultures and religions,[3] but also, for instance, between the Old and the New Testament, where laughter and mockery seem to have different (moral) connotations and consequences.[4]

The aim of this chapter, however, is not to write a genealogy of the "prohibition" of laughter. Rather, it is to examine the extent to which Nietzsche's "philosophy of laughter" can help us think about the tension between laughter and politics today. And for this it seems important to at least bear in mind the fact that the relation between seriousness and laughter, that is, between taking something seriously and laughing at it, has not always been (and therefore does not necessarily have to be) understood in terms of opposition and exclusion.

For modern liberal democratic sensibilities and the values of equality, popular sovereignty, freedom of speech, and so on, there is something undoubtedly problematic, if not ridiculous, in wanting to determine what we are and are not allowed to laugh

---

* I would like to thank the members of the Nietzsche Werkgroup in Leiden and my students at UvA for their insights in the process of writing this chapter.

at. Thus, the very thought of comedians being censored might appear to "us" as blatantly undemocratic. It is less straightforward perhaps when it comes to explicit self-censorship, such as when we see stand-up comedian Kenny Sebastian explaining, through jokes, why he does not address political issues in his shows (Sebastian 2018).[5] Still, one might like to think that "consolidated"' liberal democracies are above or beyond these tensions. And yet, at least since the shootings in the offices of the French magazine Charlie Hebdo (CH) in 2015, and more recently, the beheading of a French teacher outside a school in the Paris-region,[6] it has become clear that this is not the case.

In relation to these events, much has been said about freedom of speech, secularity, religious fundamentalism, as well as Islamophobia, the clash of cultures, and so forth. Although I cannot do justice here to the complexities in these debates, I briefly consider the responses of condemnation (mainly in Europe and the United States) to these attacks. In response to the 2015 attack on CH, demonstrations in defense of the magazine (and freedom of speech in general) were organized in many cities worldwide under the slogan *"Je suis Charlie Hebdo."* However, in interviews and social media, the motto was very often accompanied with some form of side-remark regarding the inappropriateness, distasteful, or controversial character of the satirical cartoon, as in "I am Charlie Hebdo—*even if I actually never really liked their sense of humor.*"

Soon enough, the press was full of columnists declaring "I am not Charlie Hebdo"[7] and criticizing the magazine for Islamophobia.[8] In other words, the nonetheless categorical condemnation of the attack included the acknowledgment that Islamophobia is a problem that needs to be taken more seriously, as well as a somewhat wary debate about comedy and humor and their roles in Western, democratic cultures. The beheading of Samuel Patty in 2020, in contrast, seems to have provoked a much simpler, unambiguous reaction. There has been no space for a debate about appropriate or inappropriate humor. And the predominant feeling, it seems, has been one of urgency and the imperative need to *unequivocally defend freedom of speech*, Western values of secularity, and so on.

To be clear: I am not suggesting that the response to these killings should be nuanced in any way whatsoever. That is not the issue. Rather, the question underlying this chapter is whether it is adequate to address the relation between comedy and politics in terms of freedom of speech, as has been done so far. My claim is that the result of this approach has proved to be insufficient if not totally counterproductive, precisely because it does not enable us to address the complex nature of comedy, nor the violent, disruptive, or transgressive potential of humor and laughter in general. Thinking about the tension between comedy and politics in terms of freedom of speech forces us to "forget" or disregard the rather simple fact that laughter can be extremely destabilizing and hurtful; or as Nietzsche put it in his Zarathustra, that 'one kills not by wrath, but by laughter' (Z I, KSA 4:49). What is more, addressing the tension between comedy and politics in terms of freedom of speech creates a false dichotomy between comedy and violence that forecloses any enquiry into the relation between laughter and violence or into what might be the "appropriate" response to violent jokes.

But how then should we think about the relation between comedy and politics? And how can we understand the tensions between them? Are these tensions inevitable? Does this mean that comedy should be either banned or always be "politically correct"? Do we need to wait until we (all) have attained the right degree of democratic "maturity" in order to make jokes about ourselves and others? Or can comedy be seen, as has been argued by politicians and scholars alike, as an essential tool precisely for achieving that "maturity"?[9] To put it differently, is there perhaps a right and a wrong way of laughing? These are important questions that we need to address if we really want to take the problem of laughter and democracy seriously(!). My aim is not to offer an answer but to show how Nietzsche can help us to begin answering them, and perhaps more importantly, help us to ask new ones.

1. *The Gay Science* and the Art of Laughing at One-Self

Nietzsche uses and thematizes laughter throughout his writings in many different ways. He talks about laughter, comedy, and jokes, but he can also be very funny, he makes jokes about himself and others and arguably uses writing techniques that strictly speaking do not belong to a philosophical genre but could very well be considered to be typical of comedies (hyperbole, exploiting the counterintuitive, contradictions, unfinished thoughts, interruptions, ruptures, changes of direction, parabasis, etc.). *The Gay Science* (GS) and *Thus Spoke Zarathustra*, however, are undoubtedly the works in which laughter is most explicitly thematized, and it is for this reason that I will briefly examine them here.

That laughter, and more concretely the ability to laugh at oneself, plays a central role in Nietzsche's GS is made clear from the very start, when Nietzsche writes, as a motto to his new book:

> This house is my own and here I dwell,
> I've never aped nothing from no one
> and – laugh at each master, mark me well,
> who at himself has not poked fun.
> Over my front door. (GS, KSA 3:343)

The fact that this should be seen as evidence of a significant move in Nietzsche's philosophical uses of laughter becomes most tangible when we compare the uses of laughter in GS and *Dawn* (D). For, what predominates in the latter is a mocking kind of laughter turned toward those (ideas, beliefs, characters, philosophies) that Nietzsche seeks to criticize and overcome. This difference is also reflected on a linguistic level: the word *spotten* (to mock) and related appears in *Daybreak* twice as much as *lachen* (to laugh), whereas in GS, *lachen* appears almost five times more than *spotten*.

In D, Nietzsche exposes and ridicules, for instance, the inconsistencies within religious beliefs, and in general our misconceptions and prejudices regarding knowledge, morality, freedom, but also regarding our own self-understanding and how we see the relation between our feelings, our drives, and our reasoning.[10] An example of the kind of mocking laughter that we find often in D would be when Nietzsche reduces *ad absurdum* the idea that there may be anything noble in respecting moral customs (*Sitten*):

> *Suspicious.* – To take on a belief merely because it is a custom [*Sitte*] – but that actually means: to be dishonest, cowardly, lazy! – And so dishonesty, cowardice and laziness would be the preconditions of morality [*Sittlichkeit*]. (M 101, KSA 3:90)

If we accept that there is something funny and mocking about this aphorism, we see that laughter itself is only a vehicle for ridiculing *our* understanding of what it means to be moral and in this way exposing *our* misjudgments, in the expectation that this will illuminate us and persuade us to engage in a transvaluation of values.[11] But laughter is not something that we necessarily need to transform the way in which we relate to things, as will be the case in GS.

It is in this sense not surprising that in D, Nietzsche's use of *spotten* is not supported or accompanied by a theoretical analysis of mocking or laughter in general. This is different in GS. And although laughter appears here in different contexts and takes on different meanings across the aphorisms, it is undeniable that it acquires its full weight and significance as it participates in the underlying project of the book. In other words, in Nietzsche's GS, laughter becomes the very symbol of the realization or the promise of a form of knowledge and wisdom where seriousness (taking things seriously) is not defined anymore in opposition to laughter and joy but is able to include them. This special connection between laughter and the very project of a gay science appears already in the first aphorism, where Nietzsche asks whether "perhaps laughter still has a future" and will be able to form "an alliance with wisdom" so that "only 'gay science' will remain" (GS 1, KSA 3:370). But it is most directly expressed in GS 327: "*Ernst nehmen*":[12]

> *Taking seriously.* – For most people, the intellect is an awkward, gloomy, creaking machine that is hard to start: when they want to work with this machine and think well, they call it "taking the matter *seriously*" – oh, how taxing good thinking must be for them! The lovely human beast seems to lose its good mood when it thinks well; it becomes "serious"! And "where laughter and gaiety are found, thinking is good for nothing" – that is the prejudice of this serious beast against all "gay science." Well then, let us prove it a prejudice! (GS 327, KSA 3:555)

Nietzsche's main claim here seems to be that it is wrong to assume that laughter and joy (and one might include lightness and superficiality)[13] do not enable us to consider things seriously. Nietzsche refers to "most people" and the "lovely human beast," but at the same time this aphorism could be seen as a response to Kant's (and other "serious" thinkers') position regarding laughter; namely that, being an affect, laughter is the opposite of reason and does not enable us to think, in the sense that it affects, disturbs, interrupts thinking.[14] The question is, though, how to understand the relation between laughter and reason that Nietzsche proposes. Is it just a matter of affirming the possibility of enjoying the process of thinking, is it perhaps a matter of changing our attitude to knowledge, of becoming more cheerful and light?

At the end of this short aphorism, Nietzsche presents the task of "gay science" to be this: to prove that to assume that thinking properly (*gut-Denken*) must exclude laughter is a mere "prejudice." Now, what is important about this is that it already indicates that Nietzsche is not positioning himself at the antipode of reason. For a prejudice is a (usually mistaken) opinion that needs to be overcome *for the sake of thinking and knowledge*. In other words, the argument seems to be that we (lovely human beasts) still do not know what it really means to think properly, and that we will only be able to take things seriously (a problem, morality, history, knowledge, politics?) to the extent that we are able to incorporate laughter into the process of knowing and thinking in general. That is to say: the task is that we change our understanding of what it means to *think well*. So it is not just a matter of making science and knowledge more agreeable, but of making them "better." From this point of view, it is interesting to pay attention to the way in which Nietzsche conveys his point, because it is through his particular form of communication that he is able to fulfill the very task he announces.

In a very obvious way, this aphorism is funny. To instantiate the opposition between laughter and seriousness (reason) as a prejudice is, at the very least, counterintuitive, which very often is the essential ingredient for a good laugh.[15] The same goes for the way in which Nietzsche defines those who do not include laughter and joy in their ways of thinking as "serious beasts," suggesting that it is laughter, and not reason, that makes us human or less bestial. Then there is his portrayal (or rather caricature) of serious thinking as a silly, awkward if not futile, enterprise, attempted by the "charming beast"—otherwise known as "man" (die *liebliche Bestie Mensch*). Also, the way in which he depicts thought as a painful, "creaky machine," all of these can be taken as jokes and puns. But, more importantly, these are special kinds of jokes, in the sense that one can assume that Nietzsche, as well as (most of) his readers, are invested in the importance of what it means to take things seriously and to "think" properly, so that it is most likely *our* prejudice(s) that "we" are invited to laugh at. In other words, in this aphorism "we" (let's say we seekers of knowledge, or we "serious beasts') are invited to laugh at ourselves, at our own prejudices about what it means to 'think seriously'. However, the wonderful thing about this provocative invitation is that, in accepting it (if we accept it), we will *de facto* be overcoming those very prejudices and inherited misconceptions that we were trapped in.

Through his own humorous, light, and funny example, Nietzsche ultimately *proves* that to assume that thought and laughter are incompatible is just nonsense—a *prejudice*. Moreover, I would argue that Nietzsche at the same time *proves* that laughter enables us to think better because, in this case at least, to "get the joke" already means to have understood that in order to take the problem of thinking seriously we also have to learn to take ourselves (and all the values, norms, assumptions that we attach to our task as knowers) *lightly*. Not just for fun, but because this might be the only way in which we will be able to debunk the prejudices that are so strongly inscribed in us that we normally cannot see them, let alone question them. As we said earlier: it is not about making knowledge more agreeable, more bearable, more livable, but about transforming knowledge *from within*—for the sake of knowledge itself.

From this point of view, the reason why laughter is important for GS is that it enables us to play with and test our preconceptions concerning the things that are closest and most dear to us, without totally undermining or negating their value. It is for this reason, I contend, that Nietzsche incorporates laughter into his very style of writing, radically transforming philosophical discourse, giving laughter a very particular function. Laughter is used as a philosophical tool to engage in a radical and immanent self-critique, but one that in its radicality and sternness is not rigid, nor totally destructive. It is able to both negate and affirm. We can see this not only in his obvious jokes but also, and perhaps more effectively, in his playful, irreverent style that dares to ask the most unexpected questions, making the usual, obvious, and well-known seem strange, awkward, and wrong, turning everything upside down, like a jester or a clown: could the most damaging be the most useful?[16] Does morality really make us better?[17] Indeed, through laughter Nietzsche takes the cake and eats it ... *and he gets away with it!*

For even if the questions are deadly serious, the playfulness with which they are presented is an indication that the intention is not to destroy, but to construct. It is not recklessness, but profound care.[18] We can learn about this special form of laughter in GS 1, where Nietzsche invites us to see ourselves from the perspective of the species (*Gattung*) and describes the changes in our values throughout history as a cyclical process of overcomings in which laughter, reason, and nature always have taken and always will take the lead.[19] Throughout the aphorism it seems as if Nietzsche is ridiculing our adherence to values altogether, as he shows, for instance, how our acquired need to give meaning or purpose to the world[20] reveals that we are still in a "time of tragedy, morals and religions." Similarly, we could interpret Nietzsche's question, whether we will ever be ready for the comedy of existence to "become aware of itself" (GS 1, KSA 3:370), as a question about our ability to relativize all values. But at the very end of the aphorism, suddenly, the tone changes. Here, through the voice "of the most cautious friend of man" (*der vorsichtigste Menschenfreund*), Nietzsche remarks that we must acknowledge that the "tragic" (such as the need to take things seriously) is necessary for us to live.[21] So that even if we may need to overcome or at least revise our values, we cannot overcome our need to adhere to values altogether. In this way, suddenly, to laugh at ourselves acquires a new meaning or nuance, because we now have the task of making our laughter compatible with this (serious) insight. In other words, we must see that laughing at ourselves "*from the whole truth [aus der ganzen Warheit heraus]*" (GS 1, KSA 3:370), as he puts it, must involve laughing at ourselves in such a way that we are able to embrace the necessity of the fact that we are (still) "tragic," that we have specific needs that we *cannot* laugh away nor negate—even if we can laugh about them. Perhaps this specific twist is what Nietzsche means about the comedy of existence becoming aware of itself. Perhaps this is also what Nietzsche means in *Twilight of the Idols* when he turns the common saying and claims that "he who laughs today best, also laughs last" (GD, KSA 6:66), where "last" would stand for a perspective that is in some way out of time or beyond time, and yet does not negate, but instead affirms the temporal.

Laughing at ourselves (*as knowers*) enables us to question the nature and value of our values and preconceptions in the most radical ways; it enables us to make them into a problem, but a problem that we embrace and recognize as our own (as opposed to a problem that concerns only *others*[22]). By laughing at ourselves, we question ourselves, but without falling into despair, (self-)negation, and most importantly, without losing sight of the necessity to understand what our needs really involve.[23] One could further argue, to laugh at oneself (*properly*)[24] is also a way of affirming one's own finitude in the aftermath of the death of God; which means a way to understand and affirm this vacuum without falling into new forms of life-hatred and life-negation.

2. The Problems of Laughter and Laughing at Oneself: Hannah Gadsby's *Nanette*

Although the uses of laughter that Nietzsche develops in his GS are specific to his writing, the possibilities they afford do not come as a total surprise. In a way, they highlight aspects of laughter that we know well and can relate to easily. From this point of view, it is not surprising that jokes, good humor, comedies, or what Josef Früchtl has recently called a "positive-aggressive" laughter could be seen as an asset for any community, but especially for (agonal) democracies that encourage respectful disagreements and depend on 'relaxed but severe' forms of self-reflection to thrive (Früchtl 2020: 103). In this sense, laughter is seen as enabling the formation of an open and safe space for enjoyable, while at the same time challenging and constructive, interactions. Thus, and thanks to its intrinsic "irreverence,"[25] its "anarchic" tendency (Früchtl 2020), that is, thanks to its potential for undermining values, traditions, and power structures, laughter—and humor in particular—has be seen as "the most democratic from of speech" (Bowen 2019). Or, as Früchtl puts it, "human beings who can laugh at themselves are at home in a democracy" (2020: 106).

Conversely, it would be wrong to assume that these very particular aspects or possibilities of laughter, which Nietzsche exploits in his GS, could be taken to exhaust what laughter does or can do in general. Nietzsche himself is well aware of this, as becomes clear in GS 346, where he asks, "As laughers [*Lachende*], haven't we simply taken a step further in the contempt for man?" (KSA 3:581)—reminding us of the other side of laughter, the one that despises and negates, wondering whether through laughter we are not falling into life negation or nihilism in the form of hatred and contempt for the human. This is why Nietzsche does not merely tell us *that* we have to laugh, but more importantly he *shows* us, through his own example, how to do it and warns us (as in this very aphorism) about the dangers we might encounter. In this respect it is important to keep in mind that when Nietzsche talks about dangers, he very often means the dangers of nihilism, understood as the abstract notion of decay, but also loss of diversity, loss of possibilities for individual self-realization, loss of imagination (as in the fact that we have lost the ability to surprise ourselves and are becoming awfully predictable), and so forth.[26]

One could, however, argue that the danger that laughter may negate and oppress rather than affirm and liberate can be addressed by stressing that the kind of laughter in need of cultivation is one in which subject and object converge: laughing at oneself as we have seen in GS. This seems to be what Früchtl refers to as the laughter that is also inherently anti-dogmatic and coincides with a "humorous self-reflection": a humorous, kind, and amicable laughter that enables us to distance ourselves from ourselves, accept our weaknesses as human beings, and question ourselves (our sense of identity, our values, etc.).[27] I argue, however, that this assumption needs to be questioned. For, even if it is true that by laughing at ourselves we create a split within ourselves (the "I" who laughs and the "I" who is being laughed at are not the same "I"), a split that resembles the split inherent to self-reflection,[28] this does not necessarily mean that the "I" who laughs occupies a "better" (more reasonable, cooler, wiser, more enlightened) perspective. By laughing at ourselves, we are in effect splitting ourselves (at least) in two, and we cannot assume that the first will be emancipated, anti-dogmatic, liberating, and so on; we cannot even assume it will be kind and uplifting. The question therefore remains: who is laughing at whom and from what perspective, from what set of values? In other words, it is wrong to assume that in laughing at ourselves we are questioning the ideologies, morals, power structures, or hierarchies in which we are immersed. For the truth is that the exact opposite may be the case, and that those very life-negating, oppressive values are being internalized and reinforced instead, without us even noticing (which is also, by the way, why authors such as Henri Bergson have seen in laughter a social, corrective function).[29] Perhaps this is also why Zarathustra asks at one point: "Who among you can laugh and be elevated [*erhoben*] at the same time?" (Z I *On Reading and Writing*, KSA 4:49).

In her 2017 stand-up comedy show *Nanette*,[30] Hannah Gadsby highlights this very problem as she reflects on her own use of jokes and humor as a lesbian comedian, a lesbian who grew up in a place and time where homosexuality was illegal and for whom "coming out" was not in any way easy.[31] About a third of the way through the show, Gadsby turns the show upside down and announces that she has to quit comedy. The stand-up comedy then gradually turns into a harsh reassessment and critique of the presumably affirmative and positive or healing aspect of comedy, and laughter in general. It is, nevertheless, a critique from within, in the sense that the show never really stops being a comedy. But what is perhaps most interesting is the way in which Gadsby analyzes or deconstructs the very jokes that she had made in the past and that arguably had enabled her to affirm herself and "come out" to the world as a lesbian comedian. As she puts it, comedy had enabled her to find a space, from which she had the "right" to speak, the "right" to affirm herself. But what was the price?

By laughing at herself, she says, she had been able to affirm herself in a "light," nonconfrontational way. Through jokes she had been able to break taboos, as well as laugh away and overcome, together with the audience, traumatic experiences of violence, verbal abuse, and injustice in general. But Gadsby's point is that, in doing so, she had not actually grown or become better in any way.[32] Those very jokes that in principle had given her "the right to speak" (as she puts it), or a possibility of affirming her homosexuality, were actually reinforcing the very principles and values that had made it so difficult for her to affirm who she was in the first place. For it was only in the context of a joke, only as a lesbian comedian, that this affirmation was made possible. And not just any joke but jokes that ultimately did not expose or question homophobic patriarchal prejudices but actually *depended* on them to be funny.[33] In other words, those apparently self-affirming jokes were in fact a hidden form of self-deprecation and self-hatred.

In her show, Gadsby denounces her own jokes and comedy in general for falling too easily into what she calls "self-deprecating humor" (Nanette 2018), and in this way she offers us a perfect example of the dangers underlying the all-pervasive assumption that laughing at ourselves is a sign of growth and liberating self-reflection. The main danger is that in laughing at ourselves we may be reproducing and reinforcing the very self-negating values that we are supposedly aiming to challenge and overcome.[34] So, from this perspective, it becomes increasingly difficult to ascribe any positive value to laughter without further qualification. Conversely, we can also see how problematic it is to assume that not finding a joke funny or refusing to laugh at oneself in a given context should be seen unequivocally as a lack of lightness and humor, a deficit of democratic spirit or inability to question one's values.

To be sure, laughter and the art of laughing at ourselves becomes increasingly problematic once we begin questioning the "I" (or the "we") who is actually laughing at herself. From what standpoint is this laughter coming? Yet this does not necessarily mean that we should condemn or give up on laughter altogether (which is what Gadsby says she will do, although in the end she did not[35]). But it does mean that determining the positive or negative, uplifting or hindering, liberating or oppressive effects of laughter can only be done by taking these issues into consideration. In other words, if Nietzsche can help us think about the relation between laughter and politics, it is so to the extent that he thematizes and addresses these questions too, that is to say, only to the extent that, without giving up on its undeniable potentials, he does not forget that laughter can be extremely alienating, divisive, and damaging, and more importantly that laughing at oneself is *per se* no guarantee of life-affirmation (understood as the affirmation of the diversity and plurality of life)—it is not even a guarantee of self-affirmation but could just very well be a closet-form of self-hatred and life-negation, that is, nihilism.

Now, as helpful as GS is for understanding Nietzsche's philosophical investment in laughter, it does not seem to address what has now become the most pressing question, namely, from what perspective are we supposed to laugh at ourselves, if the existing perspectives available to us might be *de facto* harmful, rather than elevating, liberating, or enhancing for *us*? Could it be that any existing perspective we may draw on will necessarily be complicit in the hierarchies, injustices, exclusions, and prejudices that we aim to question? Or, to put it differently, how can we avoid reproducing in our laughing self-criticism the very same prejudices and values that we intend to undermine?

On the other hand, one could argue that Nietzsche already addresses these questions in GS insofar as the perspective that we are offered to occupy in order to laugh at ourselves is blatantly inexistent. "The whole truth," "the perspective of the species," "the future," "gay science"[36]—all these seem to be quite explicitly philosophical fictions. The point of view that Nietzsche is inviting us to adopt in order to laugh at ourselves properly is the standpoint of a yet to come, imagined community of life-affirming seekers of knowledge. In this sense, Nietzsche is involving us in the creation of the very standpoint from which we have to learn to see, criticize, and laugh at ourselves. Finding, or construing, this standpoint is as important as laughter itself. And yet, it is arguably not until *Thus Spoke Zarathustra* that Nietzsche engages with the issues we have raised above as he elevates the art of laughing at oneself to one of the key moments in his project of self-overcoming. It is here that Nietzsche, while maintaining the value he has found in laughing at oneself in GS, considers the social or ethical dimensions of it. Laughter is indeed completely bound up with the figure of the *Übermensch* through which Nietzsche thematizes the complex relation between the individual and the herd, that is, the community (the "we" that he constantly refers to: everybody and no one). And I take it that when he tells us now that we need to learn to laugh (at ourselves), it has all to do with learning about how to envisage this community.

3. Zarathustra and the Intricacies of Laughing at Oneself as *Self-Overcoming*

In the chapter *On the Higher Man*, toward the end, Zarathustra presents himself as the one who makes laughter holy and says the following:

> This crown of the laughing one, this rose-wreath crown – I myself put on this crown, I myself pronounced my laughter holy. I found no other strong enough for it today. (Z IV *Higher Man*, KSA 4:366)

A few lines later:

> How much is still possible! So *learn* to laugh over and past yourselves [*über euch hinweg lachen*]! Lift up your hearts, you good dancers, high! higher! And don't forget good laughter for me either!
> This crown of the laughing one, this rose-wreath crown: to you, my brothers, I throw this crown! I pronounced laughter holy; you higher men, *learn* from me— to laugh! (Z IV *Higher Man*, KSA 4:368)

As perhaps becomes more explicit in his late preface to *The Birth of Tragedy* (where Nietzsche quotes these same passages), laughter as an "antidote" or a "solution" needs to be understood within Nietzsche's critique of metaphysics, his critique of Romanticism and Christian values in general. In *Thus Spoke Zarathustra*, laughter is unequivocally connected to life-affirmation and the overall project of self-overcoming and hence to the transvaluation of all values. Throughout the book, Zarathustra seems to suggest that in order to overcome ourselves, we need to learn to laugh at ourselves. From this point of view, though, the solution that Zarathustra presents to such complex problems is suspiciously simple. And one is immediately confronted with the question, what *is* this laughter actually, what does it involve, and what does it actually do? What is its role in the process of self-overcoming?

These problems are not easy to resolve. Not only because of Nietzsche's metaphorical and riddle-style of writing—taken to an extreme in this book—but also because there seem to be different kinds and meanings of laughter at play. Zarathustra's own laughter, for instance, is not the same as the "cold" laughter of those who mock him at the market and cause him so much distress.[37] Likewise, Zarathustra's relation to the very laughter he wants to teach us is not simple or straightforward in any way: contrary to what the passage above may suggest, Zarathustra is not always able to laugh and has to learn how to do it properly. In addition to this, laughter very often appears without a clear object or in the total absence thereof, as if laughter were to signify a state of pure joy and detachment.[38] Also, some of the laughters we come across seem to be beyond and above the human, such as when *Life* laughs at Zarathustra himself. Finally, being intrinsically related to the figure of the *Übermensch*, the laughter Zarathustra teaches us is fundamentally ambivalent: on the one hand, it points toward absolute or unconditional life-affirmation, while on the other, it is bound up with radical life-negation, since Zarathustra repeatedly demands that we "perish" or "go to ground" (*zu Grunde gehen*) in order to "build a house for the *Übermensch*" (Z I Preface, KSA 4:17). Laughter affirms and negates, and "whoever wants to kill most thoroughly, laughs" (Z IV, KSA 4:392).

My aim here, however, is not to solve these puzzles. Rather, by focusing on the problems that arose in the last section, I hope to indicate how we might approach them. From this point of view, when Zarathustra tells "us" that we must learn to laugh (and Nietzsche emphasizes "learn" twice in a row), I take him to mean that we must learn to occupy a specific perspective. Therefore, the question we need to ask is whether Nietzsche/Zarathustra tells us anything about this perspective from whence we must learn to look and laugh (at ourselves, at others, at "us" as a community). We need to see whether he gives us any clues as to how to understand this perspective and occupy it.

If we go back to the quote above, where Zarathustra claims that he wants to make laughter holy, it is helpful to situate it within the overall argument of the chapter. Nietzsche/Zarathustra begins this chapter by warning us against the rabble and reminding us of the death of God,[39] the death of the idea that there are unquestionable values, that things have a definitive, unchangeable meaning. The following eighteen sections of the chapter can also be seen as an invitation to overcome this event in a positive way, an invitation to be fearless, to be creative, to be assertive, and most importantly to be humble enough to accept that we are not perfect, to accept that we will inevitably fail, but that these failings do not necessarily make us into failures.[40] Consequently, we could say that laughter and the art of laughing at oneself appears in the context of a message of encouragement, one that says something like *don't take things too seriously, and especially don't take yourselves and your sufferings too seriously; focus instead on what still needs to be created*, and so on.[41] But from which perspective is this discourse that belittles our sufferings legitimate, and who is occupying this position? The simplest answer seems to be that it is Zarathustra himself, so that in the end it is all about becoming a bit more like Zarathustra—seeing things as *he* sees them and taking him and his laughter as our model for self-overcoming. There are certainly many instances that seem to corroborate this interpretation.[42]

Yet this conclusion not only contradicts one of the main themes of the book as it unravels in Part IV (where we see how those who listened to Zarathustra have grotesquely misinterpreted him precisely because they began to follow him, taking him as a leader); but, more importantly, it does not take account of the fact that Zarathustra is much more fragile and unstable than these passages suggest. Indeed, if we look at Zarathustra's own journey, we will find that although he claims to be the one who can teach us to laugh, he does not always know how to do it himself. Zarathustra is himself going through the process of learning how to laugh at himself (properly). Looking into those moments of fragility and brokenness will help us find an answer to or a direction for our questions.

There are several moments in which Zarathustra is overcome by a sense of failure and despair. In these moments he is also overtaken by an unbearable sense of gravity, unable to find any laughter and lightness. And it is in these moments that an almost other-than-human voice or force comes to him and laughs at him, mocking him. In "The Dance Song" (even if we learn about this from a song that Zarathustra sings to fight the spirit of gravity), it is life itself that "pulled [him] out with [her] golden fishing rod" and "laughed mockingly."[43] In "The Stillest Hour," Zarathustra hears a laugh that "tore [his] entrails and slit open [his] heart!"[44] Now, what becomes clear in both passages is that, from time to time, Zarathustra also needs to overcome himself, which necessitates that he learn to laugh at himself in the way these figures, which are larger than life, do. Unlike the laughter of those who mock him in the market,[45] and which he must learn to shake off.[46] This is a kind of laughter that Zarathustra understands he must make his own. In other words, it is not the laughter of just any "other." But where, then, is this laughter coming from? How to interpret these figures that seem to come from nowhere and everywhere, that are both silent and loud, alien, and close, within and beyond or above Zarathustra? How to interpret them, in the knowledge that it would be profoundly problematic to read them as some form of *deus ex-machina* magically resolving the plot? In effect, the only way to read these interactions between Zarathustra and "Life," or Zarathustra and his "heart," is to see them as inner dialogues. It is Zarathustra himself who comes to save Zarathustra, but he is coming as an image of what Zarathustra wants to become: as the shadow of a perfection he could become.[47]

Coming back to a passage from the preface, where Zarathustra asks,

> What is the ape to a human? A laughingstock or a painful embarrassment. And that is precisely what the human shall be to the *Übermensch*: a laughingstock or a painful embarrassment. (Z I Preface, KSA 4:14)[48]

We can now say that the *Übermensch* does not stand for an ideal beyond the human. The *Übermensch* stands for a perfection that "we" could become, and hence, it is fundamentally futural.

Moreover, the *Übermensch*'s futural character also means that it must be understood not as a finished, fixed, well-defined, and known goal but as a constantly evolving project: *our* project. And *our* task is then to learn to see ourselves, laugh at ourselves—with all the love and cruelty that belong to laughter—from this new standpoint, that is, from the standpoint of what we could become. Put differently, if laughter and laughing at oneself are to be the key to the realization of the project of self-overcoming, it is not just any laughter, but one that we achieve once we learn to occupy this radically new perspective: a perspective that does not yet exist but is a promise (of a perfection) that we make to ourselves. To learn to laugh at ourselves means, then, to learn to imagine this perspective, to be engaged in its construction. The standpoint that we were looking for is not yet there, but under constant construction and reevaluation—and we are involved in its construction from the start. That is the task.

It goes without saying that Nietzsche/Zarathustra cannot tell us what this new perspective, what "our" project, should be like. But they do give us some criteria—even if mostly by pointing toward the dangers of reproducing the hegemonic standpoint of unquestioned (Christian) values, such as the standpoint of the "despisers of the body" (Z I, KSA 4:39–41), the standpoint of the "virtuous" (Z II, KSA 4:120–3), or the standpoint of the rabble who mocked Zarathustra as "he found and walked his own path" (Z II, KSA 4:188–9). From this we can infer that the new standpoint from which we must learn to laugh at ourselves must be one that embraces our body's intelligence (our "great reason") and pays attention to its needs; one that does not devalue or condemn life; one that allows for difference, for the singular and plurality to emerge. The crucial point, though, is that the new standpoint we are looking for is one that we can never truly possess or embody because we are always in the process of becoming it.

Nietzsche writes his *Zarathustra* for everyone and no one (*für Alle und Keinen*). The story itself, Zarathustra's story, is narrated in the third person, and we are repeatedly reminded that it took place in the past (*thus spoke Zarathustra*). And yet, the book speaks to the reader, it engages her as individual in the present. Indeed, the project of self-overcoming can only be performed by individuals as an activity that comes from within. On the other hand, though, this process cannot be performed in isolation. The problem of nihilism and the project of life-affirmation and self-overcoming are not pitched at the level of the individual. It is not about *my* self-overcoming and *my* self-creation, about *me* finding *my* perspective from where to laugh at myself alone, but about the self-overcoming of the human (*der Mensch*).[49] It is, thus, a shared and diverse project that can only be engaged collectively, by a plurality of individuals. This means that the task must also be to collectively imagine or envisage a community that is able to embody such project. The perspective we are looking for must be one that "we" construct together. At the same time, though, since this very community is part of the project, it must necessarily remain unfinished, in process, under construction, which ultimately means that we must learn to identify with an entity that is *essentially not yet determined*,[50] and hence, unknown, in other words: fundamentally open.

Conclusion

I began this chapter by indicating that to address the relation between laughter and politics in terms of freedom of speech creates a false dichotomy between comedy and violence that forecloses any enquiry into the relation between laughter and violence. From our engagement with Nietzsche's texts, we can now say that the problem with this approach is that it makes it almost impossible to even consider, let alone question, the standpoint from whence a particular form of laughter, a joke, is operating or the violence it may be doing. In other words, it becomes impossible to analyze the kind of values that this or that particular laughter may be incorporating and reinforcing, as well as the forms of life that it may be negating. This is because, by approaching the issue in this way, by considering that comedy is a priori an expression of freedom of speech, its particular standpoint is almost inevitably conflated with that of the right to free speech itself and democratic values in general. (Clearly, to exercise the right to say something doesn't make what you actually say a symbol of freedom or anything remotely similar.) Hence, an insurmountable division emerges between "us" and "them", between those who laugh and those who don't, between those who laugh and those who feel attacked, offended, or excluded. Suddenly, questioning a particular standpoint (a particular joke) is read as being opposed to democratic values *tout court*. In this way, a conflict that should be seen and addressed as internal to a living democracy, part and parcel of the very complex project that we are aiming to attain, becomes a conflict between those who are already "in" and represent a democracy that coincides with democratic values, and those who were always out.

What I have tried to show is that addressing the relation between laughter and politics in terms of freedom of speech almost inevitably leads us to take the project of democracy as being already accomplished and embodied by a series of "enlightened" individuals and institutions; instead of confronting its failure and seeing that for it to be truly open to change, critique, and improvement, it must conceive of itself as being always underway, in the making, a work necessarily in progress. This, however, should not be taken as a condemnation of laughter and comedy. To the contrary. But it does seem—to borrow Zarathustra's idiom—that we still have to learn to laugh! We have to create new comedies, new jokes, and new laughters, and imagine new horizons in an attempt to anticipate or prefigure the very standpoint that we aim to attain. In this way, perhaps one day, by laughing at ourselves with a laughter that includes and addresses everyone, we will have to laugh at the hubris of those who preach free speech as "good" democrats against others.

Notes

1. Aristophanes's comedy *Lysistrata* from 411 BC is one of the oldest documented cases of censorship; it was considered subversive. Cf. Halliwell (1991: 48–70).
2. Although if we follow recent studies focusing on the evolutionary origins of human laughter and see it linked to survival functions, one might conclude that its relation to danger or threat was there from the start. See Raine (2016).
3. As F. Schlegel notes in his 1794 essay "On the Aesthetic Value of Greek Comedy" (*Vom aesthetischen Werte der Griechischen Komödie*), Ancient Greek culture and religion had a different attitude to laughter, joy, and humor than Christian cultures do. As he puts it (silently quoting Plato), according to the Ancient Greeks, "all Gods like a good joke" (Schlegel 1794: 20, my translation). For the relation between humor and other religions/cultures, see Koenraad Elst, who argues that in Hinduism, "mockery and worship go together" (2011: 37).
4. As Stephen Halliwell has pointed out, the Old Testament seems to be more indulgent with laughter and jokes than the New Testament (2008: 471–83).
5. In this show, however, Sebastian arguably does joke about political or religious "issues," as he puts it, if indirectly, like when he says he prefers to joke about tea and coffee: "Coz biscuits are non-violent" (2018).
6. Samuel Patty taught a class on freedom of expression and used CH cartoons for this.
7. See, e.g., Brooks (2015) or Sjaastad (2015).
8. As Brian Trench has argued, "the claimed 'hysteria' of the '*Je suis Charlie Hebdo*' movement became the prime target of criticism" (2016: 184).

9. The podcast/discussion between Matt Wuerker, Pulitzer Prize winning editorial cartoonist for *Politico*, and Derek Mitchell, President of the National Democratic Institute in the United States, is a good example for this line of thought (Bowen 2019); see also Goldman (2013).
10. See M 89, where Nietzsche rather wittily exposes the "a-moral" roots of morality in five lines, or M 91, where Nietzsche wonders how it might be possible that an almighty God did not manage to make his intention (*Absicht*) clear to his creatures (*Geschöpfe*).
11. In his essay, "Nietzsche, Re-Evaluation and the Turn to Genealogy," David Owen (2003) convincingly shows how this project fails and leads Nietzsche to rethink his analysis and critique of Christianity through a genealogy.
12. It would be wrong, however, to assume that the relation between seriousness and laughter in GS is always thematized or approached in the same way as in GS 327. In GS 107, for instance, Nietzsche seems to claim that the only possible relation between them is one of alternation, which suggests that they ultimately remain mutually exclusive. Cf. Siemens and Hay (2015).
13. Nietzsche is working with images: The "gloomy, creaking machine" indicates a heavy duty that cannot be done lightly. That Nietzsche is working on a reevaluation of superficiality is clear also in the preface to GS, where he says that "the 'Greeks were superficial—out of profundity!'" (GS Preface 4, KSA 3:352).
14. Cf. Hay 2017.
15. Thus, the incongruity theory of laughter locates the cause of laughter in the absurdity of a given situation, plot and so on. We laugh "when we experience something ... that violates our expectations" (Morreall 1982: 245). I find John Morreall's classification(s) of the different theories and types of laughter unhelpful, especially when it comes to reading Nietzsche's uses of laughter, so I consciously avoid using them.
16. Cf. GS 1, KSA 3:369.
17. Cf. *Genealogy of Morality* (GM) Preface 6.
18. I use this term in the knowledge that it is polemical. The simple point I want to make is that Nietzsche's investment in philosophy and his entire critical project is not coming out of indifference for the human, but something else.
19. See GS 1, KSA 3:372: "There is no denying that *in the long run* each of these great teachers of a purpose was vanquished by laughter, reason and nature: the brief tragedy always went back and towards the eternal comedy of existence."
20. See GS 1, KSA 3:372: "Man has gradually become a fantastic animal that has one condition of existence more to fulfil than any other animal: from time-to-time man *needs to* believe to know *why* he exists."
21. See GS 1, KSA 3:372: "'Not only laughter and gay wisdom but also the tragic, with all its sublime unreason, belongs to the means and necessities of the preservation of the species!' And therefore! Therefore! Therefore! Oh, do you understand me, my brothers?"
22. Although Nietzsche also indulges in laughing *at* others.
23. To understand what our needs truly are is arguably one of Nietzsche's main concerns in GS, as becomes clear in GS 335 *Long live Physics!*
24. I.e., "To laugh at oneself as one would have to laugh in order to laugh from the whole truth" (GS 1, KSA 3:370).
25. Cf. Derek Mitchel, in Bowen (2019).
26. See GM P 6 (KSA 5:252–3) and GM II, 1 (KSA 5:291–2).
27. In this, Früchtl is following Simon Critchley's analysis of Freud in his book *On Humor* (Critchley 2002).

28. This is one of the thoughts underlying Alenka Zupančič's analysis of the comical and its potential in *The Odd One In* (2008).
29. According to Bergson (1900), through laughter, social norms and values are reinforced as laughter corrects the eccentric.
30. Hannah Gadsby's stand-up comedy film *Nanette* is a recording of a live performance at the Opera House in Sydney. This show, which Hannah Gadsby started in 2017, went on for over a year.
31. Homosexuality in Tasmania was not decriminalized until 1997.
32. It is interesting to compare the values that Gadsby defends in her show with Nietzsche's project of transvaluation of all values and his critique of metaphysics in general, for there are, in spite of the differences, important affinities. Though not the place to develop this, I note that both are engaged in a radical critique of the human, while at the same time showing extreme concern for the phenomenon that we could call hatred of the human (especially in the form of self-hatred). In other words, they are both committed to the "growth" or perfection of the human. They both criticize the masses, the "herd," and the idea that the individual could ever be defined with general categories of identity. Moreover, Gadsby, and I believe Nietzsche too, strongly believes that differences, pluralities, and diversity is what makes us strong and allows us to learn and grow, whereas everything else impoverishes us.
33. In her show, divided in two parts with different kinds of jokes and puns, the audience is invited to experience this very paradox and to question the perspective from which it had laughed at the beginning.
34. This is why Critchley's assumption that whenever we laugh at ourselves suddenly our "superego becomes our amigo" proves to be quite problematic (2002: 93–111).
35. In 2020, she created a new show: Douglas (also for Netflix).
36. All these refer to GS 1. The perspective of the species is perhaps the least obviously fictive or most seemingly real and attainable perspective of all, but it is also the most problematic one. While it helps Nietzsche to denaturalize and question all values, in the end it is too vague. Nothing remains but the life of the species. The important question is, what *kind* of life are we talking about? Nietzsche addresses this question in *Thus Spoke Zarathustra*, and it goes hand in hand with the pursuit and creation of a different point of view from where to look at things.
37. Zarathustra complains about the people in the market who laughed at him and in doing so expressed their hatred. Thus, he says to himself, "My soul is calm and bright as the morning mountains. But they believe I am cold, that I mock and I deal in terrible jests. And now they look at me and laugh, and in laughing they hate me too. There is ice in their laughter" (Z I Preface 5, KSA 4:21).
38. It would be wrong, too, to consider that Zarathustra's laughter is always intransitive.
39. "But now this God has died!" (Z IV, KSA 4:357).
40. "And when you failed at something great, are you yourselves therefore—failures? And if you yourselves failed, did humanity therefore fail? But if humanity failed: well then, well now!" (Z IV, KSA 4:364) I take Zarathustra's key message to be about the *sufficiency* of human nature.
41. "Cheer up, what does it matter! How much is still possible! Learn to laugh at yourselves as one must laugh!" (Z IV, KSA 4:364).
42. For instance, when Zarathustra reflects on the life and death of Jesus and proclaims,

> If only he had remained in the desert and far away from the good and the just! Perhaps he would have learned to live and to love the earth—and even to laugh!

Believe me, my brothers! He died too early; he himself would have recanted his teaching if he had reached my age! He was noble enough for recanting! (Z I, KSA 4:95)

It is unclear how seriously to take Zarathustra's reflections here. What does seem clear, though, is that Zarathustra presents himself as having attained the right perspective from whence to judge and laugh.

43. Z II, KSA 4:140.
44. Z II, KSA 4:189.
45. "'There they stand,' he said to his heart, 'they laugh, they do not understand me, I am not the mouth for these ears'" (Z I Preface, KSA 4.18).
46. "What does their mockery matter!," asks his heart in "The Stillest Hour" (Z II, KSA 4:189).
47. In a Nachlass note called "Zarathustra's Holy Laugh," Nietzsche introduces the idea that beauty is a sign of a perfection to come. He calls this the shadow of the *Übermensch*: "Perfection throws its shadow ahead: I call this shadow beauty—the lightest and stillest of all things came to me as a shadow of the *Übermensch*" (NL 13[1], KSA 10.467).
48. See also NL 1 [49], KSA 10:24: "Whoever has seen the ideal of someone, finds the real one to be like a caricature."
49. Although it is important to stress that this is not to be understood as a nihilistic rejection of the human, but of its transformation.
50. Cf. BGE 62, KSA 5:81, where Nietzsche, like Kierkegaard, defines man as "*das noch nicht festgestellte Tier.*"

References

Bergson, H. (1900), *Le rire. Essai sur la signification du comique*, Paris: Éditions Alcan.
Bowen, L. (2019), "How Does Humor Help Democracy?," *Democracy Works*, October 9. Available online: https://www.demworks.org/how-does-humor-help-democracy.
Brooks, D. (2015), "I Am Not Charlie Hebdo," *New York Times*, January 8. Available online: https://www.nytimes.com/2015/01/09/opinion/david-brooks-i-am-not-charlie-hebdo.html.
Critchley, S. (2002), *On Humor*, London: Routledge.
Elst, K. (2011), "Humor in Hinduism," in *Humor and Religion. Challenges and Ambiguities*, ed. H. Geybels and W. Van Herck, 35–53, London: Continuum. Available online: https://theconversation.com/the-evolutionary-origins-of-laughter-are-rooted-more-in-survival-than-enjoyment-57750.
Früchtl, J. (2020), "Sensus and Dissensus Communis: The Comedy of Democracy (Following Cavell)," *Aesthetic Investigations* 4 (1): 96–111.
Goldman, N. (2013), "Comedy and Democracy: The Role of Humor in Social Justice," *Animating Democracy*. Available online: https://animatingdemocracy.org/resource/comedy-and-democracy-role-humor-social-justice.
Halliwell, S. (1991), "Comic Satire and Freedom of Speech in Classical Athens," *Journal of Hellenic Studies* 111: 48–70.
Halliwell, S. (2008), *Greek Laughter: A Study of Cultural Psychology from Homer to Early Christianity*, New York: Cambridge University Press.

Hay, K. (2017), "Reason and Laughter in Kant and Nietzsche," in *Nietzsche and Kant: On Aesthetics and Anthropology*, ed. K. Hay and M. Joao Branco, 197–217, London: Bloomsbury.

Morreall, J. (1982), "A New Theory of Laughter," *Philosophical Studies: An International Journal for Philosophy in the Analytic Tradition* 42 (2): 243–54.

Nanette (2018), [Comedy] Dir. M. Parry, written by H. Gadsby, Australia: Netflix.

Owen, D. (2003), "Nietzsche, Re-Evaluation and the Turn to Genealogy," *European Journal of Philosophy* 11 (3): 249–72.

Raine, J. (2016), "The Evolutionary Origins of Laughter Are Rooted More in Survival than Enjoyment," *The Conversation*, April 13.

Schlegel, F. (1794), "Vom ästhetischen Werte der Griechischen Komödie," in *Kritische Friedrich-Schlegel-Ausgabe*, 1 *Studien des Klassischen Altertums*, ed. E. Behler, 19–33.

Sebastian, K. (2018), "Why I Don't Do Jokes about Politics in India," Stand Up Comedy, April 23. Available online: https://www.youtube.com/watch?v=azFe8b6yfb0.

Siemens, H., and Hay, K. (2015), "Ridendo dicere severum: On Probity, Laughter and Self-Critique in Nietzsche's Figure of the Free Spirit," in *Nietzsche's Philosophy of the Free Spirit*, ed. R. Bamford, 111–36, Lanham, MD: Rowman & Littlefield.

Sjaastad, M. (2015), "I Am Not Charlie," *Open Democracy*, January 15. Available online: https://www.opendemocracy.net/en/can-europe-make-it/i-am-not-charlie/.

Trench, B. (2016) '"Charlie Hebdo", Islamophobia and Freedoms of the Press," *Studies: An Irish Quarterly Review, FREEDOM OF SPEECH HOW FAR CAN YOU GO?* 105: 183–91.

Zupančič, A. (2008), *The Odd One In: On Comedy*, Cambridge, MA: MIT Press.

10

Nietzsche on Masculinity:
The Joys of Danger and Play

Jeffrey Church

There is a pervasive sense in contemporary culture that "traditional masculinity"—whatever that means—is discredited and, if not dead, then at least moribund. Mention a John Wayne movie at a party with academics and you will be met with eye rolls. There is also the strong feeling that what has replaced it—"toxic masculinity"—is, well, toxic for society as a whole, as well as for men and women. The incel movement, for example, has become at times lethal, as when a seventeen-year-old incel killed a woman with a machete. However, there is much less clarity about what should replace these forms, what ideal or ideals of masculinity could discipline, focus, and elevate the development of men. Nevertheless, there remains a pressing concern for finding a new ideal, born out of a rejection of tradition's narrowness and hierarchy, and our current oppressive, often cruel, hedonism. In light of this concern, it is important for us to examine and assess the forgotten ideals put forward by thinkers of the past, in our hope that their ideals could be retrieved in the present.[1]

This chapter examines Friedrich Nietzsche's view of masculinity, in part because, as Harvey Mansfield has argued, "Nietzsche is *the* philosopher of manliness in modern times" (2006: 110). Despite Nietzsche's importance on this matter, there has been little scholarly work done on Nietzsche's view of men—most of the attention in Nietzsche scholarship has been devoted to his view of women.[2] As a result, what remains is the impression that Nietzsche envisions masculinity as being macho in the face of the death of God, asserting yourself not just in society or politics but also creating and asserting your being in an empty cosmos (Mansfield 2006: chapter 4). As I will argue below, I think this is the wrong way to think about Nietzsche on masculinity or what he calls "*Männlichkeit*" (BGE 209). I argue that for Nietzsche, masculinity's central concern is not with a meaningless cosmos but with one of the tensions or contradictions characteristic of being human.[3] In the conclusion, I will suggest that this view can help address some problems facing men in modernity.

1. Mansfield on Nietzsche on Manliness

One of the few scholars to discuss Nietzsche's view of manliness is Mansfield. According to Mansfield, Nietzsche's central preoccupation is with the death of God and hence with the implication of that truth, namely the nihilism of "nothing is true, everything is permitted." As a result, "any extreme action can be expected" (2006: 111). However, Mansfield's Nietzsche finds, nothing extreme results. In fact, in modern times, there is a tremendous constriction of extreme deeds, a feminization of the human spirit.

For Mansfield's Nietzsche, the manly response to the death of God is not to "unbend the bow" but rather to extend masculine assertiveness beyond the personal, beyond the political, to the existential. The man in modernity, first, can endure "truthfulness," the embrace of modernity's grasp of a meaningless universe (2006: 113). Second, manliness for Mansfield's Nietzsche consists in a creative assertion of human significance, embodied above all in the "superman" who is the "manly man who does his own thinking" (2006: 116).

Mansfield critiques Nietzsche for his nihilism. Though Nietzsche himself had a personal preference for artists and philosophers, Mansfield argues that Nietzsche's nihilism has no principled limit to masculine assertiveness. In other words, "although Nietzsche himself would never have been a Nazi, his influence helped create what has been called 'German nihilism,'" which was "at its worst" in "Hitlerism" (2006: 118). Nietzschean nihilism has no resources to condemn Hitler and may have been instrumental in leading to him. As such, masculinity needs a check, a restraint from natural or divine morality (2006: 119). Mansfield concludes his book by returning to Plato and Aristotle, who provide such a limit to masculine assertiveness.

There are several problems with Mansfield's interpretation. The root problem is with his understanding of nihilism in Nietzsche. Very few Nietzsche scholars interpret nihilism in the way that Mansfield does. In fact, many scholars understand nihilism to be a feature of the Platonic-Christian-modern tradition, that it has destroyed itself and become nihilistic, rather than a view embraced by Nietzsche himself.[4] In addition, several scholars recently have begun to develop an approach to Nietzsche's ethics that denies Mansfield's assumption that for Nietzsche "everything is permitted."[5]

Since I am part of this latter movement, I have a dog in this fight. So let me briefly sketch my approach to Nietzsche's ethics and direct readers to a fuller treatment elsewhere (Church 2015, 2019). To begin, it is useful to place Nietzsche and the "death of God" within the context of post-Kantian German philosophy. The "death of God" does not consist of an original argument of Nietzsche's but was rather a crystallization of the modern tendency away from God as the center of the universe and toward humanity as the center of the universe (Pippin 1999). One might profitably see Kant as a key figure in this tendency, especially in his Copernican Revolution that turned philosophy away from its abiding concern with metaphysics to its central concern being human reason and human freedom. Kant is such a key figure here because he asserted the primacy of practical philosophy over theoretical philosophy and sought to base ethics not on nature or God but on the aspiration of human beings toward freedom. Kant's philosophy of freedom dominated German philosophy after him, in the Hegelian and post-Hegelian thinkers, as well as the efforts on the part of the first generation of neo-Kantian thinkers in the mid-nineteenth century to find some accommodation for human freedom within a naturalistic (and eventually Darwinian) universe (Beiser 2014). Arthur Schopenhauer, for instance, seeks to understand the value and significance of human existence within the frame of Kant's Critical Philosophy, and Nietzsche as well was steeped in the debates among neo-Kantian philosophers, especially the *Pessimusstreit* of the mid-nineteenth century, inaugurated by Schopenhauer (Beiser 2016).

As a good neo-Kantian philosopher, then, Nietzsche's abiding ethical ideal was to defend and discern the conditions for the possibility of human freedom.[6] Also as a good neo-Kantian, Nietzsche understood that simply liberating the human will to do whatever it wants—what Kant called *Willkür*—was not truly freedom. It was not freedom because following our whims or our destructive tendencies (as in the case of the Nazis) involves abandoning one's will to our natural selfishness or pride or viciousness. For this reason, Nietzsche does not celebrate the "blond beasts" or master morality—who can do whatever they want—because they are "stupid" and shallow animals, expressions of their nature rather than their own self-determining will. It is only when slave morality comes along, when the saint demonstrates a greater will to power than the soldier in mastering his desire to master others, that human beings begin to develop the capacity to transcend and master their natural and social surroundings. In this way, as Nietzsche emphasizes again and again in his portraits of "higher men," the achievement of freedom is not an easy task as might be suggested by "everything is permitted." Instead, it involves tremendous self-development and cultivation so as to achieve genuine freedom. In other words, as in Kant, the formal conditions of the ideal of freedom provide substantive ethical standards to evaluate human action, such that not everything may be permitted.

In general, Mansfield is right that for Nietzsche masculinity's fundamental nature involves some sort of assertion of humanity's worth or significance in a silent universe. At the same time, he is wrong to assume that this assertion can take any form. In what follows, I will develop an account of masculinity as containing a standard immanent to its nature, one that reveals Nietzsche not to be an irresponsible nihilist but a philosopher wrestling with the conflicting demands modernity places upon us.

2. The Contradiction at the Heart of Humanity

In all of Nietzsche's scattered discussions of modern masculinity, he emphasizes the tension inherent in its nature. For example, in *Assorted Opinions and Maxims* (AOM 274), Nietzsche argues that "through the woman nature shows the point it has by now reached in its work on the image of mankind." By contrast, with regard to men, nature "shows what it had to overcome in attaining to this point," but also "what its intentions are with respect to mankind." Masculinity is both retrospective and prospective, an account of human self-assertion in the past, as well as an account of whither humanity will go next. These two perspectives need not harmonize, and in fact quite often emphatically do not. The past can be seen as a fetter on our creativity, or as unjust, or as base and lowly. Indeed, it seems built into the nature of masculine self-assertion to transcend the past, to make one's own mark, rather than simply following in the footsteps of what has come.

It is helpful at this point to back up and understand why masculinity on Nietzsche's view is characterized by an inherent tension. Consider the famous account of master morality and slave morality in *On the Genealogy of Morality* (GM). According to Nietzsche's philosophy of history, masculinity first emerged in the ancient world in the aristocratic classes, whether in the primitive societies of the "blond beasts" or the more developed ancient civilizations. The ideal of masculinity in this class consisted in a certain mode of "valuation"—through action, the aristocratic man "grows spontaneously, seeking out its opposite only so that it can say 'yes' to itself even more thankfully and exultantly" (GM I 10). The aristocratic man asserts his being unreflectively, through "governing unconscious instincts" (GM I 10). He impresses his being on the surrounding world, and takes pleasure in recognizing his own being after besting his "opposite." Or, in the language of Nietzsche's notion of the will to power, this class seeks to exert its agency in the world and incorporate the world around it as part of its agency.[7] The assertion of this agency almost always involved risk and hence the virtue of courage or "daring" in sometimes "unpredictable" and "improbable" ways (GM I 11). The manifestation of this power was material in nature: aristocratic classes were stronger physically and could coerce the bodies of the weaker, and in later aristocratic societies they were richer, more powerful, more physically impressive.

The problem with the aristocratic or master morality, as is well known, is its unreflectiveness. The aristocratic class was similar to animals or "blond beasts" in its "innocent conscience" that it does not reflect, or bring a normative judgment upon, its own actions (GM I 11). However, this lack of reflection means that "the history of mankind would be far too stupid a thing if it had not had the intellect [*Geist*] of the powerless injected into it" (GM I 7). "Man first became an interesting animal on the foundation" of slave morality, such that the "human soul became deep in the higher sense" (GM I 6). The slave class effected this transformation by introducing an alternative form of moral valuation. This moral valuation is reflective in nature, in the sense that it negates the given, the natural with its inequality of strength, power, and prestige. It raises the question of the value of the master's valuation. In so doing, it creates a form of agency that transcends the master's agency, a kind of superego reflecting on the ego (GM I 13). This agency, an "unbiased 'subject' with freedom of choice," was a fiction, but it was a "sublime self-deception," sublime because it allowed humanity to continually sublimate its drives and achieve higher and higher states of the soul (GM I 13). The slave moral valuation entered humanity's consciousness and took on a logic of its own. It negated master morality and introduced its own form of Jewish and Christian slave morality. Yet the negating gaze of slave morality turned against itself, its particular form of slave morality, calling it into question, creating a new modern democratic moral system, and so on. We might think of slave morality as that part of human freedom which annihilates the given.

Slave morality was victorious because it could turn the will to power against itself, demonstrating a higher or governing manifestation of it. That is, the aristocratic class manifested its agency in visible deeds. The slave class then proceeds to manifest its agency spiritually, that is, it governs these physical actions by conferring on them a particular normative character, either good or evil, and by creating in individuals the need to achieve this ideal of goodness, an ideal legislated by the community, as opposed to the various, unique displays of individual goodness by the aristocratic community. Those unique displays become governed by the communal goodness of slave morality.

Finally, however, the self-negating character of slave morality necessitates a sublation of master and slave morality. Eventually slave morality turns against our embodied natures so much as to be ascetic, life-denying. For Nietzsche, the return of master morality does not mean that we abandon slave morality and turn back the clock to the blond beast—this is impossible. Instead, the human soul becomes the battlefield of two competing modes of valuation—"there is, today, perhaps no more distinguishing feature of the 'higher nature,' the intellectual nature, than to be divided in this sense and really and truly a battle ground for these opposites" (GM I 16). This conflict is the context in which it is best to understand the nature and ideal of masculinity for Nietzsche.

3. Masculinity in *Thus Spoke Zarathustra*

A fuller treatment of masculinity in *Thus Spoke Zarathustra* might examine the character of Zarathustra and what his behavior expresses for Nietzsche's ideal. In this section, I will confine myself to Zarathustra's most extensive discussion of *der Mann* in "On Little Old and Young Women" in part 1. In this passage, Zarathustra states that "a real man [*ächte Mann*] wants two things: danger and play." Danger and play exist in distinct tension with one another. Danger appears when our life or reputation is at risk, when life is serious and there is often only one course of action. The early manifestation of this masculine desire is of course in the "warrior," so that "man should be educated for war." Why do men seek out danger? For Zarathustra, the "happiness of man [*der Glück des Mannes*] is: I will." In other words, it is in times of danger where we can most clearly demonstrate our agency. In times of peace and calm, there is little need to transform the world to confront problems. We can passively go on, our will hidden from view. Times of peace, then, dissatisfy the man, because he cannot find satisfaction in changing the world around him. It is only in danger when the man can achieve satisfaction, because then he can externalize his being into the world, risking being incorporated into someone else's activity and becoming governed by them, and hoping for success, in which he can contemplate his own will as reflected back at him from others. Though *Thus Spoke Zarathustra* predates his account of master and slave morality, we can see in his account of danger a view of master morality. The aristocratic man asserts his will in dangerous times, whether this be times of physical danger, as in wartime, or in times of spiritual danger, in the conflict over the normative ideals of an organization or community.

Play is quite different than danger and is difficult to imagine in trying times. In play, we can be cheerful, we can take joy in our creation and destruction because nothing really is at stake. Danger demands immediate, unreflective activity, while play calls for a depth of soul, and, indeed, "man's disposition ... is deep." This desire for play,

Zarathustra states, derives from the "child" hidden "in a real man [ächten Manne]." Nietzsche view of childhood play stretches back far in his career, particularly to his famous description of nature in *The Birth of Tragedy* (BT) as a "playing child who sets down stones here, there, and the next place, and who builds up piles of sand only to knock them down again." This activity is a "playful construction and demolition of the world of individuality as an outpouring of primal pleasure and delight [*Urlust*]" (BT 24). Why do men desire play? Men do so in order to manifest a higher level of agency and freedom than is manifested in danger. Play upends the results of previous actions, or creatively reconfigures their meaning. In play, men can take joy in the negation and creation of the order of things, a Dionysian joy in the dissolution of the Apollonian. Danger inclines men to necessity, while play allows men the freedom to transform circumstances to reflect their agency's capacity for transcendence.

In this way, Zarathustra anticipates the double consciousness that exists in GM. Master morality calls for courageous valuations, while slave morality adopts a reflective, even an ironic distance toward those very valuations. In sum, then, the Zarathustra discussion of masculinity reflects the tension we saw elaborated in GM. Men love danger and play because these amount to, in compressed form, the ends of both master and slave morality. The tension between these two is the same as the tension between the two moralities: the immediate assertiveness of master morality and the reflective assertiveness of slave morality. So what is a man to do? How can masculinity synthesize these quite distinct ends?

The passage, as I mentioned, is entitled "On Little Old and Young Women" and is mainly concerned with describing femininity. Nietzsche offers some of his characteristically unkind and demeaning remarks about women's nature: "everything about woman is a riddle, and everything about woman has one solution: that is pregnancy." The function of women here is to employ her love in service to eliciting the child out of the man so that the child will grow to be the overman. If we set aside these particular teleological remarks, however, and focus on the overall account, then we may read this passage as holding that men cannot achieve their ends on their own, through a promethean independence or self-sufficiency that is often a hallmark (or stereotype) of masculinity. To synthesize their divergent ends, men need to love and be loved in turn. It is difficult to love men, because they arouse "fear," with their courting of danger and their ironic play. Nevertheless, only through the creation of a community bound together by love can men achieve the synthesis of their ends.

How does love achieve this purpose? In *The Gay Science* (GS 363), Nietzsche has his most extensive discussion of love and how the different sexes conceive of love. For Nietzsche, masculine love is the love of possession, while feminine love is the love of self-surrender. When putting them together, we do not find the beautiful complementarity of, say, Aristophanes's speech in the *Symposium*, but a "harsh, terrible, enigmatic, and immoral ... antagonism" (GS 363). That is, men seek possession in love, and women withhold their surrender until they find the right man. The role of the feminine in Nietzsche's thought, then, is to sublimate male assertiveness, to find a higher object of male agency than physical possession. In the Zarathustra speech, Zarathustra calls on women to be "the most dangerous plaything," bringing together danger and play. What this love does is elevate men's striving from the physical to the spiritual, to those relationships men can take on with their partners in which they can engage in mutual play, but its very mutuality is prone to danger, because the partner can turn around and dominate or adopt an ironic distance toward the man. In other words, a loving relationship is a difficult, fragile ideal, because it is built upon antagonistic dispositions. Yet because of its difficulty and fragility it can be a satisfying object of men's striving for both danger and play.[8]

4. Masculinity in *Beyond Good and Evil*

In the previous section, I argued that *Thus Spoke Zarathustra* characterizes masculinity as riven between two conflicting ends, and that personal relationships of love can supply one possible way to harmonize these ends. In *Beyond Good and Evil* (BGE), I will argue, Nietzsche provides another path.

In BGE 209, Nietzsche recommends to us the notion of "masculine skepticism." To illustrate this concept, he tells the story of Frederick the Great's father, a man of aristocratic morality who held that in the modern age such "men were lacking." Instead, everyone in Europe seemed to be "falling prey to atheism, esprit, and the entertaining, happy-go-lucky spirit of clever Frenchmen," and above all, "that enormous bloodsucker, the spider of skepticism in the background." The elder Frederick, in other words, witnessed the corrosive effect of the negating element of slave morality. The ultimate result of this negation was a self-negation, a "shattered will that no longer commanded, that was no longer able to command." Since men assert their agency and command, and Europe no longer has a will, then the prospects for masculinity in modernity looked dim.

However, Nietzsche remarks, a "harsher and more dangerous new type of skepticism was growing in his son," Frederick the Great. This is the "skepticism of a bold masculinity [*Männlichkeit*], which is most closely related to the genius for war and conquest," which appeared in Germany in the character of Frederick the Great. This masculine skepticism demonstrates the same duality we have seen characteristic of masculinity: it "despises and nevertheless appropriates; it undermines and takes possession; it does not believe but does not die out on this account; it gives the spirit a dangerous freedom but is severe on the heart." According to Nietzsche, this skepticism, born in war and conquest, becomes sublimated in the form of Goethe, and in "German philologists and critical historians," and is an essential tool for the emergence of the philosopher of the future.

How is such a skepticism possible? It combines elements that do not mesh well with one another. It despises an object and undermines it, yet appropriates it, nonetheless? Why? It believes in nothing but does not die? How does it sustain itself? Finally, it liberates itself, yet gives itself limits? How? The synthesis in this passage is carried out in an exemplary form by Frederick the Great, so it is best to begin with him. Unlike the military leaders who preceded him, Frederick was concerned not simply with accumulating political power, through the physical extension of territory, for example. In addition, Frederick, influenced by French Enlightenment figures such as Voltaire, saw the need to supplement his political rule with popular enlightenment. As a result, he supported policies to open up free discussion and invited philosophical and scientific luminaries from across Europe to join his court.

Frederick in this way combined disparate ends in a political life. He satisfied his aristocratic morality by appropriating, by exerting his will in the material domain, that is, in governing his subjects and winning his wars. Yet he satisfied his slave consciousness by adopting a reflective distance toward political life through his philosophical writing and discussion. From this spiritual perspective, those material possessions appear to be objects that one may despise, undermining their significance. Frederick could maintain his atheism and not die out because he could replace the authority of the divine with the authority of human self-conscious reflection as expressed in philosophic inquiry. Finally, he could grant some "freedom" to his "spirit" precisely in those spiritual activities of self-reflection in his court. Such freedom of the spirit resembles the "play" that we saw in the masculinity of Zarathustra. For Nietzsche, philosophy above all involves cheerfulness or playfulness, as it is not subject to strict rules and strict necessity but consists in an activity of free, creative self-determination, a legislation for oneself and others of the "whither" and the "for what?" of humanity (BGE 211). Yet Frederick could be severe on the heart, restricting and disciplining his passions based on the necessities of the serious business of political rule.

Nietzsche is quite clear that the political life is not the only vocation that can bring together the diverse ends of masculinity—the scholar and the poet can as well (the philosopher is wholly different, incorporating and transcending skepticism in the subsequent two sections of BGE). As such, Nietzsche suggests here that life within a political regime is always bifurcated. On the one hand, politics and the many vocations that constitute a regime and make it possible—the scholar and poet included—have certain material necessities that must be addressed in the most serious fashion. Sometimes, these political imperatives come with attendant dangers, which arouse the desire of the masculine. Such imperatives are of the emphatically material kind, but they need not be the sort of basic, existential threats to states such as war. There are many more mundane forms of material demands comprising political life—modern commercial society demands risky decisions; the arts and letters involve risk to reputation or honor; medicine, law, justice all require difficult decisions in which the lives of individuals are often on the line—and such demands are serious, calling for the assertion of human agency within their boundaries in order to rise to meet the danger, to protect the political regime, to advance and enrich the business, to bolster your firm's credibility, and to save the lives of others in medicine or law. Such activities require tremendous discipline and courage and calls on the masculine desire to take possession of the situation, to understand it and master it.

On the other hand, life within the political regime always points beyond it, because the reflective slave consciousness cheerfully transcends what is given around us, calling into question its assumptions and its significance. This is most easily seen in the case of the political life, in which "my state right or wrong" is easily challenged when one recognizes that there are many other states in the world with their own material needs and valuations. We can take on a reflective distance to such conflicts, despising them as the result of petty concerns or bruised pride. Yet many other activities within the regime admit of such reflective questioning—the lawyer who reflects on the ethics of her firm, or the businessman who wonders about the value or importance of his product. In transcending our vocations, we can take joy in our liberation from our individual role, a joy in our capacity to make or remake our vocations in any number of ways or directions. We take joy in our freedom, which effects a kind of Dionysian creative destruction of our Apollonian political life.

Such a reflective distance does not come into outright conflict with the material imperatives because it ends up having a salutary effect on the performance of the vocation. The reflection is not simply a nihilating gesture but comes with it the masculine desire for play, as suggested by the Zarathustra passage. The reflection on political, business, legal, and medical ends can lead to a creative rethinking of those ends. It can check the worst excesses of the "manly" assertion in the material domain by calling into question the necessity or seriousness of its imperative. Yet it can also improve the performance by adopting a more cheerful disposition toward these ends, adopting a willingness to destroy even what one has worked for a lifetime. For Nietzsche, this is the sign of masculinity, not the brute assertion of physical power, but the ability at once to assert one's will and to assert one's will against one's own will.

This balancing act in political life is not easy, just as the romantic relationship we discovered in the last chapter was quite hard. As we saw, the tendency in the German spirit was toward an enervating form of skepticism, as opposed to the older form of unreflective masculinity. It is easy for masculinity to fall into brute assertiveness without any reflection, and it is also easy for masculinity to be swamped by reflection and turn into an ironic, simply playful self-consciousness, either a form of immediate agency or a nihilating spirit.

Conclusion

These key passages in Nietzsche's late period works help clarify the initial description of masculinity Nietzsche developed in AOM. As we saw above, through masculinity nature shows what it has had to "overcome" up to this point. This backward-looking form of masculinity describes its master morality side, as master morality involves the assertion of one's will in order to meet some danger, reconfigure the world, thereby impressing the world with one's will, leaving a lasting trace on it. At the same time, through masculinity nature also points toward humanity's aim or intentions. This forward-looking form of masculinity describes the slave morality side, since slave morality involves the abstraction from the given in order to project some ideal, an ideal that is the product of human free play. We have seen in the previous discussion the two contexts in which masculinity's inner tension can be reconciled: in a personal loving relationship and in a vocation of the political regime.

This account of masculinity also shows how there can be an internal check or limitation on the ethics of masculinity. Everything is not permitted for the man. As we have seen, masculinity exists within a personal or political context, in which certain norms govern those relationships. In order to assert one's will, the man must assert his will in service to this personal or political community. The man cannot act whimsically—since his action will be unintelligible to others—nor can he act immorally according to this community—or else he will not be regarded as serving that community. At the same time, however, masculinity calls for free play, some liberation from these communities, but play is only possible with the particular contexts which one transcends. There is no play *ex nihilo*.[9]

Nietzsche's view of masculinity could have some contemporary significance. First, it provides a basis for the criticism of one-sided understandings of masculinity. The "traditional masculinity" of John Wayne or of more recent movie action heroes—the gruff, macho, taciturn type—represents only one expression of masculinity's duality and, moreover, essentializes what is a particularly early form of masculinity's historical development, namely, the heroism of physical strength. The traditional view flattens masculinity and fails to recognize its capacity for sublimation into the heroism of the intellect, or of "spirit." In addition, it provides a basis for criticizing contemporary skepticism or irony about any such normative role as masculinity. The ironic, playful self-consciousness is once again a one-sided form of masculinity and hence not fully satisfying to us. Traditional masculinity squelches our desire for reflection and distance, while the contemporary skepticism about gender roles frustrates our desire for the assertion of agency.

Second, Nietzsche's ideal of masculinity is compatible with contemporary liberal democratic life. In fact, contemporary liberal democratic life seems to call for exactly the type of dualism embodied in this masculine ideal, namely, a longing to serve a cause higher than oneself, a cause full of danger in which one can make a difference in the world, as well as that longing to question and challenge, to take nothing for given and subject all claims and institutions to a skeptical gaze. Democracy requires assertive citizens, for instance, and liberalism requires skeptical ones. At the same time, Nietzsche's ideal goes some way in addressing what is the contemporary confusion that many men experience about their roles in modern life. It all seems quite confusing how men should act—should we be macho and tough, or intellectual and cold, or sensitive and emotional? Nietzsche's account demonstrates that some confusion or ambiguity is warranted, because it is built in to the very ideal. The highest task of masculinity is to find some sublation of those divergent ends, a task that is full of danger—in this way, one's own self can be the greatest object for masculine mastery and command.

Notes

1. In what follows, I do not assume that sex must be connected to gender. Instead, I am interpreting Nietzsche's understanding of the nature and purpose of the masculine gender. As such, nothing at all prevents women from sharing in masculinity, nor does it exclude a pluralistic understanding of gender (that is, more than two genders). Indeed, there is a case to be made that Nietzsche himself is an important figure in the constructivist approach to gender that distinguishes between the cultural origins of gender and the biological bases of sex.
2. See, e.g., Young (2013), and the pieces included in Oliver and Pearsall (1998).
3. I do not have the space here to substantiate this claim, but my own sense is that Nietzsche also conceives of femininity not in terms of an essential category but in

terms of a concern for a different tension or contradiction of being human, between the desire for a caring absorption in the other and a desire to distinguish oneself from the other. I make this point only to clarify my overall argument here—I am not claiming that for Nietzsche the masculine (*männlich*) is identical with the human (*menschlich*). Rather, the masculine and feminine emerge on Nietzsche's view as two distinct ways to navigate two tensions of being human.
4. See several of the pieces collected in Metzger (2009).
5. See Berkowitz (1995), Leiter (2002), Reginster (2006), and Katsafanas (2016).
6. See especially Hill (2003) and Church (2015) on Nietzsche as neo-Kantian, and Gemes (2009) and Pippin (2009) on Nietzsche and freedom.
7. See Richardson (1996) for an excellent account of the will to power in Nietzsche, an account I follow here.
8. Again, I stress that Nietzsche conceives of these as gender roles, but there is no particular reason why we must connect these gender roles to biological sex, or indeed to any one particular individual. It might be that all individuals participate in, or could participate in, both masculinity and femininity.
9. I do not discuss Nietzsche's ideal human beings—the overman, philosopher of the future, sovereign individual—in this chapter, as they are more comprehensive ideals than that of masculinity.

References

Beiser, Frederick (2014), *The Genesis of Neo-Kantianism: 1796-1880*, Oxford: Oxford University Press.
Beiser, Frederick (2016), *Weltschmerz: Pessimism in German Philosophy, 1860–1900*, Oxford: Oxford University Press.
Berkowitz, Peter (1995), *Nietzsche: The Ethics of an Immoralist*, Cambridge, MA: Harvard University Press.
Church, Jeffrey (2015), *Nietzsche's Culture of Humanity: Beyond Aristocracy and Democracy in the Early Period*, Cambridge: Cambridge University Press.
Church, Jeffrey (2019), *Nietzsche's Unfashionable Observations: A Critical Guide*, Edinburgh: Edinburgh University Press.
Gemes, Ken (2009), "Nietzsche on Free Will, Autonomy, and the Sovereign Individual," in *Nietzsche on Freedom and Autonomy*, ed. Ken Gemes and Simon May, 33–50, Oxford: Oxford University Press.
Hill, R. Kevin (2003), *Nietzsche's Critiques: the Kantian Foundations of his Thought*, Oxford: Oxford University Press.
Katsafanas, Paul (2016), *The Nietzschean Self: Moral Psychology, Agency, and the Unconscious*, Oxford: Oxford University Press.
Leiter, Brian (2002), *Routledge Guidebook to Nietzsche on Morality*, London: Routledge.
Mansfield, Harvey (2006), *Manliness*, New Haven, CT: Yale University Press.
Metzger, Jeffrey, ed. (2009), *Nietzsche, Nihilism, and the Philosophy of the Future*, London: Bloomsbury.
Oliver, Kelly A., and Marilyn Pearsall, eds. (1998), *Feminist Interpretations of Friedrich Nietzsche*, University Park: Penn State University Press.
Pippin, Robert (1999), "Nietzsche and the Melancholy of Modernity," *Social Research* 66 (2): 495–520.

Pippin, Robert (2009), "How to Overcome Oneself: Nietzsche on Freedom," in *Nietzsche on Freedom and Autonomy*, ed. Ken Gemes and Simon May, 69–88, Oxford: Oxford University Press.

Reginster, Bernard (2006), *The Affirmation of Life: Nietzsche on Overcoming Nihilism*, Cambridge, MA: Harvard University Press.

Richardson, John (1996), *Nietzsche's System*, New York: Oxford University Press.

Young, Julian (2013), "Nietzsche and Women," in *The Oxford Handbook of Nietzsche*, ed. Ken Gemes and John Richardson, 44–62, Oxford: Oxford University Press.

11

The Free Spirit's Dionysian Mirth: A Laughing Storm to Herald Philosophers of the Future

Michael J. McNeal

> *When nothing else from today has a future, our laughter is the one thing that does!*
> (BGE 223)

Imbued with a joviality that distinguishes them from those of other philosophers, Nietzsche's works are enlivened by jokes, puns, and facetiousness.[1] Their characteristic cheerfulness demonstrates that, as Lawrence Hatab observes, laughter is "far from an incidental matter" (1988: 67) in his thought. Rather, it demonstrates the joyful temperament central to his lived philosophy.[2] Yet as relatively few scholars have analyzed the significance of gaiety to Nietzsche's thought—let alone to its political implications—the subject warrants further analysis.[3] Specifically, there remains much to consider regarding the reigning sensibility he associates with his free spirits and the sociocultural (and ultimately political) transformations he expected it to produce.[4]

Nietzsche's positive vision of the future necessarily deals in hypotheticals. He postulates what might be according to the sort of world he hoped his philosophy would produce, compelling us to contend with prospective outcomes that assume his free spirits' success. And while his vision cannot therefore advance specific organizational or prescriptive recommendations about future political institutions, it is implicitly political in that it envisages a fundamental revaluation of all values, the transformation of the communities those values foster, and ultimately, the transfiguration of humankind.[5] For this reason I use the conditional mood throughout this chapter to convey the possibilities Nietzsche expected the free spirit's striving to reveal.

I argue that it is through the affective disposition I label "Dionysian mirth" that the revaluation of values Nietzsche advocated is possible. By extension it makes the distant appearance of philosophers of the future likelier, too, as the capacities enabled by the free spirit's inimitable laughter transform the sociopolitical order. Through the laughter it produces, this inclination conceals its own political significance, so is inherently subversive, which distinguishes it from the typically guileless laughter of the majority.[6] But why call it "Dionysian mirth"? In conceiving the phrase, I follow Nietzsche's characterization of the free spirit's temperament as arising from their insight into the tragicomic nature of existence and the heightened perspective on the agonic striving and suffering of human beings that it affords. It facilitates the laughter required to contemplate the most abysmal thought.[7] In this, Nietzsche recovers the *joie de vivre* of the ancient Greeks—which arose from their acceptance of the tragic nature of existence and their cultivated vitality—and deploys it throughout his oeuvre to connect his philosophical concerns. According to Nietzsche, this affective disposition is symptomatic of its possessor's great health. It corresponds with their innate drives and the distinguishing experiences those drives compel, each reciprocally ramifying the other to increase the free spirit's manifoldness and capacity for self-creation and overcoming. From oneiric, Dionysian revery and a longing to become who it is they are, free spirits undertake their revaluation of values. Therefore, the phrase "Dionysian mirth" encapsulates the characteristics Nietzsche associates with his free spirits and aptly conveys their affective disposition.

In demonstrating this thesis, I consider related questions pertaining to the political significance of the free spirit's Dionysian mirth and how the latter subverts the conventional values Nietzsche disdained, which continue to dominate human societies. First among these is, how does the free spirit's laughter aid them in identifying their individual tasks and shared aspirations? Second, what practices does their joyful disposition commend? Third, how may the free spirit's gaiety serve as a method for disrupting the reigning values of our decadent age? Fourth, how does the "laughing storm" of these subversive *farceurs* sweep away those anti-natural, life-denying values, and what remains in its aftermath? I answer these questions in corresponding sections that structure the chapter to show how Dionysian mirth facilitates a revaluation of values. By incorporating numerous of his assertions on the subject I demonstrate the constancy of Nietzsche's concern with laughter across his works, then conclude by reiterating their relevance to the revaluation of values he anticipated.

Symptomatic of the free spirit's psychophysiological state, Dionysian mirth—their "Olympian laughter" (UM II 2), or "laughter of the heights" (Z II Tarantulas)—informs Nietzsche's critiques of culture and values, his campaign against morality, and his war "on the 'atomistic' [and] 'metaphysical need'" (BGE 12). Among other things, it links combatting the "un-Dionysian spirit … of [Socratic] 'Greek cheerfulness'" characteristic "of the theoretical man" (BT 17) in his earliest work, to the critique of decadent values that occupied his final productive year during which he sought a "return to nature, health, cheerfulness, youth, [and] *virtue*!" (CW 3). As an orientation arising from "the same species of inner experience" that "reveal[s] something about the structure of [their] soul[s]" and their "genuine needs" (BGE 268), the exuberant feeling of life driving them and the humor it enables are key means by which these artist-philosophers challenge the myopic worldviews authorized by slave morality while overcoming and perfecting themselves. Their lampoons of decadent values entail a *kynical* ironism that discredits nihilism and diminishes its ability to paralyze future exemplars of a re-naturalized humanity.[8] Yet they "refrain from giving [their] insights universal attributes … [so that their] own critical distancing from traditional values and structures of thinking might [inspire] others to recognize their capacity for critique and motivate them to pursue a similar path" (Elbe 2001: 280). Zarathustra's assertion that "all good things laugh" (Z IV Higher 17) reflected Nietzsche's view that the power to laugh from Dionysian mirth is a hallmark of great spirits and thinkers who emancipate themselves from the "morality of custom" (D 9) to "become free" (HH WS 182). Antipodes of modern "free thinkers," free spirits strive to revalue dissipative values, instantiate a new, culturally edifying myth, and ultimately realize a natural rank order of types. In *Thus Spoke Zarathustra* (Z), Nietzsche evocatively likened them to "a laughing storm," underscoring their laughter's disruptive potential and the possibilities it presents:

> Praised be this spirit of all free spirits, the laughing storm who blows dust into the eyes of all fusspots and pus-pots! ... How much is still possible! So *learn* to laugh over and past yourselves! Lift up your hearts, you good dancers, high! higher! And don't forget good laughter either! (Z IV Higher 20)

Importantly, the type of laughter Zarathustra praises is both learnable and practicable. Those possessing the great health needed for Dionysian mirth may come to appreciate its force and utilize it productively. "Spirit" in the above-cited passage references the disposition from which the free spirit's laughter erupts.[9] Rooted in sober recognition of "the terrors and horrors of existence" (DW 2), their "tragic insight" concerning humankind's condition conduces the "*Dionysian* pessimism" (GS 370) that makes their laughter possible. Joyful warriors who "*live gaily and laugh gaily*" (GS 324), they affirm "things that are questionable and terrible" (TI Reason 6) as they battle life-demeaning values. Nietzsche describes them, thusly, as

> at home in many countries of the spirit, at least as guests; repeatedly slipping away from the musty, comfortable corners where preference and prejudice ... have driven us; full of malice at the lures of dependency ... curious to a fault, researchers to the point of cruelty, with unmindful fingers for the incomprehensible. ... This is the type of people we are, we free spirits! (BGE 44)

Dionysian mirth mediates the free spirit's experience in every country of the spirit they transit, elevating them to "transcendental heights of ... Aristophanean world mockery" (BGE 223) and providing them with means to destroy decadence values,[10] as Zarathustra suggested when he asserted, "Whoever wants to kill most thoroughly, laughs" (Z IV Festival 1).[11]

1. The Free Spirit's Identification of Their Task and Shared Aspirations

In his so-called middle period ("free spirit") works, Nietzsche stated, "Perhaps there will one day be laughter at that which nowadays counts as moral" (D 183), an assertion that simultaneously indicates his hope and his goal. It also suggests his strategy for overcoming the decadent, post-Christian secular morality of his age. But to undertake the revaluation of values he attempted to inaugurate, free spirits would have to recognize their tasks and shared desires.[12] How, then, would laughter enable free spirits to identify their individual task, which "is and remains above all not to mistake [them]selves for someone else" and their shared aspirations? (GS 381). To start, a free spirit's Dionysian mirth conditions their interpretation of their experiences. In keeping with Nietzsche's theory of the self as an assemblage of hierarchically ordered drives (BGE 6), he suggested that the capacity for laughter—or Dionysian mirth—indicates their psychophysiological health and the corresponding scope of their worldview.[13] Disparate responses to laughter, including the experience of being laughed at, have their origin in the drives. For free spirits, such an experience would not be humiliating; rather, they would "be glad to have involuntarily augmented the amount of cheerfulness and sunshine in the world" (D 119). A person's ability to laugh, its ease and range, expresses their openness, integrity, and resilience, and gradually refines the discernment constituting their "intellectual conscience" (BGE 230). This corresponds with their ability to reimagine, develop, and overcome themselves. These yes-sayers nurture the cheerful disposition needed to liberate themselves from metaphysical consolations for the world, laughing so that their amusement "will someday send all attempts at metaphysical solace to Hell" (BT A 7) and contribute to the "task of *revaluing values*" (EH Clever 9).[14]

The laughter of Nietzsche's yes-sayers contributes to their discipline of self-cultivation, which actualized his hopeful response to the crisis of nihilism. Rather than a "letting go" (*laissez aller*), his praxis of life-affirmation (gay science) aims to generate "the sentiments and virtues ... [Nietzsche] requires for a rebirth of tragic, aristocratic culture," an ethos through which the ebullience of his daring experimenters may generate unanticipated possibilities for organizing and governing human communities (Ansell-Pearson 1994: 72).[15] Related to such a "letting go," Nietzsche disdains uncritical acceptance of conventional virtues, received values, and what is taken as "known" for stymieing the appearance of ascending forms of life. This contrasts with the doubt and intellectual curiosity at the heart of the free spirit's discipline of self-cultivation, which fosters awe with existence, as Nietzsche indicates when he states,

> To stand in the midst of this *rerum concordia discors* [discordant harmony of things] and the whole marvelous uncertainty and ambiguity of existence without questioning, without trembling with the craving and rapture of questioning ... that is what I feel to be contemptible, and this is the feeling I look for first in anyone. (GS 2)

His courageous "argonauts of the ideal" recognize one another's shared wonder at life's—and our world's—ultimate unknowability (GS 382). The incredulity of free spirits, who oppose "the *degenerate* instinct that turns against life with subterranean vindictiveness" (EH Books BT 2), comes through in their laughter to undermine certainty in conventional beliefs. That skepticism, through which they perceive "behind every word the laughter of error, of imagination, of the spirit of delusion" (D 423), propels the amusement they derive by challenging received truths, which expands their possibilities for constructive contests and self-perfection. Their struggles further arouse the *eros* of other exceptions in a process likely to foster the aforementioned new modes of ascending life (see McNeal 2020a: 199–200). But it is the free spirit's

Dionysian mirth, which promotes incredulity and contests, that reveals "the probable paths and trials that would enable a soul to grow tall and strong enough to feel the *compulsion* for these tasks" (BGE 203). Laughter is a key means by which tragic artists precipitate the trials through which they may overcome themselves and revalue decadent values.[16] By undermining confidence in their culture's mores and taboos, the free spirit's subversive laughter eases their individual tasks and shared aspirations, namely realizing the sociopolitical ramifications of their valuations. Their instinctive rejection of anti-natural values—our post-Christian, secular "*ressentiment* morality" (A 24)—brings them into conflict with ascetic priests, whose authority devalues "*every valuable type of person*" and whose laughter (from contempt for difference) compels conformity to dissipative norms that further stultify the herd and persecute every exception (TI Skirmishes 45).

Conversely, ascetic priests perceive the laughter of free spirits as a threat for exposing the "hidden need for revenge" (A 59) that generates their "monstrous method of valuation" (GM III 11).[17] With souls squinting from ressentiment (GM I 10) they condemn those lucky strikes—"individual successes ... [and] a higher type ... of overman in relation to humanity in general" (A 4)—as heretics, radicals, or criminals for violating the precepts of their life-devaluing morality. Contesting ascetic values and the priests who enforce them, Dionysian mirth conveys transgressive possibilities that multiply the options free spirits have. Through their acts of defiance they come to recognize the arbitrariness of language and concepts, and the contingency of the ascetic values they challenge. Further, the laughter of such lucky strikes indicates an implicit proposition about its source, enticing those attune to it to consider alternative value-judgments, and—among those who share their instincts and the desires it commends—other possible worlds, corresponding with their affective disposition.

It follows that creating new modes of being necessitates a new language to justify and sustain salubrious new beliefs. This insight played a role in the "campaign against morality" (EH Books D 1) Nietzsche launched in *Dawn*:

> What is laughter? How does laughter originate? We have thought the matter over and finally decided that there is nothing good, nothing beautiful, nothing sublime, nothing evil in itself, but that there are states of soul in which we impose such words upon things external to and within us. We have again taken back the predicates of things, or at least remembered that it was we who lent them to them. (D 210)

Laughter reveals the ultimate contingency of the meanings we impose on the world and the potential of language as a means by which creative free spirits may transform it. He suggests that the laughter of a genuine philosopher, who has "run through the range of human values and value feelings" so is "*able* to gaze with many eyes and consciences," feels a commensurate growth of her power via the insights it confers (BGE 211).

Toward identifying their individual tasks, Nietzsche indicates that free spirits will not only need to overcome themselves but deepen their comprehension of existence. "To laugh at oneself as one would have to laugh in order to laugh *from the whole truth*—for that, not even the best have had enough sense of truth, and the most gifted have had far too little genius!" (GS 1). Only audacious individuals with the strength to deride ascetic values and "sacrifice [much of value] to [their] desire for the heights" (GS 27) may attain the Dionysian summits of perspective from which new modes of valuation—ones beyond the customary truths that inhibit the all-too-many from laughing from the whole truth—may come into view. Toward this matchless laughter and consistent with his aim of showing his reader its utility, Nietzsche employed gaiety as a means of illuminating and living with difficult truths. As Kathleen Higgins noted, "Nietzsche's levity reflects his being a very serious man" (2000: 3); he took seriously and made serious philosophical use of jokes and playfulness to resist "the absurd spectacle of moral indignation, which is an unmistakable sign that a philosopher has lost his philosophical sense of humor" (BGE 25). A distraction to those for whom his insights are not intended (and who likely dismiss him as a serious philosopher), he delivered some of his most incisive criticism through jocularity. This served to synthesize his philosophical concerns with the "concrete problem of existence," namely life's inescapable suffering (Acharya 2014: 19, 47).

In the opening lines of *The Gay Science* (GS), Nietzsche avers that "at present, the comedy of existence has not yet 'become conscious' of itself; at present, we still live … in the age of moralities and religions" (GS 1). The heights of perspective required to become conscious of the comedy of existence augment the Dionysian mirth necessary to combat anti-natural moralities and the religions that reproduce them. As "comedians of [the post-Christian, secular ascetic] ideal," free spirits are its "only … real enemy and injurer" (GM III 27).[18] But what precisely does their subversion entail; what role does their provocative mockery play in this undertaking? While he expected these tragic artists to cast doubt upon decadence values, he does not (as aforementioned) prescribe the institutional arrangements or forms of life that should follow their revaluation of values, their own downgoing, or the distant overcoming of humankind. By leaving these possibilities open, Nietzsche may frustrate readers desirous of prescriptive political programs, but he maintains intellectual honesty by not constraining the options open to future legislators who will struggle to perfect themselves and create new modes of being.

The individual tasks and shared aspirations of Nietzsche's free spirits corresponds with his response to the secularization of Judeo-Christian values and modern reign of scientific reason, about which he observed that the

> demand for certainty that today discharges itself in scientific-positivistic form among great masses—the demand that one wants by all means something to be firm … is … the instinct of weakness that, to be sure, does not create sundry religions, forms of metaphysics, and convictions but does—preserve them. (GS 347)

Tasmin Shaw observes that "secularization involves, for Nietzsche, acceptance of the view that reason is the only legitimate guide to belief and value." This is a problem because "reasoning does not … lead to normative consensus" (2007: 8). However (in)coherent or lacking in consensus, a set of ideologized secular values are disseminated throughout our world today via globalization. It is therefore clear that to make the "comedy of existence … 'conscious' of itself," Nietzsche's free spirits have their work cut out (GS 1). Importantly, Nietzsche's critique of modern Europe's decadence does not equate with declinism, for he specifies its source and theorizes how it may be overcome, though he did not expect the conflicts this overcoming would generate to be resolved for centuries.[19] Against the bovine satisfaction characteristic of his (and our) decadent age, Nietzsche argued that "happiness and virtue are not arguments" (BGE 39). This applied to the bourgeois standards of respectability enforced by the late nineteenth century's secular "men of *ressentiment*" (GM III 24), but rather than avoid life's pain or minimize its grief, free spirits embrace suffering through their distinctive cheerfulness. Nietzsche indicated the need for this when he wrote, "Perhaps I know best why man alone laughs: he alone suffers so deeply that he *had* to invent laughter. The unhappiest and most melancholy animal is, as fitting, the most cheerful" (KSA 11:36[49]). Acting in accordance with "predetermined decisions and answers to selected, predetermined questions" (BGE 231), free spirits identify their individual tasks—and shared desires—via an intuitively understood cheerfulness, the mutual knowledge imparted via their inimitable laughter. But what of the practices their disposition commends toward the realization of their task?

2. The Jocular Practices Commended by Dionysian Mirth

What practices, vis-à-vis the revaluation of values, does the joyful disposition of free spirits commend? This question goes to the central motivation of Nietzsche's philosophical project and the content of his "gay science." Through the latter he responded to the issue of suffering and the seriousness with which individuals approach themselves. When Nietzsche asks, at GS 383, "Was there ever a better hour for gaiety?," his fearless ones certainly would not have thought there was, for in the wake of the death of God the discombobulating effects of nihilism on individuals and societies has made plain the need for jocular practices through which free spirits may first increase and then sublimate their suffering. It is through laughter that free spirits mine their gold, explore philosophical labyrinths, consider old questions anew, and ridicule life-denying ascetic values to awaken the passions of the complacent and unsettle the self-satisfied, just as their *Schadenfreude* and fun-making subverts the dogmas of priestly philosophers (HH I 27; GS 200). But do these constitute practices, and if not, why does Nietzsche not prescribe practices for cultivating Dionysian mirth? First, the latter symptomatizes the affective disposition (originating in their instincts) from which the free spirit's evaluative orientation, desires, and subsequent actions arise. Second, that temperament is improved and refined by unpredictably transformative contests. What can be taught is recognition of the innate capacity for Dionysian mirth among those exceptions who have denied and/or repressed it in themselves. His own spontaneous laughter and occasional charientism illustrates the strength of one capable of living without either metaphysical consolations or the approval of their promoters. By undermining the religious-moral pathos, Nietzsche sought to "make [free spirits] braver, more persevering, simpler, fuller of gaiety" (GS 338) through an ennobling laughter that provides a tonic to late-modernity's enervating decadence, increases their feeling of power, and urges them further out on the tightrope of becoming. They thereby herald the appearance of the yes-saying philosophers of the future Nietzsche envisaged, who would be capable of revaluing all values through "act[s] of humanity's highest self-examination" (EH Destiny 1).

How does Nietzschean cheerfulness empower free spirits to combat cultural decadence and contribute to the overcoming of nihilism? Faced with the crisis of nihilism and challenged by the disgust induced by humanity's diminution, their cheerful sensibility strengthens their joy with life and (re)focuses them on affirmative projects. Free spirits comprise a "character type [that, accommodating a range of disparate outlooks] can be embodied in a large number of particular characters," corresponding with their broadened mindset (Nehamas 1985: 38). A part of their discipline of self-cultivation and open-mindedness, Dionysian mirth permits them to "laugh *from the whole truth*" (GS 1), while subduing the counterproductive impulses that are rewarded in a decadent society (Bamford 2015: 100); cf. D 560). It immunizes them to spiritual corruption—the morality of pity—and any antipathy for humanity that their ailing culture transmits. Cheerfulness distances them "from the happiness of weaklings, from 'resignation'" (A 1), inducements to which they sublimate into their abiding delight with existence.

Related to its role in their distinctive practices, the free spirit's corrective laughter is the opposite of thoughtless. Echoing Higgins (2000), Babette Babich observes that Nietzsche's "deeply serious ... 'gay' science [is] gay out of profundity" (2006: 56), and it is in GS that Nietzsche expounded the praxis corresponding with his philosophical insights through which tragic artists could cultivate

> a mocking, light, fleeting, divinely untroubled, divinely artificial art that, like a bright flame, blazes into an unclouded sky! Above all: an art for artists, only for artists! In addition we will know better what is first and foremost needed for that: cheerfulness—any cheerfulness, my friends! (GS Preface-4)

As opposed to the plebeian laughter Nietzsche scorns, the jocular practices of his tragic artists emerge from deep insight into the flux and contingency of existence. For "all fusspots and pus-pots" (the decadent majority), this penetrating laughter, qua laughter, obfuscates its transformative potential. While the free spirit's laughter blows dust into the eyes of ascetic priests, the dull herd's communal scotosis suffices to prevent it from perceiving these "good dancers" at the height from which they laugh, let alone the threat their gaiety poses to customary morality. Yet even as the free spirit's mockery of the priestly philosopher's morality of taming derives from the same source of spiritual strength that enables them to meet life's unpredictable challenges—namely Dionysian mirth—it also jeopardizes their security. For while Dionysian mirth enhances "the feeling that power is growing, that some resistance has been overcome" (A 2), and girds free spirits against nihilism, its agonic character increases their prospects for suffering, including their likelihood of being maltreated.

Life's ineliminable suffering is also relevant to the free spirit's comprehension of their task. By responding to suffering and the pity for all that suffers through laughter,

Nietzsche's free spirits recognize those who share their sensibility and encourage one another.[20] Rather than avoid suffering, free spirits welcome it, for

> such philosophers are cheerful and ... like to sit in the abyss below a perfectly clear sky: they need different means from other men for enduring life; for they suffer differently (namely, as much from the profundity of their contempt for man as from their love for man)—The most suffering animal on earth invented for itself – laughter. (KSA 11: 37[3])

Genuine philosophers, who experience a higher spiritual exhilaration when they "are in the most—*danger*" (BGE 224), transform their suffering through laughter to generate new meanings that may help other rare exceptions better endure their suffering, too (McNeal 2019a).

For those with the great health necessary to appreciate the free spirit's jocularity, Dionysian mirth prompts a greater openness to change, spurring them to undertake tests of their own mettle that deepen their love of fate (GS 276; EH Clever 10). As the free spirit's suffering heightens their experience of life, they increase their striving for self-perfection via the contests and experiments their agonistic sensibility spurs them to undertake (GM II 16; cf. McNeal 2019a: 164). Emulating the free spirit's practices of jocularity, they may come to approach their lives as experiments. Struggling to become who they are compels them to simultaneously affirm the past (their own and humanity's) and embrace their tragic fates, which are inextricably linked, as what they pursue in overcoming and perfecting themselves is ultimately the transfiguration of all that has been and their downgoing. The capacity to cheerfully accept this is a test for the strongest individuals, as Zarathustra's laughter following his speech on redemption indicates. Insofar as this may have been in response to the "it was"—perhaps from an ironic stance?—might laughter not be understood as a means of subduing "the will's gnashing of teeth and most solitary misery" to ease acknowledgment of "thus I willed it" (Z On Redemption)?

As a practical response to suffering that exhibits the free spirit's zest for life, their experimentation includes personal tests of mettle and the contests for self-perfection that contain both "Apollonian" and "Dionysian" aspects. The former appears in the affirmative, ordered beauty artists impose upon the chaos of the world as their experiments assay possibilities for a transformed sociopolitical order; the latter via an ecstatic means of contending with the unpredictability of existence, evinced not least in the courage they demonstrate in undertaking them. By increasing their discernment of the "degrees and multiple, subtle shades of gradation [of this] well-falsified world" (BGE 24), they are better able to laugh even at their own struggles (value-creating attempts) to re-naturalize their world. In relation to such creative striving—an involuntary response to both their love of and contempt for man—Nietzsche reflected on Wagner's *Parsifal*, observing that "a great tragedian ... like every artist, ... only reaches the final summit of his achievement when he knows how to see himself and his art beneath him,—and knows how to laugh at himself" (GM III 3).

In realizing their prodigious task, free spirits make light of the solemnity associated with conventional "seriousness," further aggravating ascetic priests. As Zarathustra's laughter indicated a willingness to eschew certain social conventions, such as the utility of refraining from giving offense (as when he exposed and denounced decadence), Nietzsche's tragic artists cultivate their Dionysian mirth to overcome the inherited prejudices and misconceptions their decadent epoch inculcates in them. This simultaneously expands their capacity for suffering while promulgating their delight with the world, which—against life-denying ascetic values—engenders shared joy with other higher types who "want to become who [they] are – human beings who are new, unique, incomparable, who give themselves laws, who create themselves!" (GS 335).

What of Nietzsche's own suffering and the seriousness with which he approached the experiments he undertook to become who he was as a philosopher? A conscious undertaking that shaped his adult life and works, these included "his process of de-Germanification" via a determined transformation of his musical taste from German (Wagnerian) to Italian opera and included his "travel to the South to rid [himself] of [his] northern, moral spirit" (Prange 2013: 223). Similarly, in the lighter spirit with which he approached philosophical problems, Nietzsche's high-spirited playfulness was evident even when dealing with the gravest matters—Dionysian mirth infusing his oeuvre with wry wit. Subsequently, the maxim *ridendo dicere severum*—"through what is laughable say what is somber" (CW P)—might be taken as his personal motto, for he consistently opposed "the prejudice … against all gay science," which, consistent with the spirit of revenge, maintains that "where laughter and gaiety are found, thinking is good for nothing" (GS 327).

Provocative in a decadent society, the free spirit's unconventional happiness is unsettling to those who cannot comprehend its origins. As misfits they are unlikely to be accepted within their communities, let alone seen as leaders by the uncomprehending herd, something Zarathustra's journey demonstrated. Nevertheless (as aforementioned), Nietzsche expected the passion evident in their struggles to transmit their joy to receptive witnesses who, inspired by their agonic striving "against *great nausea at man*," might undertake similarly creative attempts to become who they are (GM III 14). As "the free spirit knows what 'you shall' he has obeyed, and he also knows what he now *can*, what only now he—*may* do" (HH P 6), namely reveal alternative liberatory possibilities by discrediting the reigning morality of pity. Accordingly, he anticipated that their playfulness would have broad sociocultural effects with implications for political life. Through jocular practices that would endow humankind with "a second innocence" (GM II 20), free spirits would contribute to the development of a pathos of distance from which they and their ilk might foster a corresponding rank order of types.[21]

3. Nietzschean Gaiety as a Method for Discrediting Decadence Values

How, then, are the free spirit's laughter-inducing practices capable of discrediting the reigning values of our decadent age to hasten their revaluation and overcoming? Keith Ansell-Pearson remarks that in such an "epoch … in which God is dead and all idols are to be overthrown," free-spirited, Zarathustra-types must employ parody to convey their disquieting insights (1994: 102). As noted above, Nietzsche models a mode of valuation in his published works that he hoped would arouse the *eros* of other strong individuals, whose "fundamental will of the spirit," includes the

> occasional will to be deceived ... perhaps with a playful hunch that things are not one way or the other, ... [the] sense of pleasure in every uncertainty and ambiguity, a joyful self-delight at the arbitrary narrowness and secrecy of a corner, ... [the] self-delight at the sheer caprice in all these expressions of power. (BGE 230)

Through playful experimentation, his free spirits legislate a *Bildung* of cheerfulness that affirms difference and galvanizes their transmutation of necessity, a process that involves "assimilat[ing] the new to the old" (BGE 230; cf. McNeal 2019b: 210). This pertains to the methods that free spirits employ to challenge conventional notions of certainty and promulgate their mood of gaiety.

As a key part of Nietzsche's method of disrupting decadence values, particularly the herd's mindless certainty in them, Dionysian mirth connects the epistemological and axiological critiques he advanced. Their laughter is intrinsically skeptical, as the afore-noted "sense of pleasure in every uncertainty and ambiguity," which orients the free spirit's reception of truth claims, indicates. This skeptical tendency is evident throughout Nietzsche's thought. Of what then may his free spirits be certain? They delight in creating meanings as they interrogate received truths and explanations of existence and ponder their world's complexity. "Convinced of the uncertainty and the fantastical quality of our judgements and of the eternal change of human laws and concepts" (GS 46), free spirits recognize that in our contemporary age, only knowledge that originates in empirical science is considered legitimate. Amused by the all-too-human impulse evinced in every knowledge claim's presumption of veracity, they tentatively reserve judgment: "Let each truth be false to us which was not greeted by one laugh!" (Z III Tablets 23).[22] The modern obsession with certainty expressed through science masks its origins, which lie in the Judeo-Christian impulse to ultimate, transcendent truth. It is a "will to know rising up on the foundation of a much more powerful will, the will to not know, to uncertainty, to untruth!" (BGE 24) As they attempt to overcome decadence values and advance life-affirming ones, free spirits recognize their will to truth in the knowledge claims they advance, which, as with all such claims, symptomizes its advocate's higher-ranked drives and the involuntary impulse arising therefrom to impose meaning upon the universe.[23]

This is especially relevant when dealing with the credulity of the herd, for whom wisdom amounts to naïve certainty and a "prudent, cowlike serenity, piety, and ... meekness" (GS 351). Consistent with his observation that "laughter means: to gloat, but with a good conscience" (GS 200), free spirits laugh derisively at the close-mindedness this entails, and at the ascetic priests whose stultifying truths aim to make healthy individuals "ashamed of their happiness" (GM III 14). Even as free spirits recognize and embrace of the contingency of all knowledge claims, this should not be conflated with the relativism that exemplifies the decadent values of our contemporary age. Nietzschean yes-sayers deride the "truths" of priestly philosophers from confidence in the higher need to discredit nihilists who calumniate life "at the expense of the future"

(GM P 6). Their laughter serves "to expose [the ascetic priest's] hiding places to the light" (Z II Tarantulas) and affectively impinges on what "truths" may be accepted and believed within the framework of new meanings his radical affirmers strive to create.

These gift-givers' confidence—which entails some certainty but falls short of conviction—derives from the strength of their drives, which enable them to recognize that "*values of decadence ... nihilistic* values, values of decline, have taken control under the aegis of the holiest names" (AC 6). Consequently, they maintain a skeptical stance toward all truth claims, for the "will to truth needs a critique ..., the value of truth is tentatively to be *called into question*" [GM III 24]), via an abiding skepticism that imbues them with the caution needed "for that long and secret labor which is reserved for the most subtle, genuinely honest, and also the most malicious consciences of the day ... [namely] [t]he overcoming of morality—even the self-overcoming of morality" (BGE 32).

Convinced that life-diminishing values inhibit a people's flourishing, the free spirit—like Zarathustra—"laughs the truth" (Z IV Higher 18).[24] The dangers of nihilism, which stymie the appearance of genuine individuals, drive them "by an even stronger instinct, in search of knowledge in the great and exceptional sense" (BGE 26), to test truth claims and the corresponding values of their age. It is through laughter that they adduce the salubriousness of truth claims, their effectiveness for enhancing life, and the perspectives they facilitate within their respective socio-cultural milieus. From the "joy of experimenting" (BGE 210) they embrace the difficult task of valuing and provisionally try out alternative perspectives through experiments with values that oppose the superficial relativism and dearth of reverence that typifies our decadent age.[25] This will strike many contemporary readers as unsatisfyingly esoteric, particularly as a means of practical resistance. However, Nietzsche thought that over time it would build into a form of effective power, for, as he asserted,

> without a doubt: these coming philosophers will be least able to dispense with the qualities that distinguish the critic from the skeptic ... I mean: the certainty of value standards, the conscious implementation of a unity of method, a sly courage, a solitary stance, and capacity for responsibility. (BGE 210)

The gaiety expressive of the "certainty" through which they apply their "unity of method" requires the "sly courage" that allows free spirits to "tak[e] pleasure in saying no, in dissecting" the corrupting values of their age (BGE 210).[26] David Owen's observation regarding the mutually constitutive dynamic between perspectives and our forms of agency is applicable here, as Dionysian mirth conditions "the ways in which we recognize ourselves as agents [and thereby] construct a field of possible ways of acting ... [which, in turn] construct a field of possible ways of 'seeing' the world and ourselves in it (and thus rule out other ways of knowing)" (1995: 40–1). The dissenting perspectives Dionysian mirth affords ramify the free spirit's practices of harming conventional truths as they develop "the will to be responsible for [themselves]" (TI Skirmishes 38).

In the preface to *Twilight of the Idols* (TI), Nietzsche disclosed a source of his confidence in the practical viability of Dionysian mirth as a destabilizing, transformative practice. There he links cheerfulness and high spirits to his (free spirit's) task, the need to "shake off a seriousness that has become [too] heavy" and the convalescence he took in "*sounding out idols*." Reflecting on the strength and audacity required to accomplish a revaluation of all values, he rhetorically queried his reader, "What could be more necessary than cheerfulness? Nothing succeeds if prankishness has no part in it" (TI P). The gloomy business of the "new war" (TI P) he declares on morality, specifically "faith in the Christian-ascetic ideal" (GS 358), requires the armor of good-humored yet mischievous determination that his gay wisdom imparts. It is through such resoluteness that Nietzsche aimed "to share not pain, but *joy* [*Mitfreude*]" (GS 338), toward "the 'humanity' of the future", and thereby foster "a new nobility the likes of which no age has ever seen or dreamt" (GS 337). He expected the free spirit's ennobling joyousness to re-dignify humankind and "produce a happiness unknown to humanity so far: a divine happiness full of power and love, full of tears and laughter!" He further anticipated that "this divine feeling would then be called—humanity!" (GS 337).

How does the gaiety evinced by Dionysian mirth reflect the characteristic mood of these tragic artists as they endeavor "to shape or interpret their environment as free nature" (GS 290)? The answer to this is suggested in Z where laughter evinces a change-driving and world-transforming affect. Zarathustra and his interlocutors are stirred, transformed, and improved by laughter, be it at, about, or with one another (Z III Riddle). Against the spirit of gravity's contempt for man the free spirit's laughter—be it golden and super-human (BGE 294), scornful (Z II child/mirror), holy (Z II virtuous), secret (Z II human-prudence), dissimulating or demonic—fosters the "rank order of psychic states," the zenith of which free spirits occupy, making the most profound concerns atop the "rank order of problems" their proper purview (BGE 213). The laughter of Nietzsche's fearless experimenters differentiates those capable of partaking in the joy that radical affirmers' share in subverting decadent modern values, from those – the irresolute majority – who cannot. In time it places all on the "long ladder of … value distinctions between men" and establishes the "*pathos of distance*" between types that impels "the development of states that are increasingly high, rare, … and comprehensive" to conduce "the enhancement" of genuine individuals capable of envisaging an alternative liberatory politics (BGE 257).

Those proto-political potentials are also suggested by Nietzsche's corresponding differentiation between the Dionysian "laughter of the heights" (Z II Tarantulas), through which his most "abysmal thought" may be accepted (Z III Riddle 2), and what John Lippitt refers to as "the conservative … 'laughter of the herd'" (1992: 47). Exemplifying the latter, a jeering crowd scorns the "madman" who announces the death of God in the marketplace (GS 125), and another laughs at Zarathustra when he addresses those gathered to view the tightrope walker (Z P 3–5). He also suggests that the free spirit's "incorporation of truth and knowledge" makes the priestly-philosopher's posture of seriousness risible (BGE 186). The former, as commanders and legislators, direct their mockery at the dissipative moral psychology spread by the latter to discredit their authority.[27] As the perceived credibility of ascetic priests declines, the laughter of courageous experimenters may unleash an eruption of suspicion toward them that blows through their community like a storm, discrediting traditional institutions and norms that validated their power and eroding social obligations to enact their decadent values.[28] Such a disruptive "storm" would likely prompt divergent ways of thinking and spur myriad contests led by the free spirit's spiritual progeny—who "learn to dream ... while awake" (Zamosc 2022)—their acts cumulatively foreshadowing the future great politics Nietzsche envisaged, including the management and safekeeping of the earth (Z P 3; BGE 254; Shapiro 2016: 13–15). Indirectly collaborating through their agonic encouragement of one another's striving to become who they are, free spirits execute a broader revaluation of values to accelerate the downgoing of humanity and distant realization of Nietzsche's futural ideal, the post-humanist *Übermensch*—that "conqueror of God and of nothingness" (GM II 24).[29]

What real prospects do the free spirits have, in the present, for challenging and transfiguring the decadent values of our age? The experiments and self-overcomings of *thymotic* individuals serve to instigate its overcoming by subverting ascetic-values to condition the possibility for the appearance of future *Übermenschen*—individuals with the requisite vitality to transmute the enfeebling values of our nihilistic age. Not imaginary figures in a salvific fantasy of redemption, these free-spirited, *kynical* ironists discredit the poisonous ascetic-consumerist ideals of our age through comic mockery, to posit viable, life-affirming alternatives that facilitate innovative, nonlinear becomings to transfigure the human.

Kynical acts by free-spirited individuals abound throughout the world. As comedians of ascetic ideals, their playful scorn discredits traditional authorities whom the nihilistic status quo serves and who cannot respond effectively to such attacks on their credibility. Some notable examples include anti-consumerist japes by *Adbusters*, the subversions of corporate authority performed by *The Yes Men*, Zarganar's seditious lampoons of the Burmese junta, Charbel Khalil's brave parodies of Lebanon's corrupt politics, Hikari Ōta's comical spoofs of Japan's parliament, and Sun Mu's wry paintings deriding North Korea's state propaganda. The courageous cartoonists of the French magazine *Charlie Hebdo*, pranks by feminist Russian punk band *Pussy Riot*, social satire of South African comic Mthawelanga "Tats" Nkonzo, acerbic anti-corruption political cartoons by India's Aseem Trivedi, and the evocative visual commentaries of international graffiti artist Banksy have all productively lampooned reactionary political powers and/or antihuman practices. Through their "desire for *destruction*, for change, and for becoming," these nascent free spirits challenge received values to transform attitudes through acts of "overflowing energy pregnant with the future" (GS 370). By exposing the absurdity of repressive social norms they hint at possibilities for becoming that may hasten the demise of post-Christian, secular slave morality and augur life-affirming futures.[30]

4. The Laughing Storm of Nietzsche's Free Spirits and Its Aftermath

What remains in the aftermath of the free spirit's laughing storm once it has ravaged anti-natural, life-denying values? Nietzsche's Zarathustra expected "the laughing storm" of the "spirit of all free spirits" to ravage the perceived veracity of anti-natural/

life-denying values (Z IV Higher 20). If, as Zarathustra suggests, the laughter of these subversive *farceurs* hits unexpecting ascetic priests and other decadents ("fusspots and pus-pots") like a storm, we ought to consider what will remain in its wake. Every act impelled by Dionysian mirth serves the task of self-creation and cultivates "the eternal joy in becoming,—the joy that includes even the eternal joy *in negating*" (TI Ancients 5). Ultimately, Nietzsche's aim of revaluing dissipative values is the promotion of joyfulness—and the laughter it makes possible—which imbued Nietzsche's own futural project of overcoming humankind with efficacy, as Zarathustra's downgoing served, in part, to illustrate.

According to Walter Kaufmann, Nietzsche thought that "happiness is found not in complacency but in joyous activity" (1974: 387), and Nietzsche's concept of happiness—which centers on struggle—should not be conflated with the plebeian "instinct for happiness ... [that] necessarily belong[s] to slave morals and morality" (BGE 260). The notion of happiness prevalent in Nietzsche's world, as in ours, advanceed a "*religion of comfortableness*" (GS 338) premised on the abolition of suffering, and a "wretched contentment" (Z P 3) that, "suspicious of all joy" (GS 329), was and is in fact, immiserating. Free spirits reject this anti-natural conception of happiness, which, centered upon the avoidance of suffering at all costs and pity for all that suffers, aims at anodyne contentedness. Furthermore, against the conventional association between goodness and happiness, Nietzsche observed that "in the great economy of the whole, the horrors of reality (in the affects, in the desires, in the will to power) are incalculably more necessary than that form of petty happiness called 'goodness'" (EH Destiny 4).

The uncommon happiness indicative of ascending life requires the radical acceptance of this world of becoming and its unavoidable suffering without recourse to traditional metaphysical illusions. Toward this, the nomothetic value creation of Nietzsche's free spirits begins as a personal undertaking that entails an exuberant agonism, but it has broad sociocultural and political ramifications. The striving for an ennobling happiness expands their capacity for joy and their strength for destroying decadence values, including modern democracy, which Nietzsche considered "not merely an abased form of political organization, but rather an abased (more specifically a diminished) form of humanity, a mediocritization and depreciation of humanity in value" (BGE 203).

This raises the question of how the free spirit's Dionysian mirth squares with Nietzsche's bellicose language and approbative references to war. The answer is not as counterintuitive as it might at first seem. In waging their axiological war through jokes, pranks, and mockery, the skirmishes for new values that his "cheerful soul[s]" undertake accelerate the deployment of their unconventional, gelogenic "weapons"— as their joyousness resupplies the forces arrayed against the will to nothingness promulgated by decadent values (HH 34). Following Zarathustra's exhortation that "not by wrath does one kill, but by laughing," Nietzsche's blissful warriors employ guerilla tactics in combatting decadence values, laughing to "kill the spirit of gravity" that is expressed in dissipative ascetic ideals that falsify the world (Z I Writing).

What prospect do free spirits have of succeeding in this battle? Nietzsche answers this through his reflections on the roles of chance and fate, subjects he relates to cheerfulness, insofar as the embrace of both serve as a means of contending with the suffering and purposelessness of existence. Laughter facilitates this acceptance and braces free spirits for the most "difficult tasks ... [which they see] as a privilege, they relax by playing with burdens that would crush other people ... which does not prevent them from being the most cheerful" (A 57). Primary among these is the individual's striving to reconcile themselves with the horror of existence (TI Ancients 5). From "the thought that life could be an experiment for the knowledge-seeker," Nietzsche's fearless ones are impelled to engage in agonic struggles. As Nietzsche's "great liberator," this thought predisposes them to risk their security (GS 324). With each dangerous experiment, test of their mettle, and attempt at self-overcoming, they embrace "the piece of fate" they are and reaffirm their love of life (TI Errors 8). This augments their prospects of exploiting chance and sublimating their desires so that they can "limit [them]selves to the purification of [their] opinions and value judgements and to the *creation of tables of what is good that are new and all* [their] *own*" (GS 335).

The insights into life's tragic nature provided by the free spirit's agonic Dionysian mirth (which the priestly-philosopher's ascetic ideals conceal) enhance their ability to delight in their fates. These insights connect with the Heraclitean insight that "joy and joylessness, wisdom and unwisdom, great and small are all but the same, circling about, up and down, and interchanging in the game of Eternity."[31] This unsettling realization, or "most dangerous point of view," which Nietzsche echoes at GS 233, suggests that as a part of the whole, the self grows through the perspectives it gains, as one's naïve confidence in received truths is worn down. Yet rather than despair over the apparent meaninglessness of existence, they affirm existence in all its seeming absurdity. This increases their resilience and provides them with a "heightened feeling of happiness and life [which] is also a heightened feeling of power" (KSA 12:9[79]). That sensibility makes "the affirmation of passing away and destruction that is crucial for a Dionysian philosophy" (EH Books BT 3) possible and provides insight into to "the whole world of becoming" (KSA 12:7[4]). In this, Nietzsche's gratitude to existence and formula for greatness intersect, in further echoes of Heraclitus:

> Such an experimental philosophy as I live anticipates experimentally even the possibilities of the most fundamental nihilism; but this does not mean that it must halt at a negation, a No, a will to negation. It wants rather to cross over to the opposite of this—to a Dionysian affirmation of the world as it is. ... The highest state a philosopher can attain: to stand in a Dionysian relationship to existence— my formula for this is *amor fati*. (KSA 12:10[3], 13:16[32])

From radical life-affirmation, which acknowledges the contingency of all truth claims, Nietzsche's tragic artists recognize the need to create invigorating values that strengthen a people's highest exemplars and conduce their cultural vitality, a task which starts with Dionysian mirth. The entirety of existence must be affirmed without recourse to metaphysical illusions if new values—and the alternative liberatory politics they may induce—are to be compellingly advanced. This includes the Enlightenment's Rousseauian concept of justice, which, spawned by *ressentiment* of all that is great, seeks to level mountains and valleys (TI Skirmishes 38) and abolish all suffering (BGE 44). Too weak to affirm their lives, the sickly majority sense something alien whenever they encounter authentic individuals who are thankful for and capable of exalting in their existences. Incapable of comprehending the laughter that accompanies "all noble morality," and "grows out of a triumphant saying 'yes' to itself" (GM I 10), they take the free spirit's Dionysian mirth as inappropriate, if not evil. Yet that laughter warns of what is sick and failing, the "objections, minor infidelities, cheerful mistrust, [and] delight in mockery ... [of Nietzsche's radical affirmers] are symptoms of health" (BGE 154). Accordingly, the free spirit's laughter is "a comedy and a concealment" that discloses their love of fate and disarms witnesses open-minded enough to embrace their own tragic destinies (BGE 273). For, as "becoming what you are presupposes that you do not have the slightest idea what you are," such receptivity to one's innate, if unrecognized, potential is needful (EH Clever 9).

The free spirit's laughing storm mocks "the hatred of the human, and even more of the animalistic, ... [as well as the] fear of happiness and beauty" (GM III 28) that those life-denying values ramify. Their exuberant feeling of life—symptomatic of a new "spiritualization and internalization of cruelty" (BGE 229)—prevails against this hatred of the human through transformed cultural practices that, by exposing the absolutist values of dogmatic moralizers as ludicrous, prefigure a future politics. Moreover, their derisive laughter goads priestly philosophers to respond, generating more occasions for laughter to undercut the latter's authority. Following Christa Davis Acampora's observation of Nietzsche's depiction of Christianity's complicity in its own demise, we should understand that the secular ascetic priest's joyless seriousness aims to "eradicate what makes one a human being" by rigging the contest over "the meaning of human existence" to promulgate nihilism (Acampora 2013: 115). The agonic dimension of the free spirit's Dionysian mirth undermines all of this, as they *kynically* lampoon the dissipative contests that exclude their striving.

From his middle works on, Nietzsche conveyed his hope that the free spirits' perspectivally broadened knowledge would merge with their incomparable gaiety in a storm of insurgent laughter to inundate ascetic priests with a rising flood of suspicion toward their values. This is evident prior to Zarathustra, as when he wrote,

> Perhaps even laughter still has a future—when the proposition "The species is everything, an individual is always nothing" has become part of humanity. ... Perhaps laughter will then have formed an alliance with wisdom; perhaps only "gay science" will remain. (GS 1)

In this gay science, he anticipates a mode of valuation emphasizing the revitalization of humankind and suggests the method by which his free spirits may achieve it, as when he rhetorically asks, "What could be more important than cheerfulness?" before stating, "Nothing gets done without a dose of high spirits" (TI P). By discrediting the ascetic priests of our age, the laughing storm brought by the free spirit's Dionysian mirth would undermine belief in the axiomatic discourses that represent democracy as the only legitimate means of realizing social and political change. This makes way for the creation of new, life-affirming myths that provide the masses with meaning and galvanize them to work in the service of a vital higher culture.

Conclusion

In this chapter I have argued that the Dionysian mirth of Nietzsche's free spirits empowers them, through an incomparable laughter, to overcome and perfect themselves as they strive to revalue all values. To explicate the individual tasks and shared aspirations of these subversive *farceurs*, I demonstrated how Nietzsche thought this ebullient temperament facilitated recognition of their duties, those healthy few who share their desires, and acceptance of responsibility for those tasks. Through shared joy, these higher individuals engage in mutually inspiring jokes and pranks to undermine decadent values. I then showed that, via Zarathustra, Nietzsche expected the contest over values that would result from his yes-sayers' laughter to strike ascetic priests like a storm. Exploiting their disorientation, the valuations of his higher types generate proto-political changes in the attitudes, sensibilities, and orientations of other vital individuals which philosophers of the future may build upon to move humankind beyond the "age of moralities and religions" (GS 1).

Foremost among Nietzsche's aims in reviving Dionysian laughter was combatting nihilism through a robust counter-ideal to decadent Socratic dialectics and morose Christian life-denial.[32] Accordingly, insofar as it generates radically affirmative modes of valuation the free spirit's joyful wisdom comprises an alternative liberatory politics for those "of the most comprehensive responsibility who ha[ve] the conscience for the over-all development of man" (BGE 61). Laughter from a profound delight with existence is the "means for their task" and through which they harness the enormous forces that its valuations unleash. To contend with secular modernity's dearth of meaning and the anarchy it spawns, Dionysian mirth induces exceptional individuals to accept the "voluntary suffering" (D 18) necessary to develop the dynamism and resiliency of their souls so their laughter may remediate the crisis of nihilism.

Nietzsche expected free spirits to sublimate any "hatred of man" they feel through their "fine joy," while striving for that "artist's freedom" by means of which they may even "laugh at [themselves] (GM III 3)" and their own "strange and insane task" (BGE 230). In "the long struggle against essentially constant *unfavorable* conditions" (BGE 262), Dionysian mirth furthers "the *ability to* contradict, [and fosters] the acquired *good* conscience accompanying hostility towards what is familiar, traditional, hallowed" (GS 297), including the leveling tendency in the doctrine of equality and democratic values. Despite disseminating negative valuations, the laughter of these radical affirmers maintains their opposition to epistemological stridency, through their acceptance of "the necessary error or untruth that is our existential condition as knowers" (Siemens and Hay 2015: 117).

It may be objected that the proto-political potentials in the free spirit's laughter and jocular practices are unlikely ever to produce the kind of change Nietzsche hoped for. However, the possible future that he envisaged (sans constraining prescriptive programs for achieving it) was one he thought the free spirits' life-affirming values—replete with errors and delusions—would inaugurate. As Nietzsche declared in his final productive year, "we free spirits already constitute a 'revaluation of all values', a living declaration of war on and victory over all old concepts of 'true' and 'untrue'" (A 13).

He maintained that the free-spirited experimenters waging this war would illuminate difficult truths to "teach humanity its future as its will, ... [and] prepare for the great risk and wholesale attempt at [the] breeding and cultivation" of a revitalized humanity (BGE 203). This corresponds with Paul Kirkland's observation that "Nietzsche's teaching on laughter supports the courage for new risks" (2009: 241). As I have argued above, the free spirit's Dionysian mirth not only exposes them to dangers but also emboldens them to fearlessly chart a course toward the distant transfiguration of humankind.

Through what I dub Dionysian mirth, Nietzsche expected free spirits to generate unforeseeable sources of happiness: "Let us go forward a few thousand years together, my friends! There is a great deal of joy still reserved for mankind of which men of the present day have not had so much as a scent!" (HH WS 183). But conventional happiness was not the goal. By increasing their delight with existence he thought they would acquire "that nature which rules the whole world through joy" and dispel the spirit of gravity, that is, subvert and transform the herd-corralling cognitive and behavioral biases enforced by decadence values (HH I 292). It is Dionysian mirth that makes the free spirit's revaluation of all values possible, as well as the prospect that future philosophers—or "Zarathustra type[s]" (EH Books Z 6)—might one day realize humankind's *"highest potential power and splendor"* (GM P 6).[33]

Notes

1. In addition to laughter, his teaching of life-affirmation (GS 324; BGE 25) advocated jokes (BGE 34), play (HH 611; GS 107; BGE 57; TI Skirmishes 48), and prankishness (TI P).
2. See McNeal (2019b) from which parts of this chapter were developed. I am indebted to the Southwestern Philosophical Society, the editors of *Southwest Philosophy Review*, and Yong Dou (Michael) Kim.
3. These scholars include Gunter (1968), Hatab (1988), Lampert (1999), Lippitt (1999), Higgins (2000), Kirkland (2009), Hay (2011), and Siemens and Hay (2015), among others. More recently, Froese (2017), McNeal (2019b), Boddicker (2020), and Hurst (2020) have published on the subject.
4. Nietzsche conceived the "free spirit" (*Freigeist*) as a quasi-ideal he "*invented* for [him]self" from his need for "companions and familiars with whom [he could] laugh" (HH P 2). Initially a futural ideal, Nietzsche's notion evolved through his middle and late works into the exemplar he took himself and his ilk—philosophical rebels who have *"become free"* (EH HH 1)—to personify, whose creative experiments *anticipate* philosophers of the future.
5. Nietzsche's thought and futural ideals are undeniably Eurocentric; it is Europe's post-Christian secular values, European societies, and European humanity that he envisaged transforming.
6. I follow Lippitt's identification of "two kinds of laughter" in Nietzsche's thought, "'the laughter of the height', and the 'laughter of the herd'" (1992: 39), a distinction hinting at the political significance of laughter in Nietzsche's thought.
7. Silenus, himself a "companion of Dionysos," delivers his terrible wisdom to King Midas via "shrill laughter" (BT 3).

8. *Kynical* is the adjectival form of *Kynicism*, a term derived from the Greek term *kynismos* that Peter Sloterdijk utilizes to refer to the playfulness I associate with Dionysian mirth that transfigures cynicism. Sloterdijk defines *kynical* acts as the "kind of argumentation [which] respectable thinking does not know how to deal with" and "a dialectic of disinhibition" characterized by a "cheekiness" that "gives a new twist to the question of how to say the truth" (1987: 101–4). This note was developed from McNeal, 2009: 521 and 568.
9. Unlike Democritus's conceptions of *euthumia* (good passion or spiritedness) and cheerfulness commending *ataraxia* (unperturbed tranquility), Dionysian mirth refers to the tragic knowledge Nietzsche specifies at BT 15, which agonically "laughs the truth."
10. Nietzsche's use of "decadence" referred to an individual's, culture's, or society's decreasing vitality (A 6); the phrase "decadence values" to Judeo-Christian and post-Christian secular moral values, "pity … the *practice* of nihilism," and other "tendencies *hostile to life*" (A 7).
11. Nietzsche uses numerous related phrases to describe his "free spirits," including "tragic artist[s]" (TI Reason 6; Skirmishes 24), "higher men" (BGE 256), "attempters" or "experimenters" (BGE 42), "genuine philosopher" (BGE 211), and "yes-sayers" (GS 276). Following him, I employ these phrases, among others, in referencing free spirits.
12. As they aim to create future values their shared desires/aspirations are proto-political.
13. The free spirit's Dionysian mirth is antithetical to the toxic positivity of our dissipative consumer culture. It is, in the Greek sense, *kynical*, skeptical, and parrhesiastic.
14. Vinod Acharya helpfully examines "how Nietzsche knows that the metaphysics he attacks actually denies life, and thus has at its basis an oppositional structure of values" (2014: 77). Justin Remhof observes that the type of metaphysics Nietzsche opposes is the dualistic, "two-world" variety, various iterations of which run through Western philosophy (2022).
15. Nietzsche's notion of what is aristocratic scorns contemporary aristocrats and leaders as "knee-jerk defenders of a woeful political status-quo in which real political power has fallen into the hands of herd politicians" (Appel 1999: 111; cf. A 43).
16. Intersecting with his notion of the free spirit, my use of Nietzsche's phrase "tragic artists" is informed by Tracy Strong's insights. See book VI on tragedy and transfiguration in Strong, 2000.
17. Dionysian mirth corresponds with Nietzsche's naturalism, which fosters "every *healthy* morality—[that] is governed by an instinct of life" (TI Morality 4).
18. Maudemarie Clark asserts that Nietzsche's opposition to the ascetic ideal lies in its "idealization of self-denial … on the basis of … a devaluation of human life" (1990: 162); by mocking its dissipative characteristics, free-spirited comedians reveal them to others. Daniel Conway argues that the absence of "alternative ideals" to which these comedians might appeal would undercut their challenges to its hegemony (1997: 105). However, I hold that Nietzsche thought the "mistrust" aroused by these comedians *could* suffice as a means of "hijacking the ascetic ideal" to reverse our post-Christian "moral interpretation of the bad conscience" (1997: 107).
19. Nietzsche foresees "wars such as the earth has never seen" (EH Destiny 1).
20. Cf. Reginster (2006: 195).
21. Nietzsche asserted, "I would go so far as to allow myself a rank order of philosophers based on the rank of their laughter—right up to those who are capable of golden laughter" (BGE 294).

22. On the multiple ways in which Nietzsche "tactically uses humor and laughter for epistemic purposes," see Alfano (2018).
23. For an illuminating explication of "the self as a structure of drives," see Katsafanas (2016: 197–200).
24. Translation by Ronald Speirs. Graham Parkes and Adrian Del Caro translate the phrase "soothlaugher."
25. Of "Nietzsche's humorous style", Hatab observes that it "is related to his critique of traditional philosophical attitudes … [and] is not accidental or incidental to his message" (Hatab 1988: 74).
26. Martine Prange helpfully suggested that this anticipates Foucault's notion of the "limit attitude."
27. This indicates antithetical, proto-political types that inform the sociocultural and, implicitly, political aims of Nietzsche's project.
28. The sexual revolution that swept the Western world in the 1960s and 1970s, and LGBTQ Pride parades over the last four decades, arguably demonstrate this.
29. Ansell-Pearson observes that "the notion [of the *Übermensch*] does not posit the transcendence of the human animal; [but] denotes its future creative possibilities … [it] is an ever-present possibility of the human. The overman fulfills the fundamental law of life (self-overcoming); it does not signify its negation" (1994: 118–19).
30. This note was developed from McNeal, 2009: 521 and 568.
31. Lucian, *Philosophies for Sale*, sect. 14, cited in PPP.
32. As "the clown who *made himself be taken seriously*" (TI Socrates 5), Nietzsche recognized Socrates as a mocking, laughing philosopher but considered him a pessimist and decadent for insisting on universal truths based on reason ("reason = virtue = happiness" [TI Socrates 4]). While the revaluation of values that Socrates's laughter instigated was antithetical to that which Nietzsche's Dionysian laughter commends, their respective forms of laughter had similarly subversive effects.
33. I am indebted to Martine Prange and our blind reviewer for their critical feedback on drafts of this chapter. I am also grateful to Christine Daigle, Gary Shapiro, and Paul Kirkland for their engagement.

References

Acampora, Christa Davis (2013), *Contesting Nietzsche*, Chicago: University of Chicago Press.
Acharya, Vinod (2014), *Nietzsche's Meta-Existentialism*, Berlin: De Gruyter.
Alfano, Mark (2018), "The Epistemic Function of Contempt and Laughter in Nietzsche," in *The Moral Psychology of Contempt*, ed. Michelle Mason, Lanham, MD: Rowman & Littlefield.
Ansell-Pearson, Keith (1994), *An Introduction to Nietzsche as Political Thinker*, Cambridge: Cambridge University Press.
Appel, Fredrick (1999), *Nietzsche Contra Democracy*, Ithaca, NY: Cornell University Press.
Babich, Babette (2006), *Words in Blood Like Flowers: Philosophy and Poetry, Music and Eros in Holderlin, Nietzsche, and Heidegger*, Albany: State University of New York Press.
Bamford, Rebecca (2015), "Health and Self-cultivation in *Dawn*," in *Nietzsche's Free Spirit Philosophy*, ed. Rebecca Bamford, 85–109, Lanham, MD: Rowman & Littlefield.

Boddicker, Charles (2020), "Humour in Nietzsche's Style," *European Journal of Philosophy*, 26 August.
Clark, Maudemarie (1990), *Nietzsche on Philosophy and Truth*, Cambridge: Cambridge University Press.
Conway, Daniel W. (1997), *Nietzsche and the Political*, New York: Routledge.
Elbe, Stephan (2001), "'We Good Europeans …': Genealogical Reflections on the *Idea* of Europe," *Millennium* 30 (2): 259–83.
Froese, Katrin (2017), "Redeeming Laughter in Nietzsche," in *Why Can't Philosophers Laugh?* Springer.
Gunter, Pete A. (1968), "Nietzschean Laughter," *Sewanee Review* 76 (3) (Summer).
Hatab, Lawrence J. (1988), "Laughter in Nietzsche's Thought: A Philosophical Tragicomedy," *International Studies in Philosophy* 20 (2): 67–79.
Hay, Katia (2011), "Zarathustra's Laughter or the *Birth of Tragedy* from the Experience of the Comic," in *Nietzsche on Instinct and Language*, ed. Joao Constancio and Maria Joao Mayer Branco, 243–58, Berlin: De Gruyter.
Higgins, Kathleen Marie (2000), *Comic Relief: Nietzsche's Gay Science*, New York: Oxford University Press.
Hurst, Andrea (2020), "An Ethos of Affirmative Laughter in Nietzsche's Zarathustra," *The Southern Journal of Philosophy*, 25 October.
Katsafanas, Paul (2016), *The Nietzschean Self: Moral Psychology, Agency, and the Unconscious*, Oxford: Oxford University Press.
Kaufmann, Walter (1974), *Nietzsche: Philosopher, Psychologist, Antichrist*, 4th ed., Princeton, NJ: Princeton University Press.
Kirkland, Paul E. (2009), *Nietzsche's Noble Aims: Affirming Life, Confronting Modernity*, New York: Lexington Press.
Lampert, Laurence (1999), "Nietzsche's Best Jokes," in *Nietzsche's Futures*, ed. John Lippitt, 82–98, London: Macmillan Books.
Lippitt, John (1992), "Nietzsche, Zarathustra and the Status of Laughter," *British Journal of Aesthetics* 32 (1): 39–49.
Lippitt, John (1999), "Laughter: A Tool in Moral Perfectionism?," in *Nietzsche's Futures*, ed. John Lippitt, 99–125, London: Macmillan Books.
McNeal, Michael J. (2009), *Becoming Good Europeans? Globality, the EU and the Potential to Realize Nietzsche's Idea of Europe*. Doctoral Dissertation (UMI 3359926), University of Denver, ProQuest Dissertations Publishing.
McNeal, Michael J. (2019a), "Nietzsche on the Pleasure of the Agon and Enticements to War," in *Conflict and Contest in Nietzsche's Philosophy*, ed. Herman Siemens and James Pearson, 147–65, London: Bloomsbury Academic.
McNeal, Michael J. (2019b), "Subversive Joy: Nietzsche's Practice of Life-Enhancing Cheerfulness," *Southwest Philosophy Review* 35 (1): 207–16.
McNeal, Michael J. (2020a), "Nietzsche Con/tra Epicurus: The Necessity of Noble Suffering for Intoxication with Life," in *Nietzsche and Epicurus: Nature, Health, and Ethics*, ed. Vinod Acharya and Ryan Johnson, 189–204, London: Bloomsbury Academic.
McNeal, Michael J. (2020b), "Good Europeanism: The Practice and Pathos of Nietzsche's Good Europeans," in *European/Supra-European: Cultural Encounters in Nietzsche's Philosophy*, Marco Brusotti et al., eds. Berlin/Boston: De Gruyter.
Nehamas, Alexander (1985), *Nietzsche: Life as Literature*, Cambridge, MA: Harvard University Press.
Owen, David (1995), *Nietzsche, Politics, Modernity*, New York: Sage.
Prange, Martine (2013), *Nietzsche, Wagner, Europe*, Berlin: De Gruyter Press.

Reginster, Bernard (2006), *The Affirmation of Life: Nietzsche on Overcoming Nihilism*, Cambridge, MA: Harvard University Press.
Remhof, Justin (2022), *Nietzsche as Metaphysician*, New York: Routledge.
Shapiro, Gary (2016), *Nietzsche's Earth: Great Events, Great Politics*, Chicago: University of Chicago Press.
Shaw, Tasmin (2007), *Nietzsche's Political Skepticism*. Princeton: Princeton University Press.
Siemens, Herman W., and Katia Hay (2015), "Ridendo dicere severum: On Probity, Laughter and Self-Critique in Nietzsche's Figure of the Free Spirit," in *Nietzsche's Philosophy of the Free Spirit*, ed. Rebecca Bamford, 111–36, London: Rowman & Littlefield.
Sloterdijk, Peter (1987), *Critique of Cynical Reason*, Minneapolis: University of Minnesota Press.
Strong, Tracy B. (2000), *Friedrich Nietzsche and the Politics of Transfiguration*, Urbana: University of Illinois Press.
Zamosc, Gabriel (2022), "Joyful Transhumanism, Love, and Eternal Recurrence in Nietzsche's Zarathustra," in *Nietzsche's 'Thus Spoke Zarathustra': A Critical Guide*, ed. Keith Ansell-Pearson and Paul S. Loeb, Cambridge: Cambridge University Press.

Notes on Contributors

Ruth Abbey is Professor and Chair of the Department of Humanities and Social Sciences at Swinburne University. She is the author of *Nietzsche's Middle Period* (2000), *Philosophy Now: Charles Taylor* (2001), *The Return of Feminist Liberalism* (2014), and *Human All Too Human: A Critical Introduction and Guide* (2019). She is the editor of *Contemporary Philosophy in Focus: Charles Taylor* (2012), *Feminist Interpretations of Rawls* (2013), and *Cosmopolitan Civility* (2020). She has written a number of articles and book chapters on topics ranging from contemporary liberalism to conceptions of marriage and animal ethics. She is currently the editor in chief of *The Review of Politics*.

Glen Baier is an Associate Professor of Philosophy at the University of the Fraser Valley in Abbotsford, British Columbia. He specializes in the history of late-nineteenth- and twentieth-century continental philosophy with a focus on Nietzsche and Foucault. His work on Nietzsche covers a variety of topics, but most recently he has written several papers on *The Birth of Tragedy*.

Jeffrey Church is Professor of Political Science at the University of Houston. He is the author of three books and several articles on Nietzsche, focusing in particular on his early period writings.

Richard Elliott is associate lecturer and teaching fellow at Birkbeck College, University of London. He has published in numerous journals and edited collections on Nietzsche, the philosophy of psychology, Heidegger, Adorno, and German intellectual history.

Peter S. Groff is Associate Professor of Philosophy at Bucknell University. He has written on Nietzsche, Arabic philosophy, and comparative questions across traditions. His most recent scholarship focuses on Nietzsche's retrieval of certain classical strategies—withdrawal, solitude, perfectibility, prophecy, and imitation of God—in *Thus Spoke Zarathustra*.

Katia Hay obtained a double PhD from the universities of Munich and Paris with a dissertation on Schelling and the Tragic. She teaches in the Department of Critical Cultural Theory at the University of Amsterdam. Among other works, she is the coeditor of *Nietzsche, German Idealism and Its Critics* (2015), and coeditor of *Nietzsche and Kant on Aesthetics and Anthropology* (2017).

Paul E. Kirkland is Associate Professor of Political Science at Carthage College. He is the author of *Nietzsche's Noble Aims* (2009) and several articles on Nietzsche and political thought.

Michael J. McNeal is Adjunct Professor of political philosophy and international studies at the University of Denver, and serves as secretary of the *Friedrich Nietzsche Society*. He is the coeditor of *European/Supra-European: Cultural Encounters in Nietzsche's Philosophy* (2020) and *US Approaches to the Arab Spring: International Relations and Democracy Promotion* (2018). In addition to journal articles on Nietzsche's thought, he has also contributed chapters to a number of scholarly anthologies.

Philip Mills is a postdoctoral fellow in French literature at the University of Lausanne. He completed his PhD in philosophy on Nietzsche, Wittgenstein and poetics at Royal Holloway, University of London. Rooted in nineteenth- and twentieth-century philosophical thought, his work lies at the intersection of philosophy of language, aesthetics, and poetry. His current research analyzes contemporary French poetry within the framework of ordinary language philosophy.

Jamie Parr is Lecturer in Philosophy at Australian Catholic University, Sydney, Australia. His principal research concern is nihilism and its avoidance, with a particular focus on Nietzsche's relationship to Blaise Pascal. This work shall be encapsulated in "Nietzsche and Pascal: Transfiguration, Despair and the Problem of Existence" (forthcoming).

Melanie Shepherd is Professor of Philosophy at Misericordia University in Dallas, PA. Her work on Nietzsche has appeared in *Philosophy Today*, *Philosophy and Literature*, *British Journal for the History of Philosophy*, *History of European Ideas*, and *The Journal of Nietzsche Studies*.

Name Index

Abbey, Ruth 22, 23, 24, 28, 39 nn.1, 3, 40 nn.5–8
Acharya, Vinod 83, 196, 210 n.14
Ahern, Daniel R. 156
Ansell-Pearson, Keith 7, 12, 15, 16, 19, 21–3, 39 n.1, 61, 77, 114, 194, 200, 211 n.28
Appel, Fredrick 210 n.15
Aristophanean 193
Aristophanes 174 n.1, 184
Aristotle 2, 40, 180

Babich, Babette 198
Ball, Hugo 6, 143, 144, 146, 147, 149, 150, 154, 155
Bamford, Rebecca 7, 39 n.1, 41, 198
Beethoven 60
Behler, Ernst 140 n.28
Beiser, Frederick 181
Berard, Tim J. 144
Bergson, Henri 168, 176 n.29
Berkowitz, Peter 189 n.5
Bertram, Ernst 118 n.1
Bishop, Paul 78 n.17
Blake, William 95
Bowen, L. 167, 175 n.9, 175 n.25
Bowie, Andrew 98 n.8
Brooks, D. 174 n.7
Brusotti, Marco 105, 114, 116, 121 n.24
Brutus 31–2
Burnham, Douglas 139 n.21
Byron, Lord 18

Carter, L. B. 77 n.3, 79 n.25
Cartwright, D. 61 n.7
Church, Jeffrey 6, 7 n.3, 62 n.13, 180, 189 n.6
Clark, Maudemarie 12, 16, 19, 61 n.5, 156 n.8, 210 n.17
Cohen, Jonathan R. 12, 16
Comte, Auguste 22, 51

Creasy, Kaitlyn 99 n.13
Critchley, Simon 175 n.27, 176 n.34

Danchev, Alex 144, 145, 148–52, 154
Davies, Malcolm 140 n.26
Democritus 210 n.9
De Certeau, Michel 120 n.16
D'Iorio, Paolo 78 n.12, 79 n.25
Donnellan, Brendan 119 n.11
Doudan, Ximénès 119 n.11
Drochon, Hugo 3, 7 n.1, 61 n.3, 62 n.13, 77 nn.1, 2
Duvergier de Haurrane, Jean 119 n.8, 120 n.17

Elst, Koenraad 174 n.3
Emden, Christian J. 132

Fortier, Jeremy 23 n.2, 39 nn.1, 4
Foucault, Michel 2, 156 n.7
Franco, Paul 22, 39 nn.1, 2, 4, 41 n.19
Frazer, M. L. 61 nn.7, 9
Frederick the Great 6, 185
Froese, Katrin 209 n.3
Früchtl, Josef 167

Gemes, Ken 99 n.13, 189 n.6
Gilman, S. L. 48, 129, 137 n.1
Goldman, N. 175 n.9
Graham, A. C. 79 n.25
Groff, Peter S. 5, 77 nn.1, 2, 3, 78 nn.12, 17, 79 nn.22, 25, 29, 81 n.48, 82 nn.55, 57
Grice, Paul 99 nn.11, 12
Gooding-Williams, R. 60, 61 n.4, 62 n.16, 77 n.8, 79 n.29, 81 nn.45, 46, 139 nn.19, 22
Guay, Robert 60, 61 n.6
Gunter, Peter A. 138 n.12, 209 n.3

Halliwell, S. 174 nn.1, 4
Handwerk, Gary 12, 18, 20, 23 nn.1, 5, 24 n.19

Harper, Aaron 153
Harris, Daniel I. 48, 49, 59, 61 n.7, 62 nn.14, 20
Hatab, Lawrence 2, 7 n.4, 123, 138 n.6, 191, 209 n.3, 211 n.24
Hay, Katia 6, 32, 33, 41 nn.20, 21, 23, 24, 25, 27, 138 n.6, 175 nn.12, 14, 208, 209 n.3
Heidegger, Martin 90, 93
Heller, Erich 22, 99 n.14
Hellwald, Friedrich von 77 n.6
Higgins, Kathleen 2, 23 n.2, 30, 40 nn.12, 14, 15, 41 n.23, 80 n.37, 81 nn.42, 45, 46, 108, 118 n.1, 129, 140 n.31, 196, 198, 209 n.3
Hill, Kevin R. 189 n.6
Huddleston, Andrew 11, 12, 15, 16, 17, 98 nn.2, 3
Huelsenbeck, Richard 143, 151
Hurst, Andrea 209 n.3
Hussain, Nadeem J. Z. 23 n.3
Hutter, Horst 77 n.1

Janaway, Christopher 138 n.3
Johnson, Dirk R. 98 n.1, 99 n.12
Jung, Carl G. 79 n.21

Kant, Immanuel 31, 34, 35, 41 n.29, 138 n.8, 146, 164, 180, 181, 189 n.6
Kaufmann, Walter 39 n.1, 40 n.5, 60 n.1, 100 n.18, 205
Katsafanas, Paul 156 n.13, 189 n.5, 210 n.22
Kirkland, Paul E. 4, 7 n.1, 40 n.9, 62 n.19, 101 n.28, 117, 209 n.3, 211 n.31
Klossowski, Pierre 156 n.13
Kofman, Sarah 134
Kress, John 138 n.5

Lampert, Laurence 2, 41 n.33, 42 n.34, 61 n.5, 77 nn.1, 3, 79 n.29, 81 nn.45, 46, 139 n.14, 140 nn.24, 30, 31, 209 n.3
Lane, Melissa 41 n.21
Large, Duncan 39 n.2
Lebreton, Lucie 119 n.11
Leiter, Brian 12, 19, 88
Lemm, Vanessa 77 n.2
Lewis, Peter B. 138 nn.8, 10, 12, 139 n.16, 140 nn.23, 25

Lippard, Lucy R. 147, 148, 151
Lippitt, John 2, 137 n.1, 139 n.13, 203, 209 n.6
Loeb, Paul 57, 61 n.2, 62 n.16, 77 n.2, 81 n.45, 110 n.26, 110 n.27, 149 n.31
Loschenkohl, Birte 61 n.4, 77 n.2
Losurdo, Domenico 22, 24 n.22
Löwith, Karl 82 n.56

Magnus, Bernd 23 n.2
Mansfield, Harvey 179–81
May, Simon 110 n.23
McIntrye, Alex 2, 41 n.32, 77 n.1
McNeal, Michael J. 7, n.4, 40 n.12, 101 n.28, 194, 199, 201, 209 n.2
Metzger, Jeffrey 189 n.4
Meyer, Matthew 23 n.4, 39 n.1, 40 n.5, 41 n.23, 61 n.5, 105, 116, 117, 121 n.24
Micheson, Katrina 41 n.20
Miner, R. C. 62 n.20
Morreall, J. 175 n.15

Natoli, Charles 119 n.11
Nehamas, Alexander 35, 41 n.30, 61 n.1, 198
Neuhouser, Frederick 98
Nussbaum, Martha 137 n.2

Oliver, Kelly A. 188 n.2
Ottman, Henning 77 n.1
Overbeck, Ida 48, 77
Owen, David 7 n.4, 175 n.11, 202

Pascal, Blaise 5, 105–22
Picht, Georg 77 n.1
Pippin, Robert 81 n.45, 82 n.56, 189 n.6
Plato/ Platonic/ Platonist 42 n.38, 65, 77 nn.1, 3, 78 n.10, 129, 135, 139 n.22, 174 n.3, 180
Porter, James 138 n.3

Raine, J. 174 n.2
Rampley, Matthew 138 n.7
Rancière, Jacques 40 n.16
Reginster, Bernard 61 n.1, 62 n.11, 90, 99 n.13, 156 n.8, 189 n.5, 210 n.19
Remhof, Justin 210 n.14
Richardson, John 189 n.7

Name Index

Ridley, Aaron 39 n.2
Rohde, Erwin 78 n.17
Rosen, Stanley 77 n.1, 80 n.30, 81 n.45, 82 n.56, 148 n.30
Russell, Olga Wester 119 n.11

Salomé, Lou Andreas 12, 40 n.5
Schacht, Richard 81 n.43
Schelling, Friedrich Wilhelm Joseph 88, 98 n.8
Schiller, Friedrich 31, 34, 40 n.13, 41 n.17
Schlegel, Karl Wilhelm Friedrich 174 n.3
Schopenhauer, Arthur 5–6, 39 n.4, 41 n.22, 48, 49–58, 61 n.7, 96–7, 100 n.26, 105, 123–41
Seung, T. K. 162, 174 n.5
Shakespeare, William 31–2, 41 n.18, 141
Shapiro, Gary 35, 41 n.30, 77 n.2, 204, 211 n.31
Shaw, Tamsin 7 n.3, 196
Shepherd, Melanie 4–5, 42 n.38
Siemens, Herman 32–3, 41 nn.20–5, 77 n.2, 175 n.12, 208, 209 n.3
Sjaastad, M. 174 n.7
Sloterdijk, Peter 210 n.8
Small, Robin 23 n.8
Spinoza, Benedict de 38, 42, 145
Staten, Henry 115, 117
Stevenson, Charles 88, 95, 99 n.10
Strauss, Leo 77 n.1

Strong, Tracy B. 7 n.2, 195 n.15
Swift, Paul 138 n.8

Taylor, Archer 133
Taylor, Seth 144
Trench, Brian 174 n.8
Tzara, Tristan 6, 144–54

Ure, Michael 21–4, 39 n.1, 62 n.14, 139 n.20

Van Tongeren, Paul 82 n.59
Verkerk, Willow 62 n.17
Vioulac, Jean 119 n.11
Voegelin, Eric 119 n.11
Voltaire 51, 85

Wagner, Richard 12, 39 n.2, 51, 97, 100 n.26, 129, 199–200
Weeks, Mark 138 n.8
Williams, W. D. 119 n.11
Woodruff, Martha Kendall 78 n.8
Wordsworth, William 100 n.24
Wotling, Patrick 156 n.6

Young, Julian 12, 16, 23 n.9, 39 n.5, 40 n.6, 41 n.26, 188 n.2

Zamosc, Gabriel 204
Zuckert, Catherine 77 n.1
Zupančič, A. 176 n.28

Subject Index

amor fati 4, 5, 37, 65, 72, 76, 80 n.36, 101 n.27, 206
Ape, Zarathustra's 65, 68, 79 n.22, 25, 80 n.3, 81 n.51
aristocratic 182, 183, 185, 186, 194, 210 n.15
art 4, 12, 16, 17, 19, 24 n.18, 27–34, 37, 40 n.7, 86, 106, 111, 124, 140, 143, 147, 148, 151, 152, 154, 163, 169, 171, 198, 19
artist, artists 24, 28–30, 37–41, 147, 192, 199, 200, 204, 210
ascetic priests 6, 195, 198, 199, 201, 203, 205, 207, 208
ascetic values 195–7, 200, 204
asceticism 29, 133

becoming 41 n.22, 58, 71, 78, 81, 90, 93, 96, 106, 108, 152, 164, 166, 167, 171, 173, 183, 198, 204–7
benevolence 17–19
blessed isles 66, 67, 69, 75, 78–80

Charlie Hebdo 162, 174 n.8, 204
Christian (Judeo-Christian/post-Christian) 3, 5, 50, 51, 52, 58, 76, 77 n.7, 87, 88–93, 95, 97, 100 n.24, 106–16, 118 n.3, 120 n.17, 145, 170, 173, 174 n.3, 180, 182, 193, 195, 196, 201, 203, 204, 208, 209 n.5, 210 n.10, n.17
comedy 6, 29, 30, 33, 40, 109, 117, 129, 131, 138, 139, 140, 161, 162, 163, 166, 168, 173–6, 196, 207
consecration (of world, self) 106, 108, 114, 116, 118
courage 115, 117, 182, 186, 199, 202, 209
cowardice 106–8, 164
creation/self-creation 3, 51, 65, 66, 169, 173, 176, 183, 184, 192, 205, 206, 207
culture 3, 5, 12, 13, 16, 19, 29, 57, 60, 79, 98, 118, 134, 144, 145, 146, 147, 148, 149, 151, 152, 154, 155, 156, 174, 179, 192, 194, 198, 207, 210

Dada/Dadaists 144–55
death of God 51, 86, 87, 89, 90, 91, 92, 97, 99, 100, 106, 108, 116, 140, 146, 156, 167, 171, 179, 180, 197, 203
democratic/democracy 6, 7, 78, 161–3, 167, 169, 173, 174, 175, 182, 188, 205, 207, 208
destruction/self-destruction 15, 29, 32, 33, 143, 147–51, 155, 183, 187, 204, 206
Dionysian 1, 7, 35, 41, 60, 115, 139, 148, 184, 187, 191–203, 205–10

earth, earthly 50, 51, 58, 69, 79, 96, 176, 199, 204, 210
ecstasy 109, 110
enlightenment 22, 24 n22, 28, 51, 52, 111, 185, 206
eternal recurrence 1, 4, 5, 6, 41 n.26, 47, 48, 56, 57, 58, 60, 62 n.12, n.21, 65, 67, 71–4, 76, 80 nn.35, 36, 81 n.54, 82 n.55, 85, 86, 89, 93, 94, 95–8, 98 n.1, 99 nn.12, 15, 100 nn.23, 25, 101 n.27
eternity 1, 5, 18, 56, 74, 76, 80 n.36, 81 n.54, 85, 86, 88–90, 93, 95–8, 98 n.9, 99 n.12, 135, 140 n.27, 206
ethical/ethics 4, 21, 27, 28, 29, 49, 100 n19, 151, 152, 169, 180, 181, 186, 187
Europe/European 90, 118 n.3, 143, 147, 149, 162, 185, 186
European, good 40 n.12

feminine/femininity/feminization 180, 184, 188 n.3, 189 n.8

Genoa 35
gravity 4, 27, 33, 36, 37, 39, 90, 135, 137, 139 n.14, 140 n.30, 172, 205, 209

great politics 2, 3, 5, 7 n.1, 47, 65, 66, 70, 71, 74, 75, 76, 77 n.2, 82 nn.57, 59, 204

hatred/hateful 30, 51, 86, 107, 124, 132, 167, 168, 169, 176 nn.32, 37, 207, 208

immortal/immortality 18, 107, 108, 112, 115, 116
incorporation 38, 39, 41 n.20, 86, 89, 94, 95, 100 nn.21, 25, 109, 116, 144, 165, 173, 182, 183, 186, 192, 203
individual 3, 40 n.14, 47, 48, 51, 52, 54, 55, 58, 61 n.4, 62 n.13, 67, 73, 94, 95, 99 n.15, 100 n.25, 105-10, 114, 115, 117, 127-9, 135, 136, 139 n.20, 148-51, 153, 167, 170, 173, 174, 176 n.32, 183, 184, 186, 187, 189 nn.8, 9, 192, 194-7, 199, 201-4, 206-8, 210 n.10
irony (ironic) 70, 81 n.45, 82 n.54, 115, 123, 127, 128, 129, 133, 134, 135, 138 n.13, 139 n.21, 140 nn.28, 29, 184, 185, 187, 188, 192, 199, 204
Isles 66, 67, 69, 75, 78 nn.11, 12, 14, 16, 17, 79 nn.25, 27, 80 n.40, 81 nn.49, 50

jokes 5, 6, 95, 123-41, 162, 163, 165-9, 173, 174, 176 n.33, 191, 196, 205, 208, 209 n.1

Lake Silvaplana 89, 94
language 7 n.2, 14, 32, 40 n.14, 41 n.22, 77 n.8, 81 n.54, 94, 107, 119 n.11, 124, 143, 146, 149-54, 182, 195, 205
levity 2, 4, 18, 27, 28, 32-4, 36, 37, 39, 41 n.26, 139 n.14, 196
looking away 5, 37, 72, 73, 74, 80 n.34, 81 n.42
love 6, 29, 30, 37, 38, 39, 40 n.14, 42 n.38, 49, 54, 60, 65, 70, 72-6, 80 n.36, 96, 107, 108, 110, 111, 114, 120 n.17, 145, 172, 176 n.42, 184, 185, 199, 203, 206, 207

masculinity 6, 179, 185-9
Mitfreude, (shared joy) 2, 5, 48, 49, 56, 62, 203
Mitleid, (pity) 2, 5, 48, 49, 52, 54, 56, 58-62
morphology 123, 125, 132-3, 134, 137

metaphysics 12, 14, 15, 16, 17, 19, 20, 22, 23 n.11, 28, 29, 53, 95, 140 n.25, 170, 176 n.32, 180, 196, 210 n.14
mockery 116, 139 n.21, 161, 174 n.46, 193, 196, 198, 203-5, 207
morality 2, 7, 17-18, 31, 33, 34, 40 n.17, 41 n.24, 48-53, 55, 56-9, 61 n.8, 62 n.11, 65, 70, 77 nn.4, 7, 85, 87, 91, 93, 97, 114, 118, 119 n.17, 124, 131, 132, 146, 156 n.5, 161, 163-6, 175 n.10, 181-8, 192-5, 200, 202-5, 207, 210 n.16

Nanette 167-8
naturalism 27, 32, 35, 36, 210 n.16
nihilism 5, 6, 85-102, 143-50, 156 n.8, 167, 169, 173, 180, 190, 192, 194, 198, 202, 206-8, 210 n.10
noble 50, 55, 65, 68, 73, 76, 94, 106, 129, 132, 137, 163, 177 n.42, 207

overcoming (self-overcoming) 2-6, 33, 34, 39 n.2, 47-50, 56-60, 61 n.4, 65 n.14, 71, 72, 76, 77 n.1, 85, 92, 94-7, 100 n.23, 113, 117, 134, 140 n.30, 165, 166, 170-3, 196-205, 211 n.28

pessimism 5, 6, 96, 97, 123-4, 132, 137, 138 n.7, 139 n.20, 140 n.23, 147-8, 193
pity 1-3, 5, 40 n.16, 47-62, 76, 82 n.54, 114, 117, 132-6, 145, 198, 200, 205, 210 n.10
play 2, 3, 6, 15, 27, 29, 31, 34-9, 55, 57, 61, 85, 96-7, 108, 118 n.3, 119 n.4, 125-6, 128, 136-7, 140 n.23, 143-57, 163, 165, 166, 170, 179, 183-8, 195-6, 200-6, 209 n.1, 210 n.8
positivism 4, 11-13, 19, 21-2, 23 n.2, 24 n.21, 27, 51
prayer 112-13
priests 6, 7, 72, 78 n.15, 80 n.31, 195, 198-9, 201, 203, 205, 207-8
probity 4, 32-4, 37, 41 n.22, 178, 212
psychology 1, 17, 98 n.5, 123, 125, 131-3, 203

relationality 4, 5, 47-62
religion 2, 12, 13, 15-20, 28-9, 40 n.7, 51, 86, 87, 101 n.28, 145-6, 161, 166, 174 n.3. 196, 205, 208

Ressentiment 95, 119 n.7, 195, 197, 206
revaluation (of all values) 3–7, 52, 58, 61 n.4, 65, 146–9, 152, 155, 191–7, 200, 211 n.30
revenge 68, 70–3, 80 n.39, 119 n.7, 195, 200
riddles 5, 6, 123–41

sacrifice 17, 29, 31, 58, 106, 111–14
science 2, 4, 6, 11–24, 25, 27–30, 33, 37, 39, 41 n.26, 58, 60, 109, 114, 117, 119, 121 n.23, 125, 146, 163–5, 169, 194–202, 207–8, 210 n.17
self-cultivation 28, 35, 41 n.30, 59, 65–9, 76, 82, 87, 98 n.5, 109, 115, 167, 181, 194, 198, 209
self-overcoming 2, 4–6, 33–4, 39, 47–50, 55, 57, 59–60, 61 n.4, 62 n.14, 66, 71–6, 77 n.1, 92, 97, 100, 113, 117, 165–6, 169–73, 192, 197–200, 202, 204, 206, 211 n.28
shame 53–5, 59, 61, 79, 107, 120, 140, 201
slave morality 6, 50, 181–7, 192, 204–5
Sorrento 78 n.12
suffering 1, 5, 15–16, 21, 33, 34, 47–62, 73, 87, 107–8, 111–14, 117, 120, 124, 132, 133, 136–8, 171, 191, 196–200, 205–6, 208

tragedy 2, 17, 29–32, 40 n.12, 62 n.19, 106, 109, 116–17, 123–4, 138 n.6, 139 n.20, 147–8, 166, 175 n.19

transfiguration 7 n.2, 66, 75, 76, 107–8, 111, 116, 119 n.10, 191, 199, 209
trust 18, 36, 78, 108, 111, 114–16, 145, 148, 207, 210 n.17

Übermensch 4, 5, 42–51, 53, 55, 57–62, 146, 169, 171–2, 177 n.47, 204, 211 n.28
utilitarianism 50–1

value(s) 2, 3, 5–7, 17, 20–3, 32, 40, 47, 50, 58, 60, 61 n.4, 65–6, 69–70, 75–6, 77 n.4,7, 78 n.10, 86–7, 90–7, 100 n.16, 106, 108, 114–15, 118, 124, 138, 143, 145–56, 161–2, 165–76, 182, 187, 198, 200–9, 210 nn.10, 12, 14, 211 n.30

'*Was liegt an mir*' ('What do I matter') 105, 118
Will 1, 5, 6, 19, 34, 41 n.27, 85–101, 112, 124, 128, 132, 145, 181, 182–8, 199–209
will to power 76, 132, 181 n.7, 205
wit 127, 200
withdrawal 65–9, 74–80, 112

Zarathustra 1, 2, 5, 8, 24, 39, 47–64, 65–84, 86–6, 95–101, 114, 116, 118 n.1, 123–4, 129, 133–42, 153, 156 n.11, 183–7, 192–3, 198–205, 208–9

Printed in the USA
CPSIA information can be obtained
at www.ICGtesting.com
LVHW010123180524
780605LV00002B/160